The Cambridge Companion to Berlioz

Still widely known as the extravagant composer of the
Symphonie fantastique, Berlioz was a subtle and complex artist
caught in the crossfire between the academic classicism of the
French musical establishment and the romantic modernism of
the Parisian musical scene. He was a thinker in an age that
invented both the religion of art and the notion of the "genius"
who preached and practiced it. This Companion contains essays
by eminent scholars on Berlioz's place in nineteenth-century
French cultural life, on his principal compositions (symphonies,
overtures, operas, sacred works, songs), on his major writings (a
delightful volume of memoirs, a number of short stories, large
quantities of music criticism, an orchestration treatise), on his
direct and indirect encounters with other famous musicians
(Gluck, Mozart, Beethoven, Wagner), and on his legacy in
France. The volume is framed by a detailed chronology of his life
and a usefully annotated bibliography.

PETER BLOOM is Professor of Music at Smith College in
Northampton, Massachusetts. He is author of *The Life of Berlioz*
(1998) and editor of *Berlioz Studies* (1992). He is also a member
of the panel of advisers for the *New Berlioz Edition* and has
edited volume 7 of the series, *Lélio ou Le Retour à la vie* (1992).

Cambridge Companions to Music

Composers

The Cambridge Companion to Bach
Edited by John Butt
0 521 45350 X (hardback)
0 521 58780 8 (paperback)

The Cambridge Companion to Beethoven
Edited by Glen Stanley
0 521 58074 9 (hardback)
0 521 56489 1 (paperback)

The Cambridge Companion to Berg
Edited by Anthony Pople
0 521 56374 7 (hardback)
0 521 56489 1 (paperback)

The Cambridge Companion to Berlioz
Edited by Peter Bloom
0 521 59388 3 (hardback)
0 521 59638 6 (paperback)

The Cambridge Companion to Brahms
Edited by Michael Musgrave
0 521 48129 5 (hardback)
0 521 48581 9 (paperback)

The Cambridge Companion to Benjamin Britten
Edited by Mervyn Cooke
0 521 57384 X (hardback)
0 521 57476 5 (paperback)

The Cambridge Companion to Chopin
Edited by Jim Samson
0 521 47752 2 (paperback)

The Cambridge Companion to Handel
Edited by Donald Burrows
0 521 45425 5 (hardback)
0 521 45613 4 (paperback)

The Cambridge Companion to Ravel
Edited by Deborah Mawer
0 521 64026 1 (hardback)
0 521 64856 4 (paperback)

The Cambridge Companion to Schubert
Edited by Christopher Gibbs
0 521 48229 1 (hardback)
0 521 48424 3 (paperback)

The Cambridge Companion to

BERLIOZ

EDITED BY

Peter Bloom

Smith College

CAMBRIDGE
UNIVERSITY PRESS

PUBLISHED BY THE PRESS SYNDICATE OF THE UNIVERSITY OF CAMBRIDGE
The Pitt Building, Trumpington Street, Cambridge, United Kingdom

CAMBRIDGE UNIVERSITY PRESS
The Edinburgh Building, Cambridge CB2 2RU, UK www.cup.cam.ac.uk
40 West 20th Street, New York, NY 10011–4211, USA www.cup.org
10 Stamford Road, Oakleigh, Melbourne 3166, Australia
Ruiz de Alarcón 13, 28014 Madrid, Spain

First published 2000

Printed in the United Kingdom at the University Press, Cambridge

Typeset in Adobe Minion 10.75/14 pt, in QuarkXpress™ [SE]

A catalogue record for this book is available from the British Library

Library of Congress cataloguing in publication data

The Cambridge Companion to Berlioz / edited by Peter Bloom.
        p.   cm. – (Cambridge companions to music)
Includes bibliographical references and index.
ISBN 0 521 59388 3 (hardback) – ISBN 0 521 59638 5 (paperback)
1. Berlioz, Hector, 1803–1869–Criticism and interpretation. I. Bloom, Peter. II. Series.
ML410.B5 C27   2000
780′.92–dc21   99–054359   CIP

ISBN 0 521 59388 3 hardback
ISBN 0 521 59638 6 paperback

Contents

Illustrations

Contributors

Jacques Barzun, University Professor Emeritus, Columbia University, was literary adviser to Charles Scribner's Sons, in New York City, from 1975 to 1993. He retired to San Antonio, Texas, in 1997. His latest book, published by HarperCollins, is *From Dawn to Decadence: 500 Years of Western Culture.*

Diana Bickley, now completing a doctoral dissertation on "The Concert Overtures of Hector Berlioz" at Goldsmiths College, University of London, is editor of volume 20 of the *New Berlioz Edition.*

Peter Bloom, the Grace Jarcho Ross 1933 Professor of Humanities at Smith College, is editor of *Music in Paris in the Eighteen-Thirties* (1987) and *Berlioz Studies* (1992). His short biography, *The Life of Berlioz,* appeared in 1998.

David Cairns, independent scholar, has been music critic for the *Spectator,* the *Evening Standard,* the *Financial Times,* the *New Statesman,* and most recently the *Sunday Times.* The first volume of his biography of Berlioz, *The Making of an Artist,* appeared in 1989; the second, *Servitude and Greatness,* in 1999. Both volumes are now published by the University of California Press.

Pierre Citron, Professor Emeritus of French Literature at the Sorbonne nouvelle, Paris, author of authoritative studies of the works of Balzac and Giono, is General Editor of the *Correspondance générale d'Hector Berlioz.*

Katharine Ellis is Lecturer in the Music Department at Royal Holloway, University of London, and joint editor of *Music & Letters.* Her *Music Criticism in Nineteenth-Century France: La Revue et Gazette musicale de Paris, 1834–1880* appeared in 1995. She is currently at work on a book on the revival of early music in nineteenth-century France.

Joël-Marie Fauquet is Directeur de Recherche at the Centre National de la Recherche Scientifique, in Paris. He is the author of, among other books, *La Musique de chambre à Paris de la Restauration à 1870* (1986) and *César Franck* (1999). He is editor of the *Correspondance* of Édouard Lalo (1989) and editor-in-chief of the *Dictionnaire de la Musique en France au XIXe siècle* (forthcoming from Fayard).

Annegret Fauser is Lecturer in Music at City University, London, and author of *Der Orchestergesang in Frankreich zwischen 1870 und 1920* (1994). With Manuele Schwartz she is co-editor of *Von Wagner zum Wagnérisme: Musik-Literatur-Kunst-Politik,* and is currently at work on a book titled *Les Voix de Marianne: Women and Music in fin de siècle Paris.*

James Haar, author of numerous and crucial studies of the music of the renaissance, is William.R. Kenan Jr. Professor Emeritus of Music at the University of North Carolina at Chapel Hill. His most recent book, *The Science and Art of Renaissance Music* (1997), includes a chapter on Berlioz and the "First Opera" and a chapter on renaissance music as viewed by the romantics.

D. Kern Holoman is Professor of Music and conductor of the Symphony Orchestra at the University of California at Davis. He is author of the *Catalogue of the Works of Hector Berlioz* and editor of volume 18 of the *New Berlioz Edition*. His life-and-works, *Berlioz*, appeared in 1989; his study of *La Société des Concerts, 1828–1967* is forthcoming from the University of California Press.

Janet Johnson is Associate Professor of Music History and Literature at the University of Southern California, in Los Angeles. She has recently completed a reconstruction and critical edition of Rossini's *Il viaggio a Reims*, the composer's last Italian opera and the first completely new one he wrote for Paris, for the *Edizione critica della opera di Gioachino Rossini*.

Katherine [Reeve] Kolb is Associate Professor of French at Southeastern Louisiana University. She has written on literature (Proust, Pascal, Balzac) and music, with particular attention to Berlioz. She is responsible for the entry on Berlioz in *European Writers: The Romantic Century* (1985) and the entry "Music and Romanticism" in the *Encyclopedia of Aesthetics* (1998).

Jeffrey Langford is Director of Doctoral Studies at the Manhattan School of Music, in New York. He is author of *Hector Berlioz: A Guide to Research* (1989) and of articles focusing on the relationship between literature and music in Berlioz and Verdi.

Ralph P. Locke is Professor of Music at the University of Rochester's Eastman School of Music, senior editor of *Eastman Studies in Music*, and member of the editorial board of the *Journal of Musicological Research*. His *Music, Musicians, and the Saint-Simonians* appeared in English in 1986 and in French in 1992. With Cyrilla Barr he is co-editor of *Cultivating Music in America: Women Patrons and Activists since 1860*.

Hugh Macdonald is Avis Blewett Professor of Music at Washington University, in St. Louis, Missouri. He is General Editor of the *New Berlioz Edition* and author of the "Master Musicians" *Berlioz* (1982). His edition of *Selected Letters of Berlioz* appeared in London in 1995 and in New York in 1997.

Julian Rushton is West Riding Professor of Music at the University of Leeds. He is General Editor of Cambridge Music Handbooks and Chair of the Editorial Committee of *Musica Britannica*. His publications include work on Gluck, Mozart, and Elgar, as well as *The Musical Language of Berlioz*, a Cambridge Music Handbook on *Roméo et Juliette*, and a general study of *The Music of Berlioz* (forthcoming).

Lesley Wright, Associate Professor of Musicology and Chair of the Music Department at the University of Hawaii, has focused her research on Bizet and his contemporaries. Her edition of Bizet's *Letters in the Nydahl Collection* appeared in 1988. More recently she edited *L'Arlésienne* (the first and second suites) for Ernst Eulenberg Ltd., and prepared the article on Bizet for the new *MGG*. She is currently at work on a study of the music of the *Exposition de Paris 1900*.

Acknowledgements

The editor is grateful to all contributors to this volume, and particularly to those who have waited with considerable patience to see their work in print. For special assistance during the preparation of the text I am indebted to Ruth Solie, Hugh Macdonald, Julian Rushton, and Cécile Reynaud. That the book exists at all is due to the good will and gentle impatience of Penny Souster, at Cambridge University Press, to whom it is a pleasure to express affectionate gratitude.

Peter Bloom

Abbreviations

CG   Hector Berlioz, *Correspondance générale*
          Pierre Citron, General Editor (Paris: Flammarion, 1972–)
CG I   1803–1832, ed. Pierre Citron (1972)
CG II   1832–1842, ed. Frédéric Robert (1975)
CG III   1842–1850, ed. Pierre Citron (1978)
CG IV   1851–1855, ed. Pierre Citron, Yves Gérard, and Hugh Macdonald (1983)
CG V   1855–1859, ed. Hugh Macdonald and François Lesure (1988)
CG VI   1859–1863, ed. Hugh Macdonald and François Lesure (1995)
CG VII   1864–1869, ed. Hugh Macdonald (forthcoming)
      Unless otherwise indicated, references here to Berlioz's correspondence are to this edition. When the precise date of a letter is included in the text, reference to this edition is assumed.

CM   Hector Berlioz, *Critique musicale*
          Yves Gérard, general editor (Paris: Buchet/Chastel, 1996–)
CM I   1823–1834, ed. H. Robert Cohen and Yves Gérard (1996)
CM II   1835–1836, ed. Yves Gérard and Marie-Hélène Coudroy-Saghaï (1998)
CM III   is forthcoming. Seven further volumes are envisioned.

Mémoires / Memoirs
      References here to Berlioz's *Mémoires* are usually by chapter number, as the various editions of the book, in French and English, are consistent on this point. The main editions are as follows:
Hector Berlioz, *Mémoires,* ed. Pierre Citron (Paris: Flammarion, 1991)
Hector Berlioz, *Mémoires,* ed. Pierre Citron (Paris: Garnier-Flammarion, 1969)
The Memoirs of Hector Berlioz, transl. and ed. David Cairns (London: Victor Gollancz Ltd., 1969; and several further editions, the latest being that issued in London by Sphere Books Ltd. [Cardinal] in 1990).
      Unless otherwise indicated, quotations from the *Mémoires* in this Companion are taken from one of the published translations by David Cairns (and sometimes modified by the authors).

Les Soirées de l'orchestre (1968)
Les Grotesques de la musique (1969)
À travers chants (1971)
      Unless otherwise indicated, references here to Berlioz's three collections of his own criticism and fiction, listed above, are to the *Œuvres Littéraires*, Édition du Centenaire, ed. Léon Guichard (Paris: Gründ, 1968–1971).

NBE [*New Berlioz Edition*] Hector Berlioz, *New Edition of the Complete Works*
Hugh Macdonald, general editor (Kassel: Bärenreiter, 1967–)

NBE 1*a-d* *Benvenuto Cellini* (1994–)

2*a-c* *Les Troyens*, ed. Hugh Macdonald(1969–1970)

3 *Béatrice et Bénédict*, ed. Hugh Macdonald (1980)

4 *Incomplete Operas*

5 *Huit Scènes de Faust*, ed. Julian Rushton (1970)

6 *Prix de Rome Works*, ed. David Gilbert (1998)

7 *Lélio ou Le Retour à la vie*, ed. Peter Bloom (1992)

8*a-b* *La Damnation de Faust*, ed. Julian Rushton (1979–1986)

9 *Grande Messe des morts*, ed. Jürgen Kindermann (1978)

10 *Te Deum*, ed. Denis McCaldin (1973)

11 *L'Enfance du Christ*, ed. David Lloyd Jones (1998)

12*a* *Choral Works with Orchestra, I*, ed. Julian Rushton (1991)

12*b* *Choral Works with Orchestra, II*, ed. David Charlton (1993)

13 *Songs for Solo Voice and Orchestra*, ed. Ian Kemp (1975)

14 *Choral Works with Keyboard*, ed. Ian Rumbold (1996)

15 *Songs for One, Two or Three Voices and Keyboard*

16 *Symphonie fantastique*, ed. Nicholas Temperley (1972)

17 *Harold en Italie*

18 *Roméo et Juliette*, ed. D. Kern Holoman (1990)

19 *Symphonie funèbre et triomphale*, ed. Hugh Macdonald (1967)

20 *Overtures*

21 *Miscellaneous Works*

22*a* *Arrangements of Works by Gluck*

22*b* *Arrangements of Works by Other Composers*

23 *Messe solennelle*, ed. Hugh Macdonald (1994)

24 *Grand Traité d'instrumentation et d'orchestration modernes*

25 D. Kern Holoman, *Catalogue of the Works of Hector Berlioz* (1987)

26 *Portraits*

Holoman NBE 25 (as above)

For detailed information regarding the contents of these volumes and the availability of scores and parts, the reader is referred to the Appendix of the article in this Companion by D. Kern Holoman.

Chronology

	Berlioz	France and beyond
1800	Birth at Ennis, Ireland, of Harriet Constance Smithson, to become B's first wife (18 March).	Napoléon's forces defeat the Austrians at Marengo (14 June).
1801		Capitulation of the French army in Egypt (August); Chateaubriand, *Atala*.
1802		Birth of Victor Hugo (26 February); institution of the Légion d'honneur (19 May); Bonaparte becomes Consul for life (2 August); Chateaubriand, *Le Génie du Christianisme*.
1803	Marriage of Louis-Joseph Berlioz (father) and Marie-Antoinette-Joséphine Marmion (mother) (6 February). Birth at La Côte-Saint-André of Louis-~~Nicolas~~-Hector Berlioz (11 December), at 5 p.m.; B's original second Christian name is crossed out in his father's *Livre de raison*.	France declares war on England (18 May); France sells Louisiana to the United States (December); Beethoven composes the *Eroica* Symphony.
1804	The Berlioz ménage at La Côte-Saint-André is one of "love and contentment" (David Cairns).	Napoléon becomes Emperor of France (20 May); birth of George Sand (1 July); Napoléon is crowned in Paris (2 December).
1805	Birth of Jean-Jacques-Humbert Ferrand, who will become B's lifelong friend.	Lesueur, *Ossian* (10 July); Mozart, *Don Giovanni*, in Paris (17 September); Napoléon defeats the Austrians and Russians at Austerlitz (2 December).
1806	Birth of B's sister Marguerite-Anne-Louise, called Nanci (17 February).	Napoléon's "Continental System" is established.
1807	Birth of B's sister Louise (August).	Peace of Tilsit between France and Russia (7 July); Spontini, *La Vestale* (15 December).
1808		Birth of Gérard de Nerval (22 May); establishment of the university system in France; birth of the future Napoléon III (11 October); France invades Spain (December).
1809	B begins his studies at the petit-séminaire nearby the family home at La Côte.	France annexes the Papal States, defeats the Austrians at Wagram (July); Napoléon divorces Josephine (16 December).

	Berlioz	France and beyond
1810		Napoléon marries the Archduchess Marie-Louise of Austria (1 April); Mme de Staël, *De l'Allemagne*.
1811	B studies at home with his father; over the years he takes up French literature, Latin, philosophy, rhetoric, and anatomy.	Inauguration of the new concert hall at the Conservatoire, in the rue Bergère (7 July); births of Théophile Gautier (30 August) and Franz Liszt (22 October), both to become B's close friends; Gluck, *Armide*, in Paris (16 December).
1812		France declares war on Russia (22 June); the French retreat from Moscow (October).
1813		Birth of Wagner (22 May); Wellington defeats the French at Vittoria (21 June); birth of Verdi (10 October).
1814	Birth of B's sister Adèle-Eugénie (8 May); birth of Marie-Geneviève Martin, who will become B's second wife (10 June).	Allied invasion of France (January); Napoléon abdicates (6 April); Restoration of the Bourbon Monarchy in the person of Louis XVIII (3 May); opening of the Congress of Vienna (September).
1815	Death of B's sister Louise (16 April); B meets and experiences a teenage passion for Estelle Dubœuf; she becomes a symbol of love that endures throughout his lifetime.	The "Hundred Days" (March–June); battle of Waterloo (18 June); Napoléon's final abdication (22 June); second Bourbon Restoration (8 July).
1816	B learns to play the flageolet and the flute, using Devienne's *Méthode* of 1795; B's mother gives birth to a son, Jules (December), who dies in 1819.	Cherubini becomes professor of composition at the Conservatoire (1 April); the *Chambre introuvable* – Joseph Faure is the representative from the Isère – is dissolved (5 September).
1817	B studies music (flute, singing) with Imbert, composes a *Potpourri concertant* (lost); B's father becomes Mayor of La Côte (September).	Rossini, *L'Italiana in Algeri* – the composer's first work to be performed in Paris (1 February).
1818	B composes two quintets for flute and string quartet (lost); Dorant succeeds Imbert as music teacher at La Côte; B takes up the guitar.	End of the Allied occupation of France (November).
1819	B proposes some youthful compositions to Parisian publishers.	
1820	Birth of B's brother Prosper (26 June).	Assassination of the Duc de Berry (13 February); birth of the Comte de Chambord (29 September); Lamartine, *Les Méditations poétiques*.

Berlioz	France and beyond
1821 B receives the *Baccalauréat-ès-lettres* (22 March); arrives in Paris (late October), enrolls at the Faculté de Médecine (16 November), hears *Iphigénie en Tauride* (probably 26 November).	Death of Napoléon (5 May); première of *Der Freischütz*, in Berlin (18 June); Habeneck succeeds Viotti as Director of the Opéra (1 November).
1822 B frequents the library of the Conservatoire (summer), composes *Le Cheval arabe* (autumn), publishes some early *romances*, subsists on allowances from his father (which vary but continue for many years).	Cherubini becomes Director of the Conservatoire (19 April); Villèle Ministry (December); Greeks proclaim independence from Turkey.
1823 B composes *Estelle et Némorin* and *Le Passage de la mer rouge* (lost), publishes his first article in *Le Corsaire* (12 August).	Liszt arrives in Paris (11 December); France intervenes in Spain to reestablish the Bourbon Monarchy.
1824 B receives the *Bachelier-ès-sciences physiques* (13 January); composes *Beverley, ou le joueur* (lost), has the *Messe solennelle* rehearsed (27 December).	Death of Byron (19 April); Beethoven, Ninth Symphony (7 May); creation of the Département des Beaux-Arts under the direction of Sosthènes de La Rochefoucauld (6 September); death of Louis XVIII (16 September); succession of Charles X; Rossini becomes Director of the Théâtre Italien (1 December); Castil-Blaze, *Robin des bois* (7 December).
1825 B composes the *Scène héroïque*, begins *Les Francs-Juges*, witnesses the première of the *Messe solennelle* (10 July).	Coronation of Charles X (29 May); Rossini, *Il viaggio a Reims* (19 June).
1826 B enrolls at the Conservatoire for composition with Lesueur (26 August) and counterpoint and fugue with Reicha (2 October), completes the overture to *Les Francs-Juges*.	Death of Weber (4 June); Rossini, *Le Siège de Corinthe* (9 October); branches of the Paris Conservatoire created in Lille and Toulouse (20 December).
1827 B sings in the chorus at the Théâtre des Nouveautés, composes *La Mort d'Orphée* (July), sees Harriet Smithson as Ophelia (11 September) and Juliet (15 September).	Rossini, *Moïse* (26 March); death of Beethoven (26 March); Hugo, *Préface de Cromwell* (December); French naval intervention in Greece.
1828 B gives his first orchestral concert with Bloc conducting the premières of the overtures *Les Francs-Juges* and *Waverley* (26 May), composes *Herminie* (July), reads Goethe's *Faust* in Gérard de Nerval's new translation.	Martignac Ministry (4 January); Auber, *La Muette de Portici* (29 February); inaugural concert of the Société des Concerts du Conservatoire (9 March); imprisonment of Béranger for political songs (10 December).

	Berlioz	France and beyond
1829	B composes *Cléopâtre* (July), *Neuf Mélodies*; writes his first article for *Le Correspondant* (4 August), gives a concert with Habeneck conducting the première of a part of the *Huit Scènes de Faust* (1 November).	Establishment in Paris of *Jeune France*, a republican student organization; Rossini, *Guillaume Tell* (3 August); Polignac Ministry (8 August); Hugo, *Les Orientales*.
1830	B begins the *Symphonie fantastique* (January), falls in love with Marie Moke (March), composes *Sardanapale* (July) – wins the Prix de Rome (August), witnesses the premières of *La Tempête* (7 November) and of the *Fantastique* (5 December), departs for Rome via La Côte (31 December).	Hugo, *Hernani* (25 February); July Ordinances (25 July); revolution in Paris (27–29 July); Louis-Philippe, King of the French (9 August); disturbances in Brussels after a performance of *La Muette de Portici* (25 August); Stendhal, *Le Rouge et le noir*.
1831	B arrives in Rome (10 March), discovers that Marie Moke has broken their engagement (April), completes *Le Roi Lear* (10 May), *Rob-Roy MacGregor* (July), and *Le Retour à la vie*, later called *Lélio* (summer).	Reorganization of the National Guard (March); Chopin arrives in Paris (October); Meyerbeer, *Robert le diable* (21 November); worker uprisings in Lyon (21–22 November); Hugo, *Notre Dame de Paris*; Balzac, *La Peau de chagrin*; Barbier, *Iambes*.
1832	B composes *La Captive* (February), departs from Rome (2 May), arrives at La Côte (June), arrives in Paris (7 November); Habeneck conducts the *Fantastique* and the première of *Le Retour à la vie* (5 December); B meets Harriet Smithson (mid-December).	Chopin's first concert in Paris (26 February); death of Goethe (22 March); Hugo, *Le Roi s'amuse* (22 November).
1833	Habeneck conducts the première of *Rob-Roy* (14 April); B attempts suicide because of Smithson's reluctance to marry (August), marries Smithson (3 October) with Liszt as one of the witnesses, continues to subsist on the Rome Prize stipend (as he will through 1835).	Death of Hérold (19 January); Auber, *Gustave III* (27 February); Guizot, *Loi sur l'instruction primaire* (28 June); Balzac, *Eugénie Grandet*.
1834	B begins *Harold en Italie* (January), moves with Harriet to Montmartre (10 April), conceives *Benvenuto Cellini*, publishes *Le Suicide par enthousiasme* (20, 24 July); birth of B's son Louis-Clément-Thomas (14 August); Girard conducts the première of *Harold* (23 November).	Schumann founds the *Neue Zeitschrift für Musik* (April); death of Lafayette (20 May); death of Boieldieu (8 October); Balzac, *Le Père Goriot*.

	Berlioz	**France and beyond**
1835	B gives a concert at the Conservatoire (3 May), receives his last payment as winner of the Prix de Rome (1 July); Girard conducts *Le Cinq Mai* (22 November).	Halévy, *La Juive* (23 February); Fieschi attemps to assassinate Louis-Philippe (28 July); Duponchel succeeds Véron as director of the Opéra (16 August); Camille Pleyel separates from Marie Moke (September); Vigny, *Chatterton*.
1836	B now depends largely on journalism for income (January), fails to obtain the directorship of the Gymnase musical (January), attends the première of *Les Huguenots* (29 January); death of Harriet Smithson's sister Anne Cecelia (June); B completes *Benvenuto Cellini* (autumn), conducts concerts at the Conservatoire (4, 18 December).	Meyerbeer, *Les Huguenots* (29 February); Louis Napoléon's failed *coup d'état* at Strasbourg (30 October); Bertin, *Esméralda* (14 November).
1837	Gasparin commissions the *Requiem* (March); Habeneck conducts the première of the *Requiem* (5 December).	Marriage of the Duc d'Orléans and Hélène de Mecklembourg (29 May); inauguration of the rail line Paris–Saint-Germain (25 August); sack of Constantine (13 October); death of General Damrémont (17 October); Balzac, *Les Illusions perdues*.
1838	B seeks the direction of the Théâtre Italien (January–June); death of B's mother (18 February); première of *Benvenuto Cellini* (10 September); B's brother Prosper arrives in Paris (20 October); the *Fantastique* and *Harold* are performed at the Conservatoire – Paganini pays homage with a gift of 20,000 francs (16 December).	Fire destroys the Théâtre Italien (13 January); birth of Bizet (25 October); Gautier, *La Comédie de la mort*.
1839	B officially becomes Associate Librarian at the Conservatoire (1 January); death of B's brother Prosper (15 January); B named Chevalier de la Légion d'honneur (10 May), conducts the première of *Roméo et Juliette* – Wagner attends (24 November).	Mendelssohn premieres Schubert's *Great* C-Major Symphony (21 March).
1840	Rémusat commissions the *Symphonie funèbre* (April); B directs the première of the *Symphonie funèbre* (28 July) and a *Festival* at the Opéra (1 November).	Thiers Ministry (1 March); birth of Tchaikovsky (7 May); death of Paganini (27 May); Friedrich Wilhelm IV accedes to the throne of Prussia (7 June); Louis-Napoléon's failed *coup d'état* at Boulogne (6 August);

	Berlioz	France and beyond
		Guizot Ministry (29 October); translation of Napoléon's remains to the Invalides (15 December).
1841	B composes recitatives and prepares *Der Freischütz* for the Opéra (March–May), composes *Les Nuits d'été* (summer); première of B's version of *Der Freischütz* (7 June); B frequents Marie Récio (autumn).	Adolphe Sax invents the saxophone; Hugo elected to the Académie française; Armand Bertin succeeds his father as director of the *Journal des débats*.
1842	B is denied the post of Inspecteur des Écoles de chant (May), gives a concert in Brussels – his first abroad (26 September), presents his candidacy for a chair at the Institute (October), visits Frankfurt and Stuttgart (December).	Rossini, *Stabat Mater* (7 January); Meyerbeer becomes General Music Director of the Royal Opera House in Berlin; Cherubini resigns from the Conservatoire (4 February), dies (15 March); death of Stendhal (23 March); death of the Duc d'Orléans (13 July); Chopin and George Sand settle in Paris (September); Wagner, *Rienzi* (20 October).
1843	B travels to Hechingen, Stuttgart, Carlsruhe, Mannheim, Frankfurt, Weimar, Leipzig, Dresden, Brunswick, Hamburg, Berlin, Magdeburg, and Darmstadt (January–May), composes *Le Carnaval romain* (September), completes the *Grand Traité d'instrumentation et d'orchestration modernes* (December).	Wagner, *Der fliegende Holländer* (2 January).
1844	Première of *Le Carnaval romain* (3 February); publication of *Euphonia* (February); official publication of the *Traité d'instrumentation* (1 March); B directs a concert for the Festival d'industrie (1 August); publication of the *Voyage musical en Allemagne et en Italie* (August); B composes the *Marche funèbre sur la mort d'Hamlet* (November).	Louis-Philippe "reigns but does not govern" (Thiers).
1845	B gives concerts in Marseille and Lyon (June, July), attends the Beethoven celebrations in Bonn (August), begins work on *La Damnation de Faust* (autumn).	Unveiling of the Beethoven monument in Bonn (10 August); Wagner, *Tannhäuser* (19 October).
1846	B directs *Roméo et Juliette* in Vienna (2 January), travels to Prague, Pest,	Louis-Napoléon escapes from Ham prison (25 May), goes to London.

Berlioz	France and beyond
Breslau, Dresden, Leipzig, and Brunswick (January–April), conducts the première of the *Chant des chemins de fer* in Lille (14 June) and the première of *La Damnation de Faust* (6 December).	
1847 B departs for Russia (14 February), gives concerts in St. Petersburg and Moscow (February–April), has an affair with a Russian chorister (April–May), directs *Faust* in Berlin (19 June), gives a concert in Versailles (29 October), departs for London (3 November).	Death of Mendelssohn (4 November).
1848 B begins his *Mémoires* in London (January), returns to Paris (14 July); death of B's father (28 July); Harriet Smithson has a stroke (mid-October); B conceives the *Te Deum*.	Revolution in Paris, abdication of Louis-Philippe (22–24 February); proclamation of the Republic (24 February); Liszt becomes Court Kapellmeister in Weimar (February); death of Chateaubriand (4 July); Louis-Napoléon elected President of the Republic (10 December); Chateaubriand, *Mémoires d'outre-tombe*.
1849 Harriet suffers from continued strokes; B plans the Société Philharmonique de Paris (December).	Death of Habeneck (8 February); Meyerbeer, *Le Prophète* (16 April); revolts in Dresden and Baden (April–May); warrant issued for the arrest of Wagner (16 May); death of Chopin (17 October); Chopin's funeral in Paris (30 October).
1850 First concert of the Société Philharmonique de Paris (19 February); B becomes Head Librarian at the Conservatoire (March); death of B's sister Nanci (14 May); B attends Balzac's funeral (19 August); beginning of the new season of the Société Philharmonique (22 October); B composes *La Fuite en Égypte* (autumn).	Death of Louis-Philippe (26 August); Wagner, *Lohengrin* (28 August), *Das Judentum in der Musik* in the *Neue Zeitschrift für Musik* (3, 6 September).
1851 Concerts by the Société Philharmonique (January–May); B presents his candidacy for a chair at the Institute (6 March), leaves for the Great Exhibition in London (9 May), departs from London (28 July),	Death of Spontini (24 January); Ambroise Thomas elected to the Institute (22 March); Louis-Napoléon's *coup d'état* (2 December), election to a ten-year term (31 December).

Berlioz	France and beyond
presents his congratulations to Louis-Napoléon (7 December).	
1852 B arrives in London (4 March), conducts six concerts of the New Philharmonic Society (March–June); Liszt revives *Benvenuto Cellini* in Weimar (20 March); B leaves Paris for Weimar (12 November); publication of *Les Soirées de l'Orchestre* (December).	Louis-Napoléon takes up residence at the Tuileries (January); Orléans family banished from France; proclamation of the Second Empire (2 December) – the Opéra becomes the Académie Impériale de Musique.
1853 B leaves for London (14 May), directs *Benvenuto Cellini* in London (25 June), returns to Paris (9 July), gives concerts in Baden and Frankfurt (August), gives concerts in Brunswick, Hanover, Bremen, Detmold, and Leipzig (October–December), submits his candidacy for a chair at the Institute (10 November).	Haussmann becomes Préfet de la Seine; Napoléon III marries Eugénie de Montijo (30 January); outbreak of the Crimean War (October).
1854 Death of Harriet Smithson (3 March); B gives concerts in Hanover, Brunswick, and Dresden (March–April), presents his candidacy for a chair at the Institute (10 August), marries Marie Récio (19 October), directs the première of *L'Enfance du Christ* (10 December).	France declares war on Russia (28 March); Nestor Roqueplan becomes administrator of the Opéra (30 June).
1855 B gives concerts in Weimar (February), Brussels (March), conducts the première of the *Te Deum* (30 April), gives concerts in London (June, July), serves as juror for the Exposition Universelle in Paris (August–September), completes *L'Art du chef d'orchestre* for the second edition of the *Traité d'instrumentation* (autumn), conducts the première of *L'Impériale* (15 November).	Wagner in London for eight concerts with the Philharmonic Society (March–June); Exposition Universelle opens in Paris (15 May) – first classification of the wines of Bordeaux; Verdi, *Les Vêpres siciliennes* (13 June).
1856 B gives *L'Enfance du Christ* in Paris (25 February) and in Gotha (6 February); Liszt gives *Benvenuto Cellini* in Weimar (16 February); B gives concerts in Weimar (17, 28 February), hears *Lohengrin* in Weimar	Crimean War ended by the Treaty of Paris (30 March).

Berlioz	**France and beyond**
(24 February), directs *Faust* in Weimar (1 March), completes the orchestration of *Les Nuits d'été* (March), moves from 19, rue de Boursault to 17, rue de Vintimille (15 April), begins work on *Les Troyens* (April), presents his candidacy for a chair at the Institute (3 June), is elected (21 June) – the annual stipend is a boon to his finances, gives a concert in Baden (16 August), moves to 4, rue de Calais (20 October).	
1857 B conducts at the Salle Herz (19 April), gives a concert in Baden (18 August).	Bizet, Prix de Rome (4 July); Liszt, *Faust Symphony* – dedicated to B (5 September); Baudelaire, *Les Fleurs du mal.*
1858 B sees Wagner in Paris (20 January), reads *Les Troyens* to colleagues from the Institute (22 January), completes *Les Troyens* (April), conducts at the Conservatoire (2 May), gives a concert in Baden (27 August); excerpts from the *Mémoires* begin to appear in *Le Monde illustré* (25 September).	Orsini attempts to assassinate Napoléon III (14 January); Offenbach, *Orphée aux enfers* (21 October).
1859 Publication of *Les Grotesques de la musique* (March); B directs *L'Enfance du Christ* (23 April), gives concerts in Bordeaux (8 June) and Baden (29 August), leads scenes from *Les Troyens* at the home of Pauline Viardot (24 October); revival of Gluck's *Orphée* in B's version (18 November).	The French government adopts a standard musical pitch (February); Gounod, *Faust* (19 March); France goes to war with Austria over Italy (12 May); Montmartre is annexed into Paris; Wagner completes *Tristan und Isolde* (6 August); Liszt is denied election to the Institut de France (3 December).
1860 Death of B's sister Adèle (2 March); B gives a concert in Baden (27 August), begins *Béatrice et Bénédict* (October).	Wagner's first concert in Paris (25 January); first rehearsal for *Tannhäuser* (24 September); France annexes Savoie and Nice; construction of two new theatres in the Place du Châtelet.
1861 B composes *Le Temple universel* (February), gives excerpts from *La Damnation de Faust* (7 April), assists at rehearsals of *Der Freischütz* (May), has *Les Troyens* accepted at the Opéra (June), assists at rehearsals of *Alceste* (June–July), gives a concert in Baden	Death of Scribe (20 February); Wagner, revised *Tannhäuser* (13 March); French intervention and war in Mexico (1861–1867); beginning of construction of Garnier's Opéra (completed in 1875); outbreak of the American Civil War (12 April).

Berlioz	France and beyond
(26 August); revival of *Alceste* with B's assistance (21 October); B completes *Béatrice et Bénédict* (December).	
1862 Printing of the vocal score of *Les Troyens* (February); Beulé elected over B as Secrétaire perpétuel of the Institut de France (12 April); publication of *À travers chants* (spring); death of B's second wife, Marie Récio (13 June), B makes the acquaintance of Amélie (June), directs the première of *Béatrice et Bénédict* in Baden (9 August).	Birth of Debussy (22 August); Émile Perrin replaces Royer as director of the Opéra; Hugo, *Les Misérables*; Flaubert, *Salammbô*.
1863 Publication of the vocal score of *Béatrice et Bénédict* (January); B conducts for the Société Nationale des Beaux-Arts (8, 22 February), parts company with Amélie (February), donates his musical library to the Société des Concerts du Conservatoire (25 March), conducts *Béatrice et Bénédict* in Weimar (8, 10 April), gives a concert in Löwenberg (17 April), is compelled to divide *Les Troyens* into *La Prise de Troie* and *Les Troyens à Carthage* (June), composes the Prologue to the latter, directs *L'Enfance du Christ* in Strasbourg (22 June), signs a contract with Choudens for *La Prise de Troie*, *Les Troyens à Carthage*, and *Benvenuto Cellini* (22 July) – the sum liberates him from journalism, directs *Béatrice et Bénédict* in Baden (14, 18 August), writes his last feuilleton for the *Journal des débats* (8 October); première of *Les Troyens à Carthage* at the Théâtre Lyrique (4 November); publication of the piano-vocal scores of *La Prise de Troie* and *Les Troyens à Carthage*, of the *Collection de 32 Mélodies*, and of a German translation of the *Traité d'instrumentation* (November); B fails to win election as Conductor of the Société des Concerts du Conservatoire (21 December).	Salon des Refusés (1 May); Massenet, Prix de Rome (4 July); death of Delacroix (13 August); death of Vigny (17 September); Bizet, *Les Pêcheurs de perles* (30 September); the French capture Mexico City, proclaim Archduke Maximilian of Austria Emperor.

	Berlioz	France and beyond
1864	B resigns from *Journal des débats* (March), returns to Dauphiné, visits Estelle Dubœuf Fornier (August–September).	Wagner is "saved" by Ludwig II of Bavaria, newly acceded to the throne (10 March); Gounod, *Mireille* (19 March); death of Meyerbeer (2 May); birth of Richard Strauss (11 June); Bismarck meets Napoléon III at Biarritz (October); Offenbach, *La Belle Hélène* (17 December).
1865	B has twelve hundred copies of the *Mémoires* printed and stored in his office at the Conservatoire (July), visits Estelle (August).	Assassination of Abraham Lincoln (14 April); Meyerbeer, *L'Africaine* (28 April); Wagner, *Tristan und Isolde* (10 June); Bismarck again meets Napoléon III at Biarritz (October).
1866	B visits Estelle (August), assists at rehearsals of *Alceste* (autumn), conducts *La Damnation de Faust* in Vienna (16 December).	
1867	B conducts selections from *Béatrice et Bénédict* in Cologne (26 February); death of Louis Berlioz in Havana (5 June); B drafts his will (29 July), visits Estelle (September), directs four concerts in St. Petersburg (November–December), meets Tchaikovsky (31 December).	Verdi, *Don Carlos* (11 March); Exposition Universelle opens in Paris (1 April); death of Baudelaire (31 August); execution of Maximilian in Mexico (19 June).
1868	B directs three concerts in Moscow (January) and two in St. Petersburg (January–February), goes to Nice and suffers two accidental falls (March), becomes Curator of the instrument collection at the Conservatoire (April), revises his will (12 June), presides over a choral festival in Grenoble (August); death of Humbert Ferrand (11 September); B attends his last meeting of the Académie des Beaux-Arts (12 December).	Five-hundredth performance of *Guillaume Tell* (10 February); Wagner, *Die Meistersinger* (21 June); death of Rossini (13 November).
1869	B dies in Paris (8 March), at 4, rue de Calais, at 12:30 p.m., and is buried in Montmartre (11 March).	Death of Lamartine (28 February); death of Sainte-Beuve (13 October); inauguration of the Suez Canal by the Empress Eugénie (November); Wagner, *Das Rheingold* (22 September); Flaubert, *L'Éducation sentimentale;* Manet, *L'Exécution de l'empereur Maximilien.*
1870	Publication of the *Mémoires d'Hector Berlioz.*	Wagner, *Die Walküre* (26 June); France declares war on Prussia (19 July); Wagner

Berlioz	France and beyond
	marries Cosima Liszt von Bülow (25 August); French defeat at Sudan (2 September); proclamation of the Third Republic (4 September); return from exile of Hugo (5 September); death of Prosper Mérimée (23 September); death of Alexandre Dumas père (5 December).

Introduction: Berlioz on the eve of the bicentenary

PETER BLOOM

In a recent novel by the popular French journalist Patrick Poivre d'Arvor, *Un Héros de passage*, a prototypically inexperienced and ambitious young man arrives from the provinces in the capital – the year is 1845 – there to seek fame and fortune. In Paris he makes the acquaintance of a darkly beautiful woman called "Queen Pomaré." This is not the historical Tahitian Queen whose fifty-year reign over the Polynesian island, from 1827 to 1877, encompassed its establishment as a French protectorate in 1843; it is rather the then fashionable cancan dancer, Élise Sergent, whose exotic and richly bejeweled appearance earned her that piquant and much bandied-about royal appellation.

What has this to do with Berlioz? It happens that in a musical *boutade* for a friend's album the composer once portrayed *himself* as chapelmaster to "Queen Pomaré" and composed "in Tahitian words and music" what he called a "morning greeting" to Her Gracious Majesty. I would not be surprised if there were a relationship between this *Salut matinal* – evidence, like so much else in his œuvre, of our man's delight in voyages both real and imagined – and the "other" Queen Pomaré, who was the licentious star of the Bal Mabille in the mid-eighteen-forties, when the undated album-leaf may well have been set down.[1] The sobriquet *pomaré*, like others applied to women of doubtful virtue, was widely known to all who made and attended to art and literature at the time. Théophile Gautier spoke of "la reine Pomaré" in his feuilleton for *La Presse* of 21 December 1846 – only two weeks after he published the review of the première of *La Damnation de Faust* in which he famously anointed Berlioz, Hugo, and Delacroix as "the trinity of Romantic Art."[2] Berlioz's friend Pier Angelo Fiorentino, a critic of "uncommon perception" on the composer's own testimony, was apparently among Queen Pomaré's lovers, and so, too, was Charles Baudelaire, who wrote some lascivious verses about their liaison.[3] Heinrich Heine wrote a poem about this "untamed beauty"[4] – and the untamed isle of Tahiti itself runs through years of Berlioz's public and private writings as an *idée fixe* of distant and wondrous adventure. So it seems fair to suggest that Berlioz's little machination was marinated in *double entendre*. And that his "appetites of the flesh," though "much weaker than the appetites of the mind," as Hugh Macdonald has recently

[1]

suggested, were perhaps not entirely satisfied by fare of the purely intellectual sort.[5]

When he returned to Paris in 1853, after giving two concerts in Frankfurt
on 20 and 24 August, Berlioz wrote letters to three different friends to
express satisfaction with the artistic results of his trip. From his letter of 3
September 1853 to the composer-conductor Gustav Schmidt, who facilitated the concerts in Frankfurt, we learn that Berlioz particularly enjoyed
the company of the players and the members of Frankfurt's musical community, among them (though not mentioned in Berlioz's letter) the
wealthy Polish Count Thadeus Tysczkiewicz. (Thadeus's father, Count
Vincenz, had been one of the Polish refugees for whose cause the not-yet
twenty-year-old Richard Wagner, we know from several emotional pages
in *Mein Leben*, felt great political and personal sympathy during his
student days in Leipzig.) It happens that Thadeus Tysczkiewicz traveled
from Frankfurt to Paris in the autumn of 1853 and remained there for a
year or so as, among other things, a correspondent for Robert Schumann's
Neue Zeitschrift für Musik. He caused a much-publicized ruckus by openly
suing the then director of the Opéra, Nestor Roqueplan, for falsely advertising and producing a version of *Der Freischütz* that in Tysczkiewicz's
view was corrupt – incomplete, mutilated, and execrably performed.

What has this to do with Berlioz? The work Tysczkiewicz had seen on
the stage of the Académie Impériale de Musique was, of course, *Le
Freischütz* – not the bastardization of the work that Castil-Blaze had performed at the Théâtre de l'Odéon in December of 1824 as *Robin des bois*
(which Berlioz became famous for excoriating), but the adaptation of the
work, first performed at the Opéra on 7 June 1841, with a French text by
Émilien Pacini and recitatives as required at the Opéra by Berlioz himself.
The prosecutorial matter, much reported in the press both foreign and
domestic, ended when the Première Chambre of the Tribunal Civil de la
Seine determined that what the Count had seen was precisely what was to
be expected in Paris, that the suit was without merit, that Tysczkiewicz
must pay court costs.

Berlioz's name was invoked by lawyers on both sides of the issue. The
composer, furious that anyone should accuse him of mutilating a masterpiece, took steps to restore his reputation as a defender of the faith,
writing to the editor of the *Journal des débats* on 22 December 1853 and to
half a dozen other editors in Germany as well to proclaim his good intentions.[6] What has heretofore not been known, what could not be known
from the letter of protest of 22 December, is that Tysczkiewicz was in fact
a personal acquaintance of Berlioz. Indeed, the two had spent some time
together in Frankfurt in August, after Berlioz's concerts there, and as a

token of his respect for the Frenchman, Tysczkiewicz offered Berlioz the first edition – a costly item – of the full score of Wagner's *Lohengrin* (published in Leipzig in 1852), with the following dedication:

Offert à Monsieur Hector Berlioz en souvenir de son passage par Francfort et comme témoignage de l'admiration la plus sincère et du plus profond respect.

Thadée Cte Tyczkiewicz, 29.VIII.1853.[7]

Someone with a conspiratorial turn of mind might therefore wonder, since he describes Roqueplan as an ungrateful and hypocritical Philistine in chapter 57 of the *Mémoires*, if it was Berlioz who encouraged Tysczkiewicz to sue.

These two episodes in the life of the artist, unrelated, offer confirmation, as that excellent collector Sarah Fenderson used so often to say, that "Berlioz leads everywhere." And that everything – at least as it pertains to the culture of the French nineteenth century, be it a Tahitian look-alike doing a prurient polka in the public square or a bona fide Polish count filing suit for a musical sort of Parisian immorality – leads to Berlioz.

The notion that Berlioz leads everywhere becomes more evident as we approach the two-hundredth anniversary of the composer's birth, to be celebrated with considerable pomp in the autumn of 2003. Concerts, exhibitions, and scholarly colloquia will mark the occasion, and, should the President of the French Republic so decree, Berlioz's remains will be translated to the Panthéon: *aux grands hommes, la patrie reconnaissante.* Berlioz, rarely in the shadows, will have an especially brilliant day in the sun. The hullabaloo should do no harm. Nor should it obscure the steadily good work of the scholars behind the scenes who are responsible for the scores, books, and articles that lead, we hope, to intelligent programming, perceptive listening, and sound appreciation.

Many of these scholars are represented in this collection, which, with its circumscribed genre studies and more wide-ranging essays, is designed to encourage general readers to deepen their understanding of the life and work of that singularly fascinating composer, conductor, writer, traveler, friend, lover, cynic, and prophet who was Berlioz. A word about each seems in order here.

In the opening piece, Jacques Barzun, quoting from memory (as was Berlioz's lifelong habit) and drawing on the learning of a lifetime, situates Berlioz in the age that invented the religion of art and the "genius" who preached and practiced it. With characteristic grace, Barzun gives broad explication to romanticism itself. On the basis of her close reading of the polemics surrounding the *guerre rossinienne* that erupted on the eve of Berlioz's arrival in Paris, Janet Johnson then shows us the young composer caught in the crossfire between the academic classicism of the Parisian musical establishment and the romantic modernism of Rossini espoused by Stendhal, Delacroix, and Balzac.

Julian Rushton prefaces a series of articles on Berlioz's principal compositions (arranged in five categories) by reflecting upon the nature of category, or *genre*, itself – this, clearly one of the most conspicuously challenging dimensions of the music of our composer. The symphony, many writers of the eighteen-twenties and thirties would have it, and Richard Wagner would later proclaim in "The Artwork of the Future" (1849), was a form that was no longer viable. In fact, though he much transformed the form by dramatizing it, Berlioz wrote four works called "symphonies" that are viable indeed, as Jeffrey Langford's treatment of them makes plain.

Robert Schumann (who wrote "viable" symphonies of his own) thought highly of the *Fantastique*, as is well known; he thought highly of Mendelssohn's symphonies, too, but offered even greater praise to his concert overtures, "in which the idea of the symphony is confined to a smaller orbit."[8] Berlioz's concert overtures, as we may conclude from Diana Bickley's essay, have been equally deserving of approbation as exceptionally original undertakings in the post-Beethovenian world of symphonic composition.

The operas and the "dramatic legend" *La Damnation de Faust* are the subject of James Haar's succinct reading, which gives us the broad outlines of their genesis and reception, and skillfully sets down the main aesthetic issues to which they give rise. In his essay on the religious music, Ralph Locke grapples, as one must, with the very definition of "religious," and speaks perceptively to Berlioz's achievement, particularly in the *Requiem* and *Te Deum*, in finding new ways of writing in forms where old-fashioned styles more commonly prevailed.

In Berlioz's songs there lie particular tensions between music private and public, music for the salon and for the concert hall, music for traditional minds and for more progressive ears. In her essay on Berlioz's better-known works in the category, Annegret Fauser engages with these and other issues such as composerly intentions versus accreted meanings, struggling to capture the musical experience as it simultaneously invites and resists interpretation.

Like the writings of Balzac, which now are seen to give "form" to the first part of the French nineteenth century, Berlioz's, too, in a more restricted arena, give shape to some of the main musical streams that flowed from the "Indian Summer" of the Bourbon Monarchy, at the opening of his career, through the autumn of the Second Empire, at the end. His

Mémoires are at once a colorful if selective chronicle of his life and a remarkable literary document of varied pace and tone; they are impulsive, satirical, enthusiastic, indignant, and as vivid as any ever written. As Pierre Citron informs us in a comprehensive reading that originally served to introduce his 1991 edition of the *Mémoires*,[9] the book allows us to feel the rebellion and the liberty that permeate the spiritual climate of the nineteenth century as a whole.

Begun in the year of Chateaubriand's death, Berlioz's *Mémoires* put one in mind of the *Mémoires d'outre-tombe*, both widely considered the crowning achievements of their authors' literary careers. By their range and variety, Katherine Kolb tells us, Berlioz's earlier collections of writings put one in mind of *La Comédie humaine* – the encyclopedic project that Balzac, whom Berlioz had by then known personally for several years, announced in 1842. In her thoughtful study of five short stories, Kolb shows how Berlioz entertains, disturbs, vents frustration, reveals principle, and forges worlds different from and more imaginative than the prosaic one in which he found himself constrained to live.

In his regular critical writings, only a small percentage of which he later collected in *À travers chants*, Berlioz had usually to use a careful combination of diplomatic skill and wit, as Katharine Ellis demonstrates in her essay here. It is ironic that the sarcasm which yesterday won Berlioz so many enemies has today won him so many new friends. Passages in which the critic indulges his passion – such as his astute and brilliant description of the Allegretto of Beethoven's Seventh Symphony (to which David Cairns returns in his contribution to this volume) – turn out in fact to be atypical.

In France today I am sometimes surprised to hear Berlioz called composer, writer, and *theorist* – since in the face of certain theoretical constructions, Berlioz was inclined to say *non credo*: "music is free; it does what it wishes, and without permission."[10] The designation is due to the widespread awareness of the importance of his *Traité d'instrumentation et d'orchestration modernes* (of which a modern critical edition is only now in the making). Joel-Marie Fauquet's essay considers the series of articles that formed the nucleus of the *Traité* (whose overmastering novelty, on its publication as a book, was the inclusion of numerous musical examples in full score), and suggests that the practical value of the tome is matched if not surpassed by its value as a treatise on aesthetics. (The chapter on conducting that Berlioz added to the second edition, in 1855, is by contrast a treatise on executive authority.)

Under the rubric of *execution*, D. Kern Holoman deals here with some of the realities of bringing Berlioz's music to life. For performers and those interested in the mechanics of performance – which scores to obtain, which instruments to use – Holoman the conductor-scholar offers practical advice.

Four *critical encounters* demonstrate in different ways the majestic reaches and unexpected perimeters of Berlioz's artistic horizons. For Berlioz, Gluck and Beethoven were both teachers and gods; on the basis of the essays here by Joël-Marie Fauquet and David Cairns we can measure their relative places in Berlioz's artistic pantheon. His admiration for Gluck grew along with his first musical stirrings and remained with him to the end: in one sense Gluck, for Berlioz, could do no wrong. However, as Fauquet demonstrates, his work could be adjusted and refined in ways that reflected our nineteenth-century composer's particular embrace of the notion of progress that was so overwhelming in Second Empire France. Berlioz discovered Beethoven only later, when he came to feel the full import of the notion of "genius"; the German composer became for him an incommensurable hero, as Cairns suggests, and Berlioz felt a deeply emotional necessity to celebrate the master's formidable scores, his fights of fancy, and even his flaws. In his Beethoven criticism, Berlioz's worshipful analyses give us, to paraphrase Berlioz's great friend Ernest Legouvé, the key to a sanctuary.

Berlioz's regard for Mozart seems to have been in a sense more intellectual, and also more dependent upon the manner in which his music was performed. Hugh Macdonald's contribution – I believe it is the first comprehensive examination of Berlioz's Mozart criticism – allows us to ponder the thought that maintaining the integrity of Mozart's music might have meant more to Berlioz than Mozart's music itself.

Wagner the man was imperfectly known to Berlioz, and his mature music remained to him a mystery. By the time of *Tristan* and the Paris *Tannhäuser*, those miracles of musical modernity, Berlioz was of little mind to celebrate the work of the self-proclaimed heir to the throne of Beethoven (to which title Berlioz, too, had a claim). Earlier, the expatriated Wagner was impressed but in some sense troubled by the composer of *Roméo et Juliette*. In my essay here I touch upon these issues, in particular considering what their meetings in person might have been like.

In the closing piece of the volume, Lesley Wright treats Berlioz's after-fame in France. As during his lifetime, Berlioz had his posthumous admirers and detractors along with fans on the fence, such as Bizet, who described his feelings in a formula whose words I have seen elsewhere – Berlioz "had genius but no talent" – but whose meaning I have never been able to fathom.

There has not been room in this last section for a study of his after-fame in Germany, where Berlioz was almost always well received, or in Russia, where he exerted tremendous influence on the members of the "mighty handful" but also on Tchaikovsky, whose memory of Berlioz as the embodiment of a "blazing love for art" – the Russian met the Frenchman in 1868 – remained with him for the rest of his life.[11] In the section on the *principal compositions* there has not been room (tautologically) for consideration of the smaller works, of which some – *La Mort d'Ophélie*, for example, orchestrated in London in 1848 – are delightful indeed. The Rome Prize cantatas, too, are largely absent here: close comparison of Berlioz's futile efforts with those of the winners might help us to understand the "talent–genius" conundrum that Bizet and others later sporadically evoked. Finally, Berlioz's writings include his letters, which can rise to the level of literature, and his librettos, which can rise to the level of poetry. Study of these would have made *major writings* too long. Is it too long already? Read the description of the reinterment of Harriet Smithson, in the *Postface* of the *Mémoires*, where Berlioz evokes the horrifying sight, sound, and smell of a corpse as it is lifted from a rotted coffin; compare this to the description of the exhumation of Marguerite Gauthier, in chapter 6 of *La Dame aux camélias*, where, to confirm his acceptance of his beloved's death, Armand Duval witnesses this same grisly process; and dare to say that Berlioz's page is any less gripping than that penned by the celebrated Alexandre Dumas fils.[12]

With the completion of the *New Berlioz Edition*, the *Correspondance générale*, and the *Critique musicale*, the foundations of Berlioz research will have been settled, on the eve of the bicentenary, for some time to come. It is difficult to imagine undertaking these kinds of critical editions again. One central item has been partly overlooked in all of this, however, and that is Berlioz's most famous book. Of *Les Soirées de l'orchestre*, *Les Grotesques de la musique*, and *À travers chants* we have Léon Guichard's attentive *édition du centenaire*. But of the *Mémoires*, though we have a fine modern edition in French and a fine modern translation in English, we have no full-dress critical edition of the original text: no exhaustive and systematic comparison of the printed version with the autograph manuscript (of which important chapters are preserved in public and private collections) or with the portions of the book that were earlier published as articles. Such an edition of Berlioz's *Mémoires*, it seems to me, clearly belongs in that celebrated series that is the *Bibliothèque de la Pléiade*.

We also need facsimile editions – Berlioz's manuscript, musical and epistolary, is of legendary expressive character – and we need a broadly inclusive picture book: perhaps the catalogue of the grand exhibition that is to crown the celebration of the bicentenary of Berlioz's birth, at the Bibliothèque Nationale de France, in 2003, will serve this purpose.

The purpose of this Companion is to point *Kenner, Liebhaber,* and self-improving readers with well-stored minds to the satisfactions and singularities of the work of a complex and enduringly inventive artist. Such readers will find some redundancies and inconsistencies among the assertions and opinions voiced by these authors; to have edited them away would have been to reduce the reviewer's delight and to lessen the contentiousness that has from the outset been associated with the subject of our endeavor.

PART I

Perspectives

1 Berlioz as man and thinker

JACQUES BARZUN

It has been well said that the pervasive elegance in the music of Berlioz is a reflection of his cultivated mind. Genius, it is true, can create master-pieces without the aid of intellect and general culture. But their presence does no harm; they develop that second-level simplicity which, when allied to conciseness, yields elegance. In every art one can distinguish those masters who have been men of thought from those in whom native gift has reigned alone. Turner and Daumier in painting, Schubert and Brahms in music come to mind as projecting the artistic power in its first simplicity. That characteristic implies no limitation of sensibility or tech-nique.

The other category – take for examples Delacroix and Schumann – is the one to which Berlioz belongs. His uncommon upbringing ensured that he would have the self-awareness and detachment of the highly liter-ate. It proved a source of imaginative richness in his music and of spiritual distress in his life.

As he makes a point of telling us in his *Mémoires*, Berlioz was reared in the Holy Apostolic Roman Catholic Church. His mother was a believer, his father an eighteenth-century "encyclopedist"; that is to say a man of advanced ideas, for whom religion had a much attenuated meaning. As a physician he rejoiced in the progress of science and passed on to his son his own broad curiosity about it. Scientific method implied an a priori rejection of the supernatural and a steady skepticism. But the doctor was a mild, not a militant skeptic; nor was it necessary for a good *philosophe* to be an atheist. Deism sufficed – the belief, free of fervor, that a Great Architect had created the cosmos and was letting it run without interfer-ence. The deity had laid down the laws by which nature, a machine in per-petual motion, took care of itself.

Reared in both the creeds that fought each other in the eighteenth century, young Berlioz reached manhood imbued with their opposite truths. This equipoise was one rather of principles and sentiments than of systematic dogmas. But to a mind as penetrating as his, the disparate conceptions of the universe, while doubling the range of his intuitions, must sooner or later confront him with an unresolved intellectual conflict.

Nor was this all. As a boy wandering in his native fields, he knew

[11]

without any need of teaching that Nature is alive. In the French Alps, where sun, wind, cloud, storm, light and dark enact spectacles ranging from placid beauty to ruthless havoc, how could it seem the push–pull of a mere machine? The naïve beholder, aware of all that lives besides himself, sees Spirit diffused through all things: Berlioz was a pantheist before he knew the meaning of the term.

When he came to compose, he drew alike on his intimacy with nature and on the human meaning of the Christian ritual. For it, too, modulates from tenderness and mercy to wrath and punishment. This two-fold vision from two sources is manifest in most of the mature works. The quiet prayers in the *Requiem* and *Te Deum* alternate with the terror of the Last Judgment; and the simple piety of *L'Enfance du Christ* recalls the child Berlioz's pastoral emotions. Yet even there wildness and gloom enter with the whirling dervishes' effort to allay by a prophecy the dark thoughts of the brooding Herod.

The third movement of the *Symphonie fantastique* embodies impressions of nature serene, with a storm in the distance; a scene of glorious sunshine opens *La Damnation de Faust*; and then toward the end, in the Invocation to Nature, the pantheist pays tribute to her thunderous mood. His adoration speaks not through the music alone: the poem is by Berlioz. But next come a credible Hell and a longed-for Heaven.

The two founts of inspiration, however inconsistent as doctrines, were all to the good for the making of music. But where do they leave the thinker? The adult Berlioz was no longer a Catholic believer, nor was he a have-it-both-ways Deist, and he felt the presence of spirit – in nature, in his works, and in art and thought at large. But he was also in touch with his time. In the nineteenth century, men of science were telling all who would listen that the true reality is bare matter. Its unbreakable chain of cause and effect determines everything that exists.

This world view, persuasively simple and sufficient, obviously takes spirit out of pantheism – as Berlioz could not fail to perceive. Just past the threshold of his *Invocation* he admits a doubt: "et je crois vivre enfin" – "I *think* I truly live at last."

Berlioz had encountered the materialist assumption in his medical training. The dogma was reinforced by his lifelong association with physicians, as well as by his reading in geology and other earth sciences that were his enduring interest. The recurrent hints in his writings of metaphysical sufferings are accounted for by this second form of the conflict between incompatible faiths.

I say hints, because in spite of appearances, he was not one to open his soul to a large circle. Besides, throughout early and middle life Berlioz was in the throes of incessant creation and preoccupied by the duties that it entailed – conducting, writing, and serving as his own impresario. In this output of energy, philosophical questions could be subdued or temporarily forgotten. To compose in one decade the *Requiem, Benvenuto Cellini, Roméo et Juliette*, the *Symphonie funèbre*, and the *Damnation de Faust*, while also performing Weber, Gluck, and Beethoven, was to plunge the whole man in a realm governed by another religion, and one seemingly free of all contradictions.

This was the religion of art, a nineteenth-century innovation. It can be readily defined by quoting Walter Scott, whom no one would call a rash enthusiast: "Our forerunners in poetry are gods or they are nothing." Berlioz would have countersigned the maxim. These gods were also being revered as "geniuses," a new use of the word. Formerly, one "had a genius for – " some particular thing, perhaps for poetry, perhaps for a trait as ordinary as a good memory. Now one *was* a genius; the "guiding genius" (the same as the ancients' *daemon* within) had become the whole self and was endowed with supernormal powers.

The religion of art arose after the French Revolution, in parallel with the revival of Catholic and Protestant piety, the old faiths and the new both being responses to the emotional void left by the *philosophes*. But the religious fervor was restricted to certain groups in each country; the artistic was widespread and international. Romanticism was its expression for two generations of artists, who did not need any catechism to be ardent worshippers. They gave Art for the first time its capital A. Art was the highest conceivable expression of Man. Art was the infallible critic of life and society. Art was the explicit condemner of the bourgeois and his gross concerns. Art bound all true artists in brotherhood against false ones, commercial and academic. Art was spirit and therefore immortal.

For Berlioz, this religion, though he practiced it fervently, became on reflection also untenable. Aware of history, he knew that art was not immortal. He saw his particular gods – Gluck, Spontini, Weber, with their works and their fame – fading from memory. He knew in addition that no agreement exists, at any time, about art and artists. Beauty, he pointed out in despair, is a matter of opinion – perhaps an illusion in certain men and women favored with a special sensitivity – but not all of them by the same illusion. Art was a will-o'-the wisp – though to each beholder as real and solid as a mountain.

So the critic, if self-aware, faced his daily task with a divided mind. He knew that mighty works (such as Beethoven's), derided at first and denounced as unintelligible ravings, turned out later to be luminous, divine, "unquestionable" masterpieces. The unhappy creator had to forge the taste by which he should be judged, only to sink back into a second obscurity in the end. And his long wait for recognition was due not alone to the obtuse public but just as much to the stubborn critic and connoisseur. Berlioz in his reviews warned against their verdicts, including his own.

It is no wonder that with such thoughts in mind he spoke out harshly against another novelty: aesthetics. Coined in the mid-eighteenth century, the word soon appeared in essays and books and has come to denote a discipline by itself. It ranks as a part of philosophy and professes, often with comic gravity, to clear up the confused debate about the form and contents of the several arts. The result has not come about. The main effect of aesthetic doctrines has been to pressure artists into explaining and justifying their work by means of theory, current or of their own making.

In Berlioz's day it was Wagner who most conspicuously acted on this plan. He expounded his views *viva voce* to Berlioz in London and got a chilling response in the midst of an otherwise extremely friendly meeting. Later, the Wagnerite slogan of "the music of the future," which promised to cast Beethoven and other masters into the shade, was bound to infuriate Berlioz. It made him commit the one willful injustice of his career, when he burst out angrily (though only in private) about the production of *Tannhäuser* in Paris. At the same time, his sense of responsibility as a professional (and ethical) critic kept him from using his authority in Paris to attack a composer of stature who differed in method and felt the need of a system to validate his art.

One may ask whether Berlioz himself did not theorize in his feuilletons, their doctrine being later reissued in book form for permanent reference. The answer is that Berlioz expounds but a single principle: music by itself is (or can be) dramatically and psychologically expressive. He does not erect a system with moral, metaphysical, or social corollaries. He denied more than once that there could be an inherently religious music. And he never explained his "methods," as a respecter of aesthetics should do. This is a pity, because it might have shortened the time it has taken to discover them. It might also have enlarged his contemporary fame, because in a journalistic civilization a work of art greatly benefits from a public argument that seems to be about merit and meaning, but is really about something else.

*

After the flood of Romanticist masterpieces, the decades of the second half of the century proved a time of despair for artists and the thoughtful in any domain. The triumphs of science and engineering persuaded the general mind that what could not be measured or counted did not exist. While Berlioz and others were still producing and celebrating Art, its support and its place in society were growing uncertain. Industry, machines, coal and iron, the railroad – in short, material progress was the center of marveling attention. As Emerson said, "Things are in the saddle and ride Mankind."

In the world of music, as Berlioz had to note week after week in the *Journal des débats*, it was spectacle – grand opera, with the real waterfall and the live goat – that attracted the crowd; or else it was the virtuoso at the keyboard – spectacle again. To create and promote as he did *le genre instrumental expressif*, which was neither spectacular nor gymnastic, was to address unheeding ears.

Equally dispiriting, politics brought on a succession of catastrophes. First, a revolution starting in France and spreading abroad subjected Europe to four years of savage war. Artists lost their livelihood; some were shot (Wagner barely missed being of the number); others like Berlioz had to take refuge in hospitable England. The issues were confused; the claims of nationalism, liberalism, and socialism concealed raw interests; *Realpolitik* bewildered the acutest minds.

Berlioz in any case could not be a partisan. As a young man he had been attracted for a very short time by the Saint-Simonian socialist movement, which promised a harmonious world. But unlike his friend Liszt, he had been unable to follow their windy rhetoric or their street parades in troubadour costume. Though he could exercise diplomatic skill in dealing for music's sake with the powers that be, he remained all his life apolitical.

What is more, in an age of increasing national hostilities, Berlioz kept displaying a cosmopolitan mind. He made warm friends all over Europe, with musicians, writers, actors, critics, and even with crowned heads. Again and again he reminded his readers that in matters of thought and art nationality made no difference. He castigated a writer who denounced Mendelssohn's works as "Jewish music," and he was impatient of "French ideas," by which he meant the parochial suspicion and rejection of things foreign.

Berlioz never had time to learn German, Hungarian, Czech, or Russian, which would have been of help in his concert tours; but he could read and speak Italian and English, and Latin was to him a second language since adolescence. His taste in literature was correspondingly broad. Though he never properly went to school – the Napoleonic years of his childhood rather stinted the lycées in remote parts – Berlioz was familiar with the French classics in poetry and prose, as one finds from his frequent quotations in his essays. Shakespeare he learned to read and worship during the eighteen-twenties in Paris, and at the same time Scott, Byron, and Thomas Moore – all favorites of the young Romanticists. To these in England, he added Dickens and James Fenimore Cooper. For his adaptation of *Faust* and of Benvenuto Cellini's *Vita*, he had recourse to translations. Of contemporary French writers, he relished especially Hugo, Balzac, Gautier, and Flaubert.

It was the Shakespearean construction by detached scenes which, reinforced by Goethe's example in *Faust*, shaped Berlioz's way of compositing his librettos. The novelistic palaver of the usual operatic recitatives is got rid of, and only those that carry live emotion and are "musicable" remain.

A noteworthy aspect of his love of literature was his strong revulsion from horror in art or life. In make-believe, such as some of his short fictions, he did describe fearsome acts of revenge. But he abandoned composing for a libretto of Scribe's that was based on *The Monk*, by Gregory Lewis, because the quasi pornographic episode chosen was that of the Bleeding Nun. For the same reason, historical scenes of carnage or cruelty repelled him. To be sure, for the *Symphonie fantastique* (actually for the earlier score, *Les Francs-Juges*) he composed a March to Execution. He associated it with the poet André Chénier's death on the guillotine. But the piece was a somber march, not a scene of mob rejoicing at the killing of a human being. Other hearsay memories of 1789 no doubt implanted the horror of horror.

The revolution of 1848, the second that Berlioz lived through, ended in France with the régime of Napoléon III, which generated an atmosphere not deliberately hostile to art nor to social betterment, but one marked, like all periods of boom and a new money crowd, by ostentation and complacency. Such an atmosphere, Berlioz described years before the fact in the account of the state of "Sicily" in his story *Euphonia*. Only in the town of that name are conditions fit for music.

What Berlioz calls for has been called utopian. Yet when Bayreuth years later came into operatic existence, a parallel was drawn. It is inexact. Berlioz wanted more than an opera house and certainly not one limited to producing one master's works. He specifies resident musicians dedicated to their art and able to perform every variety of the best music. With due exaggeration for narrative emphasis, his demands seem applicable to any musical enterprise anywhere: musicians trained to understand as well as perform; a single directing mind; respect for the composer's score; and an audience of connoisseurs in the strict sense of the term. What frustrates such an outcome in all actual towns, today or yesterday, is a trifle: the economics of the situation and the bad habits of those involved.

Euphonia is also a story of love, and one that ends in a scene of horrendous revenge by means of machinery. The love that leads to this fantasy is also beyond human measure. For the Romanticists generally and for Berlioz in particular, that passion was all-encompassing. Unlike the gallantry of the preceding age, it was not a form of entertainment through sexual conquest or light-hearted dalliance. Love took possession of the whole being; it was the twin of art as well as its source, both alike mysterious and awesome. That is why poets sang its praises and passionate souls killed or died for it. Indeed, tradition said it was as strong as death.

Modern psychologies tend to validate the linkage with art, which they find rooted in the unconscious drive they call libido. The Romanticist heightening of guiding genius into genius *tout court* made the same connection. Berlioz put it tersely: music is "our passions poetized." For unlike the gush of eighteenth-century sentiment, nineteenth-century love imposes a duty on the artist: one must "ruthlessly plow the heart-and-mind to sow inspiration."

About the listener and the experience of music, Berlioz also had much to say. That he derived sensuous delight from sheer sound, we know from his delicate blends of tone color. But when all the elements of music were fused into an expressive whole, hearing the work was to him no ordinary pleasure. As readers of *À travers chants* will recall, it affected his nervous system like a current of high voltage. The description of this galvanism has sometimes been deemed an exaggeration; but similar accounts are on record as far back as the ancient Greeks. A more recent one by the physiologist-philosopher Diderot confirms them: "There are some men," he says, "in whom the fibers vibrate with such rapidity and vivacity that in experiencing the violent motions that harmony causes, they foresee the possibility of a kind of music that would kill them with bliss."

This susceptibility need not imply physical weakness. It certainly did not for Berlioz. He could not have met the demands of his complex career as composer-conductor and organizer of concerts without a sturdy constitution. When after years of unremitting exertion he suffered bouts of illness (probably due to stomach ulcers), it was the expectable result of the strain and poor regimen to which he had subjected his organism.

But why, it has sometimes been asked, did he feel this vast effort necessary? Was it not excess ego to travel all over Europe chiefly to perform his own works? The question betrays naïveté. An artist has every right – one may even say a duty – to exhibit his productions as prominently as he can. Self-confidence is one ingredient of genius. It prompted Horace and Shakespeare to award themselves an eternity of fame. From the towering figures we must not expect the modest cough of the minor poet.

Berlioz had very good reasons for his promotive tours: his works constituted an original genre and were denied performance in Paris. And if never played, his scores would find no publisher. Unless he wanted to bequeath to posterity a collection of manuscripts, he had no other choice but to raid London, Prague, Vienna, Berlin, St. Petersburg, and other centers where he found willing orchestras and audiences, and to "forge the taste by which he should be judged."

His activity in Central Europe and elsewhere had the result he wanted and an enormous side-effect, as Wagner, Hanslick, Damrosch, and others noted: besides gaining European fame, Berlioz taught European performers the precision that modern works, from Beethoven's onward, demanded from singers and instrumentalists. Last and most important, playing his music enabled him to test his innovations by ear. His attention to detail was minute and he had cause for regret when, as it turned out, he never heard the first two acts of *Les Troyens* or that small gem, the *Marche funèbre pour la dernière scène d'Hamlet*.

*

Most scientific materialists can be happy knowing that their scheme serves their work of research. On top of this, they enjoy the game of telling the laity how foolish faith is and how groundless. But try telling an artist that the act of creation is a blind product of matter in motion. In the eighteen-fifties a good many people other than artists and religious believers – indeed, more than one scientist – rebelled against the idea. And some made efforts to prove the reality of spirit by recourse to table turning and other "manifestations" of Spirit*ism*. It captured for a time the imagination of Victor Hugo.

Berlioz was too sagacious to join in. His sense of humor also came into play and he made fun of the "revelations" of mediums, perceiving, no doubt, that they were but materialism in reverse. And when one reads him closely, one notices that he never expresses any longing for personal immortality. To be sure, his deep attachment to his father, his younger sister, and his son, together with his whole-hearted loves and friendships, would have caused him to welcome evidence of reunion in the hereafter. But if that thought ever crossed his mind, it weighed little in comparison with what he felt about the materialist philosophers' negation of thought and annihilation of art. "When will it be our turn at the bottom of the abyss?" asks the artist hero in *Euphonia*.

Urged not solely by the root desire of the mind to keep forever conscious, but also by the welling up of creative power, an artist may be tempted to accept contradiction – to believe and not to believe, simultaneously. To live thus, married to a dilemma, is not exclusively a subterfuge of the nineteenth century. In our own, Montherlant confided (in *Don Juan*): "There is in me a high excitement and a passion that require me to have recourse to God, even though I do not believe in God." Berlioz, having struggled long, in the end refused this intellectually untenable position. Late in life, in a few letters and the *Mémoires*, he declared himself an atheist. His telling expression is: "There is only Nothingness" (*le Néant*).

He had come to the very modern Existentialist conviction that the universe is blind, cold, and senseless. He saw death and dissolution as the goal of existence. For the last word in the *Mémoires* he called on Shakespeare for a definition of life: it is "a tale told by an idiot, signifying nothing."

The wonder is that with this anguish in his heart Berlioz was able to go on producing great music – *Les Troyens* and *Béatrice et Bénédict*. Here again his characteristic humor helped to sustain the balanced mind. The dialogue of the sailors at Carthage and Somarone's antics in Sicily are not the products of an embittered soul, any more than the letter from Baden to the French Academy or the private joke of composing *Nuit sereine* during a dull speech in that same Academy. True, none of these implies wild gaiety, but who does not know that humor and melancholy dwell together?

To the last also, Berlioz maintained the moral dignity that had never failed him but in the *Tannhäuser* episode. Neither in manners nor in mores had he ever been the Bohemian artist who must be forgiven a great deal, including his ubiquitous debts. In the eighteen-fifties and sixties, when this departure from "bourgeois values" was becoming expected of the true artist, along with recrimination against "his society," Berlioz observed the standards of an earlier age. He died, as Havergal Brian remarked, a Stoic.

But his nature, as all agree, was "fire and ice." The ice of Stoicism in late life did not cool the fire of love. Hence his courtship of the Estelle of his youngest days, a Romanticist love matured, but springing from the same fount as that which in the adolescent of 1815 had yielded the melody that opens *Rêveries, Passions* in the *Fantastique*. It is fitting that in writing about Berlioz, W. J. Turner came to define music as "the imagination of love in sound."

2 The musical environment in France

JANET JOHNSON

On 5 June 1821, only five months before a provincial stagecoach deposited an unsuspecting young medical student named Hector Berlioz in the "capital of the world," Gioachino Rossini's *Otello* had its overwhelmingly successful Parisian première, sparking the first skirmishes in an all-out paper war that was to be officially "declared" on the very eve of Berlioz's arrival. Written for Naples and based partly on Jean-François Ducis's French adaptation of Shakespeare's tragedy, *Otello* (1816) was the first of the twenty-nine-year-old Pesarese's serious operas to be produced at the Théâtre Royal Italien by a management still so partial to the older Italian school of comic opera that it had only reluctantly presented *Il barbiere di Siviglia* two years before. For comparison's sake, Rossini's radically new setting had been faced off against Paisiello's genteel thirty-seven-year-old one, and an aggressive advance publicity campaign waged in the press by the *paisiellisti*. When the senior *Barber* closed after only two performances, other comic operas by Rossini, including the clever *Italiana in Algeri*, were given in eviscerated versions adapted to older Parisian taste yet borrowing so promiscuously from works soon to reach the stage as to hasten Rossini's reputation for repeating himself. When the semi-serious *Cenerentola* was given in 1822, for example, the over-worked heroine had already been "deflowered" by the buffo *Turco in Italia* in 1820, her music set to new words. And *Torvaldo e Dorliska*, a lesser opera semi-seria quickly pronounced a "bad parody" of a revolutionary-era rescue opera then enjoying a revival at the Opéra Comique (Cherubini's *Lodoïska*), had been mounted that same year seemingly to provoke just such unflattering comparisons. Émile Deschamps co-authored a pamphlet that alleged sabotage,[1] and Stendhal (who ghost-wrote part of another one from Milan)[2] soon weighed in with the longest pamphlet of them all, his *Vie de Rossini* (1824).

But no amount of maneuvering could contain the exponential momentum unleashed by *Otello*, as performance statistics predicted all too clearly. Two operas by Rossini had been performed at the Théâtre Italien in 1819, four in 1820; the première of *La gazza ladra* on 18 September would make five in 1821. By the end of 1822, eight operas would account for fully half the repertory and three-quarters of performances. By 1824 Rossini would take on the direction of the Italiens (as

[20]

it was called), compose a completely new opera for the company (*Il viaggio a Reims*), personally mount his best works, and cast them with the finest Italian-trained singers he could recruit. By 1826, twelve of his operas, including *Tancredi, Mosè in Egitto, La donna del lago, Semiramide,* and *Zelmira*, would be performed so frequently that they would leave room only for some half-dozen hearings each of a few older classics such as Cimarosa's *Il matrimonio segreto*, Mozart's *Don Giovanni*, and Zingarelli's *Romeo e Giulietta*. Meanwhile, the Théâtre de l'Odéon would present French versions of four of Rossini's operas plus pastiches like *Ivanhoé* – Rossini's music (some of it possibly new) fitted by Deschamps and Gustave de Wailly with a versification of Walter Scott's popular novel. Then, between 1826 and 1829, Rossini would compose four French works for the Opéra and train French singers to sing them, the last but not least of these being *Guillaume Tell* – brand new rather than partially adapted from earlier works, and a prototype for French grand opera. And this is not to speak of the music performed at concerts and adapted for military bands and dance orchestras. In short, as Stendhal suggests in his novel about post-revolutionary French society, *Le Rouge et le noir*, Rossini was as ubiquitous as the weather. Berlioz, being what Alfred de Musset called "un enfant du siècle," was thus to come of age in the era of Rossini.

Berlioz in the age of Rossini

Contemporary Germans might have spoken of their times as "the era of Beethoven and Rossini," thinking of one of the stylistic dichotomies that would turn out to be central to the nineteenth century's historiography: German instrumental music, on the one hand, implying an inviolable "text" subject to exegetical interpretation; and Italian opera, on the other, a performative event that could be adapted to the vocal resources of a given theatre.[3] But things looked rather different from where Berlioz stood when he surveyed the Parisian musical scene in 1821. The first performances of Beethoven's symphonies and concertos and of Weber's overtures by Habeneck's Société des Concerts du Conservatoire – so revelatory for Berlioz and many others when they finally occurred – were still more than six years hence. Only a few of Beethoven's quartets were being programmed by Pierre Baillot on the public chamber music series the violinist had founded in 1814, and the late ones were still so little understood that Berlioz was one of only a half-dozen people out of some two or three hundred to stay until the end of a performance of the "absurd" and "barbarous" C-sharp-Minor Quartet on 24 March 1829, as he told his sister in a letter of the 29th. Though the magnitude of his experience can be gauged from that letter, parts of which he toned down for inclusion in a serialized biography of Beethoven published later that year in *Le Correspondant*,[4] we only learn of it retrospectively – from his music, of course, from the studies and reviews he published beginning in 1834 (those from 1829 concentrating instead on performance and reception), and from his *Mémoires*.

What was being performed regularly was opera – French, Italian, and German, though here again Weber's *Der Freischütz* was still a novelty in May 1829 when Berlioz finally heard the visiting Théâtre Allemand give it in the original version rather than in Castil-Blaze's infamous adaptation as *Robin des bois*, along with *Fidelio* and *Die Zauberflöte* (rendered unrecognizable at the Opéra as *Les Mystères d'Isis*). As we shall see, moreover, some of the French opera he heard actually served as background music for the ballet. What did he make of all this music and of the *guerre rossinienne* in which he was soon to be swept up? In what follows we will explore Berlioz's earliest musical experience in Paris and his anti-Rossinian polemics on behalf of Gluck, his idol, then take a step back to situate these in the on-going aesthetic controversies that raged during the composer's first formative decade and beyond. As should become clear, the stylistic rift opening in Paris concerned two competing notions of the relationship between words and music in opera, one of which Berlioz would extend to instrumental music – both Beethoven's and his own.

Berlioz at the Opéra: the ubiquity of Rossini

Berlioz probably heard nearly all Rossini's operas whether he wanted to or not, sometimes even when he went to his regular haunt, the Opéra. Long before *Otello* and the *Barber* were performed in translation at the Opéra's Salle Peletier,[5] and even before *Le Siège de Corinthe* was given in 1826, several of Rossini's Italian operas were premièred there by the Italian company, with a ballet performed between acts by the dance troupe of the Opéra.[6] It must have been at one such première that Berlioz happened to hear *Elisabetta, regina d'Inghilterra*, given on 10 March 1822 as a benefit for the Italiens' prima donna Joséphine Mainvielle-Fodor. This can be deduced from his later account of the months of waiting and frustrated expectations he had endured before finally seeing Gluck's *Iphigénie en Tauride* (1779), a tragédie lyrique based on Euripides given on 13 March 1822. By this time, he tells us, he had discovered the Conservatoire library and memorized the score of the opera, but had almost given up hope of ever hearing it. When he went to find out what that evening's fare would be, he was especially glum because, as he put it, "the night before I had seen Rossini triumphantly 'mount the throne' escorted by *Les Pages du duc de Vendôme*," a triple pun on Queen Elizabeth, the seat of French musical culture (the Opéra's official name was the Académie Royale de Musique), and Adalbert Gyrowetz's dated Viennese comic opera-cum-ballet.[7]

The confluence of these two musical events was what made Berlioz decide that very night, according to the *Mémoires*, to abandon his medical studies and to become a composer. But while just seeing the name of his favorite opera brought on a nosebleed and set his knees to knocking, his teeth to chattering, he clearly thought at this point that if you had heard one opera by Rossini you had heard them all. As he opined in his first foray into criticism, a polemic contributed to *Le Corsaire* in August 1823, "who could deny that all the operas of Rossini put together could not hold up to comparison with one line of recitative by Gluck, three bars of a song by Mozart or Spontini, and the least of Lesueur's choruses!" As far as Gluck was concerned, he knew whereof he spoke: by the end of 1825 he claimed to have "all of Gluck by heart," and, when he auditioned for the chorus at the Théâtre des Nouveautés in 1827, to be able to sing any air from virtually any tragédie lyrique you cared to name from the ancien régime or revolutionary era. This included the two *Iphigénies*, *Armide*, and the French versions of *Orphée et Eurydice* and *Alceste*, as well as Salieri's *Les Danaïdes*, Sacchini's *Oedipe*, Spontini's *La Vestale* and *Ferdinand Cortez*, and Méhul's *Stratonice*.

But how well did Berlioz know Rossini? The only score by Rossini he appears ever to have really studied was *Guillaume Tell*, which he proofread for its publisher, Eugène Troupenas.[8] With the exception of *Le Comte Ory*, *Tell* was also the only one of the composer's operas that he reviewed at any length. Even during the mid-eighteen-thirties, when works by Rossini still filled a third of the Théâtre Italien's schedule and Berlioz was asking the theatre's director for so many complimentary tickets that he felt obliged to apologize for his importunity, he avoided them, sticking to singers or covering exclusively new works by the generation of Bellini and Donizetti.[9]

Later, of course, he did discuss Rossini, even admiringly, in *Les Soirées de l'orchestre* and in the feuilletons he wrote around 1860 for the *Journal des débats*. But the letters he penned during his first Parisian decade give us a glimpse of the "barely believable hatred and horror" of Rossini and his admirers that he admitted still colored his judgment when he launched a four-part study of *Iphigénie en Tauride* in the *Gazette musicale de Paris* in 1834:

> If it had been within my power to put a keg of powder under the Salle
> Louvois [home of the Théâtre Italien until 12 November 1825] and blow it
> up along with everyone in it during a performance of the *Gazza* or the
> *Barber*, I undoubtedly would have. The reader will probably suppose that my

blood has cooled remarkably and that my musical opinions are much changed; yet the influence of these first impressions is such and my admiration for Gluck still so great, that I think it would behoove me, in analyzing those of his works which most affected me, to be on guard against the recollections of the one and the unreasoned seductions of the other.[10]

In a letter of October 1824, for example, he calls the audience "wretched scoundrels not even worthy of that puppet Rossini's farces." On 3 June 1829 he told his friend Humbert Ferrand that he "hated this Figaro more every day" and wished he'd been in the foyer of the Théâtre Allemand on the evening Rossini supposedly said that *Der Freischütz* gave him colic so he could have "let him have it."[11] In the same letter he reported that *Le Correspondant* had rejected a severe critique of the Italian school that he had written for the magazine, the organ of the Association pour la défense de la religion catholique, inspired by the theologian Félicité de Lammenais. "So the prostitute finds lovers even among religious folk," he concluded darkly.

Berlioz and the dilettanti: music as imitative and abstract art

Indeed, the comments Berlioz makes about *Otello* in his essay "On Imitation in Music," published in 1837, are every bit as polemical as the reviews by Stendhal to which they are surely directed. The crux of Stendhal's argument had been that Rossini was dramatic because

> Among all known composers, he is the one who is least dependent upon his librettist; he has, as far as it lies within the nature of his medium to do so, liberated his art from the inglorious fetters of a necessity which left it shorn of half its glory. [...] Rossini's music is fired with an indescribable, intangible element of reality and living emotion. [...] The operatic composer is nothing but a portrait-painter who paints in music.[12]

Here was a direct challenge to the notion of the relationship between words and music that Gluck set forth in 1773, with reference to *Iphigénie en Aulide*:

> My music is directed only to the greatest expression and to the reinforcement of the declamation of the poetry. This is the reason that I never employ the trills, the passages, or the cadenzas of which the Italians are profuse.[13]

In the first part of his 1834 essay on Gluck, Berlioz reproduced the core of Gluck's preface to the Italian version of *Alceste* (1767), including this key passage (which Berlioz internalized as his own critical and compositional credo):

> I sought [in *Alceste*] to restrict the music to its true purpose, that of
> reinforcing the poetry in order to strengthen the *expression* of feeling and the
> interest of the various situations *without interrupting the action or
> diminishing it with superfluous ornaments.* [...] I have not placed any value
> on the discovery of a novelty, unless it emerged naturally from the situation
> and was tied to the expression; and there is no rule I would not have felt in
> duty bound to break in order to achieve the desired effect [italics mine].[14]

In the later essay "On Imitation in Music" he contrived wittily to refer
to the "nonsense" about music liberated from words being "true"
defended by "a certain celebrated composer's followers" who were then
"refuted" by Rossini himself with the score of *Guillaume Tell*.[15]

Berlioz avoids discussing Rossini's opere serie by saying in so many
words that the composer himself proved their enthusiasts mistaken. The
enthusiasts whom he describes as lacking "all musical feeling and education" were the *dilettanti*, of whom it was said that the Théâtre Italien had a
clique instead of a paid claque.[16] Rossini's legions rather than his music
were more often than not the focus of Berlioz's criticism. He must have
thought of the dilettanti as the evil twins of the acolytes of Gluck whom
he gathered round himself: most sat in the parterre (the part of the
orchestra-level closest to the stage) and rendered judgment like "a true
revolutionary tribunal."[17]

In fact the word *dilettante* could describe almost anyone but *performers* of Italian opera: Chopin, for one, was a dilettante. It meant something
between the German Kenner (connoisseur) and Liebhaber (lover, or
amateur), but it also had a social connotation – as we learn from this par-
odistical definition:

> *Dilettante:* Today this is almost a form of civil service. A man who has a
> modest income and is neither a government official, nor a member of the
> Conseil d'État, nor a gentleman at the royal court, nor eligible for election,
> buys entrées to the Bouffes [the Théâtre Italien], and takes the title of
> *Dilettante*. He is then counted among our aristocracy. He has the right to be
> trenchant and to treat as ignoramuses the poor people who only go to the
> Feydeau [the Opéra Comique] or to the Opéra. He knows a hundred words
> of Italian, which he works in everywhere. He says La Pasta, La Mombelli
> [prime donne], he dreams only of Naples and Milan, and he speaks French
> only to ask for his slippers.[18]

The Théâtre Italien's audience – "everyone except the public," it was
quipped[19] – was mostly made up of the denizens of the wealthy Faubourg
Saint-Germain, an international array of dignitaries and diplomats, and
aspiring composers, writers, and artists. Only some sixty spectators were
dilettanti, but they were the most conspicuous, as one might conclude
from the *Notes d'un dilettante*, a posthumous collection of Stendhal's

reviews from the *Journal de Paris* (although Berlioz probably did not know that that classically educated, cosmopolitan critic was their author).

Another of Rossini's "followers" was "the excellent Italian critic" Giuseppe Carpani, whose ideas on imitation were the ostensible point of departure for Berlioz's 1837 essay; he mentions Carpani's *Le Haydine* (1812), but the more recent *Le Rossiniane* was among the "other things" to which he only coyly alluded. Concerning the relationship of words and music, Carpani had there argued the modern Italian view, a version of Mozart's (that "poetry should be the altogether obedient daughter of music") updated to allow for the theory of abstract artistic expression known as the "Bello Ideale." And he had challenged "the most ardent supporter of Gluck" to deny that expression had to take second place to musical thought, or to what he called "cantilena," the alternative being *Fidelio* – not an opera, but "an orchestrated declamation."[20]

In his own essay, Berlioz agreed that *Fidelio* and even the *Pastoral* Symphony – an example of what he called *le genre instrumental expressif* and a model for his own work – were too reliant on direct imitation of physical objects. But he nonetheless found Carpani's claims that music alone could portray emotions to be loose talk. He recommended a program, and distinguished between "musical depiction" and "musical metaphors." And he certainly could not endorse (as Carpani did) the aesthetic premise underlying all of Rossini's operas with the possible exception of *Guillaume Tell*: in the composer's own words, that music "is not an imitative art, but is at root entirely abstract."[21] For Berlioz, steeped in the French practice of the "explication de texte" and the history and mythology that sustained the entire classical French tradition, texted music unhinged from words bypassed the head and the heart, and was purely "sensual" and "culinary," "a sort of voluptuous emotion," "noise acting with more or less force on the human system."[22] It was not music, or at least not art music, which is why Berlioz conspicuously left Rossini – whose operas, after all, inspired Chopin, Paganini, and Liszt, and constitute the foundations of the Italian school up to and including Verdi – out of the list of romantics he published in 1830.

What "Gluck's school of dramatic expression and good sense" meant first and foremost for Berlioz was declamatory melody rather than melody embroidered with ornaments – those written out by the composer and improvised by the singer, often all too liberally, though it was an individual singer's characteristic manner of "varying" a melody that explained the style's allure for Chopin and many others. "Truth of expression," for Berlioz, meant structuring melody so as to enhance fidelity to individual words, not to employ the regular phrases and periods Rousseau had argued were the indigenous language of music. He commended the orchestrated recitatives Rossini wrote, under the influence of French style, in his Neapolitan operas. But a cadenza such as Desdemona sings after the words "Se il padre m'abbandona, da chi sperar pietà?" ("If my father abandons me, whom can I ask for pity?") at the end of her second-act aria in *Otello* was for him an example of "the rhetoric of the larynx" and thus of the triumph of the larynx over the brain, or of the singer over the composer.[23] According to his friend Ernest Legouvé, he mocked the passage by substituting his own words: "If my father abandons me," he sang, adding ("with an outburst of sardonic laughter and reproducing all the roulades of the text"), "I don't give a damn!"[24] But Berlioz would parse the poetry of the air from *Orphée et Eurydice*, "Divinités du Styx," complaining that Gluck's French translators had not reproduced the scansion of the original Italian setting, whose succession of trochees and dactyls for the line "Umbre, larve, compagne di morte" was what had produced "a powerful effect of religious terror."[25]

Of course, theory differed from practice, and neither Rossini nor Berlioz was completely consistent. The choral Preghiera from *Mosè in Egitto*, for example, with its splendidly "simple and vibrant modulation from G Minor to B-flat Major" and its opening into G Major for the reprise of the theme, was for Berlioz exemplary of the expressive style.[26] And Liszt's pianistic rendition of the anguished Introduzione, which "depicts" the Egyptians plunged in darkness, apparently reduced Berlioz to tears.[27]

But Berlioz could never fathom how four people experiencing different emotions could sing the same words and music (as he is at pains to say in chapter 43 of the *Mémoires*). This is what happens in the pseudo-canonical slow movement "Mi manca la voce" in the quartet in Act II of *Mosè in Egitto*. Characteristically, the singers are so overcome with emotion as to be speechless; according to Balzac's *Massimilla Doni*, they speak the "language of the soul."[28] But for Berlioz they seem only to have conjured up the coarse "pièces de stupéfaction" that were the speciality of popular melodramas. And worse, the orchestra is practically reduced in such moments to accompanying singers.[29] Berlioz's own answer to this aesthetic challenge was the "réunion des thèmes," the simultaneous inter-twining of different themes such as he manages in, for example, the finale of the *Symphonie fantastique*, in the Serenade in *Harold en Italie*, and in the *Fête chez Capulet* of *Roméo et Juliette*.

He had a better appreciation for such moments upon hearing the quartet in Act I of Beethoven's *Fidelio*; then he said that Rossini wrote "a host of ravishing things in this form," including "Mi manca la voce."[30] But Berlioz still complained that unlike Beethoven's canon, Rossini's was succeeded, inevitably, by a cabaletta and noisy coda, that "lash of the whip" designed to wake up the audience and move the action forward. Such large-scale effects were still alien to older French sensibilities, which

Berlioz so often shared. Compounding the effect of their sometimes brassy orchestration was the two-fold statement of the theme, usually separated by a structural crescendo that registered the role of the audience by demanding, in effect, that singers encore the theme with new embellishments. Berlioz parodied the effect in the Seventh Evening of *Les Soirées de l'orchestre* by calling the *cabaletta* "the little cabal." But Rossini's worst crime, for Berlioz, was the abuse of the bass drum, along with cymbals and triangle, in order to accentuate the downbeat – and thus to make the audience "vibrate," in a manner akin to the modern stereophonic boosted bass.[31]

The critical crossfire of the eighteen-twenties

Such a devotee of Italian opera as Eugène Delacroix could muse in his diary, after hearing *Mosè in Egitto*, that "music is the sensual pleasure of the imagination."[32] But in the confused public rhetoric employed in early nineteenth-century French aesthetic debates, the chasm that had opened between "mechanical" Italian music and "philosophical" French music seemed unbridgeable. It was this polarized artistic climate that drew Berlioz into criticism and made Gluck ever more the touchstone for both his writing about music and his own compositions. We shall miss something essential about both unless we return to a consideration of the paper war into which Berlioz was thrust upon his arrival in Paris.

The *guerre rossinienne* or "Guerre des dilettanti," as it was dubbed, differed from earlier musical quarrels in that it was not only a contest between national styles, but was also part of a larger conflict between Ancients and Moderns, *classiques* and *romantiques*, Racine and Shakespeare – or at least these were the terms in which this phase of the debate over emerging romanticism was framed. In point of fact the instigators were on the one hand the academic classicists entrenched in the various Academies making up the powerful French Institute, now restored to the king's protection, and on the other hand all those poets, painters, and composers who were not content merely to emulate the letter of the grand French classical tradition. As historians have recently come to recognize, this battle had a strongly generational basis, crossing political as well as disciplinary lines and pitting disenfranchised younger artists – the sons of the bourgeoisie to whom only the law and medicine were open – against the artistic gerontocracy Stendhal had in mind when he famously defined romanticism as the art of pleasing one's contemporaries, and classicism as the art of pleasing their grandfathers.[33] These were the composers he called "musiciens-anatomistes," more concerned with technical irregularities than originality, esprit, or dramatic verve;[34]

the label was an allusion to the *docteurs-anatomistes* who had been their colleagues in the pre-revolutionary days when music was part of the Académie des Sciences.[35]

After Berlioz had abandoned the dissecting rooms of the Hospice de la Pitié, it was only to be a matter of time before he, like Victor Hugo, would realize that his own elective affinities for the classicism of Gluck and Spontini could not bridge this generation gap. He resolved the paradox rhetorically, in the spirit of Hugo, by declaring Gluck a romantic, the Shakespeare of music, and his personal pantheon – Spontini, Weber, and Beethoven – Homeric students of Gluck, the first musical modernists.[36] But unlike Hugo, whose romantic views resonated more loudly once he had realigned his politics with the left, Berlioz was to find that the opposition camp had already been staked out by the dilettanti, leaving him recourse only to imagined acts of terrorism. It is as though he were caught between a rock and a hard place – between the *vieille roche* school of French classicism, with its critics drawn from the ranks of the hommes de lettres, and the new Italian school promoted by critics such as "Grimm's grandson," as Stendhal styled himself in the chronicle of Parisian culture he wrote for the *London Magazine* (Grimm being the encyclopedist and pamphleteer who had played a leading role in the mid-eighteenth-century Querelle des Bouffons). The moniker telegraphed both the youthful vigor of the Rossinistes and the ossification of the Opéra, where nothing much had changed since the battle of the Gluckistes and the Piccinistes of the late seventeen-seventies.

Two decades before Berlioz's arrival in Paris, the *Journal des théâtres* had already reported that the public, "fed up with the sublime productions of Gluck which it has been given now for the past twenty-five years, has not yet heard anything that can equal them," and coughed, spit, gossiped, and flirted when Alceste or Iphigénie sang.[37] By the time Berlioz heard *Les Danaïdes* on 14 November 1821, the Opéra had not had a new hit since 1817, when it presented *Fernand Cortez* in a revised version that lacked the seventeen horses supplied by Napoléon when he commissioned it in 1809. Gaspare Spontini, its composer, had also spruced up Salieri's pre-revolutionary opera before he left for Berlin in 1820, supplying it with the "sad sensuous" ballet music that so "excited and disturbed" young Berlioz.[38] The Opéra's repertory otherwise consisted of the works of the academicians who rigidly emulated classical models. And with no more than two newly composed operas a year to look forward to, the constant rotation of the same repertory put habitués in mind of Salieri's mythological maidens, doomed forever to return to the river with their leaky water-barrels.

The Opéra's coffers were similarly filled to the brim by the taxes it levied on other theatres and by more in the way of government subsidies than it ever grossed from door receipts and loge rentals. Yet still they were chronically drained just by the sheer cost of maintaining its bloated artistic bureaucracy. A slightly older and wiser Berlioz would complain about having to review such chestnuts as the "nauseating" *Rossignol*, a one-act opera programmed for the satisfaction of "provincials, medical students, and shopgirls."[39] And even during his musical apprenticeship, he and the acolytes he led as the "high priest" of the "cult of Gluck" would express on the spot their "sovereign contempt" for the last-minute substitution of such a work as *Le Devin du village*, Rousseau's amateurish contribution to the Querelle des Bouffons in 1753, by "abruptly leaving the theatre en masse, swearing like marauding soldiers who discover water in what they had taken to be brandy casks."[40] (Berlioz was on hand, though, for the curtain call on closing night in 1827, when instead of flowers a powdered wig was thrown at the heroine's feet.)

The ballet as the embodiment of the Opéra: three lithographs

According to Stendhal's chronicle in the *London Magazine*, all but die-hard music-lovers came only for the pre-romantic ballets performed between acts, of which there were also about two new ones per year. These included mostly imports by Viennese Kleinmeistern, pastiches or updatings of older composers' opéras comiques (Grétry, Méhul, and Dalayrac), and newly composed collaborative ballets, but none of Gluck's ballets en action. Most were galant or in the amatory and erotic vein of the Greek poet Anacreon, who in his old age extolled wine and love.[41] One such work was Fréderic Vénua's new setting of the choreographer Didelot's *Flore et Zéphire*, which concerned the inconstant Zephyr, the West Wind, and the nymph, Flora, goddess of flowers, who clips his wings. Created in 1815, it was parodied in 1836 by Thackeray when he was the Paris correspondent for *Le Constitutional*. Théophile Gautier, the scenarist of one of the first romantic ballets, *Giselle*, cited it as an exemplar of the outworn style romanticism would replace.[42] Ernest Miller's *Psyché* (1790) was the story of the maiden rescued by Zephyr from the jealous Venus's plans to marry her to a winged serpent, and curious to learn the identity of her lover, the invisible Cupid himself.

The one-act reduction of Dalayrac's *Nina* (1786) created in 1813 by Persuis was one of the first things Berlioz saw upon his arrival in Paris. He recognized the tune of Nina's romance "When my sweetheart returns to me," arranged for English horn, as the song his sister's friends had sung at his first communion.[43] And he marveled at the miming of Emilia Bigottini, the ballerina who would later create the title role of Fenella in

Auber's *La Muette de Portici.* As Nina, she goes mad, regaining her reason on the arms of her long-lost sweetheart and of her father, and Berlioz reports that this reunion scene, fraught with pre-romantic sensibility, was so compelling that he almost forgot to protest the omission of Baillot's famous violin obbligato. When he came to his senses, he says, he called out for it, whereupon the entire house joined in and stormed the pit.[44]

The reduction of the French lyric theatrical canon to a status secondary to the ballet was the point of a lithograph called "The Grand Opéra," published on 26 July 1821 as an insert in *Le Miroir des spectacles* (see Fig. 2.1), where a gloss explained that because the Opéra had up till then "sacrificed itself almost entirely to Terpsicore, we present it to the public supported by its *ballets*" (playing on the homophonous word *balais* – brooms).

The artist was none other than Delacroix, soon to become the leading representative of French romantic painting. Teeming with verbal-visual puns that could easily have been decoded by any contemporary French-speaking opera-goer, it concentrates the allegorical terms of contemporary debate. Délacroix presents as the embodiment of the Opéra its pirouetting sixty-one-year-old semi-retired dancer, Marie-Auguste Vestris,[45] a toothless, grinning, grizzled, and inebriated "vieille perruque" clad in little more than a Greek tunic. The superannuated dancer had specialized in the roles of Zephyr and Cupid, but was now better known as "Père l'Amour"; with Anacreontic vigor he vaults through the air using a pair of brooms as crutches. Single-handedly, he saves Psyché and Nina, and helps the abandoned Opéra keep body and soul together.

And as brevity is the soul of wit, the irony of the impersonation is underscored by the positioning upstage, as part of the scenery, of the soulful Baillot, the Opéra's famous concertmaster, who thought musical instruments could do much more than paint scenes. A popular professor of violin at the Conservatoire, and with Rode and Kreutzer author of the *Méthode* used there since 1800, he was also closely identified with the repatriated royalist émigrés who sponsored his exhumations of chamber works by Mozart, Haydn, Boccherini, and early Beethoven.[46] Here, standing, as was his custom for old-fashioned *quatuors concertants*, Baillot fiddles atop a barrel (*tonneau*) that represents at once his giant-sized sounding board and the out-sized singers' lungs that he "covers" – the hollow *tonneau des Danaïdes*, another symbol of the Opéra's diminishing returns.

Their stentorian style of French declamatory singing, known as "crying" or "howling" – a style that invited comparison with the "criers of our public squares" (hence the nickname *crifort*), had been exacerbated by a recent and rapid rise in concert pitch, which required musicians to

Fig. 2.1 Eugène Delacroix, "The Grand Opéra supported by its ballets"
Bibliothèque Nationale de France (Cabinet des Estampes).

transpose certain parts up by a whole tone ("monter un ton haut"). (Berlioz cracked that singers had now not to "give forth" high notes but rather to "extract" them, as dentists do decayed teeth).[47] As a result, the powerful dramatic bass Henri-Étienne Derivis, whom he heard in 1823 as the High Priest in Spontini's *La Vestale*, had become the *bête noire* of the dilettanti (who advocated the light, floating style of vocal production known as *bel canto*); and Mme Branchu, whom he regarded as the very incarnation of the tragédie lyrique, had refused the title role of *Iphigénie en Tauride*.

Desperate to renew its repertory in the face of such widespread humiliation, the Opéra was nonetheless saddled with commitments to mount works by its veteran composers. These included Henri-Montan Berton, a member of the Académie des Beaux-Arts, the Opéra's Jury de lecture, and a professor at the Conservatoire who had been inducted into the *Miroir des spectacles*' fictitious Order of the Weathervane for having done four political volte-faces (from Louis XVI to Napoléon, from Napoléon to Louis XVIII and back during the Hundred Days, and finally to Louis XVIII after the Settlement of 1815).[48] Berton's biblical ballet *L'Enfant prodigue* (1812) was due for a revival, and his opera *Virginie* was to be a short-lived *succès d'estime* when it was finally completed in 1823. The Opéra had kept the eager Rossini at bay since 1818 with vague promises of a dusty neoclassic libretto that had been accepted by its Jury littéraire in 1816, since which time he had composed sixteen operas (including the *Barber*, composed, rehearsed, and staged three and a half weeks from the day Act I of the libretto was delivered). *Otello* was still getting rave reviews at the Théâtre Italien.

Finally determining to exploit Rossini's popularity, after overruling the objections of an internal faction led by Berton, the Opéra promised Castil-Blaze author's rights to adapt one of the composer's serious operas – first, in January 1821, *Tancredi* (1813), then, in July, after concerns about Parisian reaction to its contralto hero were voiced, *Mosè in Egitto* (1818). Completed in January 1822, the adaptation was to be turned down in 1824: Castil-Blaze then took his case for translation to the Odéon. In the end, in 1827, Rossini himself would adapt it as *Moïse et Pharaon*, which opened at the Opéra on 26 March.

The decision to produce Rossini at the Opéra was leaked to the press, and an anonymous pamphleteer sounded an apocalyptic alarm:

> [T]he end of the musical world approaches; the antichrist has already appeared; he triumphs; the altars of Genius are profaned, and His adorers, reduced to silence, see with indignation an idolatrous crowd offer impure incense with the same hand to Mozart, whom it can't understand, and to Rossini, whom it is well worthy of admiring.[49]

It was at this point that Berton, provoked by the anonymous articles Stendhal began publishing in *Le Miroir des spectacles,* issued his own call to arms, perorating as follows in a three-part philippic he entitled "De la musique mécanique et de la musique philosophique," published in *L'Abeille*:

> We cannot deny that the enemy is at the doors of the musical empire. Let us protect ourselves from the invasion, let us defend the heritage that our illustrious masters have bequeathed us.[50]

Berton declared war on "innovators" in general (he was the "gouty old man" whom Berlioz remembered as being responsible for declaring his 1827 prize cantata "unplayable," and as advising him that novelty was a "chimera"), but his fire, here, was clearly aimed at Rossini. Speaking on behalf of the philosophical Ancients, who had "laid down the rules of musical art for all time," he asserted that the mechanistic Moderns, whose protective deity was "fashion" sacrificed everything to effect and "abandoned the true for the bizarre." Their "mannered turns of melody" and the "heavy artillery" with which they had "bent the laws of the orchestra under their imperious yoke" prompted Berton to compare them to the Gothic barbarians who destroyed Greek architecture.

An anonymous lithograph entitled *Il Tambourossini, ou la nouvelle mélodie* echoed Berton's call to arms (see Fig. 2.2).

A catalogue of French complaints about Rossinian opera, it updates the mythological judgment of Midas, King of Phrygia. Midas won his ass's ears by preferring Pan's crude piping to the music of the gods played by Apollo on his silver lyre. At the height of the war between the French Gluckistes and the Italian Piccinistes in 1778, Grétry had turned the story into an opéra comique parodying high tragic and low comic French styles of the past; these he had had Apollo liken to a contest between a cuckoo and an owl judged by an ass, all of them oblivious to the song of a nightingale. In the lithograph, Grétry's nightingale (the Opéra) has won out to Rossini's raucously cawing thieving magpie, the eponymous "star" of *La gazza ladra,* an opera so popular that when the young Balzac was researching his treatise on stimulants (the *Traité des excitants modernes*) in 1822 and a friend challenged him to a drinking contest, the standard for sobriety was whether he could be made to pass out at a performance and miss "the music of Rossini, la Cinti, Levasseur, Bordogni, la Pasta."

From its perch on the bell of a trumpet, the magpie sings its roulades, competing to be heard over the clamor made by Rossini's barbaric Moor, blowing on his horn and pounding on his Oriental drum in the Turkish manner (with a mallet and a switch of twigs) while trampling on violins

Fig. 2.2 Anonymous, *Il Signor Tambourossini, ou la nouvelle mélodie*
Bibliothèque-Musée de l'Opéra.

(and thus standing Declacroix's image of Baillot on its head). He is a kind
of Panharmonicon, an updated version of the monstrous, fire-breathing
Chimera of Greek mythology slain by Bellerophon riding the winged
Pegasus. Midas himself, enthralled by the din and oblivious to the music
of Mozart and Cimarosa underfoot, is a metaphor for the dilettanti but
also a reflection of the composer, whose image he magnifies in a mirror
(an allusion to *Le Miroir des spectacles* and to the romantic school's
notions of art as a realistic image rather than an idealized allegory of
society).[51] Apollo flees to distant Parnassus, where the rearing Pegasus
awaits Bellerophon, and where Psyche, saved by Zephyr from marriage to
the winged serpent, awaits Cupid.[52]

This verbal-visual one-two punch was matched in *Le Miroir* itself, first
with Stendhal's unsigned articles in praise of *Otello*. Stendhal also

appears to have written the taunting commentary published along with a second lithograph by Delacroix on 13 August. Entitled *Théâtre Italien* and described by Stendhal as "Rossini single-handedly supporting the Italian Opera" (see Fig. 2.3), this was the antithesis of the artist's earlier cartoon – and of the photographs of the portly septuagenarian typically encountered in the literature today.

Delacroix's Rossini was the one Berlioz had to contend with: young and fashionably dressed, his pockets overflowing with scores and his body surging with the strength of Atlas straddling France and Italy, he balances on his head and hands three characters: the jealous Otello, the clever Isabella, heroine of *L'Italiana in Algeri*, and Figaro, *factotum della città*, in such demand that he never rests. As the art historian Nina Athanassogloui-Kallmyer rightly suggests, it may have been this image of Rossini as the embodiment of the romantic notion of the "vegetable genius" that Théophile Gautier had in mind when in 1852 he referred to Rossini as "an orange tree spontaneously producing its round, golden fruit."[53]

Delacroix's idealizing image also provides a context for understanding Ingres's remark about some of Rossini's serious operas – as "the music of an ill-bred man";[54] he must have been all too aware of his younger rival's advocacy of Rossini, since it was one index of the contemporaneity that had distinguished Delacroix's work from the classicism of his own grand manner ever since the Salon of 1824 and that had caused Baudelaire to prefer the "colorist" to the "draftsman," in Stendhal's formulation, as "the true painter of the nineteenth century."[55]

Considering that Berlioz was to become one of the great harmonic colorists and to make the expanded romantic orchestra his "instrument," it seems paradoxical to find him on the other side of the generational divide from Delacroix – though to be sure, the artist's taste for "Italian color" over "German line" parallels Rossini's preference for setting dramatic situations rather than imitating specific words. But Berlioz noted that he shared more with Ingres than the artist's high opinion of Gluck. What Delacroix's lithograph suggests is just how classical Berlioz was to be even in such a quintessentially romantic work as *Roméo et Juliette*, his own response to the growing fascination with Shakespeare first seen in Rossini's *Otello*.[56] The symphony's fugal combat scene, its choral recitative, its strophic "improvisation" in the declamatory mode, its pantomime at the tomb, and so many other instances of the "imitative style" as Berlioz understood it, all proclaim an artistic identity forged during his formative decades in Paris by confrontation with what he perceived to be its antithesis, Rossini.

Fig. 2.3 Eugène Delacroix, "Rossini single-handedly supporting the Italian Opera" Bibliothèque Nationade de France (Cabinet des Estampes).

PART II

Principal compositions

3 Genre in Berlioz

JULIAN RUSHTON

Titles, cycles, collections

On the face of it, Berlioz is a composer for whom genre was a secondary issue. Working within a genre creates definite expectations, but Berlioz – unlike Monpou and Niedermeyer in their *romances*, Haydn and even Beethoven in their symphonies, Auber and Meyerbeer in their operas – seems to have preferred not to operate in this way. Berlioz's overtures, among his most popular and readily understood works, do adhere to expected outlines, but his symphonies evoke the theatre, his operas pay only nominal tribute to established categories, and his liturgical compositions (the *Messe solennelle*, *Requiem*, and *Te Deum*) present generically conventional surfaces which prove, on closer examination, to be deceptive.

Berlioz implicitly acknowledged a difficulty by providing generic subtitles for otherwise purely descriptive titles. At the time of their composition, the *Épisode de la vie d'un artiste*, *Harold en Italie*, *Roméo et Juliette*, *La Damnation de Faust*, and *L'Enfance du Christ* were the sole occupants of their generic categories – respectively Fantastic Symphony (*Symphonie fantastique en cinq parties*), Symphony in Four Movements with a Solo Viola (*Symphonie en quatre parties avec un alto principal*), Dramatic Symphony (*Symphonie dramatique*), Dramatic Legend (*Légende dramatique*),[1] and Sacred Trilogy (*Trilogie sacrée*). Despite such specificity, however, Berlioz could not always avoid misunderstanding. If the subtitle for *Harold en Italie* tells us that in this symphony there is more than a trace of the concerto, terms such as "dramatic legend" convey little about genre: some contemporaries mistakenly alluded to the *Damnation* as a symphony, for example, but Berlioz would not accept the designation "Symphonic legend."[2] And yet he was prepared to include *Le Retour à la vie* (generically, a *mélologue*) among his symphonies.[3] Even his song sets have suggestive titles (*Irlande*, *Les Nuits d'été*, *Fleurs des landes*) which effectively disguise whether they should be interpreted as coherent cycles or as collections of individual items.[4] The collection *Tristia* groups three works (chorus, song, orchestral march) with no regard for generic consistency. Despite the unity of subject-matter, the same is true of *Huit Scènes de Faust*, which includes choruses and solo songs with instrumentation varying from a full orchestra to a single guitar.

In offering idiosyncratic designations of genre, Berlioz may have been attempting to clarify public expectation and assist enjoyment and comprehension of his works. If so, he was to some extent working against genre rather than with it, by applying the rhetorical device of paradox. Genre is an aspect of rhetoric, a tool by which creative artists manipulate responses to their work. With Berlioz, then, there may be tension between his "romantic" desire to be original and his natural desire to be understood and appreciated.

The title *Symphonie fantastique*, for example, paradoxically combines the order implied by symphony with the disorder implied by fantasy. It may seem perverse to suggest that the *Fantastique* is Berlioz's most conventional work, but it is indeed perhaps less strange than a symphony with solo viola (*Harold*) or a symphony with seven movements (*Roméo et Juliette*). His symphonic design retains only enough of precedent to permit the dramatic, even operatic, elements he required to realize his parallel programmatic intentions. In what follows, I propose to discuss selected passages and works in order to suggest that Berlioz took risks with his audience precisely because he relished the potential conflict between generic expectation and musical reality.

The vocal versus the instrumental: thoughts from an early overture

Not least among Berlioz's risks with generic expectation is his blending of the idioms of vocal and instrumental music. While the same might be said of a generically conventional composer like Mozart, who combined the prevalent eighteenth-century forms of aria and concerto, Berlioz challenged expectations in the forms of individual movements and sections, and also of works as a whole. In this, from the point of view of his audiences, he may have gone too far.

The *Grande Ouverture de Waverley* was published as Op. 1 in 1839 but was composed some twelve years before. The second theme of its sonata allegro conforms to a generic lyrical type: a range of only a tenth, a single instrumental "voice" (wind in double octaves), a simple string accompaniment, and symmetrical phrasing (see Ex. 3.1a). When it is repeated, however, wind and strings exchange roles, and the melody is figured to suit the latter: its upbeat is tossed from one side of the orchestra to the other – in Berlioz's time first and second violins sat on opposite sides of the platform – and the descent, doubled in thirds, is bowed in eighth-notes across the beat (see Ex. 3.1b). A quasi-vocal idea thus becomes idiomatically instrumental.[5]

Example 3.1 Berlioz, *Waverley* Overture
(a) bars 139–147
(b) bars 179–187

In this early overture, Berlioz shows learned or intuitive understanding of the genre in which he worked, paying tribute to the overtures
of predecessors he admired, among them Weber and Beethoven, primarily, and, secondarily, Gluck, Méhul, Cherubini, and Rossini. The slow
introduction and sonata allegro was a formal model he continued to
develop and stretch until his last opera, *Béatrice et Bénédict*. Genre is a
"class, type, or category, sanctioned by convention."[6] It is not academ-
icism; it is a means to attain comprehensibility, to communicate with an
audience. Working within a genre does not preclude originality. For
example: had any overture before *Waverley* attracted attention by
opening with a single note from the second oboe? Had many transformed
the secondary material in the manner of Example 3.1 (which is by no
means all that Berlioz does with it)? *Waverley*, sometimes considered
immature or not wholly characteristic, stands on the cusp that separates
imitation from marked individuality; the technique of combining themes
(after the recapitulation of the second theme, at bar 294, the first theme
joins in, at bar 304) and the inspired build-up to the coda, which involves
playing Example 3.1a at double speed, are pointers to the way the later
Berlioz handles convention.

There is no reason to suppose that the theme in Example 3.1a originated in a vocal piece. Nevertheless, translation from vocal to instrumental genres, and the resulting instrumentalization of vocal melodies, is
common practice with Berlioz, particularly in the earlier years in which
his habit of self-borrowing was most pronounced.[7] The most common

Example 3.2
(A) The Allegro that follows the *Méditation* in *Cléopâtre*, bars 77–93.

such generic translations occur when vocal themes turn up in opera overtures, as they do in Beethoven and Weber; we hear the overture first, of course, but the themes were conceived vocally, the overture being written last. This happens in the *Benvenuto Cellini* and the *Carnaval romain* overtures as well as in the overture to *Béatrice et Bénédict*.[8]

More remote and thus more interesting instances arise when Berlioz recycles material from his despised Rome Prize cantatas. Once we become aware of the source of a melody, can we escape possible generic, and hence signifying, resonance from its earlier incarnation? If we can, it is because of Berlioz's professional awareness of the idiomatic distinction between vocal and instrumental music. When a melody from *Cléopâtre* ("Du destin qui m'accable"; see Ex. 3.2a) appears instrumentally in the *Fantaisie sur La Tempête*, the words ("Is it for me to complain of the destiny that overwhelms me?") bear no obvious relation to the new context, and the melody, eventually set to the Italian text in which the island spirits invoke Miranda, is enormously extended (see Ex. 3.2b) in an instrumental idiom rich in appoggiaturas and touches of chromaticism.

In this and similar instances, a melody is extracted as an independent unit and placed in a context which is instrumentally and poetically distinct from its original. The same cannot be said of the elegant *Rêverie et Caprice* for solo violin and orchestra, based on an aria rejected from *Benvenuto Cellini*.[9] Despite transposition up a fifth, the *Rêverie et Caprice* retains all the essentials – formal, thematic, and melodic – of the aria.

Example 3.2 (*cont.*)
(B) *Fantaisie sur La Tempête*, bars 230–289.

Nevertheless, from the outset, Berlioz reconceived the music rather than merely transcribing it. Where the aria has an eight-bar orchestral ritornello and one bar of "till ready" accompaniment before the voice enters, the *Rêverie et Caprice* has the soloist appear dramatically, in the fourth bar, with a trill that signals the character of the violin before it soars up an octave to play the tune.

As a master of instrumental composition, Berlioz was always sensitive to those aspects of genre which are concerned with the fitness of musical ideas to their presentation. He thus appropriated thematic materials from discarded works as much for dramatic as for formal purposes. Of the *Symphonie fantastique*, for example, Berlioz acknowledged that the opening idea was taken from an early song whose text ("I must leave forever my fair country, my sweet beloved") is appropriate in mood, if not in detail, to the program.[10] The entire *idée fixe* had already appeared in an aria in the Rome Prize cantata *Herminie*; now it ranges more widely, and is twice transformed into a dance (in the second movement, a waltz, and in the finale, at the grotesque apparition of the beloved as a witch). The main theme of the third movement came from the *Gratias agimus* of the *Messe solennelle* – a song of thanksgiving used, in the symphony, to signify pastoral repose. In the finale, the *Dies irae* plainchant would traditionally have been sung, of course; here it is first severely exposed by the bass instruments used in church to accompany singing, and it is then grossly parodied by trombones and woodwind in a purely instrumental style.[11]

When a song-theme of whatever origin is transferred to an instrumental context, then something closed, such as a strophic *mélodie*, is transformed into something open: a symphonic theme. The generic problem of incorporating lyrical themes into instrumental music is widespread in nineteenth-century music, and is resolved by different composers in different ways. (It continues to be perceived as problematical, for example, in Brahms and Mahler as well.) For Berlioz, the desire to expand what are naturally closed forms also enlivens his purely vocal genres. He wrote a number of strophic *romances* whose publication – on a single page in a periodical – guaranteed simplicity: the music was written out with the words of the first stanza, and the remaining poetry appeared without music. In a *romance* of 1834, *Les Champs*, thirty-nine bars of music apply identically to seven identically structured stanzas. When *Les Champs* reappeared as No. 2 of the *Feuillets d'album* of 1850, the poem was reduced to four stanzas, but the music was now through-composed in one hundred and forty-six bars, with an abundance of variation in both melody and accompaniment. Attention to detail led to similar alterations in the later published versions of *Irlande*. By such means, Berlioz turned the *romance* into the *mélodie*.[12] The various versions of his popular melody *La Captive* represent the extreme case of this type of generic transformation. Tom Wotton was even led to suggest that in its final incarnation *La Captive* approaches the status of a symphonic poem.[13] This process of elaborating a strophic outline sometimes preceded performance or publication: the sketches for *Les Troyens*, for instance, reveal that Iopas's song (No. 34) was originally planned as strophic, but was eventually reworked into a kind of rondo.[14]

At this point we may draw some preliminary conclusions. First, strophic elaboration was one of Berlioz's lifelong preoccupations, and could affect his composition in any genre. Second, vocal and instrumental genres were for him closely entwined: understanding of the latter may well be enhanced by reference to the former. Third, Berlioz disliked repeating himself: even when his works were successful, he tried other formulae in later compositions. These conclusions appear most obviously consistent with the programmatic and dramatic nature of Berlioz's instrumental works. The trajectory of his career, after early concentration on vocal works, led him to present his most original designs in orchestral forms. Then, after 1840, nearly all his works again become vocal. All told, Berlioz's symphonic music, including his overtures, remains the smaller part of his œuvre. It may seem unnecessary to problematize shorter works such as songs, although generic tension is by no means excluded there. But it is in large-scale works that Berlioz's willingness to lure the listener into a set of expectations, and then to challenge them, is most apparent. In the survey of his output that follows, I shall suggest that Berlioz and genre are slippery bedfellows even in opera and choral music, where the broader conception (comic opera, Requiem Mass) appears most conventional.

Sacred, symphonic, and operatic works

Berlioz's first surviving large-scale endeavor is a setting of the Ordinary of the Mass, which he undertook, one must suppose, to please his teacher, Jean-François Lesueur.[15] While hardly a job for an apprentice, Mass setting might seem an invitation to play safe; the church, after all, had a history of rejecting ambitious music. But Lesueur's own Mass settings, unlike those of Cherubini, provided an unorthodox model, and Berlioz's *Messe solennelle* is hardly decorous either. Cavalier treatment of a sacred text, possibly derived from Lesueur's practice, is taken much farther in the *Grande Messe des morts*, where Berlioz omits, transposes, and even confuses the texts of the different sections, bringing words from the Offertory ("Domine Jesu") into the *Rex tremendae* of the *Dies irae*.[16] The *Requiem* was never intended for strict liturgical use, and Berlioz subjugated the text to the interests of the musical plan, which concludes with a complex recapitulation of earlier numbers.[17] The *Te Deum* is still more free: Berlioz selected text from the canticle to suit a design of six grand choral movements and a concluding march, forming a sort of pageant. Traditionally used for military triumphs, the *Te Deum*, in Berlioz's hands, becomes both a celebration and an elegy for Imperial France.

Berlioz's conception of the symphony is no more orthodox. Whatever the element of disguise and possible confusion with elements taken from literature, the *Symphonie fantastique* is about Berlioz and his frustrated, distorted attraction to Harriet Smithson. Previous programmatic music was either constructed upon a conventional topic, like Beethoven's *Pastoral* Symphony (with its mildly autobiographical tincture), or upon traditional, mythical stories, like Dittersdorf's symphonies after Ovid (which were surely unknown to Berlioz). Yet Berlioz contrived to remain within the expected form of a symphony: the lyrical preface to the Allegro, the dance-movement, the Adagio, the complex finale – these are hardly unexpected. The musical consequences of the program modify the pattern by the device of musical interconnection (the *idée fixe*, transformed throughout the five movements) and, more decisively, by details: the alternate repose and dynamism of the first and third movements, the displacement of the minuet or scherzo by the waltz of the second; the insertion of a savage march as the fourth, and the extensive introduction of the finale (atmospheric prelude, arrival of the beloved as a witch, parody of the *Dies irae*), which provides nearly half the movement before the Round Dance (bar 241) gets underway.

The sequel to the *Fantastique*, called *Le Retour à la vie* (characterized as a *mélologue*) and later *Lélio* (characterized as a *monodrame lyrique*), is certainly no symphony, and its awkwardness for listeners is intimately connected with genre, or lack thereof. A monologue for an actor of an overtly autobiographical nature is used for the cunning but to many critics essentially arbitrary motivation of six musical numbers framed, in the definitive version, by touching reminiscences of the symphony's *idée fixe*. The *Fantastique*, whose last two movements are hallucinatory in the original program (the rest, as it were, being "real"), is now represented in its entirety as a dream. The first musical number of the sequel is presented as the last music heard by the protagonist before he falls into a drug-induced sleep. It is another strophic song expanded into a *mélodie* whose text, after Goethe, has a fisherman lured to his doom by a siren: the association with the artist's beloved is made explicit by a citation of the *idée fixe*.

While the monologue covers many subjects that preoccupied Berlioz at the time of its composition, its progress is determined by his musical selections. The protagonist's mind turns to Shakespeare and Hamlet; he

conceives a chorus of shades, which we then hear.[18] He thinks of escape to
the life of a brigand; an appropriate musical number follows. His mind
turning to Arcadian happiness, he hears his own *Chant de bonheur* and its
sequel, *La Harpe éolienne* (the work's only instrumental movement, a
reminiscence of the previous song, both borrowed from the 1827 Rome
Prize cantata, *La Mort d'Orphée*). Finally, he gets back to work and
rehearses his new orchestral composition, the *Fantaisie dramatique sur La
Tempête*, a rich hybrid of overture and cantata which generically anticipates the Lisztian symphonic poem. Performed with commitment, then,
Lélio is more than a revealing text for Berlioz's life and aesthetic, and more
than a collection of musical numbers from his portfolio. But it is easier to
say what it is not than what it is.

Harold en Italie is more readily located on the generic spectrum. If we
overlook the solo viola, it is clearly a four-movement orchestral composition with the hint of a program, its titles aligning it with the nineteenth-
century genre of the picturesque symphony, along with Mendelssohn's
Italian Symphony, which was conceived at about the same time. The
device of *idée fixe* is applied to three movements and then takes cover in
the finale (as does the *idée fixe* in the *Fantastique* following the grotesque
apparition of the beloved). The design of two moderate-tempo middle
movements (also used by Mendelssohn) anticipates Brahms, while the
thematic reminiscences at the start of the finale look back to Beethoven's
Ninth.[19] Here Berlioz is clearly playing generic games; in the context of a
work of vivid melodic and rhythmic life, and of only covert autobiographical significance, the relatively low intensity and high entertainment
value are persuasive.

Berlioz's next symphony, *Roméo et Juliette*, while based on an existing
drama, has intense autobiographical significance. For this Berlioz created
the genre of the "dramatic symphony," also applying the designation
"symphonie avec chœurs" – "choral symphony." The traditional symphony is buried within *Roméo et Juliette's* vaster frame: the lyrical slow
section and the Allegro appear as the second movement of seven, after an
instrumental overture and a vocal prologue; these are followed by an
Adagio (the love scene) and a scherzo ("Queen Mab"). A march is then
interpolated for the funeral procession of Juliet. Preceding the choral
finale (in the form of an operatic scene, and thus quite unlike Beethoven's
Ninth) is a frankly programmatic tomb scene. Generic coherence is
threatened and perhaps only sustained through tracing the dramatic line
as a covert opera.[20] Berlioz himself perceived his last symphony, the
Funèbre et triomphale, as generically closer to his sacred works because of
its architectural qualities, as he notes in the Postscript of the *Mémoires*,
and its element of ritual, which replaces a program. A solo instrument,

reciting as it were a speech from *Les Francs-Juges*, appears in the slow movement to link eulogy with opera. But by this date (1840), Berlioz had had his first brush with operatic production.

Benvenuto Cellini is certainly not a symphonic opera in Wagner's sense, for most of it is clearly divided into numbers. The 1838 version, rather than the simpler version made for Weimar in the eighteen-fifties, nevertheless shows Berlioz reaching imaginatively towards the symphony. There is extensive use of motivic tags (the visiting-card type of leitmotif) and there is a forging scene massively structured in a symphonic vein.[21] Still, generically, *Benvenuto Cellini* is one of Berlioz's more straightforward works. The massive volumes of the new edition notwithstanding, it is not a grand but a *petit opéra*, designed to form the larger part of an evening's entertainment completed by a ballet. The boldness of the musical language, I think, more than its genre or blend of romance and comedy, was fatal to its chance of success. From what survives of Berlioz's next opera, *La Nonne sanglante*, one might guess that despite its gothic subject-matter, a generically decorous work, one quite assimilable into the repertory, was in store. Berlioz's exclusion from the opera house following the failure of *Benvenuto Cellini* thus deprived us of more such pieces and led, instead, to the even more unconventional *Roméo et Juliette*, *La Damnation de Faust*, and *L'Enfance du Christ*.

Faust, as already mentioned, really is a concert opera, with markedly fewer symphonic elements than *Roméo* or, indeed, *Benvenuto*. Like many nineteenth-century operas, it is replete with genre pieces – songs, a march, dances, and choruses of worshippers, drunkards, demons, and angels – as well as arias, and a linked duet and trio. This last, ending Part III, is the most egregiously operatic scene, yet it follows a most unstageable conception, for we must suppose that Mephistopheles sings his serenade in the street simultaneously with the love duet of Faust and Marguerite. To make the point, Berlioz follows the serenade with an echo of Marguerite's ballad, and brings Mephistopheles on to start the trio with a reference to the serenade. Thus, paradoxically, an operatic system of cross-references is used to distance the concert opera from its theatrical model.

L'Enfance du Christ was once identified, rather too optimistically, as the first oratorio by a "Musician of the Future."[22] Like *Roméo* and *Faust*, it, too, has had few if any imitators to sanction its genre by convention; most nineteenth-century oratorios (including Liszt's *Christus*, a true "Zukunftsoratorium," also of richly mixed genre) either follow the model of Handel's Old Testament works or engage more consistently with theological issues. (Mendelssohn provides examples of both types in *Elijah* and *Saint Paul*.) *L'Enfance* is one of Berlioz's least demanding works; it takes familiar scenes and decorates them with extraordinary sensitivity, distancing the events in time by a narrative framework, and commending the events, in the prologue and epilogue, to the meditative prayers of Christendom. The form may be related to the concert opera, with genre pieces (nocturnal march, soothsayers' dance, pastoral chorus), Herod's aria, the duets of Mary and Joseph, and the dramatic scene interlarded by chamber music, when the holy family finds refuge in Saïs. Furthermore, as in *Faust*, Berlioz includes stage directions in the score. But the symphonic device of transformation, used sparingly in overtly operatic works, invades Part III of the oratorio: the opening narrative is a full reprise and transformation of the delicate fugal overture to Part II, and the recitative of the Father is haunted by reminiscences of Mary and Joseph's pleas for succor. Equally bold is the silencing of the orchestra for the epilogue, so that a work for full chorus and orchestra, having dismissed the louder instruments at the end of Part I, attains the paradisiacal beauty possible only with unaccompanied voices.

The device of simultaneity, by which musics of contradictory feeling are combined, is broached in the early overtures to *Les Francs-Juges* and *Waverley*; it reaches uproar in the combined songs of the soldiers and students at the end of Part II of *Faust*, and recurs with serious intent in *Les Troyens*, not only in the raw combination of the *Air et Duo* of Narbal and Anna (No. 31), but in the conventional lament of the descending semitone, heard earlier from the oboe and representing Cassandra, while Chorœbus repeats his tender arioso "Reviens à toi" (No. 3, from bar 186). This is not the only sense in which *Les Troyens* is the culminating work of Berlioz's career. (The opera is normally associated with "grand opera," a genre about which Berlioz had mixed feelings.) Certainly the five-act form, the organization of grand and intimate scenes, and the private tragedies of the female protagonists played out against the male-dominated march of history are all pointers to the Scribe–Meyerbeer tradition. The recurrent Trojan March in Acts I, III, and V is more architectural and symbolic, that is, "operatic," than it is symphonic.[23]

Nevertheless, scratch the surface of this vast work and among its genre pieces, ballets, choruses, ensembles, songs, and arias, less conventional elements appear. In the moving pantomime of Act I (No. 6), Andromache differs from the character who is her obvious model, the mute heroine of Auber's *La Muette de Portici*, in that she is silent by choice. Moreover, she is a character developed purely for her symbolic significance in this one scene, as she never reappears. The astonishing *Chasse royale* that opens Act IV may be claimed for the French tradition of picturesque operatic *symphonie*, but generic references include fugue, at the opening; folksong, in the gentle melody that follows (bar 30); hunting fanfare (bar 45) almost vocal in style, and recurring, perhaps ironically, at the end; and imitative music (rain, wind, thunder, and lightning). This is not interlude, it is rather accompaniment to action: Dido and Aeneas are seen to enter a cave where their love is consummated. In most operatic traditions, such an action would follow, rather than precede, the love duet, and the music itself would reflect their love. But Berlioz's music displays a Breughelesque indifference to the lovers *as* lovers. Grand opera can show no parallel to these features, which create, in *Les Troyens*, an epic design peculiar to Berlioz.

It remains to mention *Béatrice et Bénédict*, ostensibly the lightest of opéras comiques, and a swan-song as unexpected as Verdi's *Falstaff*. Genre pieces, arias, and duets are all present, together with features less traditional, such as the *Épithalame grotesque* that adds yet another twist to Berlioz's lifelong and ambivalent preoccupation with fugue. But what most separates this enchanting opera from generic convention is the virtual absence of plot. For example, one of the most musically developed characters is Hero, yet nothing happens to her in the Berlioz because the Hero-Claudio story that is predominant in the Shakespearean source, *Much Ado about Nothing*, is entirely omitted.

If we take a broad view of Berlioz's career, we may identify a peak of generic complexity and ambiguity in the decade that stretches from *Roméo et Juliette*, via *La Damnation de Faust*, to the *Te Deum*. Challenging as they are, earlier and later works (the *Fantastique*, *Les Troyens*) fall into a clear, if oblique, relationship to existing conventions. Of course, this exposition of generic complexity – in the comedy, the epic, the earlier symphonies, and the works that appear *sui generis* – should not suggest generic confusion. For many people it is precisely these middle-period works that are the most highly esteemed. But whatever his œuvre's relation to the sanctioned class, type, or category, Berlioz may be seen to have constantly exercised his imagination and skill in manipulating genre to broader artistic ends – whether rhetorical, dramatic, or musical.

4 The symphonies

JEFFREY LANGFORD

Berlioz was no ordinary symphonist. In the course of his career he wrote four works that he himself categorized in that genre, but not one of these is traditional in either form or style. By far the most famous of the group is the *Symphonie fantastique*, a work whose curious autobiographical program and unusual orchestrational effects have kept it alive in the orchestral repertory ever since its première in 1830. The other three symphonies of Berlioz are less well known, but equally non-traditional. *Harold en Italie* makes use of a concerto-like solo viola to help depict recollections of Italy. *Roméo et Juliette* draws heavily on the use of solo and choral singing to reinterpret Shakespeare's drama. And the *Symphonie funèbre et triomphale* is clearly a work for concert band. In many ways these works are not symphonies at all – at least not when measured against the familiar German repertory of Haydn, Mozart, and Beethoven. Berlioz's symphonies frustrate and defy attempts at traditional generic classification by presenting listeners with an exceptional fusion of elements drawn from both opera and symphony. The result is something completely new – an unorthodox hybrid genre for which he coined the term "dramatic symphony."[1]

Symphonie fantastique (1830)

Berlioz's first symphony appeared only three years after the death of Beethoven – a fact that bears keeping in mind as one assesses the remarkable innovations in this work. What shocked and intrigued listeners at the première was the extremely detailed program that Berlioz attached to the work and distributed to the audience in the form of a printed leaflet. That a symphony could be inspired by a "poetic idea" was something Berlioz surely learned from Beethoven, whose Third and Fifth Symphonies he had heard in performance only two years earlier. But that a symphony could be so unreservedly autobiographical and self-confessional, in the manner of contemporary French and English literature (where novels of this type had been popular for some years), was fresh to music at that time. Thus the symphonic exposé of Berlioz's unrequited love for the

Irish actress Harriet Smithson marked a new fusion of music and literature in the nineteenth century.

Berlioz's relationship to descriptive program music was as misunderstood in his own day as it is today. In an important essay titled "On
Imitation in Music," he made clear that it was never his intention to paint
pictures or tell stories in music, but rather to explore emotions.[2] The
Symphonie fantastique is thus not a narration of "an episode in the life of
an artist" (the work's original title was *Épisode de la vie d'un artiste*), but a
review of the composer's emotional response to particular dramatic
situations. Of critical importance to Berlioz's theory of program music
was the selection of only those "situations" that inherently lent themselves
to musical representation, often through the use of universally understood musical archetypes such as marches, dances, hymns, and the like.

Discussions of the *Fantastique* inevitably settle on one of its most
innovative features – the *idée fixe* – a theme specifically associated with
the qualities of the beloved woman. Such an association of theme with
character naturally calls to mind the musical technique of Wagner, whose
Leitmotif system it adumbrates by at least fifteen years. But more important than the existence of such a "character" theme in the symphony is the
cyclical manner in which it is employed (which extends the model found
in Beethoven's Fifth Symphony) and the transformations it undergoes
upon each restatement (as we shall see below). This process of thematic
transformation, here deployed for dramatic purposes, was soon to
become the basic compositional principle of nineteenth-century avant-
garde composers such as Liszt and Wagner.

A year after its first performance, Berlioz revised and expanded the
Fantastique with the addition of a sequel, *Le Retour à la vie* (later titled
Lélio), which continues the "story" of the symphony, mixing spoken
monologues with musical numbers of different kinds. Although the
sequel was well received at its first performance in 1832, it is little-known
today and will not be dealt with here.[3]

Movement I: Rêveries, Passions

The intent of this movement is to suggest the general emotions and states
of mind experienced by a young artist (i.e., Berlioz) who is tormented by
unrequited love. For this reason, it is the least specifically descriptive of
the five. Structurally it derives from the traditional first-movement
sonata form found in all classical symphonies. A long, slow introduction
leads to an Allegro in which Berlioz introduces the *idée fixe* as the main
theme (see Ex 4.1) of a sonata form in which a short exposition is followed
by sections of development and thematic restatement (recapitulation) in
free alternation.

Example 4.1 *Symphonie fantastique*, first movement, *idée fixe*, bars 71–90.

Example 4.2 *Symphonie fantastique*, second movement, *idée fixe*, transformed, bars 120–130.

Movement II: Un bal

The music of this movement is more programmatically specific than is that of the first movement because the principal theme is a waltz melody that suggests not so much the mood of a party as it does the very sound of the party itself. Near the middle of the movement (at bar 120) appears a statement of a now transformed *idée fixe* (see Ex. 4.2). Its formal function is to create a contrasting interlude – a B section in a large tripartite form. It leads fairly quickly to a reprise of the main dance tune.

Movement III: Scène aux champs

An introduction to this "scene in the country" imitates the piping of shepherds with a duet between an offstage oboe (probably the first such use of offstage music in a symphony) and an onstage English horn. The main theme then follows at bar 20. A stormy contrasting section, meant to depict the intrusion of thoughts of the beloved, serves as a backdrop for the transformed return of the *idée fixe* (see Ex. 4.3) now heard in upper woodwinds at bar 90.

Example 4.3 *Symphonie fantastique*, third movement, *idée fixe*, transformed, bars 89–95.

The opening theme returns at bar 131 (it is disguised in the middle of a complex texture) and leads eventually to the final coda in which one of the piping shepherds repeats his opening declaration, but finds no response other than a series of unusual chords played by the timpani and designed to evoke the sound-image of distant thunder (as specifically mentioned in the program).

Movement IV: Marche au supplice

Much as the second movement evokes the image of a grand ball through the use of a waltz, the fourth movement creates the mood of the procession to the scaffold through the use of a march (borrowed, then revised, from his early opera *Les Francs-Juges*). Here again Berlioz relies on musical "archetypes" to project his programmatic intention.

The movement develops with a simple alternation of two themes until a coda is reached at bar 131. In these few bars we find a striking antiphonal juxtaposition of the triads of D-flat Major in the brass and woodwinds with G Minor in the strings (bars 154–159) – a tritone relationship indicative of Berlioz's striking harmonic audacity (and one borrowed years later by Musorgsky in the Coronation Scene of *Boris Godunov*). Berlioz then appends to the march a reference to the *idée fixe* as demanded by the program – one final reminiscence of the beloved. On this occasion the theme is not transformed (as it is in the two previous movements); it is rather stated in its original form but truncated at the fifth bar by an abrupt G-Minor chord from the full orchestra – a gesture clearly meant to represent the falling blade of the guillotine, the "coup fatal" of the program. There follows an additional element of gruesome pictorialism in the next three beats of the bar, as a descending G-Minor arpeggio played pizzicato and divided between the various sections of the string family effectively imitates the dropping of the severed head.

Example 4.4 *Symphonie fantastique*, fifth movement, *idée fixe*, transformed, bars 40–46.

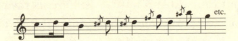

Movement V: Songe d'une nuit du sabbat

While the musical forms controlling the shape of the opening four movements are fairly regular – respectively sonata, ABA, ABA, and rondo (loosely defined) – the "Dream of a Witches' Sabbath" moves much further away from traditional symphonic structures. Here the narrative of the program is mirrored in the sectional through-composed form of the music. Berlioz begins with an introduction depicting the "strange noises" and "groans" of the assembled sorcerers mentioned in his program. The music continues with the arrival of the beloved, come to join the black mass. Her new "trivial and grotesque" character is captured by the most drastic transformation of the *idée fixe* in the entire symphony (see Ex. 4.4).

From here to the end of the movement episodic sections of music correspond closely to the program, which calls attention to a "funeral knell, burlesque parody of the *Dies irae*, Sabbath round-dance, [and] the Sabbath round-dance and the *Dies irae* combined." Especially effective in this last section is Berlioz's use of *col legno* to imitate the rattling of bones.

In all, the *Symphonie fantastique* is one of the most revolutionary works in the entire history of the genre, calling into question as it does the most fundamental assumptions of traditional symphonic rhetoric and design.

Harold en Italie (1834)

Berlioz's second symphony, written in 1834 and scored for the unusual combination of solo viola and orchestra, was inspired both by Byron's dramatic poem *Childe Harold's Pilgrimage* and by Berlioz's own recollection of the happy days he spent wandering through the Abruzzi mountains outside Rome during his sojourn there, in 1831 and 1832, as winner of the Prix de Rome.[4] Berlioz's own description of the symphony (in chapter 45 of the *Mémoires*) suggests several similarities with the *Fantastique*, including the use of an autobiographical program and a cyclical form based on a repeating motto theme that represents a character in the "drama" (in this case the hero, Harold/Berlioz).

What Berlioz does not fully explain in his *Mémoires* is the checkered history and evolution of this symphony, which only later in its genesis became associated with Byron. The original reason for undertaking a work for solo viola and orchestra was a request from Paganini, who commissioned Berlioz to write something that would show off his new Stradivarius viola. Berlioz's first idea was for a piece titled *Les Derniers Instants de Marie Stuart* to be scored for solo viola, chorus, and orchestra. At some point this plan was abandoned in favor of a symphony composed after Byron (four movements with solo viola but without the chorus). Paganini eventually rejected the "symphony" on the grounds that it was not sufficiently virtuosic, but he later regretted doing so, after hearing the work in performance.

Movement I: Harold aux montagnes. Scènes de mélancolie, de bonheur et de joie

Several parallels with the first movement of the *Fantastique* are apparent here. Both movements are more traditional than those that follow, being cast in modified sonata forms with slow introductions. And both are less programmatically specific than the others, dealing with the general emotional states of pensive melancholy and impassioned happiness without suggesting any specific dramatic scenario.

The motto theme that represents Harold is first heard in the introduction (see Ex. 4.5). In a way it is the *idée fixe* of this symphony, but unlike its counterpart in the *Fantastique*, this melody is not subjected to transformations when it reappears. In this manner Berlioz creates for Harold an appropriately Byronic detachment from the scenes he observes.

Movement II: Marche de pèlerins chantant la prière du soir

The source for this movement is discussed in chapter 37 of Berlioz's *Mémoires*, where he describes one of his many Italian reminiscences: peasant farmers returning home at the end of the day, passing by the rows of shrines to the Madonna along the tops of the high hills, and "singing litanies, while from somewhere comes the sad jangle of a monastery bell." Like two movements of the *Fantastique*, this movement, too, is based on a universally recognizable musical archetype: a processional hymn. Eight-bar phrases of the pilgrims' canto are punctuated at every cadence with a

Example 4.5 *Harold en Italie*, first movement, motto theme, bars 38–45.

bell-like chime of horns and harp playing the dissonant note C. This pitch is always resolved to B (fitting the E-Major harmony) at the beginning of the following phrase. The chiming of the "bell" effect is only interrupted by the appearance of the Harold theme in the solo viola. At the end of the movement, C and B are a dozen times juxtaposed until B, as the fifth of the closing tonic triad, finally wins out.

Movement III: Sérénade d'un montagnard des Abbruzes à sa maîtresse
The "Serenade of an Abruzzi Mountaineer to his Sweetheart" is also based on Berlioz's experience traveling in the countryside outside Rome. In chapters 38 and 39 of the *Mémoires* he tells of being awakened one night by a "*ragazzo* with a formidable pair of lungs" who was "roaring out a love song under the window of his *ragazza*." And he describes the music of the *pifferari*, those strolling musicians who come down from the mountains, "armed with bagpipes and *pifferi* (a sort of oboe), to pay homage before the statues of the Madonna." In selecting a mountaineer's serenade for musical depiction in his symphony, Berlioz again resorted to the principle of finding dramatic scenes in which music plays a natural role. His musical rendering of this particular tableau is constructed around two contrasting themes: a quick dance-like melody and a slower, more lyrical serenade. The movement culminates in a triple thematic and metric superimposition, masterfully combining Harold's motto, the rhythm of the dance, and the theme of the serenade (see Ex. 4.6).

Movement IV: Orgie de brigands. Souvenirs des scènes précédentes
The musical model for this "Orgy of brigands," with its "reminiscences of preceding scenes," seems to have been the finale of Beethoven's Ninth Symphony. Berlioz borrows from that work the idea of reviewing in the fourth movement themes from the previous three. Between repeated statements of a rhythmically disjunct theme (associated with the brigands),

Example 4.6 *Harold en Italie*, third movement, thematic superimpositions, bars 167–169.

Berlioz introduces portions of all the earlier main themes including the motto. But here the similarity to Beethoven ends. Rather than introducing a new theme of a hymn-like character, such as we find in the Ninth Symphony, Berlioz leads us back to the brigands' theme (the "filler" between the reminiscences), which then becomes the primary theme of the movement. This G-Minor theme is developed at length before giving way to a contrasting theme in the relative major, and a third theme of more modulatory character. These three themes are then repeated nearly exactly before the key changes to G Major and the movement concludes with a brilliant coda.

Noteworthy here is yet another reappearance of the pilgrims' hymn played by two solo violins and a solo cello, all positioned offstage. The technique recalls the offstage music at the beginning of the third movement of the *Fantastique*, and underlines Berlioz's tendency to blend elements of opera (where such offstage effects are common) into the concert symphony. In chapter 37 of the *Mémoires*, Berlioz speaks to the programmatic intent of the last movement, "where wine, blood, joy and rage mingle in mutual intoxication," and mentions specifically that as the pensive Harold was fleeing in dismay, "a few faint echoes of his evening hymn still hovered on the vibrant air."

Despite the fact that only the first movement in *Harold* conforms to structural symphonic norms, and that thereafter Berlioz finds musical forms that suit both the programmatic intent of the work and the musical material he conceived for its conveyance, one might nevertheless argue that *Harold en Italie* is the most traditional of all Berlioz's symphonies. It has a regular four-movement structure, and the ordering of the movements replicates the traditional Beethovenian sequence of a sonata allegro beginning, a contrasting slow movement, a scherzo, and an energetic finale. Overall the work represents a further evolution of Berlioz's conception of the dramatic symphony, one in which abstract musical design and programmatic meaning are brought into close balance.

Roméo et Juliette (1839)

It is possible that the idea of writing a symphony on the subject of *Romeo and Juliet* first occurred to Berlioz after he attended the series of Shakespearean productions mounted in Paris by the English troupe of which Harriet Smithson was the leading actress, during the 1827–1828 season. (Both the *Symphonie fantastique* and *Roméo et Juliette* would thus owe their inceptions to the same theatrical events.) The project was given further impetus in 1832 when Berlioz, still in Italy as the winner of the Prix de Rome, attended a production of Bellini's *I Capuleti e i Montecchi* which so offended his sensibilities, with its lack of attention to what he (mistakenly) thought was its Shakespearean source, that he wrote a bitter critique in which he listed all the essential ingredients of any musical adaptation of this play, none of which could be found in Bellini's opera.[5]

Actual work on a large-scale musical-dramatic work on this subject had to wait several more years, however, until Paganini stepped back into Berlioz's life. The great virtuoso returned to Paris in 1838, after having forsaken the viola "concerto" he had commissioned from Berlioz four years earlier, *Harold en Italie*. When Paganini finally heard *Harold* for the first time, he was so overwhelmed with admiration for the work and with remorse for his rejection of such a masterpiece that he sent Berlioz a check for 20,000 francs. This lavish sum of money – far more than Berlioz's usual annual income – facilitated the payment of many of his long-outstanding debts and the reduction of his work-load as music critic for daily and weekly press. In January 1839 Berlioz sent a scenario of *Roméo et Juliette* to Émile Deschamps for poeticizing. By September the symphony was complete.

The broad design of the new symphony was revolutionary: seven movements in all, some vocal, others purely instrumental. In its structure *Roméo et Juliette* is Berlioz's most perfect synthesis of operatic and symphonic elements – the apotheosis of his notion of "dramatic symphony." As always, he began work by identifying those scenes in his drama which he felt were inherently musical, after which he addressed the problem of how best to attach the program to the music. For *Roméo et Juliette* Berlioz rejected both the detailed written program of the *Fantastique* and the simple movement-titles of *Harold*, and substituted in their place vocal texts in the form of arias, recitatives, and choruses.[6]

Movement Ia: Introduction (Combats – Tumulte – Intervention du Prince)

The symphony begins with an instrumental introduction that evokes, first, the street fighting between the families of the Capulets and Montagues, and then, in an operatic passage of trombone recitative, the intervention of the Prince of Verona attempting to restore peace.

Ib: Prologue

Much of the opening of the story of Romeo and Juliet is narrated in an unusual choral recitative. Fearing, perhaps, that such a long recitative might lack sufficient musical interest, Berlioz cleverly adds a series of foreshadowings of themes from later instrumental sections of the work – a technique that may be said to mirror that of Beethoven's Ninth Symphony, but in reverse. This allows the listener to associate the subsequent themes with a particular dramatic message.

Ic: Strophes

The choral recitative is interrupted by the alto soloist, who contemplates the nature of first love in a simple aria-like number that Berlioz calls "strophes" – a form borrowed from opéra comique.

Id: Scherzetto

After the choral recitative returns to introduce the subject, Shakespeare's Queen Mab is described by a solo tenor and small choir in a sprightly aria accompanied by flute, piccolo, violas, and cellos. The section closes with the return of the choral recitative hinting at the death of the lovers (with a musical foreshadowing of the fifth-movement funeral march) and narrating the reconciliation of the two families that is achieved, after so much spilling of blood and tears, at the end of the drama.

Movement II: Roméo seul – Tristesse – Bruit lointain de bal et de concert – Grande Fête chez Capulet

The opening of this purely instrumental movement consists of a slow introduction based on three contrasting themes. The first of these depicts Romeo's loneliness through an unaccompanied violin melody which, in its chromaticism and rhythmic irregularity, perfectly captures the aimless wandering of Romeo's spirit at this point in the play. The ensuing section consists of a lyric oboe melody (marked Larghetto espressivo and possibly indicative, as the title suggests, of concert sounds heard from afar) followed by a dance-like Allegro. Eventually the oboe melody is superimposed in augmentation over the principal dance tune. Such thematic superimpositions are a regular and important part of Berlioz's symphonic style (we find them in the *Fantastique* and in *Harold*, too), and the dramatic contrasts that they produce through direct juxtaposition are yet another example of Berlioz's operatic inclinations.

Movement III: Scène d'amour

This movement carries a detailed subtitle that is akin to a stage direction: "Serene night – The Capulets' garden is silent and deserted. The young Capulets, leaving the ball, pass by while singing reminiscences of the music of the ball." It opens with a choral introduction to the purely instrumental love scene that follows. Here again Berlioz employs the operatic device of offstage music: two male choruses are placed in the wings in such a way as to suggest that Romeo, from his hiding place in the Capulets' garden, hears distant revelers returning home after the ball.

The fact that the love scene which follows was scored by Berlioz for orchestra alone (rather than for vocal soloists, in a wearisomely traditional operatic duet) requires some explanation – something Berlioz anticipated in the preface to the published score. Here he comments that the absence of voices is partly the result of needing to try a new mode of expression for a sort of dramatic scene that the best masters had already treated thousands of times as a vocal duet. Furthermore, he adds, in a kind of manifesto,

> the very sublimity of this love made its depiction so dangerous for the composer that he had to offer his imagination a latitude that the precise meaning of sung words would not have allowed, and thus to turn to the language of instrumental music – a language that is richer, more varied, less restricted, and by its very vagueness incomparably more powerful in such a case.[7]

The movement is cast in a free form in which varied repetitions of three main themes (one for Romeo, one for Juliet, and one composite theme containing parts of both) alternate with linking sections of contrasting material (see Ex. 4.7).

Movement IV: La Reine Mab, ou la Fée des songes

Marked "Scherzo" and fulfilling to some extent the function of a regular symphonic component, this movement – "Queen Mab, or the Enchantress of Dreams" – is cast in a traditional ABA form (scherzo–trio–scherzo) whose fine points, on close inspection, are far from conventional. The scherzo portion comprises a statement of the main theme followed by two varied repetitions. The "trio" brings a contrast of key and meter before the varied return of the opening material.

Movement V: Convoi funèbre de Juliette

This funeral march is based not on Shakespeare, but on a bowdlerized version of *Romeo and Juliet* made by the English actor David Garrick, which included a number of such "improvements" of the original text. Berlioz describes the music in a subtitle: "A fugal march, at first

Example 4.7a *Roméo et Juliette, Scène d'amour,* "Romeo," bars 146–155.

Example 4.7b *Roméo et Juliette, Scène d'amour,* "Juliet," bars 248–259.

Example 4.7c *Roméo et Juliette, Scène d'amour,* composite theme, bars 322–328.

instrumental, with a psalmody on one single note in the chorus, then *vocal,* with the psalmody in the orchestra." Accordingly, set against the intricate fugue, based on a long, sinuous, chromatic subject, is a choral chant on the note E that periodically punctuates the fabric of the fugue with short two- or three-bar interjections. At the midpoint of the movement Berlioz reverses the roles of orchestra and chorus, placing the fugue in the chorus while the orchestra takes over the chant-like recitation of the note E.

Movement VI: Roméo au tombeau des Capulets. Invocation – Réveil de Juliette
Berlioz's full title for the movement ("Romeo at the tomb of the Capulets; Invocation; Awakening of Juliet; Delirious joy, despair, ultimate anguish and death of the two lovers") again implies something Shakespeare did not write: in this case David Garrick's idea for the awakening of Juliet

before the poison taken by Romeo has had time to take effect. The two lovers are thus momentarily reunited for the tragic realization that Romeo poisoned himself needlessly.

Berlioz's music for this powerful scene is highly descriptive, unfolding in an episodic through-composed fashion, with rapid transformations of earlier themes combined with new material. Violent musical contrasts evoke the impetuous arrival of Romeo, his despair over finding Juliet "dead," his delirious joy upon her awakening, and the terrible agony of the lovers' death. Here, as elsewhere throughout his symphonies, the logic of Berlioz's musical discourse is not traditionally symphonic, but rather operatic, or balletic; the logic is that of a music, as it were, to be acted.

Movement VII: Final
The mixture of genres that characterizes all of Berlioz's symphonies is nowhere more in evidence than here in the finale, whose subtitle again reads like a stage direction: "The crowd rushes to the cemetery; Quarrel of Capulets and Montagues; Recitative and aria of Friar Laurence; Oath of reconciliation." At this point in his symphony Berlioz steps fully into the world of opera, combining multiple choruses and soloist with the orchestra in an extended ensemble-finale whose musical continuity may be heard as modeled after that found in French grand opera of the time, but whose dramatic scenario (which departs from both Shakespeare and Garrick) was that of Berlioz and his librettist, or of Berlioz alone.

Grande Symphonie funèbre et triomphale (1840)

Berlioz's last work in the symphonic genre was no less unusual than any of his other symphonies, due in part to its ceremonial purpose. In the summer of 1840 the then Minister of the Interior, Charles de Rémusat, asked Berlioz to provide music for the commemoration of the tenth anniversary of the three-day revolution of July 1830. At this ceremony, the remains of the victims of the revolution were to be exhumed and transported for reburial beneath a new monument erected especially for this purpose in the Place de la Bastille. Music was needed for the procession, for the interment, and for the conclusion of the ceremony – all of which was, of course, to take place outdoors. What was needed was thus something loud and simple, yet grandiose and effective. The model for such a work was to be found not in Berlioz's earlier symphonies, but in the colossal, patriotic music written for occasional outdoor celebrations during the period of the Revolution and the Napoleonic Empire. Although this particular kind of patriotic music had long been dead by the time Berlioz came to musical maturity, aspects of its grandiose style lived on in much of his music, including the *Requiem* and, of course, this *Symphonie funèbre et triomphale*.

Berlioz's preoccupation with some kind of a military work dates back at least ten years prior to the writing of the *Symphonie funèbre*. As early as 1831, while he was studying in Italy, he conceived of a large oratorio to be titled *Le Dernier Jour du monde*. The following year, while traveling home from Italy, he was again struck by the desire to write something large and ceremonial. His new plan was for a two-part Napoleonic symphony with chorus to be called *Le Retour de l'armée d'Italie: Symphonie militaire*. Although this work reached the sketching stage, a completed symphony never materialized. All of these aborted plans and unused sketches at last materialized into something more concrete in 1835 – a planned seven-movement symphony celebrating "the memory of the illustrious men of France" with the title *Fête musicale funèbre*. Two movements were actually completed when Berlioz abandoned plans for such a monumental work, using instead what he had already written in two other new works: the cantata *Le Cinq mai* (1835) and the *Symphonie funèbre*. The speed with which he was able to complete this new symphony – forty hours, if we are to believe what Berlioz told his father in a letter of 30 July 1840 – was further increased by the borrowing of material from his abandoned opera *Les Francs-Juges* for use in the second movement. While the job of writing the symphony was thus made easier with such borrowed material, Berlioz did have to face the task of recasting his earlier ideas in the only medium appropriate for a parade: a military wind band.

The performance in parade was apparently a disaster, for almost nothing of the work could actually be heard. The first movement lost its effectiveness because those stationed along the parade route could hear only a few bars of the music as the band marched by. The acoustics at the Place de la Bastille, where the remaining movements were performed, were impossible, and the last movement was completely obliterated by the exit of the National Guard, marching off to their own drum cadence. Nevertheless, the work was extremely well received. Audiences, conservative critics, and even Berlioz's usual detractors all agreed that this was perhaps the best thing he had written to date. But the work's popularity might have been predicted on the basis of its immediate accessibility and overall simplicity of style – all hallmarks of traditional French patriotic music.

In addition to the original version for band, Berlioz also made a version for concert performance, in 1842, which added a traditional orchestral string section and appended a choral finale to the *Apothéose*. The text for the chorus, by Antoni Deschamps, expresses the simple senti-

Example 4.8a *Symphonie funèbre et triomphale*, first movement, bars 4–7.

Example 4.8b *Symphonie funèbre et triomphale*, first movement, second theme, bars 95–98.

ment of "glory and triumph to these heroes." The *Symphonie funèbre* thus lacks the dramatic implications and autobiographical overtones of the three earlier symphonies (and of the logical successor to *Roméo et Juliette*, which is *La Damnation de Faust*); but it is a no less fitting conclusion – in its own unorthodox way – to Berlioz's experiments in the category of symphonic music. We learn from an amusing anecdote in chapter 59 of the *Mémoires* that in 1852 Berlioz did in fact contemplate the writing of another symphony. But the near certainty of losing money on producing it caused him to abandon the dream.

Movement I: Marche funèbre
The opening funeral march may be seen as a simplified sonata form based on two distinct themes in the contrasting keys of F Minor and A-flat Major (see Ex. 4.8).

The middle section of the movement (bars 125–155) functions as much as an area of musical contrast and retransition as it does of development in the traditional sense. Overall, the style of the movement, while generally simple and grand, is peculiarly intricate for parade music: it is not really surprising that the long-drawn-out twenty-bar first theme alone, with its expressive sonorities and subtle linear details, failed in the out-of-doors to create the effect Berlioz had hoped for.

Movement II: Oraison funèbre
Here again Berlioz borrows a form and style from the world of opera, as this movement (taken over from *Les Francs-Juges*) is essentially a recitative and aria for solo trombone accompanied by the rest of the band. The aria itself, which captures the quality of a religious sermon, is cast in non-repeating four-bar phrases to produce a through-composed effect.

Movement III: Apothéose

The main theme of the up-tempo march-like finale is in a rondo-like, rounded binary form (aaba). Its presentation is followed by a lengthy section that combines elements of development and contrast, leading to a reprise of the opening theme combined with Berlioz's appended chorus. It is odd that this three-movement symphony begins in F Minor and concludes in B-flat Major, and one cannot know if this is the result of pre-meditation – one more Berliozian "first" in the area of what was later called "progressive tonality" – or rather of self-borrowing from disparate source materials.

*

That Berlioz held such an untraditional view of the symphony can hardly be attributed to his experience and training in France, where symphonies were generally of little interest to composers and to the public. Nor can it be attributed to his early exposure to the works of Beethoven (which Berlioz does not better, of course, but does transcend). It is more likely that Berlioz invested the instrumental genre with elements of musical theatre simply because his was an inherently dramatic musical talent. Had the administration of the Paris Opéra been more favorably disposed toward the young Berlioz as a potential composer for the theatre, one suspects that his career would have taken a totally different track. The invention of the "dramatic symphony," therefore, might be viewed as one of those happy accidents of history, the significance of which was to become clear only years later. Berlioz's friend Liszt, for one, embraced the idea of the dramatic program as a controlling formal element in music. And at the end of the century, Richard Strauss unabashedly adopted Berlioz's principle of music as autobiography. But the most influential of Berlioz's innovations was undoubtedly the *idée fixe* – the unification of a large symphonic work through the repetition of a theme subjected to continual transformation. Hardly a composer in the later nineteenth century, from Wagner to Mahler, could be said to be free of this basic principle of Berlioz's musical construction. So while the "dramatic symphony" itself, as a blend of opera and symphony, had no direct progeny, aspects of Berlioz's symphonic style may be seen to have inspired many of the most important developments that flowered throughout the remainder of the century.

5 The concert overtures

DIANA BICKLEY

Like his symphonies, Berlioz's concert overtures raise lingering questions regarding the effect of "story" or program upon pure musical coherence. Their relative brevity – crucial to their popularity both during and after the composer's lifetime – allows observation of how he handled such matters as organization and orchestration in the approximately twenty-five-year period between the composition of the first and last works included in this category.

The genre of the concert overture excludes those composed as operatic preludes. For this reason there is no discussion here of the *Grande Ouverture de Benvenuto Cellini*, composed in February 1838 and published in full score in 1839, long before the rest of the opera, or of the overture to *Béatrice et Bénédict*. *Les Troyens* is striking for – among other things – its opening *in medias res*, with no separate overture. However, when external considerations caused *Les Troyens* to be divided in half, Berlioz felt the necessity of explicating the action of *La Prise de Troie* (the acts excised at the time of the performance) by opening *Les Troyens à Carthage* with a *Prologue*, which he composed in June 1863. This consists of a *Lamento*, a *Légende* (in which a *rapsode*, or epic narrator, gives a synopsis of *La Prise de Troie*), and the *Marche troyenne* "in the triumphal mode" accompanied by a *Chœur de rapsodes*. The *Lamento*, which uses material from the original Act I, is not properly speaking an overture, but it is a noble evocation of the fall of the Trojan nation, and its dark sonorities sustained by the low notes of the tenor trombone – "majestic, terrifying, awesome," as Berlioz called them in the *Traité d'instrumentation* – are sufficient to warrant its revival in concert performance.

The *Grande Ouverture des Francs-Juges* is included here because Berlioz clearly regarded it as a concert overture, and conducted it more frequently than he did any other of his compositions except the overture *Le Carnaval romain*. The opera *Les Francs-Juges* ("The Judges of the Secret Court"), a *Freischütz*-like tale of heroism and intrigue set in the Germanic Middle Ages, is the result of Berlioz's collaboration in the mid-eighteen-twenties with his friend and librettist Humbert Ferrand. It was never staged and never published. But the overture was completed in 1826 and published, after what must have been considerable revision, in parts (in 1833), in full score (in 1836), and in various arrangements, including one for piano four-hands by Berlioz himself (1836).

In addition to this work, then, there are six concert overtures that receive attention here; their titles and dates require brief explanation as well.

The *Grande Ouverture de Waverley* was composed after the *Francs-Juges* Overture, probably in early 1827. Both had their premières at a concert of his own music that Berlioz organized on 26 May 1828. *Waverley*, too, was much revised before its publication in 1839. This is the work to which Berlioz finally affixed the label Opus 1, a fitting designation for his first independent orchestral work to rely on no previously composed music. He had earlier published *Huit Scènes de Faust* as Opus 1, but soon came to feel that that score was defective: he withdrew it from publication, and gathered and destroyed as many copies as he could. Thus it was that his first-numbered publication became associated not with Goethe's philosophical drama but rather with Sir Walter Scott's 1814 evocation of eighteenth-century Scotland.

The *Ouverture de La Tempête*, composed in the summer of 1830 and first played at the Opéra on 7 November 1830, precisely one month before the première of the *Symphonie fantastique*, was a year later taken over into *Le Retour à la vie* as a *Fantaisie dramatique sur La Tempête, drame de Shakespeare*. Berlioz's decision to incorporate this composition into the rarely performed sequel to the *Fantastique*, later known as *Lélio*, has had the unfortunate effect of removing from circulation one of his most lively and evocative Shakespearean works whose orchestration alone – which includes one or two pianos, four-hands each, and mixed five-part chorus – should cause it to be performed on more than special occasions.

The *Grande Ouverture du Roi Lear, Tragédie de Shakespeare*, is one of the chief products of Berlioz's sojourn in Italy as winner of the Prix de Rome, along with *Le Retour à la vie* (mentioned above) and the *Intrata di Rob-Roy MacGregor*. The autograph of *Le Roi Lear* – the only manuscript of a mature work by Berlioz that resides in the United States (at the Beinecke Library of Yale University) – is marked "Nizza 7 mai 1831," a reminder that Nice was then still under the protection of the Italian House of Savoy, and did not became a part of France until 1860. Berlioz programmed this work frequently, both in Paris and abroad, and had it published in full score and parts in 1840.

The *Intrata di Rob-Roy MacGregor*, another overture inspired by Scott, was also completed in Italy, after *Le Roi Lear*, in the summer of 1831. Berlioz sent it to Paris as one of the official *envois* required of those holding fellowships at the French Academy in Rome. It is possible that he employed the Italian word *intrata* in the title as a tribute to his idol, Gluck, who had used the word at the head of the score of his opera *Alceste* (1767), which Berlioz admired and knew intimately.[1] *Rob-Roy's* first performance was given by the Société des Concerts du Conservatoire on 14 April 1833, but, as Berlioz wrote years later, in chapter 39 of the *Mémoires*, it seemed "long-winded and diffuse" and was so coolly received by the public, to his disappointment, that he burnt the score "immediately after leaving the concert." (The surviving manuscript, in a copyist's hand, is the one that Berlioz had had made to send to Paris.)

Le Carnaval romain, ouverture caractéristique, is not only the work that Berlioz himself most frequently conducted, but the work that has continued to be the most popular item in his catalogue. Berlioz composed it between June 1843 and January 1844, using as primary material two themes from the score of *Benvenuto Cellini*, the opera that had been unsatisfactorily performed and received at the Académie Royale de Musique in 1838 and 1839. As if in defiance of public judgment he created this ever sparkling overture, which was given an enthusiastic reception at its first performance on 3 February 1844, and which was published shortly thereafter both in Paris (in 1844) and in Berlin (in 1845).

It is not known with precision when the *Ouverture du Corsaire* was conceived and drafted. The score was published with this title in 1852, but on the autograph manuscript the original title, now crossed out, is *La Tour de Nice*. This, and a date set down there in a foreign hand, suggested to Jacques Barzun that the work began life during Berlioz's visit to Nice during the eventful year of 1831.[2] The title *La Tour de Nice* was later replaced by *Le Corsaire rouge*, the French translation of *The Red Rover*, and this title has suggested to others that Berlioz wrote the piece while under the continuing spell of that sea story by "the American Walter Scott," as Berlioz called him, James Fenimore Cooper. (Berlioz devoured Cooper in 1827 – the year of *The Red Rover* – and continued to read him thereafter, as his books appeared almost simultaneously in both English and French.) When the word *rouge* was crossed out, however, the overture took on its definitive title and its Byronic twist: Byron's *The Corsair* was published in London in 1814 and in Paris, as *Le Corsaire*, in 1825.[3]

In chapter 53 of the *Mémoires* Berlioz writes with nostalgia about his visit to Nice in the summer of 1844; though he provides considerable detail, he makes no mention of composing. It is only from the letter to his sister of 5 November 1844 – in which he says that he has "composed a grand overture for my forthcoming concerts" – that we know that he had by then completed *La Tour de Nice*, as it was called at the première on 19 January 1845. It was not performed again until 4 April 1854 (two years after publication), this time with the title it has today, *Le Corsaire*. In letters of 12 April 1852 and 4 April 1854, Berlioz insists – to Franz Liszt, to whom he had no reason to exaggerate – that *Le Corsaire* is a work he has *never* heard. The second version differs from the first primarily by its inclusion of a new slow theme and its overall tautening of the structure, making it more than two hundred bars shorter than the first. In the absence of further information we must assume, therefore, that Berlioz considered the revisions so substantial as to have altered the very identity of the original composition. In this case he had abrogated his normal practice of hearing a work before bringing it out in print, for the revised version had indeed been published in Paris in 1852.

The formal attributes of Berlioz's overtures are not the main stuff of their originality. The slow introductions, the loosely sonata-like allegros, the breathless perorations also fit the description of the overture found in Castil-Blaze's *De l'Opéra en France* (1820), with which Berlioz was undoubtedly familiar: "A symphonic Allegro – rapid, brilliant, impassioned – following upon a short introduction in a more deliberate tempo: such is the widely accepted form of the overture."[4] Theoretical debate about the genre of the overture, ranging from Rousseau in the mid-eighteenth century to Lacépède, Momigny, and Étienne Jouy in the early nineteenth century, focused on the appropriate relationship between the opera itself and its instrumental introduction; but some overtures were performed separately from their operas as early as the seventeen-nineties – Vogel's overture to *Démophon* (1789), Méhul's *La Chasse du Jeune Henri* (1797), to mention only two – and by the eighteen-twenties, Castil-Blaze and others acknowledged the occasional effectiveness of performing overtures as independent compositions.

Berlioz obviously knew overtures by Grétry, Gluck, Salieri, Cherubini, Méhul, Rossini, and others – but he probably did not know Beethoven's *Namensfeier* (1815) and *Die Weihe des Hauses* (1822), or Mendelssohn's overture to *A Midsummer Night's Dream* (1826), which may be said to represent the first true works in the category of the concert overture. Thus, by conceiving an overture with no reference to any opera, ballet, or play subsequently enacted on the stage, Berlioz marked a first in France, with the composition of *Waverley* in 1827.

Grande Ouverture des Francs-Juges

This overture was composed, in the traditional manner, after the opera it was designed to precede was completed. In the opening section, marked Adagio sostenuto, the presentation of the home key of F Minor is followed by a majestic if lumbering theme in the brass, in D-flat Major, associated with Olmerik, the opera's despotic ruler: this theme – proudly notated in two letters to Ferrand (the librettist) of 6 and 28 June 1828 – made a stir at the first rehearsal. Berlioz told his father (on 29 May 1828) that as the introduction came to an end, a violinist turned to him and cleverly suggested that the music had had the effect of a windstorm playing the organ – which led to a round of applause. (The words Berlioz cites are apparently a misremembered quotation from Act III of *The Tempest*, where Alonso cries that "the billows spoke," "the winds did sing," and the thunder is a "deep and dreadful organ-pipe.")

A dominant pedal prepares the return to F Minor for the Allegro assai (with its remarkably fast tempo marking of ○ = 80). Here the main business is the contrasting theme in A-flat Major, a thirty-two-bar violin melody whose resolute and four-square regularity suggests the truth of Berlioz's remark, in chapter 4 of the *Mémoires*, that he borrowed it from a quintet composed when he was barely into his teens. (That his father liked this melody gives us a rare glimpse into the elder gentleman's musical taste.)

The move from A-flat back to the tonic is via a middle section, *misterioso* and more episodic than developmental, in C Minor (with a presentation of the contrasting theme in E-flat Major). The music at the return to F Minor is more varied than the word recapitulation would suggest, and the quadratic second theme, too, is quietly and indirectly insinuated before it returns literally and boisterously in F Major. The rest is all coda, with "Olmerik" returning in D-flat before the Rossini-like rush to the end.

When Berlioz compared the players' enthusiasm at the rehearsal to the public's lukewarm reaction at the concert, he realized (in the letter to Ferrand of 29 May) that "one cannot suddenly win an audience over to novel forms." By "des formes nouvelles" he surely refers not to the repetition of blocks of material (which he rarely carries out in literal fashion) but to the thematic contrasts and dynamic intensities of his various situations and sonorities. When he heard the *Francs-Juges* Overture for the second time, in 1829, the critic F.-J. Fétis, for example, did seem to be coming around: Berlioz was consumed with "fever," but this was "by no means the fever of an ordinary man."[5] Something of this seems to have been felt by Johann Christian Lobe, too, when, after participating in the performance of the piece in Weimar, on 19 March 1837, he penned an invitation to Berlioz to come to Germany that was published in the *Neue Zeitschrift für Musik*. It was felt as well by Wolfgang Robert Griepenkerl, whose enthusiasm for Berlioz was sparked by hearing the *Francs-Juges* Overture in Brunswick in 1839.[6]

The overtures to Johann Christoph Vogel's *Démophon*, Méhul's

Stratonice, and Catel's *Sémiramis*, like Beethoven's overture to *Egmont* (1810), are fiery F-Minor pieces that end in a triumphant F Major; the overture to Cherubini's *Médée* (to which the Beethoven owes a thing or two) remains in the minor at the end. In 1826 Berlioz could not have known the Beethoven, but he admired the Vogel and the Méhul, and knew the Cherubini and, probably, the Catel.[7] A case for the influence of these works on what was, after all, Berlioz's first work to be widely performed as an independent composition, remains to be made.[8]

Grande Ouverture de Waverley

This composition follows the traditional format outlined above, in which a particularly slow introduction, ♩ = 56, leads to a spirited Allegro. Instead of commanding attention at the outset, as Berlioz's last two overtures do to perfection (with a quick and impetuous passage that heralds the slow section), *Waverley* begins with a single note in the oboe followed by a quiet descending phrase in the strings. It is difficult not to draw a parallel here with the quiet solo horn opening of Weber's overture to *Oberon*, for Berlioz admired and even revered Weber's music. But while he soon became intimately acquainted with the operas, it is by no means certain that he knew the score of *Oberon* as early as 1827, when *Waverley* was first drafted.

After a thirty-one-bar introduction, there is a broad aria for the cellos, irregular in phrase structure, curious in harmonic underpinning, imaginative in orchestration: the canonic reflection of the theme in the winds is an academic nicety, and the rhythmic figure in the timpani that accompanies the return of the principal melody is a small stroke of genius. This Larghetto is followed by an Allegro vivace with main themes in tonic and dominant that return, symmetrically, in dominant and tonic. The coda is marked by certain commonplaces that led Hugh Macdonald to wonder if Berlioz was here mocking the Rossinian style he claimed to detest,[9] but the reworking of this section demonstrated by the autograph manuscript suggests rather an attempt to meet the then celebrated opera composer on his own turf.

Indeed, between its performance in May 1828 and its publication in 1839 the work underwent considerable change: not only was the peroration revised, but so, too, was the instrumentation, as the orchestral forces were reduced from one hundred and ten players to eighty-three. The score originally included the new-fangled trompette à pistons with three valves – a small but telling indication of the young composer's fascination with freshly minted instruments and techniques. When Berlioz discovered that the three-valved model was less reliable in intonation than the model with two, he replaced the former with the latter.

Sir Walter Scott was much in fashion in France in the eighteen-twenties, and the quotation at the head of the *Waverley* Overture (taken from a poem in chapter 5 of Scott's 1814 novel of the same name) is certainly congruent with its two-part form:

> Dreams of love and lady's charms
> Give place to honour and to arms.

Berlioz dedicated the published score to his uncle, Félix Marmion, a military officer and a man of letters with whom Berlioz maintained affectionate and life-long relations, despite the temporary rift caused by Hector's marriage to Harriet Smithson. Indeed, one might wish to view the dedication as Berlioz's peace offering to his mother's music-loving brother.

Ouverture de La Tempête

Berlioz was invited to compose this overture by his friend Narcisse Girard, the concertmaster of the Société des Concerts du Conservatoire in its early years and, from 1830 to 1837, the conductor of the orchestra at the Théâtre Italien, where *La Tempête* was originally scheduled for performance on 1 November 1830. This does not explain its inclusion of a five-part chorus of "airy spirits" – surely the first time voices would play a role in a composition called "overture" – but it does explain the reason that these spirits sing in Italian, which was *de rigueur* in the theatre that first welcomed Rossini to France. When the orchestra at the Théâtre Italien proved to be inadequate at the rehearsal, Berlioz adroitly managed to arrange a performance with Habeneck's better-equipped troops at the Opéra, where the première took place on 7 November 1830.

In an article announcing the new work, Berlioz described its peculiar structure: "This overture is divided into four separate parts that are none the less linked to one another and form one continuous composition: *Prologue, Tempest, Action,* and *Dénouement.*" He then outlined the four parts in terms of the business of Shakespeare's play: the airy spirits' prediction of the coming of Miranda's future love; the storm-driven arrival of the King of Naples and his son upon the enchanted island; the disparate emotions of the timid Ferdinand, the virginal Miranda, the savage Caliban, the majestic and magical Prospero; and the eventual departure of Miranda and Ferdinand "to the accompaniment of fanfares and the joyful shouting of the entire crew."[10]

The music of the *Introduction*, which returns, refrain-like, at the end of the *Tempête* and the *Action*, is remarkable in its upper-register scoring for piccolo, flute, clarinet, muted violins, chorus without basses, and – another first for an orchestral composition – piano four-hands. (Berlioz may well have imagined this part as played by his friend Ferdinand Hiller, and by the woman whose love he had drawn away from Hiller, Camille Moke, whom he called "Ariel.") The texture is "glinting" and "diaphanous," as David Cairns has put it, "hovering seemingly weightless above the earth."[11] In his review of the concert of 7 November 1830, F.-J. Fétis had been equally moved:

> A truly remarkable work was performed last Sunday at the Opéra. [...] This
> is M. Hector Berlioz's overture to *The Tempest*, the drama by Shakespeare.
> [...] The disposition of the orchestra and chorus here is marked by great
> originality; the means the composer employs are largely new; the blendings
> of instrumental sonorities are unheard of; and the voices are handled with
> uncommon intelligence and in a singular manner.[12]

Fétis was also impressed by the second section, which Cairns calls "a marine landscape in sound [. . .] handled with exhilarating freshness." Berlioz borrowed the principal melody of the *Action* from his 1829 prize cantata, *Cléopâtre*. The fiery opening of the *Dénouement* is inventive in its use of repeated five-bar phrases, but the remainder of the peroration may be heard as galloping imitation of Rossini's already celebrated overture to *Guillaume Tell*.

The *Fantaisie dramatique sur La Tempête*, as it was rebaptized on incorporation into *Lélio ou le Retour à la vie*, has long remained hidden from view as the finale of the little-performed sequel to the *Symphonie fantastique*. (Berlioz's efforts to have it separately performed in Paris, in early 1834, and in London, in early 1848, came to naught.) The four-in-one structural organization and the close association with the action of Shakespeare's play, however, in addition to the singular instrumentation, suggest that the composition merits attention not only in its own right, but as an antecedent to such one-movement illustrative works as Wagner's *Faust* Overture and Tchaikovsky's "overture-fantasy" *Roméo et Juliette*, to say nothing of Franz Liszt's one-movement symphonic poems.

Grande Ouverture du Roi Lear

Berlioz read Shakespeare's *King Lear* at one of the great emotional crossroads of his life – during the very week, in mid-April 1831, when he learned that his long-silent fiancée, Camille Moke, was to marry another man. This episode, which forever colored his stay in Italy as winner of the

Prix de Rome (and his thinking about women, and revenge, for years to come), is brilliantly recounted in chapter 34 of the *Mémoires* and need not detain us here. What apparently cured Berlioz of his hysterical anger at the betrayal was intensive labor: on arrival in Nice on 20 April, he proceeded to spend two concentrated weeks drafting what became the *Ouverture du Roi Lear*.

This expansive work is in two parts marked Andante non troppo lento, ma maestoso; and Allegro disperato ed agitato assai. The first part can be construed as an ABA form whose middle section, a lyrical melody stated successively by the wind and brass – the latter with ravishing effect, is surrounded by sections in which the violas, cellos, and basses speak nobly and indignantly in the manner of the instrumental recitatives of Beethoven's Ninth Symphony (which Berlioz had not heard, but had read, in Paris). The second part (with the very quick marking of $\lozenge = 168$) can be construed as a near-regular sonata form: the principal themes of the exposition, in tonic and dominant, return in the recapitulation and remain, as expected, in the tonic. What is unusual is the return of the "speaking bass" from the opening, now remade into transitional and contrapuntal material, in the recapitulation and coda. The autograph manuscript, with renumbered pages and papers of different qualities, shows that over the years the work – in particular the second subject of the exposition and the coda – was considerably revised.

The term "speaking bass" comes from Tovey, who urged that "we shall only misunderstand Berlioz's *King Lear* Overture so long as we try to connect it with Shakespeare's Lear at all."[13] With far greater knowledge of the recent events of Berlioz's life, David Cairns takes issue with Tovey's "absolutist" view of the work as a "magnificent piece of orchestral rhetoric in the tragic style," asserting rather that the Beethovenian recitative is "clearly inspired" by the stubborn old king, just as the orchestral conflict in the coda is "surely an echo" not only of the destruction of Cordelia, in the play, but also, in Berlioz's biography, of the annihilation of the love of Camille Moke.[14]

Berlioz himself provides evidence of his thinking in a letter of 2 October 1858 to his admirer in Detmold, the Baron von Donop, where he says that he "intended to indicate [Lear's] madness only towards the middle of the Allegro," and in a letter of 18 April 1863 to his friends the Massarts, where he says more generally that he intended to "give voice to" (*faire parler*) the old Britannic king and his sweet Cordelia. This letter was written on the eve of his concert in Löwenberg, on 19 April 1863, of which Berlioz speaks in the Postface of the *Mémoires*. Not having heard the piece for some nine years, he wrote, "But, it's tremendous! Did *I* really write this?" *Le Roi Lear* is the only overture about which he spoke with such pride.

Intrata di Rob-Roy MacGregor

If this is Berlioz's least-known and most maligned work, it is because the composer destroyed the autograph after the first and only performance during his lifetime, and spoke ill of it in the *Mémoires*. But his submission of the piece for performance by the Société des Concerts du Conservatoire is an indication that, in March 1833, he clearly believed in its potential attractiveness. Had he made some judicious cuts and emendations after that première, this score might now enjoy greater respect.

It is possible to view the structure of the work in terms of an orchestral sonata in D Major, with an introduction, a Scottish principal subject, a Caliban-like transitional theme (to liken it, as Hugh Macdonald does, to a unison tune in the *Ouverture de La Tempête*), and several secondary subjects of which the second was soon borrowed as the second subject of the first movement of *Harold en Italie*. A brief development is followed by the recapitulation, as expected, in D Major, but this is immediately interrupted by a forty-seven-bar passage, marked Larghetto espressivo assai, whose extraordinary scoring for harp and English horn is enough to justify the occasional modern revival. The work concludes with a varied recapitulation and coda that include new thematic material and the curiously original harmonic twists that Berlioz frequently employed to alter the conventional peroration's harping on dominant and tonic sonorities.

The Larghetto of *Rob-Roy* is the direct source of the "Harold" theme in the introduction of the first movement of *Harold en Italie*. (This is the well-known theme that recurs in each subsequent movement). The passage in the overture is every bit as evocative as the passage in the symphony when the English horn – for which Berlioz later substituted the viola – is in capable hands.[15] The transfer of material to a work nominally inspired by Byron's *Childe Harold* from a work presumably inspired by Scott's novel about the "Scottish Robin Hood," *Rob Roy* (1818), again suggests the precariousness of linking the literary source to the musical texture.

Le Carnaval romain, ouverture caractéristique

Berlioz extracted *Le Carnaval romain* from *Benvenuto Cellini*, using as his principal material themes different from those employed in the formal overture to the opera – but a technique derived directly from that tumultuous curtain-raiser. The technique is the application of a swift opening summons-to-attention to the more traditional slow–fast construction. Here, at the outset, we hear a brilliant $\frac{6}{8}$ snatch of the main melodic material of the Allegro vivace – lifted from the finale of the

Deuxième Tableau of the opera, the carnival scene (No. 12), at the place where Teresa, with the women of the chorus, sings "Ah! Sonnez, trompettes! Sonnez, musettes! Sonnez, gais tambourins!"[16] If we are precise about the reference it is because of the astonishing discovery, made only recently, that the source of *this* melody, in the opera, is a phrase ("laudamus te, benedicimus te") from the *Gloria* of the early *Messe solennelle*.[17] One of Berlioz's most thrilling tunes, from the most thrilling scene of his first mature opera, thus comes from a student work (and a sacred work at that) of the mid-eighteen-twenties!

The main business of the ensuing Andante sostenuto is the three-fold presentation of another pivotal theme from the opera, the love music of the Cellini–Teresa duet in the Premier Tableau – where the central phrase, too, represents a surprising borrowing from an earlier work, in this case the 1829 prize cantata *Cléopâtre*.[18] In *Le Carnaval romain* the English horn takes center stage, as in *Rob-Roy*, singing the duet music in the key of C Major. The violas intone a second presentation in E, and the orchestra as a whole a third, in canonic imitation, in A.

A whirling passage for the winds, poco animato, leads back to the $\frac{6}{8}$ carnival music that permeates the concluding Allegro vivace. This is writing so brilliantly fitted to the instruments that it is difficult to accept the fact that in its original guise it is vocal. Sliding imperceptibly from one key to the next, in sentences and rhythms of regular and irregular duration, and with canonic and contrapuntal passages that eventually incorporate the tune of the Andante, the Allegro accumulates a simply irresistible momentum and builds to what is perhaps Berlioz's most dazzling conclusion, with a final progression of vi to I providing one last, blinding shock.

The first performance of *Le Carnaval romain* was given on 3 February 1844, in a program that otherwise featured arrangements of earlier works. The new composition, even though it had been inadequately rehearsed, was immediately encored and subsequently acclaimed by the reviewers. In the *Revue et Gazette musicale* of 11 February, Maurice Bourges offered an analysis (clearly based on an examination of the score) and an encomium:

> Opulent in its ideas and effects, intense in its expression, extraordinarily original in its construction – this work has everything. It will henceforth be numbered among the most beautiful pages that we have from M. Berlioz's pen.

Ouverture du Corsaire

This is the work which began life as *La Tour de Nice* and which was performed with that title in January 1845. In the catalogue of his works that

Berlioz appended to the libretto of *La Damnation de Faust*, the so-called "Labitte catalogue," the title of this still unpublished composition is given as *Ouverture du Corsaire rouge*. When Simon Richault brought out the score and parts, in 1852, and even before, when Berlioz submitted a list of works to the Académie des Beaux-Arts in support of his candidacy for a chair at the Institute, on 6 March 1851, the work bore its definitive title. Assuming the validity of the chronology outlined earlier, *Le Corsaire* thus originally followed upon the heels of *Le Carnaval romain*.

In offering a quick opening (in the principal key) followed by a traditional slow–fast movement – an Adagio sostenuto, in A-flat Major, and an Allegro assai, in C Major – the overture repeats the pattern established by its immediate predecessor (although the tempo markings of the two halves of *Le Corsaire*, ♪ = 84 vs. ♩ = 152, are extreme). In this case the Adagio is taken up with one of those uniquely Berliozian melodies generated by a compound of the bizarre and the divine: the line – a ten-bar unit followed by a six-bar unit that is repeated – seems to clamor for words, as Hugh Macdonald has written, and no one would be surprised if its source were eventually discovered in some earlier vocal work that has not as yet come to light.

One could describe the Allegro as a monothematic sonata form, with a principal melody of sixteen bars whose consequent is the inversion of its antecedent. But this would be to overlook the intrusion into the proceedings of a speeded-up version of the theme from the Adagio, the canons and syncopations that enliven the texture, and the harmonic sleights-of-hand that signal Berlioz's premeditated desire to avoid the commonplace at all costs. One of these miracles occurs in the peroration, when the C-Major version of the opening eight bars (at bars 402–409) glides electrically into a second return, this time in D (at bar 410). Another occurs at the final cadence, where five bars before the double bar the sudden pause on vi^6 clearly implies the conventional formula of V–I, but astonishingly introduces the rebellious formula of ♭VI–♭III – and only then V–I. The announcement for Berlioz's concert of 29 June 1848 could thus fittingly apply to *Le Corsaire*, which alone would be "worth the price of admission, were it only to hear its final cadence of original harmony."[19]

Rebellious, and, like the trombones in the *Lamento* from *Les Troyens à Carthage*, majestic and terrifying. These words apply to many portions of Berlioz's concert overtures, but their most enduring impression – the impression that ensures their continued popularity – is one of vibrant energy and high spirits.

6 The operas and the dramatic legend

JAMES HAAR

"Berlioz ne fut jamais, à proprement parler, un musicien de théâtre" –
"Berlioz was never, properly speaking, a musician of the theatre."[1] This
seems a strange judgment on a composer whose work is from beginning
to end of intensely dramatic character, and who for most of his life was
strongly interested in and closely connected with the musical stage. It is
especially odd if one considers its source. Debussy when he made this
remark (1893) was beginning work on his only complete opera, *Pelléas et
Mélisande.* Like Berlioz he considered and even began composition on
other operatic projects. And Debussy's operatic masterpiece, though it
has had better luck staying in the repertory than Berlioz's *Les Troyens*, has
always been more admired by devotees than loved by the general public,
something true of Berlioz's great work as well. Debussy and Berlioz are
surely greater composers than Massenet and Meyerbeer; but the latter
were more successful stage composers in their own day.

Debussy is not alone in his opinion. Until quite recently critics tended
toward the view, perhaps still current among music lovers in general, that
Berlioz was more successful as dramatist in his symphonies than in his
stage works. Why should this be so – the view, that is – when the reality, if
the reader will accept my opinion as a definition of that undoubtedly slippery concept, is quite different? It began during the composer's lifetime.
Reviewers of *Benvenuto Cellini* and *Les Troyens* occasionally found that
the dramatic brilliance of the orchestral writing in the symphonies did
not transfer well, even detracted from the theatrical effectiveness of the
operas. Thus Charles Merruau admonished Berlioz that he should have
realized the difference between an opera and a symphony but instead
wrote (in *Benvenuto Cellini*) a symphony to which voices were added like
extra instruments. The English horn, says Merruau, is not a lover; but the
lovers' words as sung are merely heard, their expressive intent given to
instruments which describe rather than express meaning.[2] Another
reviewer of *Cellini* remarked more perceptively that Berlioz had dramatized the symphony to such an extent that these works (*Symphonie fantastique, Harold en Italie*) "may be considered true fragments of opera."[3] And
Nestor Roqueplan, reviewing *Les Troyens*, compared Berlioz as musician
to Beethoven, unrivaled as a symphonist but composer of an opera,

Fidelio, "which will never be, truth to say, a real theatre piece." Only Mozart, he says, succeeded in both genres.[4]

Much of this early comment is simply anti-Berlioz sentiment, fed by envy or desire to cut down to size the ambitious and, in his own critical writing, outspoken and often uncomplimentary composer. Berlioz had little to say in favor of Italian opera, even less for its French imitators, and critics who viewed these works with approval felt it only natural to attack him in turn.

Some but by no means all critics responded in this way. Perhaps an equal number, friends and steady supporters of Berlioz, praised the operas as triumphs, proof that the composer belonged at the center of French opera instead of the periphery to which indifference, timidity, and even hostility on the part of theatre directors had consigned him. Many critics took a middle ground, withholding complete approval but recognizing Berlioz's talent, originality, and workmanship. Jacques-Germain Chaudes-Aigues, though troubled by what he saw as a compulsive need to be original at any cost on the part of Berlioz, deplored the vocal hostility with which parts of the audience greeted the first performance of *Benvenuto Cellini*, concluding that "despite the cabals to which M. Hector Berlioz has fallen victim, I do not hesitate to give the name of *chef-d'œuvre* to his score."[5]

Almost all the contemporary reviews of the operas stress their difficulty and the need for repeated hearings and frequent performances to make the opera audience at home with Berlioz's dramaturgy. Here there has been a continuing problem. Of the four works to be considered in what follows only *La Damnation de Faust*, operatic in many ways but not designed for the stage, has been performed often enough to become reasonably familiar to audiences. *Benvenuto Cellini*, *Les Troyens*, and *Béatrice et Bénédict* have never approached repertory status, especially in France. Good recordings, not in great abundance, do now exist for all the operas, and all have been edited with exemplary skill in the *New Berlioz Edition*.[6] The operas have devoted admirers today as they did in Berlioz's lifetime. Serious listeners in large numbers can now get to know the operas as well as the symphonies; when this has happened these operas will at last come into their own.

*

From the time of his arrival in Paris as a music-loving young medical student Berlioz was attracted by musical theatre. Frequent visits to the opera were soon followed by intense study – not of medicine but of scores, chiefly those of Gluck, in the library of the Conservatoire. On a day of great importance for his future career (6 November 1822) Berlioz saw Gluck's *Iphigénie en Tauride*.[7] From this time on dreams of conquering the operatic stage were never to leave him. At the end of 1822 Berlioz began a period of study with J.-F. Lesueur, one of the most successful opera composers in Paris at the turn of the century. Encouraged by Lesueur, Berlioz began several operatic projects, juvenilia which he later burnt. In 1824 he heard Weber's *Der Freischütz*, in a sadly adulterated version, and realized what the romantic spirit could do for opera; he was to remain a strong partisan for Weber, and an advocate for proper performance of his work, throughout his life.

Entering the Paris Conservatoire in 1826, Berlioz began to mature rapidly as a composer. Ideas for opera were ever-present, and Berlioz actually composed a good deal of music for *Les Francs-Juges*, a *Freischütz*-like libretto by his friend Humbert Ferrand, in 1825–1826.[8] During these years he thought of operas on classical subjects (*La Mort d'Hercule*), English themes (*Richard en Palestine* [Scott]), *Robin Hood*, *Les Noces d'or d'Obéron et Titania* [Shakespeare]), and Chateaubriand (*Atala*). Later ideas included *Les Brigands* (Schiller), *Hamlet*, *Roméo et Juliette* (a full opera), *Cléopâtre* (all Shakespeare), and *Méphistophélès* (a full opera on Goethe's *Faust*).

Many nineteenth-century composers picked up and then abandoned opera subjects. Berlioz stands apart in that his ideas, for completed as well as abortive projects, were centered on a few authors. Just as his principal musical models for opera were few – Gluck, Spontini, Weber – so his literary interests centered on Shakespeare, Goethe, and Virgil. Musical influences he absorbed and blended into an operatic style of startling originality. Literary themes were also blended, either in an overt mix, such as the Shakespearean love scene in Act IV of *Les Troyens*, or in character blending (Cellini has some Faustian-Mephistophelean traits, Faust resembles Childe Harold in certain ways). So much did Berlioz love his chosen authors that he came increasingly to feel that only he could transfer them to the operatic stage; from *La Damnation de Faust* onwards he wrote his own librettos.

In Berlioz's time success in the field of opera was essential if a composer was to achieve any kind of reputation, and for all his idealism Berlioz was ambitious to succeed. But the operatic stage, and particularly the state-supported Opéra itself, was not easy of access to young and unproven composers. Individual concerts, however troublesome and financially risky, were easier. Partly for this reason, and of course in large measure because of his enthusiasm for the work of his idol in instrumental music, Beethoven, Berlioz turned for his first major works to the symphony and to religious music employing a large orchestra. The first three symphonies (the *Fantastique*, *Harold*, and *Roméo et Juliette*), concert music of intensely dramatic nature, certainly reflect Beethoven as that composer's expressive message was understood by the *Jeune France* of the eighteen-thirties.[9] They were considered in the composer's lifetime as verging on the operatic, a view encouraged by Berlioz's remark in the original program of the *Fantastique* that the program must be thought of "as the spoken text of an opera." The works feature protagonists; of these the artist of the *Fantastique* and *Harold* and, perhaps, even *Roméo*, have strong autobiographical traits. They do not have smoothly consecutive plots, but then neither do the operas. Procedure common to both genres in the hands of Berlioz is selection of episodes or scenes, all well suited for musical treatment, which form not a continuous narrative but rather an assemblage of characteristic musical portraits and landscapes, a kind of gallery devoted to the subject. This procedure is very clearly seen in the *Huit Scènes de Faust* of 1828–1829, and comes to fulfillment in the larger work derived from it, *La Damnation de Faust* of 1845–1846. It is no less important in the operas, and from the beginning. A good deal of nineteenth-century opera can be described in this way, but with Berlioz it is a consciously chosen and strongly emphasized feature of his work whether symphonic or operatic.

Excitement generated by performance of the symphonies led to demands for the composer to be called to the opera stage. After a "grand concert dramatique" on 9 December 1832, featuring the *Fantastique* with its sequel, *Le Retour à la vie*, the composer's friend Joseph d'Ortigue wrote, "Let the portals of Grand Opera be opened to Berlioz!"[10] It would be nearly six years before those doors were opened to Berlioz's first opera.

Benvenuto Cellini

After his return from Italy in mid-1832 Berlioz was ready and willing to embark upon an opera. Various ideas, including that of approaching Victor Hugo for a libretto, were considered; at first nothing tangible resulted, and the composer, urged on by Paganini who wanted a viola concerto, turned to the orchestra and in 1834 wrote *Harold en Italie*. During this year more opera plans were considered. Alfred de Vigny suggested a libretto based on the autobiography of the sixteenth-century sculptor Benvenuto Cellini; Berlioz was struck by the idea and drafted a scenario which he submitted to the Opéra Comique. In the meantime Vigny got Léon de Wailly to agree to write the libretto, aided by Auguste Barbier, a friend of the composer from Roman days. The two-act libretto, which as an opéra comique was to have spoken dialogue, was rejected. Reconsidered as an *opéra semi-seria* (with sung recitatives), it was accepted by the Opéra and put on a list of works to be performed. Berlioz all but finished the opera by the end of 1836; it was finally premiered in September of 1838 – by which time the *Requiem* had been composed and, after some delay, performed.

Cellini's autobiography, circulating in a new French translation, was talked about a good deal in Paris in the mid-eighteen-thirties. Its picaresque but hardly heroic protagonist and its episodic character, with few strongly profiled incidents, would not seem to promise much for dramatic treatment; but Berlioz liked it, and this is not surprising, for what it offered was a new set of "episodes in the life of an artist," with new opportunities for identification of the composer with that artist. Cellini was perhaps not alienated from society in the manner of a good romantic, but he certainly felt his talents to be undervalued. This, along with the sculptor's recklessness and brigand-like violence of behavior, surely appealed to Berlioz, who knew the problem of the battle for recognition and who remembered fondly his Italian wanderings, with their dreams of banditry and freedom from convention.[11]

At times in the opera, notably in the second act when Cellini recounts his escape from the law after the violent fracas of the previous night's carnival, or later on when he sings an air dreaming of escape to a pastoral life ("Sur les monts les plus sauvages"), we get Berlioz-as-Cellini. The sculptor's defiant refusal to allow anyone else to cast his Perseus (Act II, sextet) and his decision to sacrifice all his treasured creations to supply enough metal to do the casting (Act II, finale) seem more aimed at depicting Cellini's actual character even though they have no textual basis in the *Autobiography*. The text for the love music, and in fact the whole Cellini–Teresa love story, are on the other hand conventional operatic stuff made up of whole cloth by the librettists without reference to Cellini as depicted by himself.

Benvenuto Cellini is a vibrant work full of first-class music. Its much-despised libretto provides a succession of scenes that Berlioz could justify himself in setting, with one, the Roman carnival, that is perhaps the most brilliant in the composer's whole operatic career. The work's basic plot, or rather plots, entwined stories of Cellini's love for Teresa and his triumphant fulfillment of the commission to cast an heroic Perseus-and-Medusa (the statue itself is real, and is now in the Loggia dei Lanzi in Florence), are comprehensible and well-rounded enough, though a careful reading of the libretto would certainly help one to follow the machinations of Cellini's rival Fieramosca and the complexities of the play-within-the-play in the Roman carnival scene.[12] The somewhat abrupt ending, with Teresa all but lost in the celebration of the successful casting of Perseus, reveals all too clearly the added-on nature of the love story. This oddity was, remarkably enough, not cited by the numerous reviewers who criticized the libretto after the opera's première, but after the first performance the fourth tableau underwent more cuts and alterations than any other part of the work. As was to be the case with *Les Troyens*, Berlioz had trouble bringing the work to a convincing close.

Cellini was subjected to so many changes and substitutions as to remind one of the fate of seventeenth- and eighteenth-century operas for which no definitive version may be said to exist. The score Berlioz delivered to the Opéra (**Paris 1** in the *New Berlioz Edition*) was doctored up with new and substitute airs even before the first performance. **Paris 2** represents the score as affected by the changes, mostly cuts, made during the opera's 1838 run. Liszt, who revived the work for Weimar in 1852–1853, called for or himself made more changes, including a recasting of the work into three acts. The *New Berlioz Edition* score disentangles the various versions but requires close attention to follow. Listeners should be aware that the admirable Colin Davis recording of 1967 (to date the only one that is complete) not only restores the two-act version and the role of Pope Clement VII (altered to a Cardinal, before the première, at the behest of the censors) but presents the work with spoken dialogue in place of many of the recitatives, a version that was never performed in the nineteenth century.[13]

What did Berlioz offer expectant – pro and con – listeners in 1838? Those who loved the symphonies were not disappointed in the orchestral music, apart from and in conjunction with the voices, in *Cellini*. It is every bit as inventive, rich, and lively as they are, from the imposing overture to the final chorus. The choruses are also full of vigor and originality – like those of the composer's next work, the "dramatic symphony" *Roméo et Juliette* of 1839. The solo recitatives, airs, and ensembles show Berlioz in a genre hitherto represented only by scattered individual songs. Here was an opportunity for the composer's supporters to proclaim brilliant success, for his detractors to say he could not write singable melody. Both views were presented by the critics. The truth is that Berlioz wrote many striking vocal melodies, but none in the familiar language of the Italian opera of the period. This disappointed, even angered critics – and the listeners for whom they spoke – who wanted to hear Bellini or as close an imitation of Italian style as possible. Berlioz's friend d'Ortigue was later driven, in a review of *Les Troyens*, to this exasperated response:

> What do we usually find in an Italian aria? Often only eight bars or so of melody; the rest is filler, commonplaces, nonsense, while in Berlioz [...] the phrase is free of these insipid and parasitical formulas used by certain composers to frame their melodic period in order to throw it into relief and make it the more striking, if at all possible, by the very poverty of its setting.[14]

Example 6.1 *Benvenuto Cellini*, Overture, Vn. 1, bars 42–64

In *Cellini* Berlioz made some effort to approach "normal" aria style; this is especially evident in Teresa's first air, "Entre l'amour et le devoir," with its cavatina-cabaletta structure, relatively symmetrical melodic line, and elaborate coloratura.[15] But he could not force himself into the Italian mode he so much disliked, and in the later operas he did not try. Berlioz wanted recitative-and-air to be listened to as if it were a symphonic construction, its logic corresponding to and dictated by the text. Few listeners at the time could manage this. For us, with our experience of Wagner (who learned so much from Berlioz), it should be easier; but some effort is still required. "Listener-friendly" arias do exist in Berlioz's work (that of Ascanio in the second act of *Cellini* is an example), but they are the exception rather than the rule.

A few details in the work may be noted here. In the overture there is a broad theme (see Ex. 6.1) reminiscent of the composer of *Harold en Italie* (and prophetic of *La Damnation de Faust*).

This asymmetrical melody, representative of everything Berlioz's admirers loved and his detractors hated about his music, is based on the *Ariette d'Arlequin* in the puppet-play of the carnival scene, the finale of Act I. A chorus murmurs about Arlequin's performance but the *ariette*, textless, is "sung" by an English horn impersonating, perhaps ironically, a "famous Roman tenor." This must be the spot that moved the critic

Merruau to say that the English horn, while not a lover, gets to deliver the composer's expressive message. What Merruau probably did not know is that this melody was taken by Berlioz from a song, *Je crois en vous*, which he wrote in 1834, at the time of *Harold*, as a supplement to a fashionable magazine.[16]

The first tableau (there are two in each act) consists largely of Teresa's air (see above) and the wonderful duo-trio of Teresa and Cellini, spied upon by Fieramosca, opening with another memorable and characteristic melody ("O Teresa, vous que j'aime plus que ma vie"). In the second tableau a rather dutiful *romance* for Cellini (a piece added to satisfy the tenor of the 1838 performance), an amusing drinking chorus during which a hapless tavern-keeper tries to get his bill settled, and an obligatory air for Fieramosca precede the great Act I finale, *Le Carnaval*. Particularly notable in this superbly complex and dashing ensemble are the announcement of the puppet-play (to the music Berlioz was to reuse in the later *Roman Carnival* Overture), the *ariette* of Arlequin mentioned above and its companion piece, the absurd "cavatina" of Pasquerello, mocking Teresa's father Balducci, and the whirlwind of music accompanying Cellini's attempt to go off with Teresa, his murder of Pompeo, and his escape as the hapless Fieramosca is mistakenly caught by the crowd.

This is, literally, a hard act to follow. It has been said that the two tableaux of the second act are dramatically weak in comparison to what precedes them. I think this is less true than that they are unconvincingly related to Act I, being completely concerned with Cellini as sculptor and with the casting of Perseus. But there are good things here. The third tableau is chiefly given over to a long and dramatically vivid sextet in which Cellini confronts all his enemies, now including the Pope/Cardinal, who is demanding delivery of his statue on pain of death. In the fourth tableau there is Ascanio's air, a popularesque piece that was one of the opera's most successful numbers at the première. The finale is dramatically exciting if a little breathless, though the musical ending, a reprise of the drinking song of Cellini's assistants, seems a bit conventional.

The critics of the 1838 *Benvenuto Cellini*, puzzled by encountering a comic drama – at the Opéra, that temple of serious musical theatre – by the composer of the *Symphonie fantastique* and the *Requiem*, were divided on the work's merits. The most glowing praise of the composer and his first opera came from someone who had not seen the work (!) but who was to be important in its future: Franz Liszt, who in 1839 wrote an atmospheric essay dated from Florence, where he went at night to look at Cellini's Perseus and to muse on the sculptor's triumph and that of the new Cellini, Berlioz.[17]

La Damnation de Faust

Strictly speaking this work does not belong here since it is not actually a stage work. Berlioz referred to it as an "opéra de concert," but his final choice for generic name was "légende dramatique." The work has been staged, for example in Monte Carlo in 1893 (the occasion of Debussy's critique mentioned at the beginning of this study) and by Beecham in London in 1933.[18] And Berlioz after completing his score thought of turning it into an opera, with the Opéra librettist Eugène Scribe supplying enough text to do the job, for performance in London.[19] In some respects the work is very much like an opera, in Berlioz's understanding of the genre. Its four parts could, with some expansion of cast and incident, comprise four acts (Berlioz told Scribe that about forty-five additional minutes would be necessary to turn his completed score into an opera). Or one might consider the first part, with Faust as lone observer of peasant revels and the *Marche hongroise*, to be a prologue followed by three acts and an epilogue (Marguerite in heaven). There is no overture, but *Les Troyens* was also to begin without one. The role of the chorus is large but not disproportionately so for Berlioz. Faust, Mephistopheles, and Marguerite have operatically dramatic roles; only a second female role and perhaps one or two minor characters would need to be added.

There is plenty of colorful incident and correspondingly little of the introspective side of Goethe's work (which so preoccupied Schumann in his contemporary *Szenen aus Goethes Faust*). Some scenes, such as Faust poking about Marguerite's chamber and then hiding as she enters to sing "Le Roi de Thulé," call out for staging. Others, Faust and Mephistopheles changing venue by sailing through the air, and especially their wild ride to hell in the fourth part, are certainly melodramatic but might be difficult to bring off on the stage (Berlioz thought that the operatic machinists in London could easily take care of this; he doesn't say anything about the singers).

In the end the *Damnation* did not become an opera, nor should one try to make it into one. In this period of his life Berlioz was thinking not of Wagnerian *Gesamtkunstwerk* but of musical-dramatic works that crossed and recrossed the border between the symphonic and the operatic. *Roméo et Juliette* belongs to this new genre as much as does the *Damnation*, the only real difference between them being the much greater role of the solo voice in the latter work. *La Damnation de Faust*, performed at the Opéra Comique (rented by the composer), though it was totally unlike what audiences there were used to, was a failure, surely in part because of what seemed its hybrid form. Berlioz thought of turning it into an opera not because he had conceived it thus but because only staged works had any

chance of success with the Parisian public of the time.[20] By another
Berliozian irony the *Damnation* was to become one of his most popular
works in the later nineteenth century.

Berlioz created the *Damnation* by cannibalizing his *Huit Scènes de
Faust* of 1828–1829. All of the earlier work is used, including such famous
numbers as Brander's Song of the Rat, Mephistopheles' Song of the Flea,
and Marguerite's two main arias. He kept most of what he had written
more than fifteen years before, adding introductory, closing, and transitional material and enriching the accompanimental texture – a stunning
example of a mature composer rethinking the work of his youth without
in any way disavowing it. New episodes were created and the order of
events rearranged to make a satisfying sequence of scenes if not a plot in
the ordinary sense. One extraordinary added bit is the fugal Amen, a
pseudo-religious blessing on the dead rat of Brander's student song. The
fugue, based on the song's opening, is woodenly "correct." The mocking
humor of the piece is made more explicit with its coda of dozens of
repeated syllabic Amens, but even so, contemporary listeners, especially
in Germany, were not sure whether it was serious or comic in intent.
Gallic wit does not always travel well.[21]

Aside from its richness of musical invention – like Mendelssohn in the
Midsummer Night's Dream music, Berlioz was able to create new material
that matched the verve of his youthful scenes from *Faust* – one of the most
striking features of the *Damnation* is its musical unity. Part of this is
accomplished through melodic development and transformation. An
example: the orchestral theme running through the work's opening scene
(see Ex. 6.2), a characteristic Berlioz melody (cf. Ex. 6.1), seems derived
from the tune dominating the *Concert* [1828–1829] or *Chœur*
[1845–1846] *de sylphes*; variants of it appear in several other prominent
places in the score.

Berlioz also uses repeated motives for character identification (particularly that of Mephistopheles) or reference to events and situations,
usually by citing a fragment of what is later to be a fully developed
melody.[22]

The richest and most satisfying character in the work, musically and
dramatically, is Mephistopheles. This is hardly surprising for the composer of the *Symphonie fantastique*. Neither Marguerite nor Faust is
equally interesting dramatically, and the latter doesn't even get as much
good music. I am inclined to think that Goethe is as much to blame for this
as Berlioz, but it is true that the liveliest pages of this rarely dull score are
those in which Mephistopheles is present. To twentieth-century sensibilities the final scene, Marguerite's reception into heaven, can be anti-
climactic after the hellish Pandemonium preceding it. Here in particular

Example 6.2 *La Damnation de Faust*, Part I, scene I, Vn. 1, bars 28–44

we must try to listen with nineteenth-century ears and be thankful that the music is not as saccharine as it might have been in other hands.

Berlioz dedicated the *Damnation* to Liszt. The close friendship between the two men gradually cooled, but in the eighteen-fifties Liszt was still an active promoter of Berlioz's music, performing both *Benvenuto Cellini* and *Faust* in Weimar. In 1857 Liszt's *Faust-Symphonie*, appropriately dedicated to Berlioz, was premiered.

Les Troyens

After dropping plans to turn *La Damnation de Faust* into an opera, Berlioz seemed finished with music for the theatre. He was called upon to supervise performances of the opera by his beloved Weber (he had written recitatives for *Der Freischütz* to enable it to be done at the Opéra) and would later supervise performances of operas by Gluck (*Orphée*, in 1859; *Alceste*, in 1861 and 1866), but no one seemed to want his own compositions. The next major work after the *Damnation*, the cantata or "trilogie sacrée" *L'Enfance du Christ*, was written in segments during the years 1850–1854. Performances of *Cellini* in Weimar (successful) and London (hissed by a hired claque) were not encouraging enough to make Berlioz want to write another opera. Yet ideas for a large work based on Virgil's *Aeneid* began to come to him as early as 1851. Urged on by the active and continuing interest of Carolyne Sayn-Wittgenstein, Liszt's mistress, Berlioz took the plunge and early in 1856 began work on the libretto. Stopping to compose the first music for the new work, the fourth-act duo of Dido and Aeneas (to become the most celebrated piece in the opera), he completed the libretto by summer and began composition in earnest. *Les Troyens* was completed, apart from numerous later additions and revisions, in April of 1858.

Cellini, planned as an opéra comique, was performed at the Opéra. In a peculiarly Berliozian ironic shift *Les Troyens*, conceived and written as grand opera on the scale of Meyerbeer's operatic triumphs, was denied access to the Opéra and was premiered – in truncated form – at the Théâtre Lyrique, a less imposing and less adequate venue, in November 1863. Berlioz went through a series of difficult negotiations, unfortunately typical of his whole career, in getting the work performed. *Les Troyens*, in five acts, as was usual for grand opera, was considered too long and too difficult to mount complete; the composer had to settle for splitting the work in two and seeing performed only the second half, Acts III–V of the original. This was done as *Les Troyens à Carthage*, with a hastily written prelude and narrative to fill in for the missing first two acts, now titled *La Prise de Troie* (Berlioz never heard this part of his great work). The performance was successful, met with respect by the audience and by most critics, with the usual extremes of admiring praise and damning criticism in the Parisian journals.[23] The work, incontestably Berlioz's masterpiece, was not performed whole until the twentieth century, and not without cuts until after the Second World War, when fine productions were mounted in the United Kingdom and later in the United States. Today, if not yet really popular, it is recognized as one of the greatest operas of the nineteenth century.

Les Troyens is sometimes thought of as a step backwards in Berlioz's compositional development, "classical" not only in subject but closer to Gluck and Spontini than to *La Damnation de Faust*, and certainly not in the spirit or technique of its great contemporary work, Wagner's *Tristan und Isolde*. Even some of Berlioz's admirers found much of the work cold, even monotonous. What they failed to see was one of the composer's most salient characteristics, faithfulness to the spirit of his literary source. Berlioz knew and loved Virgil's poetry from his youth, and tried to capture something of the dignity and epic grandeur of the *Aeneid* in the vocal music of his opera, varying this with the colorful and, as always, highly inventive orchestral marches and ballet music liberally strewn through the score. The "warmest" music in *Les Troyens*, the fourth-act duo "Nuit d'ivresse," is not only the first music Berlioz wrote for the opera – thus perhaps composed before he settled on the prevailing tone of the work – but is based on text drawn from Shakespeare (*The Merchant of Venice*, V, 1) rather than Virgil.

The music given the central characters in *Les Troyens* is neither cold

Example 6.3 *Les Troyens*, Act III, Finale, bars 86–103; 123–136

nor monotonous but it does observe a kind of decorum that is deliberately imposed with results very different from the tone of *Cellini* or *Faust*.
A few of Berlioz's contemporaries saw this and praised it, contrasting
Berlioz's opera with run-of-the-mill Italianate works in which a waltz or
barcarole suffices for every situation, every emotion, every character. But
it does take getting used to; *Les Troyens* must be heard as one reads Virgil,
recognizing that the personages of the epic drama are not free to behave
like carousing students or young lovers. The finale of Act III, in which
Aeneas steps forward to identify himself and Dido accepts his offer of military aid, is a good example of this epic decorum (see Ex. 6.3).

A feature of *Les Troyens* that has not been commented on enough is
Berlioz's addition of exotic musical touches to mark the identities of
Trojans and Carthaginians. He specifies a few ancient and oriental instruments in the score (for most of these modern substitutes are also indicated).[24] In addition there are touches of exotic color in the music itself,
first of all the ballet music, notably the wonderful dances of Act IV, but
also the *entrées* of the Carthaginian workers and sailors in Act III and the
combat of the Trojan boxers in Act I. To this might be added the Trojan
Hymne of Act I, with its odd major-minor mix; the "Phrygian" scale used
by Cassandra and her attendants at the close of Act II; the *Marche troyenne
(dans le mode triste)*, with its unusual turns toward the flat side, first heard
in Act III, and then used repeatedly; and perhaps the hunting call of the
Chasse royale opening Act IV, with its curious "blue note" in the saxhorn
solo (see Ex. 6.4).

Musical and literary exoticisms were not rare in nineteenth-century

Example 6.4 *Les Troyens*, Act IV, No. 29, *Chasse royale et orage*, E-flat saxhorn, bars 45–52

France. In the eighteen-forties Berlioz performed and spoke admiringly of Félicien David's "oriental" *Le Désert*. While waiting for the first performance of *Les Troyens* he read and admired Flaubert's *Salammbô* (1862); he may well have anticipated a bit of the exotic Carthaginian detail abounding in that work.

Les Troyens is a magnificent work, in several senses of the word. Its subject-matter – the fall of Troy, the rise of Carthage, the tragic love between Dido and Aeneas, the inexorable call of Italy to the Trojans – is of genuine grandeur, put into words by the composer with taste and skill. It calls for resplendent sets and costumes. Here its not having become a repertory staple is an advantage; so far no enterprising director has set *Les Troyens* in nineteen-twenties Chicago or with Beckett-like spareness. The major roles – Cassandra, Dido, Aeneas – are in every way commanding while at the same time enabled, through the words and music Berlioz has given them, to preserve their humanity. And the music is glowing throughout, reaching in the fourth act, especially the incomparable septet and the following duo, an incandescence elsewhere rarely attained.

Béatrice et Bénédict

As he was finishing *Les Troyens* Berlioz was approached with a commission to write an opera for the opening of a new theatre in Baden-Baden. Full of compositional energy, he quickly settled on an old idea, first bruited about in the early eighteen-thirties: an opera based on Shakespeare's *Much Ado about Nothing*. As he had for *Les Troyens*, Berlioz wrote the two-act libretto himself, drawing out the comic love story of Beatrice and Benedick and discarding almost all the rest of Shakespeare's play while adding Somarone, a farcical character of his own invention (but in part based, a bit unkindly, on Spontini), in place of Shakespeare's Dogberry and Verges.

Berlioz was a passionate reader of Shakespeare all his life. Quotations from the plays fill his letters and his *Mémoires*, and are to be found in his scores as well (notably in the *Huit Scènes de Faust*). At various times he contemplated operas on Shakespeare plays. Completed works on Shakespearean themes include *La Mort de Cléopâtre* (the 1829 Rome Prize cantata), the *Ouverture de La Tempête* (1830; later included in *Lélio*); the *Grande Ouverture du Roi Lear* (1831), *La Mort d'Ophélie* (1842; a scene for chorus and orchestra); and a *Marche funèbre pour la dernière scène d'Hamlet* (1844). And of course there is the Shakespearean symphony *Roméo et Juliette* of 1839. All serious subjects, but in the end Berlioz, like Verdi, turned to comedy, and this time he wrote a genuine opéra comique, full of spoken dialogue on the whole translated or paraphrased from Shakespeare's text.

Béatrice et Bénédict is a perfectly rounded work, balancing witty elegance with charmingly half-serious sentiment, mixing the style if not the intensity of *Les Troyens* (the duo of Hero and Ursula ending the first act) with reminiscences of Weber (Hero's "Je vais le voir" in Act I) and even Mozart (the first-act duo of Beatrice and Benedict). Aside from the overture, the chief piece of instrumental music is a wonderful *sicilienne*, full of syncopations and colorful pitch inflections, heard early in the first act and again as an entr'acte.[25]

Like Shakespeare's play, the opera varies its witty language with broad farce: Somarone's "chef d'œuvre" chorus in Act I, his drinking song in Act II, and the *enseigne* memorializing Benedick as married man, heard first in the trio of Act I and again near the end of Act II, when porters bring on signboards with a mock epitaph: "Ici l'on voit Bénédict, l'homme marié" – "Here you see Benedick, the married man." The work is formally symmetrical as well. Beatrice and Benedick each have a single aria; there is a duet for the two in each act; a male trio in Act I is balanced by a female trio in Act II; the quicksilver opening of the overture uses the beginning of the duo that closes the work. Berlioz, after composing what seems like a businesslike ending for *Cellini* and a perhaps overly terse ending for *Les Troyens* (where Dido's revenge, Hannibal's ascent, and Rome's eventual victory are closely telescoped), finally found a perfect ending, for a work that brought his career as operatic composer to a perfect close.

7 The religious works

RALPH P. LOCKE

We may well wonder which of his works Berlioz – and his contemporaries – understood as "religious." In the eighteenth century, the phrase "religious music" would have been widely understood as indicating the repertories used in worship services by the Catholic Church and by the various Protestant denominations. It was certainly not music for the concert hall or opera house, since, as everyone knew, these were places of secular entertainment, where at times immodest socializing and even licentious behavior could easily be found.[1] Furthermore, these secular venues were in those years developing the apparatus of the modern public concert scene: the musicians' pay derived from the take at the box office, and thus the audience's curiosity and approval needed to be repeatedly won through newspaper advertising and wall-sized placards, journalists' reviews, and word of mouth. Only one genre – the oratorio – crossed over between these sharply distinct cultural spheres; in the hands of Handel, Haydn, and, in France, Mondonville and Rigel, it brought Bible stories into the hurly-burly of public concert life.

But the oratorio prefigured larger changes within the musical life of the West. The increasing cultural importance of the concert hall and opera house in the decades around 1800 allowed composers and audiences to take more seriously the kinds of music that could be made there; and this frank, if by no means consistent, incursion of seriousness made those places as natural a home as the church for the occasional exploration of religious and other spiritual (philosophical, ideological) thought and imagery.

In some cases, such exploration unfolded indirectly. Certain instrumental concert works begged to be "read." Beethoven's Fifth Symphony, for instance, was widely understood as portraying the struggle and triumph of the individual spirit. Liszt even attached to his symphonic poem *Les Préludes* a vague program based on a consolatory poem by Lamartine about the meaning of life and death.

In other cases, such exploration was more explicit. From the romantic era to our own day, prominent composers have produced works that are not "sacred" in any strict sense yet are patently inspired by or else invoke God, biblical figures, the clergy, or some other element of religious tradition. Numerous concert works with chorus have been based in whole or part on some liturgical text, most notably the Catholic Mass for the Dead (the *Requiems* of Verdi and Fauré, for example, and the *War Requiem* of Benjamin Britten). Oratorios (and works plainly influenced by the genre) have proliferated in great variety, from Mendelssohn's *Elijah*, Félicien David's *Le Désert*, and Liszt's *Christus*, to Debussy's *Le Martyre de Saint-Sébastien*, Honegger's *Le Roi David*, and Leonard Bernstein's *Kaddish* Symphony and *Mass*. And many successful and durable operas – ranging from Gounod's *Faust* to Verdi's *Don Carlos* – have evoked powerful images of salvation and damnation, divine inspiration and ecclesiastical authority, diabolical temptation and saintly forbearance.

At the beginning of his public career, Berlioz would have observed this shift in emphasis from sacred music intended strictly for use by the church to music rather evocative of religion and intended for use in the broad secular arena. The ambiguities of such a situation might have doomed a lesser composer. But Berlioz's insightful manipulation of genre and style allowed him to exploit those ambiguities for highly creative ends, and to produce what are unquestionably three of his greatest works: the *Grande Messe des morts*, or *Requiem*, of 1837; the *Te Deum*, of 1849; and *L'Enfance du Christ*, of 1850–1854.

Berlioz and "le religieux"

These three are clearly not Berlioz's only works to emanate "religion." The *Chant sacré* (1829) and *Méditation religieuse* (1831), the *Prière* in Act II of *Benvenuto Cellini* (1838), the *Prière du matin* (1846), the *Chant de la Fête de Pâques* and other scenes from *La Damnation de Faust* (1846) are all tinged with religious sentiment, as is that grand inspirational piece for double chorus and organ, *Le Temple universel* (1861). The three post-humously published motets, *Veni Creator*, *Tantum ergo*, and *Invitation à louer Dieu*, are quite serviceable for use in church, as is, of course, the early, extended, and altogether remarkable *Messe solennelle* – composed in 1824, revised in 1827, "burnt" by Berlioz and long presumed lost, but miraculously rediscovered in 1991. This will be the only other work, besides the three celebrated masterpieces, to be discussed in this chapter. Nonetheless, it is worth noting here that many of Berlioz's other "non-religious" works likewise contain movements or sections that plainly evoke religion – and in a variety of ways: by describing, via a sacred style, an individual engaged in religious reflection (as occurs at the end of the first movement of the *Symphonie fantastique*) or pilgrims praying as they march (in the second movement of *Harold en Italie*); by satirizing the Gregorian *Dies irae* (in the finale of the *Fantastique*) or the fugal Amen (in

Part II of *La Damnation de Faust*); or by portraying clerics whose utterances carry the weight of churchly authority (in the figures of the Pope, in *Benvenuto Cellini*, and of Père Laurence, in *Roméo et Juliette*).

This recurrent fascination with religious matters was rooted in early experience. In the opening chapter of the *Mémoires*, Berlioz speaks of his first communion, when he heard the choir singing what was a sacred retexting of an aria from Dalayrac's opera *Nina*:

> [The music] filled me with a kind of mystical, passionate unrest which I was powerless to hide from the rest of the congregation. I saw Heaven open – a Heaven of love and pure delight, purer and a thousand times lovelier than the one that had so often been described to me. Such is the magic power of true expression, the incomparable beauty of melody that comes from the heart! […] It was my first musical experience.

In addition, other, quite different memories and inheritances would feed Berlioz's religious preoccupations. Historically, the French monarchs had long served as head of the nation's Catholic establishment. High art had often served at once king and church: many *grands motets* were composed for use at the chapel of the Palace of Versailles, and there was a longstanding Bourbon tradition of performing a *Te Deum* on the occasion of a military victory. The French Revolution, in its convulsive first decade (1789–1799), co-opted the latter tradition for its victories against the royal troops. It also commissioned new "hymns," some of them employing multiple choruses and soloists, to celebrate the heroic self-sacrifice of those who had died in the fighting, to commemorate the ferociously anti-ecclesiastical spirit of Voltaire (whom the Revolution's leaders took as an inspiring forerunner), or to sing the praises of various worthy groups of citizens: mothers, farmers, children, the aged.[2]

A return to the established conjoining of music, Catholic tradition, and state coincided with the reign of Napoléon, particularly after his 1802 Concordat with the Pope, and was resuscitated in full force for coronations and other state occasions during the Bourbon Restoration (1814–1830).[3] It was dealt a hard blow by the dissolution of the Chapelle Royale (in the Tuileries Palace) in 1830, but it continued nonetheless in attenuated form during the reign of the "bourgeois monarch" Louis-Philippe (1830–1848) and the Second Empire of Napoléon III (1852–1870).

The three Latin works and their roots

Berlioz's three major works on liturgical texts are linked in two different ways. First, they overlap in content. That is, Berlioz reused some of the best episodes from his youthful *Messe solennelle* in the *Requiem* and *Te Deum* (as well as in the *Symphonie fantastique* and elsewhere). Second, and more importantly, the three works form a kind of conversation with the various traditions of sacred and religious music in use in France at the time. Certain eighteenth-century works (by Durante and other Italians, for example) continued to be performed in church, as did old liturgical chants, some from the medieval Gregorian repertory, others from seventeenth-century *plain-chant musical*.[4] Recent comic-opera numbers were given Latin religious texts (as Berlioz reported, in the *Mémoires*, regarding the aria by Dalayrac), and impressive new works continued to be composed in the style of Italo-Viennese classicism. A grand Mass and *Te Deum* by Paisiello, the prominent Italian composer whom Napoléon had brought to Paris in 1802, adorned the latter's coronation as emperor in 1804.[5] For the young Berlioz, though, the two looming figures in sacred music were his teacher, Jean-François Lesueur, and the director of the Conservatoire, Luigi Cherubini. Lesueur composed imaginative if quirky masses and oratorios that, most often, were relatively brief, avoided fugal and other polyphonic textures, and favored a plain harmonic style. Cherubini's various mass settings could be stirringly dramatic while remaining sober, dignified, and, in substantial sections, skillfully polyphonic. His Requiems of 1816 and 1836 (the first, greatly admired by Beethoven, for mixed chorus and an orchestra dark-toned by the omission of violins; the second, for men's chorus TTB) were widely performed throughout the nineteenth century. Lesueur and Cherubini tended to write for three- or four-part chorus STB or STTB – with a single high choral part for women and/or boys, rather than with separate parts for sopranos and altos. Sometimes all three main voice "sections" were divided so as to create a six-part texture (SSTTBB).

Lesueur was the more powerful influence on Berlioz. He lectured insistently to his protégé on the importance of making church music "particular to each solemn occasion."[6] At the Chapelle Royale, which he directed or co-directed from 1804 to 1830, Lesueur inserted additional biblical but non-liturgical texts at various places in his masses and eliminated certain traditionally required texts, such as the lengthy *Credo*. Furthermore, in many of his works for Catholic worship, the singers represent specific biblical characters. In his early Mass for Christmas, for example, from the seventeen-nineties, we are to imagine that the chorus singing "Adoramus te, glorificamus te" (from the *Gloria*) stands for the shepherds at Jesus' crib. In all these ways, Lesueur established a tradition, parallel to oratorio but within ecclesiastical precincts, of a music that was fully "religious" or, indeed, even "sacred," but no longer bound by liturgical constraint. Berlioz would eventually take this freedom and run with it.

Finding a voice

Berlioz's earliest surviving large-scale work is a Mass which, perhaps because it was written for the church of Saint-Roch rather than for the Chapelle Royale, includes the traditional text in its entirety and in addition interpolates several motets, all of this typical of grand masses written by Gossec, Cherubini, Lesueur, and others.[7] In 1824 Berlioz was a mere twenty-one years of age; he had been studying privately with Lesueur for scarcely a year, and had not yet applied for admission to the Conservatoire. The work's successful reception in 1825 and, much revised, in 1827, encouraged the young composer to believe in his ability to forge a musical career, despite continued opposition from his parents.

When the work was brought to its first modern performances and first recording, in 1993, listeners familiar with Berlioz's mature works were struck by what Hugh Macdonald carefully calls "the extraordinary diversity of style and achievement" of this student work.[8] Some of its movements are conventional (such as the energetic but occasionally awkward *Quoniam* fugue) or palely pretty, though always in a way appropriate to the text (such as the *O salutaris* – "Oh, saviour, ... give us strength"). Other movements suggest a mimicking of standard stylistic conventions or even of specific works by famous composers: the Offertory begins with a dotted-note arpeggio such as was often used in the Baroque era to portray the majesty of God or king, and the broad $\frac{4}{4}$ tune in the *Resurrexit* resembles the contrasting theme in Weber's overture to *Der Freischütz* both in its rhythm and in its gradual upward arpeggiation to the third degree of the scale, here high G (see Ex. 7.1a–b).

In contrast, the almost operatic *Agnus Dei*, for solo tenor and choral sopranos, sounds freshly minted and perfectly accomplished: in 1849 – twenty-five years later! – Berlioz inserted this movement into his *Te Deum*, changing only the text, yet for more than a century thereafter no one suspected its early origin.

Even more surprising to Berlioz lovers were several other later borrowings from the *Messe solennelle*. Among these the most important are the opening of the *Gratias* ("We render thanks unto Thee"), which became the main theme of the *Scène aux champs* in the *Symphonie fantastique* (the music's contemplative tone works well in both contexts), and the "Laudamus te" of the *Gloria*, which became a kind of first draft for a passage in *Benvenuto Cellini* that would in turn become the saltarello-like main theme of the overture *Le Carnaval romain*.

In contrast, certain distinctively Berliozian conceits in the *Messe solennelle* make for music that is perhaps less immediately entertaining but richly repays a listener's close attention. The beginning of the *Kyrie*, for

Example 7.1a *Messe solennelle*, movement 8: *Resurrexit* (at its final appearances, in E-flat Major).
Example 7.1b Weber, Overture to *Der Freischütz*, contrasting theme (at its third and final appearance, in the same key).

instance, sets two distinct ideas in counterpoint: a stately, prayerful tune sung by the basses (later reused in the fugato-like orchestral lines of the Offertory of the *Requiem*), and angular, short-breathed exclamations from the sopranos; all of this is interrupted periodically by open-octave stabs, *fortissimo*, in the strings. Sharp contrasts and spatial oppositions such as these would become some of the most striking features of Berlioz's later religious music, and of his monumental works in general.

At "Christe eleison" Berlioz experiments in a different way. The key of F Major, the orchestra's static pedal on the tonic (later an explicit open-fifth drone), and the flowing triple-meter vocal line, regular in phrase structure and emphasizing the raised (Lydian) fourth, combine to evoke an eighteenth-century compositional topos familiar especially from comic opera: the sound, as reimagined by city folk, of peasant tunes played on a hurdy-gurdy or bagpipe. Berlioz's application of these stylistic markers to sacred music is not unprecedented: we find this pastoral topos invoking shepherds, for example, in Gossec's Christmas Oratorio *La Nativité*, in "And he shall feed his flock" of Handel's *Messiah*, and in scenes from Lesueur's *Ruth et Boöz*. Still, the text of the *Christe* offers no such obvious invitation, consisting as it does of nothing but a two-word cry for Christ's mercy. Berlioz's decision to allude to more specific concepts and images – rural peaceableness and, by implication, Christ as the Good Shepherd – must therefore be considered a conscious, and successful, leap into the descriptive or programmatic.

Visions of death and salvation

The unevenness of the *Messe solennelle* helps us appreciate all the more the consistency and keen sense of musical design that Berlioz achieved thirteen years later in his *Grande Messe des morts*. The *Requiem* was commissioned by the Ministry of the Interior, early in 1837, as a grand public statement of support for the government of Louis-Philippe. The occasion was the seventh anniversary of the 1830 Revolution that had brought down the Bourbon Restoration, strengthened the parliament, and given France a new king (who was to be her last). The event was also intended to commemorate a foiled assassination plot the previous year, in which several government officials lost their lives.

The project spoke deeply to Berlioz. The traditional text of the Mass for the Dead, with its visions of the end of the world on the "Day of Wrath" (*Dies irae*), touched a chord in him that had been vibrating since 1824, when he wrote the *Resurrexit* of the *Messe solennelle* – a movement he later reworked as *Le Jugement dernier*, in 1828, and again, as a part of a never-completed oratorio called *Le Dernier jour du monde*, in 1831. The *Requiem* commission also resonated with several heroic or patriotic projects from the past, among them *Le Retour de la grande armée*, sketched in 1832, and a seven-movement *Fête musicale funèbre*, contemplated in 1835. Berlioz thus seized the opportunity, composed the new work in a white heat of inspiration (even inventing a musical shorthand to keep pace with the upwelling of his ideas), paid to have the parts copied, and started the rehearsals – only to learn, in July 1837, that the ceremonies had been canceled for political reasons.

A few months later, the death of a French general wounded in the war of conquest against Algeria gave occasion for a true state funeral, complete with the long-delayed première of Berlioz's *Requiem*, in the vast stone chapel of the Hôtel des Invalides (a hospital and residence for military veterans). The work proved to be a masterpiece, at once somber and alert, or, as the poet Alfred de Vigny put it, "beautiful and strange, wild, convulsed, and dolorous."[9]

The structure of the text of the Requiem no doubt helped Berlioz give the work a coherence that the 1824 *Messe solennelle* lacked. The biggest single chunk – the eighteen three-line strophes that comprise the *Dies irae* – is in rhymed verse, which readily lends itself to musical setting. In any case, the Requiem text had never been treated as fully sacrosanct by composers. Berlioz followed the distinguished precedents of Mozart and Cherubini, among others, in omitting the Absolution ("Libera me") and in carving up the *Dies irae* into a number of manageable movements, each with its own distinct images and character (numbers 2 through 6). But he went further, making bold changes in the Latin texts both to sharpen the depiction of an image and to increase the expression of a phrase. In particular, his shuffling of certain stanzas between several of the *Dies irae*-based movements and his insertion into one of them (*Recordare*) of a passage from the Offertory, reworded in the first person ("Deliver me from the lion's mouth"), bring about a more frequent and systematic oscillation between descriptions of the "imagined cataclysm" of the Last Judgment (to use Edward T. Cone's phrase) and the "terrified personal reaction" of the individual sinner.[10]

These visions of punishment and quaking fear are brilliantly rendered through unprecedented musical contrasts. The *Hostias* alternates chordal chanting – "We offer sacrifices and prayers to You" – with a series of long-held high chords in three flutes over unison low pedal tones in eight trombones; this weird and wonderful instrumental sound seems a metaphor for the vast, unbridgeable space between human need and the unattainable Ideal. The *Lacrymosa* opposes a lurching orchestral rhythm to a melody line that cycles obsessively through short, mostly descending (sighing and groaning?) fragments; together, the two elements form a vital and imaginative response to the text's images of the "tearful day" on which "guilty humankind arises out of the ashes for judgment."

The single most striking moment in the 1824 *Messe solennelle* is the brass fanfare of the *Resurrexit*; it is at once preserved and utterly transformed in the *Requiem*. The music had been well suited to its first text: "And He shall come again with glory to judge both the living and the dead." Nothing more natural, then, than to use it for the equivalent scene in the Mass text: the *Tuba mirum* in movement 2 (the *Dies irae* proper). But now Berlioz assigns the fanfares to four separate bands, located at the four corners of the combined choral and orchestral forces, and overlapping in rhythmically disturbing patterns. And the men's chorus answers with stentorian unison declarations over truly frightening chords for eight timpani that are then obliterated by menacing loud rolls on the bass drum. The extraordinary amount of noise-making here, as always with Berlioz, is fully motivated and, in the large sense of the word, poetic.

The innovation in other movements lies more in the choral writing. In the Offertory (*Domine, Jesu Christe*), the entire chorus intones a kind of psalmodic recitation on two stubbornly alternating pitches (A and B-flat) against a constantly fluctuating, modulating orchestral background, based (as noted earlier) on the *Kyrie* of the *Messe solennelle*, complete with its intrusive open-octave stabs.[11] In one edition of the score, Berlioz made it explicit that the voices represent the "chorus of souls in Purgatory" pleading to be spared; still, one could equally imagine the chant being sung by a deceased person's survivors on his or her behalf. At the midpoint of the *Quaerens me*, the movement that sounds most ecclesiastical, due to its accomplished imitative polyphony, the men's voices begin a speechlike muttering on a constant pitch – a device plainly suited to the humility of the words, "My prayers are not worthy." And in the descending chromatic countersubject of the opening Introit, a movement likewise rich in imitative polyphony, Berlioz inserts a rest after each note – something that lends to the whole an air of weary dejectedness.

The *Requiem* was met with wide-ranging acclaim from dignitaries (including the duc d'Orléans, the music-loving eldest son of King Louis-Philippe), newspaper reviewers, and discerning creative artists such as Heinrich Heine and, later, Camille Saint-Saëns. Nonetheless, despite such positive responses, Berlioz would long remember the frustrations of mounting the première and the difficulty of procuring proper payment for his labors. Later in life, he succeeded only rarely in arranging full performances of the work and thus took to programming its individual movements, on his own concerts, along with other items from his catalogue. Enterprising performers today might profitably follow his example, since this is music that, more than most, thrives in live performance.

A satisfying grandeur

The same is true of Berlioz's last massive Latin composition, the *Te Deum*. This resolutely public, ceremonial work was not commissioned by either church or state. Its conceptual origins go back to the sketches for the Napoleonic *Retour de la grande armée* mentioned earlier. The impulse to complete the composition in late 1848 and 1849 surely relates to the ever-growing Napoleonic legend and, more specifically, to the convulsive events of the revolution that broke out in February 1848, and which led, within a matter of months, to the arrival of a new leader for France. Louis-Napoléon Bonaparte was the nephew of the "real" Napoléon; elected president in December 1848, he would dissolve the parliamentary assembly in December 1851 and a year later declare himself Emperor.

Berlioz revised the (still unperformed) *Te Deum* in 1852 and sought to have it mounted in conjunction with the Emperor's coronation, in 1852, and again, in 1853, in conjunction with his grandiose marriage to Eugenia de Montijo. The work finally reached performance in 1855 in the imposing church of Saint-Eustache, but under very different auspices, namely as part of the festivities surrounding the opening of the Festival of Industry, a kind of world's fair involving thousands of international exhibitors.

The *Te Deum* is the most resolutely "architectural" of Berlioz's major works, which is not surprising given its pointedly celebratory origins. It begins with a slow chordal colloquy in which orchestra and organ "commune" (as Berlioz put it in the Postscript of the *Mémoires*) from the two ends of the nave of the church. The principle of dialogue continues in most of the remaining movements through the use of two choirs, each consisting of sections for sopranos, tenors, and basses. Furthermore, before the première, Berlioz, having recently heard a vast children's choir at St. Paul's Cathedral, in London, added a part for a six-hundred-voice unison children's chorus. In the *Mémoires* Berlioz says that this third choir "represents the people adding their voice from time to time to the great ceremony of sacred music," a populist and loosely Napoleonic claim, but one fully merited by the stirring result.

As in the *Requiem*, Berlioz rearranges the text substantially, mainly in order to end with yet another grandiose vision of the Last Judgment, in the *Hymne et prière* of the *Judex crederis*. The music, though, is rarely as quirky in its inventiveness as is that of the earlier work. Indeed, the *Te Deum*, in its relative restraint, its obvious sense of self-discipline and return to certain traditional procedures, marks the beginning of Berlioz's late period. But, perhaps because of those very features, the work sometimes cuts deeper, or surges forward more irresistibly, than the *Requiem*. In the *Judex crederis*, for example, the insistent, impulsive fugal theme ends a half-step higher than it began; the next entry of the theme – naturally, but still breathtakingly – always starts in a key likewise a half-step higher. The music is thus kept in constant motion, tonally as well as rhythmically, befitting the anguish-driven text.

No less remarkable is Berlioz's increasingly subtle expertise at combining expression and form. The liturgical words of the *Tibi omnes*, for example, offered the composer only a bare list (the angels cry aloud, the Apostles praise Thee, the holy Church acknowledges Thee, etc.) and included the ancient *Sanctus/Pleni* formula but once. Berlioz creates a more metaphorical and aesthetically more satisfying version by breaking the list into three separate sections and capping each with a homophonic and fascinatingly modal setting of the *Sanctus/Pleni* – broad and unpredictable chords that fill a large and resonant space with a blend of grandeur and wonder (see Ex. 7.2).

Even more magical a construction is the *Dignare*. The various choral statements, often stated in canon, sensitively reflect the contrasting successive phrases of the text. But Berlioz goes further, creating a coherent whole of the movement by building each section on one of a slowly unfolding series of ten pedal points, first rising from D up to the E an octave and a step higher, then descending again to D (by a different route). A new change of perspective and emotional tone comes with each shift of pedal point and prevailing harmony, including unanticipated shifts between major and minor.

Example 7.2. *Te Deum*, movement 2: *Tibi omnes* (excerpt from the first *Sanctus/Pleni* refrain). The succession of four minor chords at bars 58–59 is tonally ambiguous, arguably "readable" in any one of several keys or church modes.

Sacred trilogy

In contrast to the three major Latin works, *L'Enfance du Christ* is in no way liturgical: it is an oratorio, on a vernacular text, intended from the outset for the concert hall. Indeed, performance in a church, especially a large and resonant one, can, on certain pages, yield a wretched blur. And yet the work, despite being rooted in the concert hall, is surely as religious in feeling as the Latin works, and Berlioz does call it not simply a trilogy, but a *trilogie sacrée.*

Here the composer was building on a distinctively French tradition that, in the previous decades, had included oratorios on such stories as the crossing of the Red Sea (Berlioz himself composed such a work, now lost, in 1823) and the fateful return of Jephtha's daughter. His adored teacher, Lesueur, had written not only church works containing non-liturgical movements but also more extended, oratorio-like operas, one of which recounts the story of the death of the Adam (*La Mort d'Adam*; 1809). And Étienne Méhul had had success with his restrained yet compelling biblical opera *Joseph* (1807).[12]

As with certain other works by Berlioz, *L'Enfance du Christ* grew from an independent seed, in this case an unlikely one. In 1850, as a joke, Berlioz penned a seemingly simple, faux-ancient chorus, *L'Adieu des bergers à la Sainte Famille*, and had it performed on one of his concerts, identifying it on the program as the work of a seventeenth-century composer named Pierre Ducré. He was delighted when listeners were easily convinced that they had encountered an authentic bit of early music, and he soon added an extended tenor recitation after the chorus and preceded the whole scene with an orchestral introduction in an "ancient style." (Here, in score and parts, he carefully noted each occurrence of the lowered seventh degree in order to make sure that the players produced the intended quasi-Renaissance Aeolian mode instead of a more normal G Minor.) This mini-oratorio, entitled *La Fuite en Égypte*, subsequently became Part II of the three-part *L'Enfance du Christ*. Parts I and III deal respectively with Herod and with the Holy Family's eventual refuge among the Ishmaelites.

Particularly keen is Berlioz's portrait of Herod, whose pride in power is shattered by his dawning awareness of a higher, more powerful morality, represented by the newborn Jesus. The scene in Herod's Palace is reminiscent of passages in Méhul's *Joseph* (notably Siméon's scene of remorse), but it also comprises an imaginative reworking of the standard scena form typical of Italian and Italianate operas of the early nineteenth century: a cantabile aria ("O misère des rois!" in which Herod voices his depression, Andante misterioso) is followed, first, by a chorus that arrives in order to move the action along (the Jewish soothsayers, spinning in the highly unusual meter of $\frac{7}{4}$), and then, a concluding cabaletta for the soloist and chorus, Allegro agitato, full of rage and newfound decisiveness. Another quasi-cabaletta, a scarce four bars of Allegretto for Mary and Joseph, in $\frac{4}{4}$, is immediately halo-ized by a flowing-triplet "Hosanna" from a choir of angels that bring us to the end of Part I.

If *L'Enfance du Christ* is not strictly sacred, despite its generic subtitle, it remains one of the most touching retellings of a core religious tale in the entire oratorio repertory. True, one too-solemn northerner, Alec Robertson, opines that "the only moment in which[. . .] Berlioz sounds a truly religious note is in the wonderful unaccompanied close [the last forty-six bars of Part III], when he suddenly seems to have fallen on his knees."[13] The deeply devout Anton Bruckner offered a similar objection to the *Te Deum*: "Kirchli is' do' nöt!" – Austrian dialect for "Church music it ain't."[14]

But surely religious spirit can be found in more than just *a cappella* paeans to the divinity. The romantics, after all, tended to reject the clergy's traditionally narrow definitions of "the spiritual." Instead, they found solace, ethical challenge, moral guidance, and a new, broader sense of the religious and the sacred in nature, human relations, history, philosophy, story, and even staged drama. In this, as in other respects, Berlioz was a chief romantic, bringing to listeners his own religious yearning and doubt and desire for transcendence in ways that remain troubling and stirring even thirteen decades after his death.

8 The songs

ANNEGRET FAUSER

Berlioz's *romances* and *mélodies* – in particular *Les Nuits d'été* – occupy a key position in the historiography of French song. Berlioz, the "renovator" of so much French music, has been seen as the composer whose various accomplishments include the transformation of the apparently insipid *romance* into a serious form on the model of the German *Lied*.[1] His admiration for Schubert's songs, expressed directly in his reviews and indirectly in his orchestration of *Erlkönig* as *Le Roi des aulnes* (1860), serves as evidence of his esteem for the more exalted genre just as much as does his oft-stated scorn for salon *romances* and for the dilettante musicianship usually associated with them. Thus, to the notion of Berlioz the creator of the ideal romantic symphony has been wedded the notion of Berlioz the creator of the ideal romantic song.

Similarly, *Les Nuits d'été*, his "masterpiece," seems to tower over all other "normal" contemporary song production. How then, in the "shadows" of *Les Nuits d'été* (to use Peter Bloom's expression), are we to view normal works in the category – including Berlioz's own – and how can such normal works enlighten our understanding of French song as a whole?[2]

Romances

Berlioz's *romances* pose a problem for musicologists who adhere to the ideology of musical progress which demands that a composer canonized as a "genius" compose art for art's sake and put his stamp both upon the music of his own period and upon posterity. Indeed, Berlioz himself was instrumental in creating the concept of the "great composer" – his prime example was Beethoven – as the progressive genius who transgresses the conventions of musical genre. His *Symphonie fantastique* became the prototype of the artwork that breaks the boundaries of form and tradition; and his almost obsessive self-exposure through carefully created autobiographical documents both musical and literary – from *Lélio* to the *Mémoires* – supports the claim for such revolutionary innovation. Berlioz, like other poets, artists, and writers of the time, tended to explain himself on the "authority of personal experience" and in so doing to shape the union of subject and object in romantic art in ways that, despite the contentions of deconstructivists such as Roland Barthes, still influence us today.

Berlioz's strategy can be understood, then, as attempting to control not only the creation of a musical work but also its reception, to limit the text to his own authorized reading. But while the *Symphonie fantastique*, the *Damnation de Faust*, *Les Troyens*, and even the *Neuf Mélodies* have been provided with an aura of romantic inspiration and autobiographical meaning, most of Berlioz's *romances* resist such appropriation: they were commercial ventures, written in familiar forms and for specific markets.[3] Their strength lies not in transgression but rather in adherence to convention.

By the eighteen-thirties, the *romance* had become an established genre overlaid with contradictory strata of reception history, which, paradoxically, guaranteed its continuing place in contemporary French music. On the one hand, the *romance* was explained by the dominant culture as a staple of the repertory of the bourgeois woman's salon (and may thus have been seen as feminized); on the other hand it was more broadly appreciated through a nationalist discourse that saw it as genuinely French vocal music.[4] Famous *romances* could therefore have considerable shelf-lives, with pieces such as Martini's *Plaisirs d'amour* (1785) part of a musical experience that continued throughout the nineteenth century. Indeed, Berlioz orchestrated this piece for concert performance, after completing *Les Troyens*, as late as 1859. For the young Berlioz, *romances* were important elements of his musical upbringing: as he wrote in the first chapter of the *Mémoires*, his first "moving" musical experience was hearing Dalayrac's *Romance de Nina* (1786) sung by the choir at his first communion, when he was eleven years old. Four or five years later, he copied popular *romances* from opéras comiques and other sources and made them into his *Recueil de romances avec accompagnement de guitare* (1819–1822).

When Berlioz began to compose *romances*, the genre had been in existence for more than a hundred years, bridging the social space between public and private performance by contributing substantially to the opéra comique and by defining musical performance in the salon.[5] Not only could *romances* move from the stage to the salon as a part of the dissemination of opera, but popular *romances* could also move from the salon to the stage: such singers as Adolphe Nourrit, for example, sometimes inserted them into performances of opéras comiques.[6] During the revolutionary years after 1789, *romances* were also commonly sung in the

Fig. 8.1 A musical soirée in the Paris of the eighteen-twenties illustrated by Achille Devéria. The pose and expression of the women represented in this lithograph reflect the *romance*'s typically languishing emotional content, such trivialized romanticism having become an essential element of the composition and performance of salon *romances* of the period – something revealed in (among other places) a comment by Pauline Duchambge (1778–1858), a successful composer and singer of *romances* in the eighteen-twenties: "J'ai composé mes romances avec mes larmes" ("I composed my *romances* with my tears").

streets as vehicles of political expression.[7] Such promiscuity of genre is a characteristic trait of the *romance*, as Berlioz surely understood. He composed *romances* for dramatic works – the *Romance de Marguerite* in *Huit Scènes de Faust* (and later in the *Damnation*); the *romance* "La Gloire était ma seule idole" sung by the hero in the Deuxième Tableau of *Benvenuto Cellini* – and for the salon, although *Je crois en vous*, for voice and piano (1834), did later become the *Ariette d'Arlequin* in the finale of Act I of *Benvenuto Cellini* (in the form of a sublime if ironic solo for the English horn).

But Berlioz also catered to popular taste with *romances*. Most of these were probably composed for consumption in the salon, a social institution whose musical practice was dominated by the performance of such works. Wagner's report from Paris is only one of numerous accounts that are characteristically dismissive of the custom: "The singers of the salon are usually dilettantes, or rather female dilettantes, of whom there are many, because they all seem to find it easy to dabble in singing. They generally sing *romances* by Demoiselle Puget."[8] We find representations of the salon in paintings and engravings by various artists of the period, among them Achille Devéria (see Fig. 8.1).

Here the performance sets the stage for the objectification not only of the singer but also of the other women present, an effect particularly obvious in the expression of the woman to the right, who seems to be posing for the camera as though complicit in the male gaze. The man at the piano focuses his own gaze less on the music than on his female partner, while the piano and the pillar form a slyly phallic pictorial ensemble at the center of the picture.

The veiled and domesticated eroticism of these social rituals may also be seen in Sophie Gay's account of the performance of *romances*, which speaks of

> these young women who had been advised to manifest deep feeling (as though such an affliction could actually be acquired), and who thus believe that, by raising their eyes to the ceiling and by pronouncing the word "baiser" in *La Folle* as though it had four B's, they could attain a paroxysm of dramatic emotion from the music. Is it not rather unseemly to hear such erotic moans from such virginal voices?[9]

Gay, herself a fine singer and professional composer, reacts with disdain to the "cheap thrills" produced by over-emphasizing sexually evocative words, such as "kiss," in the repressed social context of the salon.

These *romances* were published by the thousands in the eighteen-thirties and -forties. Specialist journals such as *L'Abeille musicale* (edited by the famous *romance* composer Antoine Romagnesi) and *La Romance* continuously fed the demand. And other periodicals – *Protée: Journal des modes* and *Le Monde musical*, for example – used annual albums of *romances* by well-known composers as an incentive to subscribe. This was big business, for a single *romance* could earn its author up to 500 francs, and a collection of six, by a fashionable composer, could bring her as much as 6,000 francs. The 200 francs that Berlioz received for his *Le Chasseur danois*, commissioned by Bernard Latte for the annual *Album de chant* of *Le Monde musical* in 1844, was thus, by comparison, a wholly modest sum.

This was the fifth *romance* that Berlioz had composed for such publications; the earlier ones include *Les Champs* (1834), *Je crois en vous* (1834), *La Mort d'Ophélie* (1843), and *La Belle Isabeau* (1843). It is possible that *Zaïde* (1845) was also written with Latte's *Album* in mind,[10] but the vocal part, too demanding for a dilettante, might have caused that publisher to reject it.

We know, from their separate publication as sheet music, their texts, and their structures, that Berlioz's earlier *romances* (from the period in and around 1820) were also aimed at the salon market. Frits Noske finds that these compositions follow the traditional mold of the *romance* with their *bergerette* texts (texts, that is, of a gently pastoral and amorous sort), mainly strophic forms, melodic formulas, and generally unassuming musical language reminiscent of that of the *ancien régime*.[11] However, simplicity, regularity, and popularity of tone are musical signifiers that are hardly innocent in the context of French song. For more than a hundred years they were identified as *the* characteristic elements of two musical genres understood in a philosophical sense as quintessentially French – the opéra comique and the *romance*. Here, then, a nationalist discourse offered aesthetic justification for a kind of music which, in compositional terms, was no longer in the vanguard. *Romances* retained musical and aesthetic *raisons d'être* in spite of contemporary notions of musical progress, which was usually measured with reference to German music and, in this context, to the *Lied*.

Berlioz's *romances* are thus compositions that allowed him to participate in the musical marketplace, but they are also works that underline his identity as a French composer. His allusions to earlier *romances*, whether through his choice of poetry, his musical means, or his reworking of a piece such as *Plaisir d'amour*, may be seen not only as signs of a tradition-based approach to music that critics have more often tended to find in Berlioz's later compositions, but also as signifiers of what one might call cultural continuity.

Neuf Mélodies (1830)

Of all Berlioz's major works, the *Neuf Mélodies*, which Berlioz often called *Mélodies irlandaises* (*Le Coucher du soleil, Hélène, Chant guerrier, La Belle Voyageuse, Chanson à boire, Chant sacré, L'Origine de la harpe, Adieu Bessy, Élégie en prose*) is probably the one most neglected by Berlioz scholars. Like other *romances*, those of this collection pose problems for historians who search for progress and linear consistency within his œuvre as a whole. Although no one now cares to repeat Adolphe Boschot's verdict that they represent "a halt, if not a step backward,"[12] one does have the impression that they are widely considered inferior to Berlioz's other compositions of the period in and around 1830. The composer himself seems to suggest as much in an anecdote recounted in the *Mémoires*, when, in his Roman days, he spent time bantering with Mendelssohn:

> [Mendelssohn] was also fond of getting me to hum, in my plaintive voice and in the same horizontal position [in which Berlioz had just sung an aria by Gluck], two or three of the tunes which I had written to poems by Moore, and which he liked. Mendelssohn always thought rather highly of my … *chansonettes.*"[13]

Is Berlioz here rejecting the "little songs" of his youth? Or is he rather simply relating a moment of shared *ennui* – two romantic musicians stirring their refined sensibilities with music that was in fact deliciously naïve. (The scene lacks only the pipe and the opium.) Much speaks for this second reading, in particular the suggestive ellipsis and thus the ironic twist of Berlioz's last sentence, whose delicate self-deprecation is an occasional feature of his more playful prose.

The *Neuf Mélodies* pose a hermeneutical challenge. At first sight they appear to be a heterogeneous group of vocal pieces linked only by their texts – all taken from Thomas Moore's *Irish Melodies*. The settings include solo *romances*, duos, and choral pieces, all accompanied by the piano (see Table 8.1).

Hugh Macdonald calls the collection "a miscellany, not a cycle"; D. Kern Holoman laments that its diversity "tends to preclude performance."[14] However, a closer look at the work – spread over two volumes of the *Old Berlioz Edition* and the *New*[15] – reveals, I think, that it is a well-structured and premeditated entity whose wholeness lies not in the traditional zone of the performable score but in an imaginative realm not entirely different from that of the *Symphonie fantastique*.

Like *Huit Scènes de Faust* (Berlioz's Œuvre 1, issued in the spring of 1829), the *Neuf Mélodies* are marked with an opus number (Œuvre 2) on

Table 8.1 The structure of the *Neuf Mélodies irlandaises*

1	*Le Coucher du Soleil* (Rêverie)	Tenor	A-flat Major	$\frac{6}{8}$
2	*Hélène* (Ballade)	Tenor (or Soprano), Bass (or Contralto)	G Major	$\frac{6}{8}$ (prelude and interlude) $\frac{2}{4}$ (strophes)
3	*Chant guerrier*	Tenor, Bass, Chorus	C Major	$\frac{4}{4}$
4	*La Belle Voyageuse* (Ballade)	Tenor	A Major	$\frac{6}{8}$
5	*Chanson à boire*	Tenor, Chorus	F Major	$\frac{2}{4}$
6	*Chant sacré*	Tenor or Soprano, Chorus	A-flat Major	$\frac{3}{4}$
7	*L'Origine de la harpe* (Ballade)	Soprano or Tenor	G Major	$\frac{4}{4}$
8	*Adieu Bessy*	Tenor	A-flat Major	$\frac{6}{8}$
9	*Élégie en prose*	Tenor.	E Major	$\frac{3}{4}$

S	2S	Ch	S	Ch	Ch	S	S		S
1	2	3	4	5	6	7	8	//	9
A♭	G	C	A	F	A♭	G	A♭		E

S = soloist; Ch = chorus

the lower left corner of the title page; the earlier work bears a quotation from Moore's *Irish Melodies*, while quotations from *Faust* can be found as epigraphs for some of the *Neuf Mélodies*. Such cross-references suggest that Berlioz's Œuvres 1 and 2 may well be more closely connected than merely by their appearance as "miscellaneous" settings of texts from a single literary work and etched (as they seem to be) by the same engraver.[16] The rich web of intertextuality that Berlioz created between these two works, among others, refers to a kind of "private mythology" in which such cross-references grow into a poetic narrative that would be understood by the literate listeners and other Parisian intellectuals of the eighteen-thirties – of whom some, despite Wagner's deprecation, were clearly found in the salon.[17] Berlioz could rely on his peers, men and women, to comprehend his internal and external references and in a sense to create their own text from what was a kaleidoscopic maze of fragments. Their readings would, however, be controlled by his choice of referents.

The genesis of the *Neuf Mélodies* permits a further glimpse of their meaning. Berlioz composed the first eight *mélodies* in the summer and autumn of 1829, using translations in verse by his friend Thomas Gounet, and closely monitored their engraving, as we see in his correspondence from December 1829 through February 1830. Only late in the process, on the spur of the moment, probably after the first eight works were engraved, did he compose the *Élégie en prose*. In this case the text came not from Gounet, but from Anne-Louise Swanton-Belloc's 1823 prose translation, *Les Amours des anges et les mélodies irlandaises de Th. Moore*. It is therefore appropriate to ponder the logic of the first eight songs, and only then to interrogate the last.

The autobiographical references here have often been mentioned: not only was Berlioz's "distant beloved" Irish (I refer to Harriet Smithson), but Moore's poetry seemed to echo Berlioz's own concept of self-reflective creation.[18] Furthermore, Ireland (despite incipient famine and violent rebelliousness against the English landlord) could be stylized into a place of exquisite, utopian exoticism – not the sensuous "east" of Victor Hugo's *Les Orientales* (which attracted Berlioz only months later, and which provided him with a remarkable *succès de salon* with his setting of *La Captive*),[19] but rather (merged with vague images of her English-speaking neighbors) the idyllic "north" of Ossian, Shakespeare, and Walter Scott. Gounet and Berlioz arranged their eight poems to evoke a range of images: the longing for a distant island, where women love shepherds, where warriors make war and drown their pain in drink, where people seek comfort in the deity, where maidens move about freely with their honor safely intact. As in a classical tragedy, the penultimate piece, *L'Origine de la harpe*, may be interpreted as the moment of crisis – when song is borne from suffering, as the body of an Ophelia-like mermaid is transformed into a harp, and her hair into golden strings. The final poem of the eight, *Adieu Bessy*, then, takes on the character of an epilogue, removing us from the island:

> Plaisirs passés que je déplore
> Auriez-vous fui pour toujours?

> [Pleasures past, for which I weep, are you gone forever?]

The first and eighth poems provide a frame of longing and memory which lends a circular character to the narrative as a whole. The island, whatever it might represent (some remembered truth? some myth of musical creation?), is distant, not present, and "in the distance," as Novalis has it, "everything becomes *poetry – poem. Actio in distans*. Distant mountains, distant people, distant events, etc., everything becomes romantic . . ."[20] Indeed, we *see* this sort of romantic contemplation in Barathier's lithograph for *Le Coucher du soleil*, where the romantic island is itself not visible (see Fig. 8.2.).

Berlioz's settings strengthen the bonds of the narrative in these eight pieces with changing forces and tonal relationships that are, it turns out, carefully calculated, as can be seen in Table 8.1. The two framing *romances*

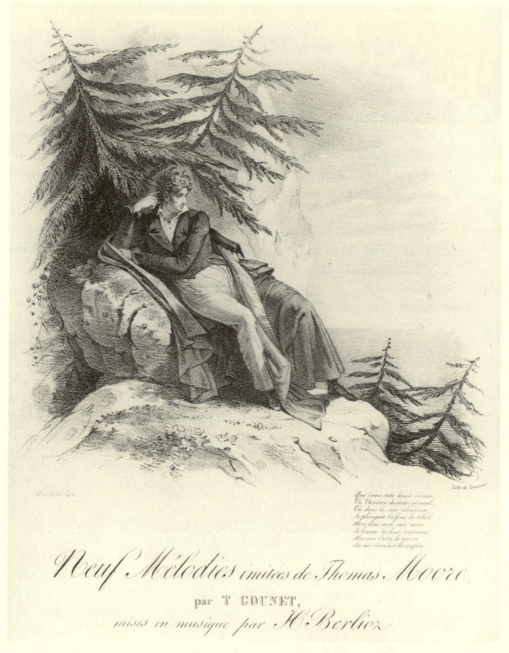

Fig. 8.2 Lithograph by Barathier with the text of the first stanza of *Le Coucher du soleil*. Hector Berlioz, *Neuf Mélodies irlandaises* (Paris: M. Schlesinger, 1830) (British Library, Hirsch IV. 699).

are in A-flat Major and are sung by a tenor. The second and seventh pieces are *ballades* in G Major, for solo voice or voices; the central, fourth piece, *La Belle Voyageuse*, is also a *ballade* for solo voice, this one in A Major. *La Belle Voyageuse* is framed by two choruses (which relate to each other as dominant, C, to tonic, F), linking these three middle numbers into a vignette of rural life in Ireland. The three scenes with chorus also feature soloists; the chorus sings the refrain.

Any of these eight pieces might have found a place in a contemporary *opéra comique*; indeed the piano writing seems almost to evoke that of a reduction of an orchestral score. And the epigraphs in the first edition, especially the conversation between John, Dick, and Max before *Hélène*, could well be literal cues from an opera's piano-vocal score. It is almost as though these *mélodies* were segments of some unknown drama, making reference to some narrative preexistent to the one created by Berlioz and Gounet – possibly an autobiographical meta-drama, returned to life in this composition.

A key role in such an autobiographical fiction of the *Neuf Mélodies* is played by the last number, the *Élégie en prose*, whose anonymous epigraph, with its Ossianic resonance and its images of the graves of Orpheus and Fingal, prepares us for the song's crucial part in the narrative: "He died. His lyre was placed on his tomb. On stormy nights the winds drew from it harmonious moans, with which the strains of his last forlorn lament seemed to mingle still."[21] The *Élégie*, presumably dedicated to Harriet Smithson (the initials "T. H. S." on the title page have been interpreted to mean "to Harriet Smithson"), turns the other eight *mélodies* around. The words are by Moore but the text (by a different translator) is in prose, not verse, and the music is through-composed, not strophic. Its emphatic melodic gestures and tremolo accompaniment are far closer to opera than anything found in contemporary collections of songs.

The *Élégie* seems to suggest that we read the preceding eight as an illusion, as a dream; it seems to transform what went before into a reading of Berlioz's life as it turns itself into a document of self-referentiality. It shatters the earlier, melancholic "autobiography" of the first eight, now "distant" (romantic) songs, and, with prosaic immediacy, exposes their character as delusional. Indeed, the *Élégie* creates romantic irony in a Heinesque manner, and gives the *Neuf Mélodies* a potency well beyond that of the typical salon piece. In chapter 18 of the *Mémoires* Berlioz leads us to such a reading in a passionate narrative where he has himself returning from a soul-searching walk in the country to find Moore's text open on the table in his room. Music for it welled up from the depth of his soul and led to the "sole occasion," he tells us, on which he was able to express a feeling of the sort "while still under its active influence." The fiction is thus complete: subject and object are no longer alienated; Berlioz would have us believe that we witness his innermost self whenever we hear the music or read the score.

When two of the *Neuf Mélodies* were performed in 1830, critics took them as serious additions to the repertory.[22] As late as 1834, François Stœpel dedicated three pages in the *Gazette musicale de Paris* to the *Neuf Mélodies*, first considering the relationship between the composer's character and that of his work, then examining various pieces to see if they ought to be considered beautiful or bizarre. (Simple *romances* were almost never accorded so much space – as much as that of an opera review – in this important journal.) Stœpel, clearly a conservative thinker (and therefore disapproving of the irregular form of *Le Coucher du soleil* and of the "violent passions" of the *Chant guerrier*) but nonetheless a colleague of Berlioz's at the *Gazette*, was constrained to find positive aspects of the *Neuf Mélodies*. His comments on the centerpiece of the group, *La Belle Voyageuse*, consist of a sequence of exhilarated exclamations: Berlioz "seems to abandon himself with a kind of magic charm, and everything that he produces thus breathes the divine pleasure of a pure joy, of a delicious ecstasy. What grace! What exuberance in the melodies of these scattered verses! What originality, even within the confines of rhythmic symmetry!" In the end Stœpel's verdict is negative, but he does set the *Neuf Mélodies* apart from the normal fare for dilettantes and reveals the work as a product of the new romantic school, in which Berlioz "submits to the influence of a poetic idea to the point of passing successively from rapture to bitter grief, from tears to violent despair."[23]

Les Nuits d'été

Les Nuits d'été, six settings of poems by Théophile Gautier (*Villanelle, Le Spectre de la rose, Sur les lagunes: Lamento, Absence, Au Cimetière: Clair de lune, L'Île inconnue*), is the best-known collection of songs by Berlioz. Like the *Neuf Mélodies*, it represents an engagement with a single poet, with verses carefully selected to form a narrative of crisis and transformation. The six pieces are bound together by their tonal disposition and their symmetrical grouping (see Table 8.2).[24]

Although the strophic *romance* is still predominant as a musical model, through-composed songs (*Le Spectre de la rose* and *Sur les lagunes*) play a role of some importance. By this time (the fourth decade of the century), Berlioz was familiar with the *Lieder* of Schubert, having called him, in a review of 1835, "one of the greatest geniuses ever to honor the art of music."[25]

Table 8.2 The Contours of *Les Nuits d'été*

Title	Form	Key in 1841	Key in 1856
Villanelle	Strophic	A Major	A Major
Le Spectre de la rose	Through-composed	D Major	B Major
Sur les lagunes	Through-composed	G Minor	F Minor
Absence	Strophic (ABA)	F-sharp Major	F-sharp Major
Au Cimetière	Strophic (ABA)	D Major	D Major
L'Île inconnue	Strophic with refrain (ABACA'DA'')	F Major	F Major

The poems Berlioz chose came from Gautier's *La Comédie de la mort*, published in Paris in 1838. Like Gounet, who provided translations for the *Neuf Mélodies*, Gautier, too, was a close friend of the composer, and a member of that lively, intellectual inner circle of artists and critics who were active in defending the cause of romantic art. With its rich images, attention to the positioning of key words and careful vowel placement, the poetry of *La Comédie de la mort* was well suited to musical setting and inspired many composers to attempt it, among them Bizet and Fauré. To give but one small example, the opening of *Le Spectre de la rose* plays with the alternation of light and dark vowels, strategically placed to emphasize the contrasting images of innocent virginity and sexual awakening as evoked by the symbol of the rose:

> Soulève ta paupière close
> Qu'effleure un songe virginal,
> Je suis le spectre d'une rose
> Que tu portais hier au bal.

Apart from *Villanelle*, Berlioz's selections loosely follow the order of Gautier's fifty-seven poems, four of Berlioz's six being neighboring pairs. These form a narrative which leads from a spring-born *joie de vivre* (*Villanelle*) and a loss of innocence (*Le Spectre de la rose*), to the death of a beloved (*Sur les lagunes*), a dirge (*Absence*), the obliteration of her memory (*Au Cimetière*), and the beginning of a new future (*L'Île inconnue*). This sequence has sometimes been interpreted in autobiographical terms as reflecting the breakdown of Berlioz's marriage to Harriet Smithson and his turn towards a future with his mistress, Marie Récio,[26] though this is a far from verifiable proposition.

The significance of the title is similarly unclear: *Les Nuits d'été* is Berlioz's expression, not Gautier's. Alfred de Musset's collection of poems, *Les Nuits*, was published in 1840 (when Berlioz's work was composed), and so, too, was a collection of short stories by his friend Joseph Méry, *Les Nuits de Londres*. The preface of Méry's book in particular speaks of summer nights in which he and his fellow wanderers tell stories to the break of dawn, following the maxim that "It is the hour of living under the stars; the nights are the days of summer."[27] More generally, Berlioz's title could suggest some sort of fantastical night-piece in the tradition of E. T. A. Hoffmann, or even another Faustian dream.

The emotional roller-coaster of the poems is reinforced by Berlioz's musical settings, which explore the expressive range of Gautier's language through a variety of musical means – structural, harmonic, rhythmic, and melodic. The opening song, *Villanelle*, is deceptively simple and cheerful; it is a strophic piece in A Major celebrating the advent of spring. In fact subsequent occurrences of the principal melody are slightly varied in ways that are peculiarly subtle and revealing. As Julian Rushton has shown, the gesture in the second part of the first verse, for the words "que l'on voit au matin trembler" (bars 27–31), which rises to a dramatically flattened sixth, F-natural, causes the expected diatonic sixth, F-sharp, at the second verse's "pour parler de nos beaux amours" (bars 67–71) to sound exceptional: "diatonicism," quite remarkably, "becomes an expressive nuance."[28] *Villanelle* thus offers important musical material to which Berlioz alludes, with similar chromatic adjustments, in the later songs.

Such melodic interrelationships take nothing away from the individuality of each setting. Whether the larger tonal organization is a unifying force is more questionable: the version of the 1841 publication proceeds down a circle of fifths to *Sur les lagunes* and, after a semi-tonal shift, through a circle of thirds from *Absence* to the end; in the later orchestral version no such obvious progression is apparent, though the persistence from one song to the next of emphasized chords and pitches again suggests some larger continuity. In neither version do we find tonal closure in the key in which we began.

As already noted, Berlioz reworked and orchestrated *Les Nuits d'été* in 1856, although one song, *Absence*, had earlier been orchestrated for performance by Marie Récio in 1843. There is no doubt that he considered the orchestral version as a "whole," as a "work" in its own right, for he lamented both the fact that it was "completely unknown in France" and that he, himself, had "never heard it in its entirety."[29] What occasioned the orchestral version of 1856 was a request from the Swiss publisher Jakob Rieter-Biedermann, who had been impressed on hearing *Le Spectre de la rose* in Gotha in February of that year. The new keys for two of the songs could seem to contradict the notion that the collection is a cyclic unity, since they now make it necessary to have at least two singers on hand for performance: if only one is available, transposition is required – and for a composer who was highly sensitive to orchestral register and to the colors and sonic nuances of all of the instruments, transposition is highly undesirable.

Indeed, the orchestra of *Les Nuits d'été* is carefully balanced; its weight – always the great danger in the orchestral song – is never too heavy for the voice. At the beginning of *Le Spectre de la rose*, for example, the singer's line is enveloped in a dream-like soundscape of contrasting winds and strings, the latter taking advantage of the "most erotic range of the viola," as Holoman has put it.[30] In the original version for voice and piano, the chromaticism of the melody and harmony emphasize the eroticism of Gautier's text, but the atmospheric quality of the orchestral sound clearly brings its sensuality more immediately to the fore.

Whether Berlioz is the "creator" of the orchestral song and the forebear of Gustav Mahler's large cycles is debatable, but there is no question that now the orchestral *Nuits d'été* are almost universally considered one of the finest examples of the genre.

Autobiographical construction

Given Berlioz's extensive experience as composer and conductor, we may well ask why he produced such an unperformable or at least problematically performable score as that of *Les Nuits d'été*. The self-evident answer – that he sought to take advantage of the frequent presence of several singers on his concert programs – is perhaps not entirely satisfactory. Like the *Neuf Mélodies*, *Les Nuits d'été* can also be understood as a document of aesthetic autobiography, as a kind of romantic fragment, in which the "tension between the revealing and the concealing" creates "rich ambiguity" and "symbolic artistry."[31] Indeed, for both works, the matter of complete performance may well be irrelevant, and even, in a sense, counterproductive.

In the case of the *Neuf Mélodies*, it is not the performance that may be understood to constitute the "work," but rather the published text of 1830. Later incarnations of the collection – under the title *Irlande* (1850) and as incorporated in the *Collection de 32 Mélodies* (1863) – add to it new layers of meaning, as Berlioz attempts to redirect its reading and its reception. When Berlioz reissued the *Neuf Mélodies* as *Irlande*, for example, the dedication to Harriet Smithson and the Ossianic epigraph (among others) simply disappeared. The composer now dedicated the *Élégie* to the memory of the Irish freedom fighter Robert Emmet, and attached an explanatory note to the score regarding Emmet's destiny and love for "Miss Curren," adding a new layer of meaning and suggesting a new reading of the whole. Thus, despite the fact that the *Mémoires* give us only the Harriet Smithson story, the *Neuf Mélodies* may now be seen to have become a drama of futile freedom fighting, of paradise yet to come.

That the orchestrated songs of *Les Nuits d'été* are individually dedicated to specific singers at the court theatre in Weimar could also, in
similar fashion, be an effort to create romantic distance from the first
layer of the autobiographical fiction of the original version for voice and
piano. If we assume that that original version was composed at the time of
Berlioz's waning passions for Harriet Smithson and waxing ones for
Marie Récio, then the theme of *Les Nuits d'été* – mourning but then
leaving a deceased love and departing to an unknown island with a new
one – could easily be related to an episode in the life of the composer.
However, a simple transposition from "life" to "work" would be reductive
and has so far been avoided by most scholars, following the lead of Berlioz
himself, who, in Macdonald's words, "was shy to the point of silence about
one of his most beautiful works."[32]

But this silence may be a part of the autobiographical fiction, like
the "unperformability" of the orchestral score. Both the *Mémoires* and the
orchestrated version are retrospective in relation to the moment of the
creation of the cycle. Berlioz's silence – and his reworking of the score –
perform a role similar to that of the re-dedication of the *Élégie en prose*:
they create romantic distance, they transform a piece that was an immediate interpretation of a biographical event as a part of a "hermeneutical
experience" into a fragment from the past whose context the reader may
or may not (re-)create.[33]

In the context of this interpretation, the final publication of the two
works in the *Collection de 32 Mélodies* of 1863 adds yet another level of
reading to both. Here the *Neuf Mélodies* appear immediately *after* the
Nuits d'été. They become the second "adventure" of, or a flashback to, a
new narrative in the later cycle. The final song of *Les Nuits d'été*, invoking
the "île inconnue" to which "la jeune belle" sets out (is she the "ma belle"
of *Villanelle*?), renders concrete something of which the hero of the *Neuf
Mélodies* only dreams. And beyond juxtaposing *Les Nuits d'été* and the
Neuf Mélodies, Berlioz creates new layers of meaning for others of the *32
Mélodies* as well, by carefully arranging the various items he selected for
inclusion. What ought we to make of the fact that the centerpiece of the
new collection is the patriotic *Hymne à la France* (1844), followed by *La
Menace des Francs* (1848)? Of the fact that the *La Mort d'Ophélie* (1848)
and several other orchestral works were reduced for piano for the 1863
publication? Of the fact that the concluding item, *La Belle Isabeau* (1843),
was originally composed for Marie Récio – who died in June 1862, only
some eighteen months before these thirty-two songs were published?

Precisely when Berlioz began to compile the *32 Mélodies* is not known,
but the lithograph that adorns the Richault edition (see Fig. 8.3) turns it
into one large and unified opus.

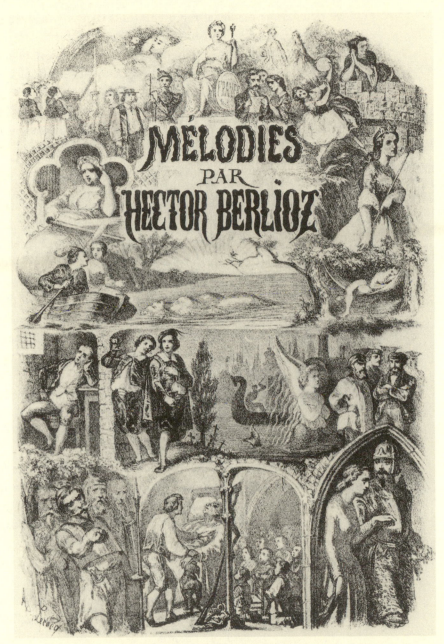

Fig. 8.3 Pictorial title by A. Lecoq for Hector Berlioz, *Collection de 32 Mélodies pour une ou plusieurs voix et chœur* (Paris: Richault, 1863). All the songs in the publication are given their place in this lithograph, from down-to-earth drinkers and workers placed in the lower regions to a representation of France as "Francia" (in the space normally reserved for Jesus Christ) at the top – referring to the centerpiece of the collection, the *Hymne à la France*. In the center of the lithograph we see Ophelia floating – or is it the unnamed mermaid of *L'Origine de la harpe*, lamenting her lover, whose body is transformed into the Irish harp?

Modeled after medieval representations of the world, the title page seems to weld the different *mélodies* into one narrative universe, into a "private mythology," again to use Dahlhaus's expression. Given Berlioz's characteristically interventionist approach to publication, we may well imagine that the artist's rendering was at least prompted by a suggestion from the composer. Be this as it may, the lithograph obviously reflects an awareness of the range of Berlioz's *romances* and *mélodies*, as it does the very act of creating layers of aesthetic autobiography via the continuous transformation of song.

The fluidity between the real and imaginary spaces of the stage and the salon, between genres, and between the meanings of particular works in their incarnations as individual items and as members of collections, provides one of the riches of the corpus of Berlioz's *mélodies* as it does of mid-nineteenth-century French vocal music in general. In this light it is thus less important to consider the question of whether Berlioz is the "creator" of French art song – probably not – than it is to recognize that he took part in an on-going process, responding to developments in the genre and contributing his own strategies, innovations, and audacities to it. Berlioz appropriated song for his autobiographical project, one might also say, and provided us with a dense web of possible readings of it both by way of his *Mémoires* (leaving aside the eternal question of their actual veracity) and through the act of republication in successive editions and in changing guises.

Not only *Les Nuits d'été* but also Berlioz's more normal *romances* and *mélodies* are unusual works even when they remain within traditional molds. Particularly read in context (the *Neuf Mélodies* as a "twin" of the *Huit Scènes de Faust*, for example), they cause us to see the advantages of an approach, such as Suzanne Nalbantian's, which would have us understand that what constitutes a musical work goes beyond the musical text and its performance and on to its existence as a document of aesthetic autobiography – a document that does not necessarily reflect the author but that *creates* him or her in the person of the listener or reader.

PART III

Major writings

9 The *Mémoires*

PIERRE CITRON

Many celebrated authors, Rousseau and Chateaubriand among them, have written memoirs that became the crowning achievements of their literary careers. But such achievements have been rare among musicians, and it is surely Berlioz who gives us the first great example. Grétry preceded him, of course, by beginning to bring out memoirs (while he was still living) in 1791. Berlioz probably knew this book – an amalgamation of biographical matters and technical details – but his musical and literary skills were frankly superior to Grétry's. One of Berlioz's heroes, Carl Maria von Weber, also wrote a somewhat autobiographical novel, but Berlioz, though probably aware of its existence, could not have read the whole text, which was published only in German. So Berlioz was a pioneer, and a rather unique one at that, for most composers, when they felt the need to express something, usually expressed it in music. How is it that Berlioz did so in writing?

For this to have come about, it was surely necessary that Berlioz *not* be one of those children who, from earliest childhood, are destined for music either by family tradition or by recognition of extraordinary skill, and who are thus encouraged first and foremost to develop their musical talents at the expense of all others – something that, for such individuals, usually leads to underdeveloped literary skills and ineptitude in confronting the written word. Berlioz – son of a doctor, recipient of a bachelor's degree, medical student, and, from the moment of his arrival in Paris, companion to young people literally starved for literature – was in no way devoted solely to the cult of music. Along with Gluck, Weber and Beethoven, his gods, let us remember, were Virgil, Shakespeare, Goethe, and Byron. Throughout his life he exhibited a literary turn of mind. For evidence one need only open his *Mémoires*: after an epigraph taken from Shakespeare's *Macbeth* – the very lines from which, in more recent times, Faulkner would construct the title of *The Sound and the Fury* – we find a two-page preface with citations from both Rousseau and Virgil, a preface in which the ghost of Chateaubriand seems to lurk just beneath the surface.

It was also necessary that his existence be rich in intrigue, in excitement and misery, in triumph and failure, in travel, in contact with famous women and men, and in love both varied and intense, in order for all of this to be worthy of continued interest and of recounting in written form.

And perhaps it was most of all necessary – this third condition subsumes the second, at least in the main – that Berlioz live during the romantic era, that is to say during a period in which the arts and literature were closely united not by chance, but by one grand and common impulse. Indeed, it is noteworthy that in the domain of the plastic arts, the same phenomenon would occur, with a Delacroix keeping a journal of great literary vitality, and a Hugo manifesting tremendous talent in drawing.

At the age of twenty, not long after his arrival in Paris, Berlioz began to publish articles on music in various periodicals. There he developed the style – combative, virulent, ironic – that would remain with him, in his feuilletons, until the end of his life. The long articles that he wrote on Beethoven, and the other early pieces in which he exposed more or less directly his own musical ideas, were soon to make of him a writer. His regular contributions to the *Journal des débats*, starting in 1835, continued to refine his now easy style. And if, for his *mélodies*, he used the texts of others – Hugo, Béranger, Gautier, Lamartine, Musset, Dumas, Barbier, Goethe, Thomas Moore, and others less well known – he contributed words of his own to some of his large-scale compositions, first, with some awkward exaggeration, in *Le Retour à la vie* (later *Lélio*), then with gradually greater skill, in large parts of *La Damnation de Faust*, in *L'Enfance du Christ*, in *Les Troyens*, and in *Béatrice et Bénédict*.

From the very beginning of his literary career, Berlioz made it a practice to intrude himself into his writings, as did others at the time, to make his presence felt and his individuality apparent. He is never impersonal; his own views always taint his observations and color the facts. The same thing happens in his music, as we see from the program of the *Symphonie fantastique* and even more from its sequel, *Lélio*, in which the artist-hero, as conductor, has a speaking role on the stage. It is thus perfectly natural that early on Berlioz should think about writing a volume of memoirs in which he would at once inscribe his opinions, his musical experiences, and – hardly separable from the rest – his autobiography.

It was in March 1848, after being in London for some four months, that he conceived the idea of writing his memoirs. Apart from the general need to commit his recollections to paper, we may suggest three rather more precise reasons that led him to do so at this time. The first has to do with the notoriety of the *Mémoires d'outre-tombe*, which everyone knew were to appear immediately upon the death of their author, François-René de Chateaubriand. On the model of the writer whose work dominated French romantic literature, the composer whose work dominated French romantic music might also have determined to leave a portrait of himself and a narrative of his life. Second, about a year before he concretized his idea, Berlioz took one of the most serious and least deserved blows of his career – the failure of *La Damnation de Faust,* which led him to wonder, as he would at various times in the years to come, whether his work and his name were heading for total oblivion. Writing memoirs could be a way of explaining and defending himself before posterity, and a way of portraying himself as he actually was, since during his lifetime so much hue and cry had obscured his voice. Finally, Berlioz was abroad when the revolution of February 1848 broke out, with its after-effects in the German states and the Austro-Hungarian Empire – the very countries, that is, in which he had been most warmly received. On 15 March, eight days before setting pen to paper, he wrote to his friend Joseph d'Ortigue:

> To further my musical career I can now think only of England or Russia; I long ago gave up hope for a future in France, and the latest revolution has made my determination even more urgent and firm. Under the former government I had to do battle with the ill will generated by the articles I wrote decrying both the ineptitude of those who controlled the theatres and the indifference of the public. Now, in addition, I would have to do battle with the whole host of great composers newly hatched by the Republic, with their popular, philanthropic, national, and economic music. The arts in France are now dead, and music in particular has begun to decompose. I hope it will be buried sometime soon, for I can smell from here its rotten stench.

The story of Berlioz's life is thus that of the existence he led up to this moment, which he took to be a decisive turning point, but which he experienced alone, with a certain melancholy spirit, in the midst of a people whose language he could barely manage to speak.

By a curious coincidence, the *Mémoires d'outre-tombe* began to appear in October 1848, just over three months after their author's death. It was in the final months of the very same year that Berlioz wrote, revised, and adjusted the greater part of his own *Mémoires,* which he, too, intended for posthumous publication: posthumous because – and it is here that he distanced himself from Rousseau and Chateaubriand – he had not painted the picture of his life as he lived it, starting with his birth, that is, and following along in chronological order. He does open the narrative in this way, but he soon begins to add chapters that had already been published, some many years earlier, in various journals and books. For even before he reached the age of thirty, without explicit intention, he had already begun to write his autobiography in fragmentary form, at first in little episodes, and then in somewhat larger segments. Up to 1836, we have only certain articles in the *Revue musicale* and the *Gazette musicale* (the two magazines merged in 1835), as well as in the *Revue européenne, Le Rénovateur,* and the *Journal des débats.* In 1836 we get the first extended piece and the first to appear in a bound volume, when the "Voyage musical en Italie" – twenty-four pages in quarto format, with two compressed columns per page – was printed in a collective volume entitled *L'Italie pittoresque*. Even here Berlioz made use of previously published articles, now somewhat modified for the present purpose.

In 1843 and 1844 another large and homogeneous group of writings appeared. After his concert tour through the German states, in 1842–1843, Berlioz published a series of feuilletons in the *Journal des débats* (from August 1843 to January 1844) as ten "Lettres sur l'Allemagne." He used these, with only very few changes, in the two-volume work he published in August 1844 as the *Voyage musical en Allemagne et en Italie* in which Germany, which he had visited most recently, rather oddly occupies the first volume, and Italy, which he had visited twelve or thirteen years earlier, occupies the second. (Berlioz never explained why he structured the book in this way.) Various other musical writings – essays and novellas – complete the ensemble. Six further letters, concerning his concert tour of 1845–1846 in Austria, Hungary, and Bohemia, appeared in the *Journal des débats* and in the *Revue et Gazette musicale* in 1847 and 1848. And then, in March 1848, at age forty-four, Berlioz began to put together his *Mémoires*, with the obviously deliberate intention of incorporating a goodly number of his previous writings.

What results from this method of construction is a volume whose reliability is highly variable. The account of the expeditions in Germany and Central Europe is essentially true, but the account of the trip to Italy is far less so. The chronology of the latter is chaotic, largely because Berlioz freely stitched together certain events that he had recounted earlier, at various times and in various publications, in articles that were themselves perfectly coherent. This, then, is the part of the *Mémoires* that is most fictionalized – but it is also the part that is most literary, if only for its evocation of the Italian landscape, something that is much reduced in the letters from Germany. As for the chapters in which Berlioz evokes his personal and professional life in Paris, these, too, are for the most part trustworthy, although two factors tend to limit their veracity: first, the time that had elapsed between the events and their retelling, which sometimes caused confusion, as Berlioz was always vague about dates; and second, the need to spare the feelings of certain persons who were still alive. It is simply impossible, for example, accurately to reconstruct Berlioz's love-life solely from what is told in these pages.

Of the four women who meant a great deal to him, only one is here depicted as she actually was: Estelle Dubœuf, later Estelle Fornier, six years Berlioz's senior. He first saw her when he was twelve years old; he worshipped her in silence for three years, from 1815 to 1818; he saw her for an instant, probably without saying a word, in 1832, when she had already been married for several years. He remembered her in 1848, when he revisited the place where he had first known her, and he sent her a letter, though we do not know if she received it, since no reply has been preserved. It was only in 1864 that he would write to her again, and eventually see her. He was now sixty-one years old, while she was sixty-seven and a widow. He would ask her to marry him (although he doesn't say so in the *Mémoires*), but in vain. Their occasional encounters would extend over a period of three years. This was a dream-like love, Platonic, tenacious, profound, the most constant and ethereal of Berlioz's entire life, and the only one about which practically none of the details is misrepresented in the *Mémoires*.

Then there was the great explosion in 1830 for the beautiful young pianist Camille Moke, whose actual name is nowhere to be found in the *Mémoires*. She threw herself at Berlioz, became his fiancée and his mistress – he tells us colorfully that he allowed himself to be "Potiphared" – only to leave him in the lurch one year later, ignominiously leaving it to her mother to tell Berlioz that she was going to marry someone else. Of the entire episode, we have here only a few elliptical allusions, and two ironic narratives – one about the seduction of the naïve genius by the libidinous virtuoso, the other about the jilted musician's comical voyage from Rome to Nice, possessed as he was by the desire to kill the infidel along with her mother and her newly intended before doing away with himself. (How much of this adventure found its way into the story of the *Symphonie fantastique* remains entirely untold.)

Berlioz's love for the Irish actress Harriet Smithson, whom he adored from afar for some five years, is told in a far more detailed narrative that extends to their marriage in 1833 – a narrative that is largely truthful, although one attempted suicide is here passed over in silence. About many episodes however – the disappointment that followed the marriage; the couple's poor relations and mutual misunderstandings; the psychological problems that tortured a woman who was excluded from exercising her profession because of her foreign accent and who, to console herself, took to drink, suffered a series of strokes, and finally arrived at a state of total ruin and paralysis; the drama experienced by their son, troubled by the increasingly wide gulf between his parents, rebellious and unstable until he was twenty, at times little understood by his father – Berlioz was constrained to say nothing.

The last is Marie Récio, the only one of this group who attracts almost no sympathy. She was, it would appear, not only more than mediocre as a singer, but also possessive, petty, arrogant, selfish, and resentful. Still, she was good at taking care of the affairs of a household and, probably, of taking care of the man to whom she was attached with talents of a different sort. For information about all of these things, however, one must look elsewhere than in the *Mémoires*, where her person – in what may be a case of posthumous revenge – is almost nowhere to be found. We hear of her in 1842, when Berlioz was about to leave for Belgium, as "a traveling companion who, since that time, has accompanied me on my various excursions." Later, evoking Harriet at the time of her death, Berlioz speaks of his wife's "incessant jealousy that finally became justified." Of his marriage to Marie, Berlioz writes with a brevity that is as bitter as it is brutal: "I had to do it." Finally, he makes mention of Marie's death, which occurred in 1862. But one would search the *Mémoires* in vain for any more precise comments about this woman, even though the book was written under her "reign": in fact Berlioz lived with Harriet for only eight or nine years, while Marie Récio shared his life for more than twenty, twelve as his official mistress and eight as his second wife.

The silences and lacunae in the narrative reflect the various stages of Berlioz's intimate existence: first legally married, then separated from his wife, then, in 1854, briefly widowed but soon thereafter remarried. Still, if there is one point that he underlines, it is that only twice in his life was he truly and deeply in love, once with Estelle and once with Harriet.

It is true that the method of composition of the *Mémoires*, which more resembles careful alignment of pre-existent elements than it does architectural construction with new materials, hardly encouraged Berlioz to be exhaustive. We find here almost no trace of his important friendships, such as the one he had with Alfred de Vigny, and almost no trace of other events that were of tremendous impact, such as the death in 1839 of his nineteen-year-old brother Prosper, who was at boarding school in Paris at the time, whom Berlioz saw often, and in whose studies he took great interest. Berlioz is similarly silent about his feud with his parents – out of respect for conventional propriety, and for his sisters – which would distance him from them for several years after his marriage to Harriet.

Even the chapters written with the intention of constituting a true autobiography are not all of the same tone. The first three, written in March and April of 1848, tell the story of his childhood and the beginnings of his adolescence. But in the middle of chapter 4, the narration takes on the appearance of a diary, with notations of the precise date: 10 April, 12 July, 16 July 1848. The chapter is divided between the end of his stay in England and his return to France. He continued to work on it in September 1848: in chapter 8 he mentions the recent death of Prince Lichnowsky, which occurred in that month. By the end of 1848 about four-fifths of the text of the *Mémoires* had been drafted, but then his writing nearly came to a halt. Berlioz always wrote more prose – this is

true of his correspondence, too – when he was not writing a lot of music.
But from October 1848 to 1850, he would compose the *Te Deum* and *La
Fuite en Égypte,* which was incorporated in 1854 into *L'Enfance du Christ.*
A few pages of the *Mémoires* – notably chapters 48 to 51 – probably date
from 1851. It would be only in 1854, after Harriet's death, in March, and
perhaps after the completion of *L'Enfance du Christ,* in July, that Berlioz
finished chapters 52 to 59, thus bringing the *Mémoires* to a close. The date
of completion, inscribed at the end of the last chapter, is 18 October 1854
– the eve of his marriage to Marie . . .

It is in this last section that we find chapter 54, devoted to *La
Damnation de Faust,* chapter 57, on the aborted opera *La Nonne
sanglante,* and chapter 59, containing Berlioz's artistic will and testament. From that point on Berlioz considered his *Mémoires* completed.
Already ill, having no idea how much longer he had to live, and sometimes literally pleading for death because of suffering both physical and
mental, he had hastened to finish the autobiography. He had the manuscript bound, and kept it not in his apartment but – hidden from the possible gaze of his wife – in his office at the library of the Conservatoire. For
a time he thought about bringing out a foreign edition, since he was still
far from appreciated in France. On 9 May 1855 he sent the manuscript to
Liszt, with a view towards having Richard Pohl make a translation into
German that would be published after his death. In fact he gave Liszt a
number of very precise instructions: if he were to die before the manuscript could be sent back to him, Liszt was to have it sent directly to the
Parisian firm of Michel Lévy for publication, with the royalties to be
divided between his wife and his son. Further, when Liszt wrote back to
acknowledge receipt, he should be sure to speak only of a "package," for
Marie was to know nothing about the book. In the end this all came to
naught. In May 1856, when the journalist Eugène de Mirecourt expressed
interest in devoting one of his little biographical studies to Berlioz,
the composer sent him the manuscript of the *Mémoires,* from which
Mirecourt in fact extracted very little of genuine interest. The long letter
that Berlioz included in the packet for Mirecourt was itself to find a place
in *Mémoires,* where it is entitled "Post-scriptum"; here he speaks of the
fundamental opposition between his own musical sensibilities and those
of the Parisian public.

In February 1858, when Berlioz published in the weekly *Monde illustré* a well-received account of his work on *Der Freischütz* at the Opéra in
1841, the director of the magazine asked the composer if he had written
anything else about his life, and Berlioz sent him the manuscript.
"Inscribed here," he wrote, "are the innumerable changes in the stormy
atmospheric conditions in which I have lived up to this day. This, if I may

use a nautical expression, is the log-book of my painful voyage." From 25 September 1858 to 10 September 1859, with a few interruptions, *Le Monde illustré* would publish these "Memoirs of a Musician." The chapter numbers of the original manuscript are maintained, but those devoted to the excursions to Italy and Germany are omitted, since they had already appeared earlier in book form. As for the rest, Berlioz made a number of cuts, which are sometimes indicated in the text by several dotted lines, and sometimes not indicated at all. Naturally, since the domineering Marie Récio would have read them, all the passages having to do with Harriet Smithson were suppressed. So, too, were passages critical of living musicians, such as the conductor Narcisse Girard, and of deceased musicians, such as Boieldieu, so as to avoid speaking ill of the dead. As for Cherubini: Berlioz does evoke the squabbles he had with the Italian musician, but he excludes the ridicule of his Italian accent, perhaps because it would have been considered unseemly for one member of the Institute to make sport of a predecessor. These satirical passages were nonetheless restored when the book was published, posthumously, in its entirety. But even with these cuts, Berlioz appears as singularly imaginative and hardly stuffy in the manner of a proper academician. This partial publication is of especial interest, then, because it highlights what Berlioz was willing to say publicly during his lifetime. The rest would appear only after his death, when he would no longer be present to suffer the consequences.

The story of the publication does not quite end here, however, for in the spring or summer of 1864, a "Postface" was added to the text, into which ten years are squeezed in fewer than twenty pages that recount the story of the two last great works, *Les Troyens* and *Béatrice et Bénédict*. Immediately thereafter, Berlioz would see Estelle Fornier, whom he had loved so passionately. He relates their encounter and once again enlarges his manuscript by adding to it his recent correspondence with her. This third series of supplementary pages, entitled "Voyage en Dauphiné," did in fact become the last. But its final words changed the tonality of the end of the *Mémoires*: the "Postface" concludes with a reflection upon the stupidity and cruelty of man, and with an appeal to Death to come as soon as it should like. But at the conclusion of the "Voyage en Dauphiné" – in a last-minute shift from the darkness of the minor mode to the light of a final major chord – Berlioz writes that "I shall now be able to die with neither anger nor bitterness."

It remains to be said that Berlioz, who, in May 1858, wrote to his sister Adèle that he had been correcting and refining his style for six years "without being able to render it wholly satisfactory," would, after October 1854, never modify the arrangement of the first fifty-nine chapters: the three texts that followed suit were for him simply complements to the larger work, as though he were dead as a man in 1854 but continued to live thanks to some sort of extension of indeterminate length.

Berlioz always insisted that after his death his text should appear in its entirety, with neither modifications nor cuts. To maintain the integrity of the work he was counting on his brother-in-law Marc Suat, but Suat died before Berlioz. There was also his son, Louis, of course, but he was sailing the high seas and could not supervise the publication. How could he be sure that the work would appear according to his wishes? He decided to have the book printed at his own expense, at the beginning of 1865. In July, after the proofs were corrected, twelve hundred copies of the work were printed; these were stored at the Conservatoire, in the library office that remained at Berlioz's disposition. In August, he presented a bound copy of the book to Estelle Fornier, whom he saw at her son's home in Geneva. He also gave copies to a few of his close friends. The rest were put on sale only after his death.

These *Mémoires* thus in no way constitute the serene and melancholy recollections of a man approaching the end of his life. They rather present a chronicle, written from day to day, or shortly after the events described took place – as in the case of the voyages in Italy, Germany, Central Europe, and Russia, which occupy such a large part of the book. The chronicle was of course revised, here in small detail, there in depth, at times with cuts, at times with additions. When his point of view had changed between first writing and rereading, he often troubled himself to add only a note to this effect, sometimes dated, sometimes not. One might attribute this to laziness in certain cases, but in others it serves consciously to highlight the successive stages of his writing. The reader, without forewarning, is thus invited to identify with Berlioz in all periods of his life, sometimes arranged in non-chronological order, as in certain twentieth-century novels and films, where unannounced previews and flashbacks remove us from the central axis of the narration: indeed, this is one of the reasons for the modernity (not always premeditated) of Berlioz's autobiography.

Given the way they were composed, we might well wonder if the *Mémoires* are unified at all. Certain chapters, as we have seen, are given as they were first written, as early as 1832. Others came as much as a third of a century later. From the young hatchling of less than thirty to the old eagle withered by failure, sadness, and illness is, after all, no small distance! But most of the book is equally balanced between these two extremes, written in full maturity between the ages of forty and fifty, in the years that surround the composition of *La Damnation de Faust*, at a time when Berlioz had already had the double experience of triumph and defeat – an alternation that would pursue him throughout his life. He was sufficiently close to his youth to relive its ebullience, since he still felt it bubbling within him. But he was also able to distance himself from his youth long enough to write about one or another episode of his past with irony – regarding his excessive irritability, rage, or despair. Never blasé, never going back upon what he has said, he appreciates with a clear head his actions, his dreams, and his spontaneous impulses with a lucid and discerning smile.

Should the work be taken as an historical document? It is not difficult to find in it contradictions and inexactitudes, to which many commentators have enjoyed drawing attention. The story of the "suicide" of 1831 is hardly believable. Berlioz describes the Sistine Chapel without in fact having seen it. He did not have as much difficulty getting paid for the *Requiem* as he suggests in the book. And one could go on. But it is of very little use to scoff at every single distortion of "objective" reality. First of all, such distortions are not so numerous as some have suggested on the basis of testimony opposed to Berlioz's – testimony that is in fact less reliable than his own. Some are due simply to the memory lapses that one would expect after so many years had gone by. It happens that Berlioz mistakes one concert for another, and thus confuses his chronological narrative. In fact he had little sense of the clock and the calendar. From time to time he gives a precise date, but most often he speaks in approximations by saying "one year later," for example, when in reality the time elapsed could be less than eight months or almost two years. His quotations, whether from Virgil, Shakespeare, La Fontaine, or Hugo, are always from memory, and often faulty – sometimes deliberately so, so as to make them fit the context into which they are introduced. Furthermore Berlioz does not always indicate that he is quoting – something that makes identifying his sources difficult indeed. At the time of publication, he made only hasty revisions, and let slide a number of inconsistencies, lacunae, and errors.

Second, certain distortions are the result of the secret workings of a frenetic imagination upon episodes that had touched him profoundly and which he found it impossible to write about with a cool head. Is it possible, as one sometimes feels from these pages, that Berlioz suffered from a persecution complex? Perhaps. Is it not difficult to believe that an experienced orchestral conductor such as Habeneck, at the time of the first performance of the *Requiem*, would have put down his baton, at the crucial moment when the brass choirs make their entrance, and taken up his snuffbox, thus risking a disaster whose shameful consequences would have redounded as much upon him as upon the composer?

But when a man is conscious of being the only great musician of his own country as well as the greatest living orchestral composer in all of Europe, at least for the several-year period between the deaths of

Beethoven, Schubert, and Weber and the ascensions of Schumann and Liszt; when such a man has spent his life confronting the most severe material difficulties, seeing his family opposed to his calling, and chained for survival to a column of music criticism that he detested and dreaded almost to the point of apoplexy; when he could not obtain the conductor's post at the Paris Opéra, even though he was one of the best conductors of his day and was admired across the European continent; when he found himself denied the harmony class at the Conservatoire, even though he was one of the greatest harmonists of the century; when the only official post offered to him for many years by the magnanimous powers-that-be was that of associate librarian at this same Conservatoire; and in view of the fact that the public failed to appear at his concerts, that intrigue or indifference led to the ignominious failure of masterpieces such as *Benvenuto Cellini* and *La Damnation de Faust,* that the doors of the halls of the Conservatoire and Opéra were closed to him, and that he saw himself rejected by the Institute in favor of Ambroise Thomas, Onslow, and even Clapisson – in view of all of this, can we really reproach Berlioz with a kind of indulgent smile for having let himself be carried away by his more fiery emotions?

It is certain that the distortions of reality in the *Mémoires* do not always occur unconsciously. Sometimes Berlioz carefully embroiders the facts, minimizes his adroit self-publicity, or otherwise gives himself the leading role. But where is the great man, especially during the romantic era, who did not consider himself to be one of the principal elements of his work, who did not sculpt his own statue with a view towards preserving his image for posterity? Rousseau and Chateaubriand provided the example. Like the *Confessions* of the former and the *Mémoires d'outre-tombe* of the latter, the *Mémoires* of Berlioz are a justification, but also a work of art; their distance from reality is the same as that of a painting (in comparison to that of a photograph). Sometimes Berlioz added details in order to make the picture more colorful, only later to rectify the matter by adding a note such as: "This is a fabrication and results from the tendency that artists always have to write something simply for the sake of effect." If certain contrasts and oppositions are accentuated, it is to confer upon the work a larger unity and a greater concentration, to underline what is essential: so the detail and disorder of reality disappear here in the light of a truth that has been felt and lived.

On the whole, then, Berlioz's *Mémoires* give us a faithful portrait of the man and his work. He was in actual fact the impulsive and passionate man portrayed in the book, the man so uncompromising about what was for him of absolute value – namely, music; the intransigent composer who, despite various requests and despite obvious financial advantages, always refused to write both for solo piano, because what he had to say could not be expressed by that instrument alone, and for small orchestra, because he felt a need for large masses of sonority. He was in actual fact the combative fellow so fanatical in his defense of those whom he admired, so forceful in his attacks upon manipulators and mediocrities, but sufficiently modest to render service to other musicians – Weber and Gluck first of all, but also Couperin, Méhul, Schubert, Padre Martini, and Bortniansky – by making transcriptions, arrangements, and adaptations that attempted to remain faithful to their essence as he perceived it, and to recognize the merits of his adversaries.

He was in actual fact the man who, in the fullness of his happier years, when he enjoyed a period of prolonged creative intoxication, was struck from time to time by the cruelest of blows, not only because his own impulsiveness brought them on, but also because, it almost seems, he was pursued by a kind of inevitable doom. He was in actual fact the man whose entire life was a struggle to have his music heard, a struggle to counter the traditional routine, prejudice, indifference, and incomprehension of the public, the press, and the persons in power. He was in actual fact the man who, almost fifty years old, had to give up on the idea of writing a symphony that he was meditating in order to avoid increasing the financial difficulty in which he was mired because of the illness of his wife; the man who proclaimed on two occasions, in his full maturity as a composer, that he hoped to be able to resist the desire he felt to compose new works because he knew that they would lead only to failure, despair and financial ruin; the man who – and this is perhaps the saddest fact of all – was never privileged to have performed, and thus to hear, certain of his works: not only most of the cantatas written for the Prix de Rome, not only fragments of the incomplete operas *Les Francs-Juges* and *La Nonne sanglante*, but the compositions that are now recognized as his masterpieces: the orchestral versions of most of *Les Nuits d'été*, the *Marche funèbre pour la mort de Hamlet*, and especially the first two acts of *Les Troyens*. If it happened that he did hear his comic opera *Béatrice et Bénédict*, it was only because it was performed in Germany, never in France.

Finally, he was in actual fact the man who literally found himself portrayed in several of the great romantic myths, who lived with such profound intensity the lives of Romeo, Hamlet, Childe Harold, and Faust that his own life became one that went beyond individual adventure to take on a genuinely universal resonance. Such a man, the reader of the *Mémoires*, whatever his presuppositions may be, cannot fail, it seems to me, not only to admire but also to love – as did certain of Berlioz's friends who, over the course of his lifetime, remained as faithful to him as he was to them. For

Berlioz was one of those men who believe in friendship; whenever he encountered it in others, he underlined it with especial warmth.

But let us not pretend that he was perfect. Indeed, the very notion of perfection is inconsistent with the notion of romanticism, whose very ardor implies excess. Not only in his youth but throughout his life, Berlioz was sometimes inconsiderate and unjust, even in his own field of endeavor. At a time when the writing of music history was beginning to develop, he remained ignorant of the music of earlier centuries. We observe him belittling Palestrina and totally misconstruing Bach, and in one of his letters he is equally reckless with regard to Handel; we are surprised to see him criticizing certain "unpardonable" excesses in *Don Giovanni*: "it is now time to have done with all this admiration for Mozart, whose operas are all alike, and whose cool beauty is tiresome and distressing," he writes in the *Mémoires*, though elsewhere he does recognize Mozartian grandeur. Even his friends did not always escape his severe regard, and it seems clear that he failed to appreciate the genius of Chopin, "who went far beyond mere rhythmic independence" and was simply "*unable* to play in strict time." In old age he understood neither the evolution of Wagner's musical style nor Liszt's, while he harbored an admiration for Spontini that has hardly been ratified by posterity. But his other great heroes – Gluck, Weber, and especially Beethoven – underline the vitality and penetration of his musical judgment. He also was fair to some of those whom he utterly disliked (and who returned his "affection"): he praises Cherubini's *Messe du sacre* in the *Mémoires*, Rossini's *Barbier de Séville* and *Guillaume Tell*, and Donizetti's *Lucia di Lammermoor*.

He is never lukewarm; his enthusiasm and indignation persist to the end. And on many levels he remains full of sharp contradictions. Strong as he was in writing music and in getting it played, Berlioz was surprisingly weak in dealing with women, sometimes even to the point of running away. He left on tour to Belgium without even telling Harriet of his departure. And in Germany, a few months later – though he doesn't mention this in the *Mémoires* – he left Frankfurt surreptitiously, leaving Marie Récio behind. But she made inquiries, found him in Weimar, and insisted on remaining by his side. Several years later, he had to construct an elaborate subterfuge in order to take off without her for Russia and, subsequently, England. Elsewhere, as "Mme Berlioz" – a title she did not yet enjoy – she would accompany and keep an eye on him, without his being able to escape.

Another contradiction: he found it difficult to stomach the disdain of the Parisian musical establishment and the nullity of the artistic life of the capital, and he never missed an opportunity to drag the town in the mud. And yet, when he was offered a post abroad, whether in Germany or

Russia, he found it impossible to accept, unable as he was to live far away from the very Paris he claimed to detest.

In his feuilletons and his conversations he rarely hesitated to exercise his caustic wit, even and indeed especially upon those who were in a position to assist or to hinder his efforts. He refused to make concessions himself – but never failed to express indignation when he was not treated with kindness by others. He lit tooth and nail into the Académie des Beaux-Arts, to which he presented his candidacy on four occasions, finding it scandalous to be passed over by others while doing almost everything possible to guarantee his exclusion.

But it is not only a musical personality that transpires through these *Mémoires*, it is a musical technician, whose narrative brings to life the concerts of his day, the instrumentalists, the conductors and choruses, the concert-halls and managers – the whole kit and caboodle of the musical world with all of its idiosyncrasies, aberrations, prejudices, enthusiasms, and devotions. And around this mass, with both brio and simplicity, he brings to light an entire era with which he was profoundly engaged. Naturally, writers and artists occupy the front rank. The literary profiles that grace these pages include those of Victor Hugo, who intervened in 1848 in such a way as to maintain Berlioz's position as librarian at the Conservatoire, of Balzac, who gave Berlioz advice about his trip to Russia, and of Heine, Lamennais, and Dumas. The most striking figures are those of the musicians who stood at his side and who, almost to a man, were born outside of France: Chopin, who participated in a benefit concert for Harriet; Paganini, who bowed down in public before Berlioz and who, with a gift of royal proportion, enabled him to write one of his greatest masterpieces, *Roméo et Juliette*; and especially Liszt, who was won over by Berlioz on hearing the *Symphonie fantastique* and who was devoted to him for more than thirty-five years, sparing neither effort nor time to arrange performances of his friend's music, and inviting the public to recognize his genius. If Berlioz found the reception he deserved abroad, in Germany, Austria, Hungary, Bohemia, and Russia, it was particularly due to a group of musicians, most of them German: Mendelssohn, whom Berlioz met in Rome and later in Leipzig, and who worked tirelessly on his behalf, playing a bass part on the piano, correcting copyists' errors in the parts, and conducting the chorus of *Roméo et Juliette*; Schumann, who wrote an enthusiastic article about the *Symphonie fantastique* on the basis of the piano transcription alone, and who expressed to the composer his own great admiration for the *Offertoire* of the *Requiem*; and Wagner, who applauded *Roméo et Juliette* in Paris, welcomed the French composer in Dresden, and put his own labor and prestige at the disposal of a man with whom he would only later fall out.

The spiritual climate of the nineteenth century can also be felt in these *Mémoires*. Berlioz's romanticism is that of 1830, the year that opened with *Hernani*, that climaxed with the "three glorious days" of the July Revolution, and that culminated with the *Symphonie fantastique*. Its musical dynamism is but one of the manifestations of a new vitality that uplifted an entire generation, a vitality sparked by a desire – felt or expressed in a thousand different, sometimes bizarre and sometimes contradictory ways – to be involved as humanity marched forward in history. One aspect of this desire was necessarily "political" in the larger, noble sense of the term, implying the idea of liberation, or rather, rebellion. And Berlioz had been a rebel from the moment of his arrival in Paris – against his family, which opposed his musical career; against the *dilettanti*, who embraced Italian music only; and against Cherubini, who barred him from one of the doors of the Conservatoire.

Rebellion and liberty: these notions appear frequently both in Berlioz's œuvre and in his life, and they are readily found in his *Mémoires* as well. As early as 1826, he wrote *La Révolution grecque*, "an heroic scene for large chorus and large orchestra," as a tribute to the combatants in a war of liberation. In 1827 and 1828, he began to work out his opera *Les Francs-Juges*, which highlights a struggle against tyranny (the opera was never completed), and he composed a *Waverley* Overture, inspired by the novel by Walter Scott, which glorifies the Scottish uprising against their oppressors. He furthermore considered writing an opera on Robin Hood, in which the common people would clearly be portrayed more favorably than certain classes of the nobility. In these same years Berlioz set two poems on the subject of bandits and pirates that give evidence of a theatrical but sincere sort of anarchistic imagination.

At the time of the July Days, in 1830, while Liszt dreamt of a *Symphonie révolutionnaire*, Delacroix conceived his *Liberté défendant les barricades*, and Hugo wrote the *Chants du crépuscule* devoted to the "Trois Glorieuses," Berlioz – just after quitting the tiny studio at the Institute where he wrote the soon-to-be victorious Rome Prize cantata – ran through the streets of Paris, armed and ready to fire if and when the occasion was right. Of all the young romantics, he was the only one, along with Alexandre Dumas, to seek action in this way. Later, in a covered gallery, he led a group of Parisians several hundred strong in the singing of the *Marseillaise*, which he himself had arranged. He also arranged the *Chant du neuf thermidor* by the same poet, Rouget de Lisle. And in 1831 he proclaimed his allegiance to the Saint-Simonian "faith."

In 1831, in Italy, he took up the theme embodied in *Waverley* by writing the *Rob Roy* Overture. The overture *Le Corsaire* and particularly the admirable symphony *Harold en Italie* make reference to Byron – who died at Missolonghi, where he had gone to fight alongside the insurgent Greek patriots. The cantata *Le Cinq Mai* sings of Napoléon who, in our day, may be viewed as a symbol of despotism, but who was the veritable god of the liberal thinkers during the period of Berlioz's formative years in the eighteen-teens and twenties. At first glance, the *Requiem* may seem at odds with these tendencies, and yet it was conceived for a service to honor the memory of the victims of the Revolution of 1830. Furthermore, although Berlioz had long since renounced the Catholicism of his youth and had become a confirmed non-believer, it would be a mistake, in the context of the romantic era, to suggest that this sort of atheism was radically opposed to religious faith, for the religion of the progress and achievement of humanity was, for many figures of the period, nothing if not a new form of belief: like a wave, which rises and breaks upon its predecessor, so, too, did the new religion, spawned by the same forces as the old, supersede that which had gone before. Herein lies one of the explanations (of which others are to be found in the realm of aesthetics) of the "atheist's Mass" that is Berlioz's *Requiem*.

The opera *Benvenuto Cellini*, too, seems at first rather removed from the historical circumstances of the moment, but August Barbier, one of the authors of the libretto, tells us in his *Études dramatiques* that the work was at first supposed to begin with the sack of Rome, where Cellini, who would have raised an independent army to defend the city, was himself to take part in the execution of the attacking Bourbon constable. Thus the sculptor – the symbol of the composer – was originally designed as a freedom fighter. In this context there is hardly any need to remark upon the *Symphonie funèbre et triomphale*, written for the tenth anniversary of the July Revolution. The *Chant des chemins de fer* at once glorifies the scientific techniques that were engines of progress and the workers who realized their potential – yet another manifestation of the Saint-Simonian ethic. And when, in February 1846, Berlioz wrote the *Marche hongroise* (soon incorporated into *La Damnation de Faust*), he knew perfectly well that he was lending an orchestral hand to the insurgent Hungarian partisans. The following year, in October 1847, at the opening of his "Letter from Pesth," he wrote ironically of Hungarian and Bohemian "devotion" to the Austrian Empire in "body, soul, and estate, much like Irish devotion to England, Polish to Russia, Algerian to France, and all subject peoples' attachment to their conquerors." This was clearly to indict territorial and especially colonial occupation, and thus to affirm a stance that was in no way reactionary. Again, in March 1848, only eight days before setting out to write his *Mémoires*, Berlioz made an arrangement of Méhul's *Chant du départ* and Rouget de Lisle's *Mourons pour la patrie*, something which suggests that he was hardly opposed to a change of regime.

These liberal ideas were to undergo radical change during the Second Republic. After the uprisings in February 1848, Berlioz, henceforth horrified by such violence, dismissed both camps without pronouncing favor upon either. Soon, however, both the collapse of Parisian musical life and the demagogic rhetoric of such political figures as Ledru-Rollin gave birth to an about-face that led Berlioz not only to reject his earlier ideas but even to position himself in the opposite camp: in his letters and in a note in the *Mémoires* we see him proclaim a sympathy for the Prince-President, Louis-Napoléon, that persisted even after the coup d'état by which Louis became Napoléon III. Perhaps there was a whiff of self-interest in such expressions of support, for Berlioz surely hoped that the Emperor would see to it that his works were performed and, more generally, that he would govern in a way that would be advantageous to the institutions controlling musical life in France. Such hopes were disappointed: Napoléon III was no more interested in music than Charles X or Louis-Philippe. But Berlioz's reactions were never motivated by self-interest alone, for age and experience, too, caused him to abandon certain youthful illusions.

Age and experience also lessened the virulent intensity of his creative imagination, for it is in his work from before 1848 that we find most of the innovations he brought to the art of music: the new kinds of orchestration – pianos used as orchestral instruments, basses played *divisi*, extreme high and low registers combined with no interior sonorities, brass fanfares played away from the orchestral mass, percussion sections augmented and diversified; the irregular rhythms, sometimes curiously superimposed; the substitution for traditional modulation by occasionally brusque tonal shifts – in short, the rejection of everything that Berlioz considered the "tyranny" of acquired habit (a rejection that opened the way to innovators such as Musorgsky and Debussy (for there are a number of passages in Berlioz that are indeed impressionistic) and especially to the great tradition-shatterers of the twentieth century, among them Stravinsky, Bartók, and Boulez.

In his work after 1848, we find abatement in his search for novelty. Despite what has been written, *L'Enfance du Christ* marks not a mutation of his aesthetic (as was claimed by certain critics of the time) but rather a cessation of his desire to conquer new worlds. And a work such as *Les Troyens* capitalizes upon previous discoveries more than it breaks new ground (as had the *Requiem, Roméo et Juliette,* and *La Damnation de Faust*). Only in isolated moments here is Berlioz the romantic of his youth; now he has become a classic in the broadest and most profound sense of the word.

All of this appears beneath the surface in the *Mémoires,* where Berlioz only hints at the evolution of his musical style, perhaps fearful of giving the impression – which he would have been horrified to do – of repudiating his earlier work.

What is abundantly clear, by contrast, is his capacity, while following the story of his life as a creator, to move from one strong emotion to another, and to cause these to be felt by the variety of his style and the freshness of his narration. These *Mémoires* are as vivid as any ever written. If Berlioz occasionally enters into technical detail regarding the worth of the different German orchestras or the evolution of the different wind instruments, if he is occasionally didactic (in a constructive way) regarding the courses that ought to be added to the curriculum of the Conservatoire, he nonetheless moves on quickly to something else, for he wants above all to change tempo and thus to keep the reader in suspense. Whether confronted with Shakespeare, Byron, Virgil, Schiller, or the Italian countryside, Berlioz writes with exalted lyricism; his lyricism becomes elegiac when he distantly recalls his first communion and his first meeting with Estelle; and it becomes dramatic when he relives the falling-out that he had with his mother. We sense a frenzied romanticism on reading such (untranslatable) expressions as "Mort et furies!," "Cinq cent mille malédictions!," "Sang et larmes!," "Feux et tonnerres!," "Extermination!" We feel his enthusiasm when he hears and analyzes the music of Weber, Mendelssohn, and Gluck; and we feel his virulence when he settles his accounts with the Institute, Italian music, Fétis, Castil-Blaze, Costa, and Girard – who mutilated the scores of the masters or who, out of personal interest, blocked his path.

Berlioz takes himself seriously as a musician, but he is able to laugh at himself as a man as he recounts a number of his experiences: learning to play the guitar and the flageolet as a child, dissecting corpses as a medical student, living penniless as a fledgling artist, witnessing the fiasco of the rehearsal of his first Mass, creating a scandal by shrieking out (with his band of conspirators) during a performance at the Opéra, watching the catastrophic performance of his Rome Prize cantata or the abortive first rehearsal of the *Symphonie fantastique*, auditioning as a chorister for the Théâtre des Nouveatés, planning vengeance against Camille Moke and attempting suicide on the Ligurian coast (from which he creates a chapter out of a comic novel), conversing happily about hunting in Italy, complaining bitterly about choral singing in Paris. Whenever possible he transcribes his conversations directly, in a theatrical manner. The humorous way in which he describes the reception he received from his colleagues at the Villa Médicis sounds like something out of Balzac: this kind of artist's joke can also be found in *La Rabouilleuse*. Also like Balzac is

Berlioz's habit of imitating in prose the foreign accents of Cherubini and Guhr, or the Italian of the outlaw Crispino and of the wife of the Roman countertenor, or the elementary French spoken by the usher at the Institute. Berlioz reproduces his comical conversations with a policeman in Nice, with the directors of the Opéra and Théâtre Lyrique in Paris, and with various persons who came to him with extravagant requests for favors, but he also reproduces his more serious conversations with the King of Prussia and the King of Hanover, who bestowed upon him their compliments, and with Estelle Fornier, whom he loved until the end. He gives musical quotations when music communicates better than words. He is especially sensitive to contrast, such as that between the grandeur of Saint Peter's Cathedral and the insipid music that he heard there. He knows well how gradually to vary an atmosphere: one of the most admirable pages of the *Mémoires* may be found in the letter addressed to Liszt, from the *Travels in Germany*, where Berlioz recounts the anguish of his life as an itinerant composer who must constantly direct concerts in foreign cities with orchestras he does not know, the difficulty of preparing the materials, the desperation of the first rehearsals, and then, little by little, after four days of trial and tribulation, the mastery of the score and its triumphant performance under the baton of the composer who, filled with rapture, speaks of having "played the orchestra."

Such moments, when a long-meditated dream had become a carefully crafted work of art, were for Berlioz his true *raison de vivre*. In these singular *Mémoires*, where wisdom and enthusiasm, reflection and haste, gravity and humor, evasiveness and passion succeed one another with tremendous vitality and élan, let us recognize, sometimes in the foreground, sometimes more concealed, the image and the voice of an artist who was free, proud, truthful, and exacting: a prince.

Translated by Peter Bloom

10 The short stories

KATHERINE KOLB

Berlioz made it easy to become acquainted with his short stories when he included them in *Les Soirées de l'orchestre*, a comic masterpiece that appeared in 1852 and has remained in print to this day. The creation of that volume out of previously published stories, biographies of composers, and other journalistic writing about music was a stroke of literary genius parallel to the musical inspiration, six years before, of *La Damnation de Faust*, which cast into dramatic form the individual scenes he had set from Goethe's poem in 1828. Of such mid-career recastings the most famous contemporary example was Balzac's *Comédie humaine*, announced in 1842 on the basis of previous and projected writings, and still in progress at the writer's death in 1850. It seems fitting that Berlioz should mention Balzac at the start of both *Les Soirées* and its sequel of 1859, *Les Grotesques de la musique.* By their extraordinary range and variety, Berlioz's two volumes put one in mind of a human comedy of the musical world – comedy both in the usual sense of farce, wit, irony, and humor, and in the Balzacian sense (derived from Dante) of drama in the world-theatre of human events.

In *Les Soirées de l'orchestre*, the Balzacian voice of high drama is accentuated by the prominence of three melodramatic short stories, all of which feature idealistic artist heroes at odds with the prosaic world around them.[1] Their outlook is reproduced in the framework of the volume, which invites us to a series of "evenings" (*soirées*) at the opera – not on stage, but in the orchestra pit of a provincial opera company during the performance of insipid, currently fashionable operas. What goes on in the pit, among a cast of characters listed at the opening, thus parallels the stage action but in effect cancels it out. The musicians' conversation and readings perform in the volume as a whole what is epitomized in the Eighteenth Evening under the name of *feuilleton du silence*: a piece of writing that deals entertainingly with something – anything – other than the work in question. (The *feuilleton* was the literary "feature" of the major French papers, in particular the *Journal des débats*, where Berlioz was music critic from 1835 to 1863.)

This indirect approach to music characterizes much of Berlioz's writing. Relatively little of his journalism corresponds to what we now think of as music criticism – the commentary or analysis of a specific piece of music. (He collected the essence of what he wrote in that genre – of which, along with E. T. A. Hoffmann and Robert Schumann, he was one of the creators – in *À travers chants.*) Such criticism – Berlioz called it *la critique admirative* – was fundamentally suspicious of words; its spirit prevails in a kind of silence that stops all conversations, in *Les Soirées*, when a masterpiece is performed. Whereas words suppress bad music, great music resonates through their absence. The literary silence is broken only by the title of the revered work (the others go unnamed), and by various expressions of emotion – again resorting to words. On one such occasion, in the Twenty-second Evening (*Iphigénie en Tauride* is being performed), excess of emotion generates a brief story: the concertmaster Corsino, whose name and fiery character are in keeping with the Napoleonic theme that pervades the volume, is overcome by the music and must be led away; whereupon he and "the Author" commune silently before a bust of Gluck.

Like Hoffmann, then, whose musical *Novellen* were popular at the time, Berlioz was a creative writer for whom music happened to be the chief concern. His colorful *Mémoires*, his exuberant correspondence, even his classic *Traité d'instrumentation* have a literary appeal independent of what they say about music. But to those concerned with music they are doubly important for what they reveal of Berlioz's musical values and beliefs, and in that respect few of his writings are as revealing as his fiction. The stories discussed below belong to the same imaginative world as the symphonies, the opera *Benvenuto Cellini*, the *Requiem*, and *La Damnation de Faust*. Like the *Symphonie fantastique*, they are "episodes in the life of an artist" – variations of that symphony's story of an artist who falls in love, is betrayed, and takes revenge.[2] They were published as the equivalent of romantic manifestoes in the *Revue et Gazette musicale*, a music journal dedicated to the cause of high art (and of music as the highest of the arts) espoused by their heroes.[3] Fictional counterparts to *la critique admirative*, midway between the satirical *feuilleton du silence* and the worshipful silence of the musical evenings, they force us to question the relation between their narratives of love and violence and the artistic ideals they propound.

Le Premier Opéra (1837)

The *nouvelle du passé* or "story of the past" that opens the First Evening is the product of an unusually precise historical circumstance: it is a revenge fantasy provoked by the cancellation of the première of Berlioz's *Requiem*. The setting derives from the memoirs of the renaissance sculptor Benvenuto Cellini, hero of Berlioz's recently composed opera.

In a letter to Cellini, the young composer Alfonso della Viola rages over the blow he has suffered to his career and his pride. The Grand Duke of Florence, who had invited him, on the occasion of wedding festivities, to fulfill his dream of a revolutionary music drama, has called the great production to a halt: he has changed his mind. Della Viola is dissuaded from violence by Cellini who, though no stranger to murder, recommends success and fame as the best revenge. Cellini supplies the money to produce the new work, stipulating only that his friend never again allow the Duke to benefit from his favors. Yet two years later, much to Cellini's disgust, that is what the now-celebrated composer appears to do. He is in fact carrying out his revenge. As all Tuscany gathers to hear his latest work, he spirits away the music and sends a message: he, too, has changed his mind. The disappointed populace breaks out in a riot, venting its fury on the Duke.

Love is missing, at first glance, from this plot; women figure only as "that malicious bitch," Mme d'Étampes, Cellini's enemy at the French court, and as hovering ladies who attest the hero's fame. On second look love is omnipresent, beginning with the plot of "the first opera," whose subject – disconcerting in view of the wedding occasion – is the adulterous passion of Paolo and Francesca evoked in Dante's *Inferno*. It is an "exquisite love," full of "abandon, melancholy, and chaste passion," violently crushed by the avenging husband but subsisting even among the "frenzied screams" of the damned – a scenario recalling the apocalyptic parts of Berlioz's *Requiem*. Della Viola's own story follows a similar course. His tale is none other than a metaphorical love story in which music is the object of passion. "Music is my Juliet," he declares, "and by God, she loves me!" The expletive has literal force. Passionate, reciprocated love – the Romeo-and-Juliet form of love, which is also that of Paolo and Francesca – is itself a sacrament; to cross it is sacrilege. Seduced by "golden words" that had "filled an artist's heart and kindled an artist's imagination," Della Viola is like a lover betrayed. The Duke's "incredible violation of the most positive promises" constitutes a crime worthy of a Dantesque punishment.[4]

Le Suicide par enthousiasme (1834)

At the end of his *Mémoires* Berlioz asks, rhetorically, whether love or music is the greater power, hinting at an answer – music can evoke love, love cannot evoke music – but leaving it in the air. At the very center of *Les Soirées de l'orchestre* he places a story that answers the question unequivocally. "This story proves that music is a passion like love," declares

Corsino, its author. But more than analogy is at stake. For the hero, musical and human love are rival passions of which the musical one proves immeasurably superior, because its object is so far superior to mortal women.

The two kinds of love occupy two intersecting stories: one of love for a woman; one of love for an opera. Both stories concern a young violinist who earns his living (like the conversationalists in *Les Soirées*) in the pit of a provincial opera orchestra. In the first or "frame" story Adolphe, a fanatical admirer of Gluck in the glory years of the Napoleonic empire, observes with suspicion the growing reputation of *La Vestale*, a new opera by Spontini. Yet when his company performs it, he finds it a revelation: he falls in love. Tormented by the "beating and torturing" of his idol under inadequate performances, incensed by the enthusiasm it nevertheless excites, he insults the audience, loses his job, and – undaunted – travels to Paris to hear the work at the Opéra. After the performance, dreading a return to ordinary life, he shoots himself.

Such a musical love-death forms a seamless ending for the simple story that "proves" Corsino's analogy. Helpfully, the chosen masterpiece bears the name of a woman. Adolphe's passion for the opera encompasses his love for the character Julia to whom the title refers and, further, his admiration for the great singer (Mme Branchu) who performs the role.[5] In anticipation of the performance, he rushes about like a romantic lover, "talking, singing, gesticulating like an escaped lunatic"; during the weeks preceding, he refrains from entering a theatre in order to preserve his "musical virginity."

If he is so careful to be worthy of the virginal *Vestale*, it is partly because he was once unfaithful to "her" – an adventure that forms the subject of the second, inner story. On the point of leaving for Paris, Adolphe is diverted from his goal by Hortense, a brilliant but superficial musician with whom he falls passionately in love. The affair unravels in a scene that anticipates the aftermath of the climactic performance of *La Vestale*. Lying at the feet of his mistress, Adolphe revels in "the melancholy happiness [. . .] that follows the great climaxes of voluptuous bliss" and envisions death as the only possible sequel. Art alone might offer an alternative. Suddenly recalling *La Vestale*, he speaks "her" name – and the spell is broken: Hortense makes a face and calls the work "boring." Adolphe jumps up, as though finding an "unclean animal" in the grass, and paces the floor in fury. Hortense bursts out laughing – a "high, cackling laugh [. . .] harsh, impudent, and shameless" that confirms her as "unclean" and marks her as not only shallow but monstrous. In a swift and decisive exorcism, Adolphe insults her – a token retribution – and departs.

By an ironic twist, Hortense turns up once more after his death, as though the storyteller (if not the hero) cannot quite let go. She recognizes him in front of the opera house and shamelessly identifies him as a rejected suitor, thereby substituting a grotesque, socialite version of his story for his grand gesture. "Poor Adolphe!" exclaims the narrator. The hero is right to quit an existence in which, as he concludes, "all women are more or less like Hortense" and society, by extension, is like "all women."

Yet "poor Adolphe" is not Berlioz's last word on the artist-hero, any more than Werther was Goethe's. However idealistic its motives, suicide verges dangerously on impotence and defeat: it lands Adolphe at his mistress's feet, once again, but without the power to rise up and denounce her.[6] In *Le Retour à la vie (Lélio)*, the monodramatic sequel to his *Symphonie fantastique*, Berlioz had already provided an alternative outcome, summoning the Artist to live for his art. One of the chief signs of his resurrection is satire: the witty combative tongue with which the speaker (Lélio) lashes out against current ills. Satire infiltrates *Le Suicide* through the narrator, wise to the heroine's wiles and prone to stepping outside the First Empire time-frame to ironize about Parisian high society hostesses of the eighteen-thirties. Like many romantic heroes, Adolphe is best rescued from the appearance of feminine weakness by his brusque dealings with women – besides Hortense, officious women on the stagecoach to Paris, whose attentions he wards off with sardonic humor.

Euphonia, ou la ville musicale (1844)

If the hero of *Le Suicide par enthousiasme* is incomplete as an artist, it is partly because he lacks a mentor (though the composer Persuis, who aids him in Paris, hints at one). Cellini plays such a role for the composer of *Le Premier Opéra*. In the third part of Berlioz's narrative trilogy, the story *Euphonia* that occupies the Twenty-fifth Evening, a mentor figure not only counsels the hero but ends up – with disastrous results – taking his place.

In this "story of the future," a mini-novel in length and complexity, the hero, to be precise, has split in two. Shetland, whose name hints vaguely at British reserve and control, is a mature, celebrated composer occupying the highest offices of the "musical city." By contrast, the younger composer-hero bears a name evocative of turbulent emotions – "Xilef" reverses the Latin *felix*, happy – and even, with its graphically expressive initial, of destructive violence. In the course of the story, during which they successively love and are betrayed by the same woman, the heroes partially change roles. Xilef learns self-control, though only to carry out with cold-blooded precision a horrifying Judgment Day vengeance followed by suicide. Shetland, his Olympian calm already undone by love, goes mad.

Images of cataclysmic violence in the beginning intimate the cosmic stakes involved in this undoing of men by a woman. The theme of fidelity, explicitly linked with music, binds the love story to the musical utopia of the title.[7] As a city dedicated to the faithful performance of great music, Euphonia worships Gluck, the famous reformer of Italian musical "promiscuity" in the name of textual fidelity. The story's climactic scene includes a festival performance of Gluck's opera *Alceste*, the ultimate story of patriarchal fidelity – that of a woman prepared to sacrifice her life for her husband's. Like Alceste, women in Euphonia know their place. Indeed all Euphonians exist to serve a city that is both orchestra (or opera house) and conservatory writ large. As a performing unit it is under the absolute rule of a "master," either conductor or composer. (Shetland, like Berlioz, is both.) As a music school it operates under a Spartan regime that regulates living quarters, course of study, and behavior to the minutest detail: unruly concert applause is banned, for example, in favor of choral acclamation. Emotional expression is the supreme value, but emotion itself is absent, or at least very rigidly controlled.

Shetland incarnates the Euphonian paradox of the absence of emotion in the service of emotion. Whereas Xilef is unhappily in love, Shetland, whose beloved is dead, is free of passion and suffering and in consequence, he declares, artistically the more alive.[8] The ideal woman, it would appear, is a dead woman.

That is indeed the message of the story, which tells the calamitous intrusion of an untamed woman into the gentle Euphonian harmony. The heroine, a new Eve, appears to Shetland in an Edenic garden, both as "goddess" and "dangerous animal" – a snake to be crushed. She begins by disrupting the form of the story. Although *Euphonia* is preceded (like *Les Soirées* as a whole) by a list of *dramatis personae*, it opens (like *Le Premier Opéra*) as an epistolary "novel." In two letters to Shetland, Xilef satirizes musical conditions in Italy – an anti-Euphonia in which singers are gods, composers their slaves – and confesses his jealous love for a brilliant and beautiful but unworthy singer.[9] Before Shetland can respond, their correspondence is interrupted by a dramatic interlude that takes us to meet the heroine in her dressing room in Paris. Tired of Xilef and intrigued by the reputation of Shetland, she resolves to go to Euphonia to sing in the Gluck Festival, meanwhile sending Xilef on a wild-goose chase to America. The men's correspondence resumes with a letter from Shetland telling his love story with a beautiful stranger – both a new version of Genesis and a

Pygmalion story (or Taming of the Shrew) in which the heroine, intending to seduce, is herself seduced and transformed.

But the transformation is illusory; disaster is merely postponed. We hear the dire ending in a third-person narrative – the heroes' dialogue is beyond repair – that tells of Xilef's return to Euphonia and discovery of the object of his pursuit, already unfaithful to his friend. No vengeance is too extreme for her multiple betrayals: of two men and two artists, of love and music, of society and art, threatened to their very foundations by her sexual and artistic promiscuity.[10] Spurred by a righteous zeal, Xilef plots an elaborate punishment. To the sounds of a newly invented piano-orchestra, the heroine, her lovers, and all in attendance are crushed in a gruesome finale that reduces the musical city to silence.

Despite elements of science fiction, *Euphonia* remains squarely within the realist tradition. Berlioz was little interested – his *Symphonie fantastique* notwithstanding – in the fantastic as a mode of storytelling, popularized in France by Hoffmann, in which the reader is drawn into an unsettling hesitation over uncanny events. The miraculous and the supernatural serve him chiefly, as they had the neoclassics, for satire and humor: the sea creatures and birds who escort Jenny Lind in P. T. Barnum's hyperbolic staging of the singer's reception in America (recounted in the Eighth Evening);[11] the piano which, subjected to thirty examination performances of the same concerto, begins to play the piece on its own (as told in the Eighteenth).

Yet the sources of hesitation in his writings are many. Humor creates its own uncertainties: at what point, we sometimes wonder, is Berlioz pulling our leg? Where are the boundaries between history and fiction?[12] At what point does satire tip over into sympathy, comedy into tragedy – or the reverse? To what extent is Berlioz to be identified with his heroes? And – when we wish to study his stories – what, in his writings, are we to count as story? Besides the eight labeled *nouvelles*, much of the historical material – biography, travel narrative, depiction of the strange customs of the musical world – is often indistinguishable from fiction. In the Second Epilogue, the biography of Méhul, an enthusiast and protégé of Gluck, reveals another Adolphe or Alfonso della Viola; at the end of the volume, the narrative of the composer William Wallace's adventures among New Zealand cannibals replays the carnage of *Euphonia* in a comic vein reminiscent of *Candide*.

The narrative impulse, in Berlioz, related to the dramatic impulse, is in fact a constant that generates stories at every turn. Single words, letters, or sounds are enough to trigger a story: the tragi-comic tale of a prompter, for example, undone by the conductor's relentless "tack" on the prompter's box; or the tale of a composer misreading his librettist's handwritten "s" and turning innocence into high drama. These, and the countless stories arising in the span of a mere sentence or paragraph, betoken a mind quick with word-play, fertile in metaphor, and alert to the dramatic potential of personification and allegory. Because *la musique* is grammatically feminine, for example, music is readily personified as a woman. "She" is then allegorized in different guises – as Andromeda, Cassandra, Juliet, or a simple "street girl whom the world wants to turn into a prostitute." The Tenth Evening, a "pamphlet" on "The Present State of Music," stages a lengthy dialogue between "Music," pleading abandonment and misery, and a government minister who harangues her for her sins. (An equal opportunity satirist, Berlioz aggressively targets the male criminals of the music world as well, including the Emperor of "the Romans" – the opera claque – in the Seventh Evening, and the tenor whose rise and fall enact a moral tale of a different sort, in the Sixth.)

Besides the three *nouvelles* discussed above, two others were also published separately, as such, and deserve special attention here.[13]

Le Harpiste ambulant (1849)

This Second Evening tale, latest in original date of the five discussed here, is furnished in *Les Soirées* with a double frame. Asked by the players to relate an adventure from his German travels, the Author recalls his meeting with the harpist of the title, who then tells his story. *Le Harpiste* is a "story of the present" as opposed to *Euphonia*, a "story of the future," and to *Le Premier Opéra*, a "story of the past." (*Le Suicide* – "a true story" – is from the recent past.) In time and setting it thus comes closest, in Berlioz's fiction, to a typical story by Hoffmann, Balzac, or Mérimée, in which a participant-narrator evokes a scene from ordinary life that takes an unexpected turn. First published as a "Letter from Bohemia," the story could almost be mistaken for one of Berlioz's travel letters about music, a genre he inaugurated during his concert tour of 1842–1843.

The narrator – "Berlioz" – describes being halted, on a rail journey from Vienna to Prague, by a washed-out portion of track. Conveyed unceremoniously by cart to a connecting station, he and the other travelers await another train. During this interval unexpectedly cleared by the elements, in this unidentified no-man's land where class distinctions and social schedules are temporarily washed away, he encounters an itinerant harpist. Music acts as a prelude to their conversation, and as signal that we have left the domain of "reality": whereas in *Euphonia* the lovers meet to the ominous strains of the *idée fixe* (from Shetland-Berlioz's first symphony), here the harpist and composer meet to the whimsical theme of the Queen Mab Scherzo from Berlioz's symphony *Roméo et Juliette*.

Queen Mab sets the tone of this high-spirited tale, at times almost a parody of the dramatic ones.

Though of different social conditions, the two traveling musicians turn out to be brothers under the skin. The harpist is another Berliozian double, prone to melancholy, swooning ecstasies in listening to music, and technical experiments with his harp. He too has a love story – one of simultaneous love for two women, incarnations of the two heroines of Weber's *Freischütz*, whom he visits on alternate days. At the discovery that one of the women is deceiving him, he flies into a jealous rage, shoots his rival, and is instantly "cured" of his double love. (It occurs to him that his rival has equal cause for complaint; it does not occur to him that the same is true of the women.)

Satire takes over the remainder of the story, sparked by the harpist's quixotic plan to give concerts in Paris. A cascade of anecdotes conveys – and mimics – the glut of music in the French capital, and spills over into the burlesque tale (quite irrelevant, as the harpist points out) of a singer of *romances* and her husband who, performing for an unappreciative sultan in Constantinople, narrowly escape being thrown into the Bosphorus.

Vincenza (1833)

A brief "sentimental story" by label, *Vincenza* has no musical theme, nor did it appear in the *Revue et Gazette musicale*; it was published in the short-lived cosmopolitan journal *L'Europe littéraire*. Set in Italy, it is placed in *Les Soirées* after the Italian story of the First Evening (*Le Premier Opéra*) to which it supplies, as it were, the missing love episode. But the heroine, an Italian mountain girl, is the very opposite of the Parisian Hortense. Passionately in love with G***, a painter and fellow-resident of the narrator's at the French Academy in Rome, Vincenza is unjustly accused of infidelity; the painter banishes her without mercy. In despair, she resolves to kill herself. The narrator ("Berlioz") speaks in her defense, arguing – to her rather indifferent lover – that her despair could serve as the subject of an "admirable" painting. G*** agrees to verify the facts, and promises – if she is innocent – to leave a key at the door of his studio. Relaying the good news, the go-between neglects to mention that the painter has changed studios. Vincenza sees the key missing, like Aegeus the black sails, and throws herself into the Tiber.

From its audience in the orchestra pit, the story merits only a hiss and a bit of raillery: the sentimental French storyteller (Turuth, in Berlioz's *dramatis personae*) should stick to his flute-playing. But if Berlioz is here mocking himself (he is, after all, a former flute player), he has retained the story, an early variation on his familiar theme of jealousy in love. In *Le Suicide*, Alphonse reaches for "Othello's pillow" at the sound of Hortense's shrill laugh; in *Euphonia*, Xilef threatens to "imitate Othello" should he find his beloved unfaithful. What is significant about *Vincenza*'s version of the Othello plot is that it is imagined from Desdemona's point of view. It is a difficult point of view to maintain: even the sympathetic narrator forgets Vincenza's innocence long enough to promise that she will be "forgiven." Yet it is with the passionate Vincenza that Berlioz most deeply identifies, not her colorless lover, just as he identified from adolescence with the suffering of Dido abandoned.[14] In "loving" *La Vestale*, he (or Adolphe) likewise identifies not so much with Julia's lover, Licinius, as with Julia herself – and with Mme Branchu, who impersonates Julia so magnificently that Adolphe, for her sake, might be reconciled to her sex. Suffering and emotion are the great levelers, even of gender: Corsino, overcome with emotion in performing Gluck, resembles Mme Branchu, who – modeling a kind of "suicide from enthusiasm" – faints on stage in *La Vestale*.[15]

As a critic, Berlioz warned (like Shetland) of the practical consequences of such emotion, capable of making a concertmaster or a star soprano lose control on the stage. As a writer of fiction, he conjured up some of the deeper anxieties triggered by the romanticist opening up to feminine emotional states, and dramatized some of the strategies marshaled in self-defense. Three of those strategies stand out: the claim for genius of god-like mastery and power; the solidarity of (male) artists; the starkly polarized image of women. Genius admits – even requires – "feminine" emotion and suffering, as long as it remains under masculine control. Woman's image admits – even idealizes – her brilliance and power, as long as it is in the service (and under the control) of men.[16]

Of the stories, *Euphonia* best illustrates just how volatile those conditions can be. For one brief moment, the otherwise reviled heroine is a model of feminine glory – a statuesque Mme Branchu. Her performance of an aria from *Alceste* is an act of multiple submissions: a recanting of florid ornamentation and its licenses; a corresponding pledge of allegiance to the composer and to the ethos of textual fidelity; an identification with the nobly sacrificial heroine of the opera; a gesture of obeisance to Shetland, who has "created" her as an artist. Yet it is also a demonstration of power. She produces an effect such that it eclipses the festival performance of Gluck's opera, even Shetland's own success. His response is correspondingly ambivalent. Stirred by the "august scene" but moved by a jealous urge to contain an enthusiasm that is getting out of hand, he strikes up the instrumental march from *Alceste*. Order returns with the silencing of the solo voice and the orchestral worship, to the conductor's beat, of the common god, Gluck.

As in *Le Suicide*, the tragic ending is prefigured in another moment of excess, that of bliss after love-making. Shetland proposes a joint suicide. At the heroine's refusal, he has a premonition of her relapse into unworthiness: could she be "a mere woman" after all? Yet his own aspiration to die in the arms of his beloved is attended by the same ambiguities as the suicide of Adolphe. The self-annihilation that he urges as proof of nobility of spirit uneasily foreshadows his lapse into "mere" womanhood in his final, Ophelia-like madness.

Music, declared Berlioz, should not simply entertain; it should also disturb. His stories likewise disturb, and deserve, like all his writings, a reading alert to their nuances and contradictions. Beyond the text, such a reading needs to consider the various madnesses – political, social, and personal – threatening at the time of their writing. *Euphonia* was born during a period of mounting revolutionary (including feminist) rumblings, on the one hand, and of professional and private crisis in Berlioz's life, on the other. Fairly bristling with allusions to both, the story seems to offer early allegiance to a Second Empire. When that Empire came into being simultaneously with *Les Soirées*, in 1852, *Euphonia* served to crown the volume, epitomizing Berlioz's musical philosophy and enhancing the Napoleonic theme that he emphasized throughout. But whereas Napoléon I, who had commissioned *La Vestale*, stood for a society open to talent and generous towards art, his nephew Napoléon III was to prove as unworthy a patron, for Berlioz, as the Grand Duke of *Le Premier Opéra*. Disillusioned and embittered, Berlioz turned again to his writings, where he could both vent his frustration and forge a world to his liking. His *Mémoires* constitute, in that sense, his ultimate story, one of awakening in adolescence to music and to love, and of comfort in old age through the unexpected return of the woman he loved as a youth. In the still-ardent glow of his early passions, his "tale of sound and fury" – to borrow from his own Shakespearean epigraph – finds a tenuous happy ending.

11 The criticism

KATHARINE ELLIS

For Berlioz, music journalism was a double-edged sword: a financial necessity and a burden, on the one hand; an opportunity to make his views heard and to change public taste, on the other. During nearly four decades of activity as a music critic he left over nine hundred journalistic items ranging from opera and concert reviews to stories, discussions of aesthetics, and technical articles on conducting, organology, and pitch.[1] Musical insight and literary flair combined to produce a body of criticism unparalleled in its richness but tinged, for the modern reader, with the regret that in writing so much journalism Berlioz necessarily wrote less music. Yet in using criticism to justify his art, Berlioz was at the forefront of a nineteenth-century tradition presaged by E. T. A. Hoffmann and continued by both Schumann and Wagner – a tradition of educative and even propagandistic writing (at its Wagnerian extreme) that acknowledged and attempted to close the gap between avant-garde composition and a predominantly bourgeois public with considerable purchasing power but conservative taste.

The peril of such didactic writing lay in the critic's duty to denounce what he saw as artistically suspect, which in Berlioz's case meant the music of contemporaries almost all of whom were more commercially successful than he. As a critic of integrity, Berlioz had little option but to allow his readership to know, or at least to glean, his own points of view; as a composer in need of support from more established figures at the Opéra, Conservatoire, and Académie des Beaux-Arts, he could ill afford to be perceived as a petulant spoiler of reputations. Inevitably, the critic's mantle, which gave him the power to judge others (and a defensive "weapon," as he notes in chapter 47 of the *Mémoires*, without which he felt unacceptably vulnerable), became an obstacle to his own career. His central problem was that he canonized only the dead and lampooned too many of the living.

Although Berlioz contributed to a dozen newspapers during his journalistic career, his regular paid work came from only two, on which I shall concentrate here: the Bertin brothers' daily and politically mobile *Journal des débats*, for which he was music critic from 1835 (and, in addition, opera critic from 1837) until 1863; and Maurice Schlesinger's *Revue et Gazette musicale de Paris*, on whose masthead his name appeared from its

foundation in 1834 until the year before his death. Readers who sub-
scribed to the *Journal des débats* looked to the feuilleton running across
the bottom of each page for light and largely non-technical relief from
the weighty political matters discussed above. By contrast, the *Revue et
Gazette*'s readers were both musically literate and, at least during
Schlesinger's directorship (through 1846), part of an experiment to bring
elements of German romanticism to French musical consciousness. Here,
Berlioz's reviews were emblematic of a new aesthetic in which "professional" critics such as François-Joseph Fétis and Castil-Blaze were supplanted by artists – both literary and musical – whose authority to write
about music came not from technical expertise but from first-hand experience of the processes of inspiration as applied to their own art.[2] In its
bringing together of writers and musicians, the *Revue et Gazette* provided
the ideal platform for a romantic idealist who had already, in articles
dating from 1823 onwards, proved his literary ability.

The literary stylist

Berlioz's most poetic moments are to be found in his "admirative criticism" of heroes, particularly Beethoven and Gluck.[3] His role in such articles is not to judge the quality of the music directly, but rather to explain
its beauties in such a way that a reader who has never heard it can nevertheless experience something of its effect through poetic description. The
technique is characterized by certain recurring elements, which may be
outlined as follows: sensitivity to rhythm in prose, often reflecting the
overall shape of the music; an ability to suspend closure and build to a
climax, thereby observing what Berlioz calls the *loi du crescendo* – "the law
of crescendo";[4] a drawing in of the reader through exhortations such as
"Listen!" or "See how . . .";[5] integration of technical explanations relating
to harmony, instrumentation, and phrase structure into poetic prose;
reference to the category of the romantic sublime, expressed either in
terms of the listener's extreme emotional reaction, or by means of analo-
gies of vastness and natural tempestuousness applied to the music itself;[6]
interpolation of literary quotations, often from Shakespeare or Virgil;
and, finally, an explicit distinction between Berlioz's own view and that of
(postulated) uncomprehending philistines – a device that neatly inter-
locks with the drawing in of the reader by encouraging a sense of solidarity: critic and reader become fellow initiates.[7]

Such elements are thickly scattered in one of the centerpieces of
Berlioz's criticism: the series of essays of 1837–1838 on the Beethoven
symphonies.[8] In this limited space, a single example of their application,

from the essay on the Allegretto of the Seventh Symphony, must suffice. Here, Berlioz mirrors the effect of cumulative rhythm reaching towards a climax and, finally, dying away as the movement reaches its close. Such prose is so organically – one might even say contrapuntally – written as to be impossible to excerpt without doing violence to the overall sense.

> It is rhythm again, a rhythm as simple as that of the first movement but different in form, that is the chief source of the incredible effect produced by the Allegretto. It is merely a dactyl followed by a spondee, struck without cease, sometimes in three parts, sometimes in one, then in all parts together. Sometimes they serve as an accompaniment; often they hold center stage; now they furnish the first theme of the short episodic fugue with two subjects in the strings. The rhythm first appears *piano* in the lower strings, and is soon repeated in a *pianissimo* full of sadness and mystery. It then passes to the second violins, while the cellos sing a kind of lament in the minor mode. The rhythmic phrase keeps rising from octave to octave until it reaches the first violins; they transmit it by way of a crescendo to the winds in the upper regions of the orchestra, where it explodes with full force. Thereupon the songful lament, now stated more energetically, becomes a convulsive wail, and incompatible rhythms compete harshly one against the other. These are tears, sobs, entreaties; they express a boundless sorrow, an all-consuming anguish. But after these heart-rending strains a glimmer of hope appears: a nebulous melody, pure, simple and sweet, sad, resigned, *like patience smiling at grief.* The basses alone keep up their inexorable rhythm beneath this melodious rainbow. To borrow again from English poetry:
>
> > One fatal remembrance, one sorrow that throws
> > Its black shade alike o'er our joys and our woes.
>
> After alternating several times between anguish and resignation, the orchestra, as if exhausted by its arduous struggle, is reduced to playing only fragments of the main theme; then it collapses and dies away. The flutes and oboes take up the theme again but in a faint voice; they are too weak to complete it. It is the violins who do so with a few barely audible pizzicato notes, after which the winds, reviving suddenly like the flame of a dying lamp, breathe a sigh over an indecisive harmony and – *the rest is silence.*
>
> The plaintive cry that begins and ends the movement is created by a tonic six-four chord that tends always toward its resolution; its harmonic incompleteness is the only way of concluding so as to leave the listener in uncertainty and increase the impression of dreamy sadness inevitably produced by all that precedes.[9]

Close attention to the beginning of this passage reveals structural features related to those of the music itself: repetition, stasis, and short phrases. Like the famous repeated-note theme that opens Beethoven's movement, the phrases at the beginning of Berlioz's description are cumulative, their internal structure delineated by direct repetition of individual words (such as "rhythm"), or by tripartite grammatical constructions involving either repetition ("sometimes . . . sometimes . . . then" – *tantôt . . . tantôt . . . puis*) or the use of parallel verbs with related modifiers ("Sometimes they serve . . . often they hold . . . now they furnish" – *quelquefois servant . . . souvent concentrant . . . ou fournissant*). Gestures similar to the 2 + 2 + 4 or AAB form of Beethoven's melody (one might wish to call it a "bar") are detectable not only in the two tripartite constructions mentioned (in which, it should be noted, the second follows directly from the first, thereby enhancing the rhythmic effect), but also in the first sentence, where the repetition of "rhythm" marks the second section of an AA′B structure with a parenthetical interpolation at the phrase "but different in form."

As Berlioz's attention shifts from analysis of the repeated-note theme to a consideration of the whole movement, two things happen: firstly, the taut structures of the opening give way to a more expansive narrative style devoid of internal repetition; secondly, the vocabulary becomes more emotive (the "songful lament," the "convulsive wail"), particularly with reference to the movement's lyrical elements. There is, however, no abrupt change, since Berlioz overlaps the beginning of the narrative ("The rhythm first appears") with the final phrase of his discussion of the repeated-note theme. Instead, there is a gradual acceleration and concomitant intensification – the *loi du crescendo* – as layer upon layer of poetic description leads from the static opening to the climactic reference to "all-consuming anguish" at the height of the movement. Such was the sophistication with which Berlioz could suggest the dynamics of music in prose.

But the Beethoven essays in *À travers chants*, rightly regarded by Berlioz and later commentators as the pinnacle of his critical art, are in fact unrepresentative of his criticism as a whole. Adapted from a set of reviews of concerts given by the Société des Concerts du Conservatoire, they were, even in their original versions, a spectacular example of Berlioz's ability to turn a conventional review into an occasional piece in which he was able to indulge his own passions. Comment on other pieces on the Conservatoire's programs was squeezed out as he concentrated virtually all of his attention upon the Beethoven. For *À travers chants*, the process of winnowing was further taken to its logical conclusion. Such selectivity and reordering, practiced on a larger scale in *Les Soirées de l'orchestre* and *Les Grotesques de la musique*, present an image of Berlioz the critic which is self-consciously literary. To recapture the experience of Berlioz the critic rather than Berlioz the literary perfectionist we need rather to return to the original context of his work: the journalistic articles themselves.

In a glass house

Much as he would have liked to, Berlioz could not choose the subjects of his reviews. His position at the *Débats* forced him to cover a succession of second-rate works which were only occasionally interspersed with operas that moved him to genuine enthusiasm. In his criticism of weaker offerings he was aided by a tradition, stemming from the late eighteenth century (when opera criticism was written by drama critics), that caused readers of the *Débats* to expect that an analysis of the libretto would precede an evaluation of the music. On occasion Berlioz gave them little else, allotting approximately three-quarters of his review to the libretto and the remaining one-quarter to the score and the performance. Alternatively, Berlioz used the strategy of truth by omission: rather than evaluating a weak opera in its entirety, he found it more palatable to home in on a few discernible artistic peaks, leaving most of the music judiciously hidden in the clouds below. (Since space in the *Débats* was restricted, this practice could plausibly be defended as a practical necessity.[10]) Such *feuilletons du silence* in the face of low-grade yet potentially successful works featured throughout Berlioz's critical career, and formed part of an extensive repertory of critical ruses intended as exercises in damage limitation.

One of the most important among such ruses stemmed from Berlioz's genuine view that no composer could make up for the deficiencies of a weak libretto if he faithfully followed its dramatic implications (as he believed any opera composer should). The circular fatalism of such an argument was invaluable to Berlioz in that it offered him the opportunity to express disapproval of certain passages while absolving the musician of blame: application of the technique to the unblushingly decorative and static music for the opening of Act II of Meyerbeer's *Les Huguenots*, for example, meant that he could avoid reproving Paris's most influential opera composer (with whom he shared the favor of the publisher Maurice Schlesinger). Indeed, it became a perverse, if unconvincing, proof of Meyerbeer's dramatic capacity that he should have failed to turn undramatic verse into dramatic opera.[11] As late as 1862, we find the same procedure in a review of Gounod's *La Reine de Saba*:

> It seems to me that this libretto is difficult to set, and must have made the composer's job arduous. M. Gounod is such an adroit [*habile*] musician that he has nevertheless succeeded in conveying the main dramatic situations. It is not his fault if he has not always been able to avoid the pitfall of monotony.[12]

Neither passage leaves the reader in any doubt as to Berlioz's opinion, but an almost courtly decorum is nonetheless preserved.

Berlioz likewise attempted to maintain propriety, when reviewing works that tested his diplomatic skills, by employing a deft and imaginative vocabulary. While his reviews of favored works are replete with superlatives and sublime oxymorons intended to overwhelm the reader, those treating music of lesser quality (as Berlioz perceived it) engendered a less powerful vocabulary, of which the word *habile*, applied to Gounod, is a prime example. Yet such "secondary praise," to borrow Kerry Murphy's term,[13] loaded with sarcasm and obviously pejorative, was arguably more damaging to Berlioz's compositional future than even outright condemnation would have been. His main objects of derision were the established composers of opéras comiques: Auber, Hérold, Adam, and, from the next generation, Ambroise Thomas – composers who, in Berlioz's opinion, had presided over the degeneration into vaudeville of a once-noble French tradition.[14] The following demolition of Adolphe Adam's *Le Toréador*, from the *Journal des débats* of 9 June 1849, is typical of the genre.

> On this canvas – a highly amusing one, I assure you – and for scenes of dialogue constructed in an extremely witty fashion (though you would hardly guess so from reading my own retelling of them), M. Adam has embroidered [*brodé*] some fine and charming arabesques [*charmantes arabesques*]. His music is upbeat [*gaie*], vivacious, farcical, and even, when the subject demands it, agreeably demoralizing.

The vocabulary of "secondary praise" makes up at least ten per cent of Berlioz's prose, the words *broder*, *charmant*, and *gai* being among his commonly employed expressions. The undermining of each positive with a negative is also characteristic. Moreover the bathetic oxymoron that ends the passage subjects Adam to cruel ridicule in a reworking of the "fidelity to the libretto" principle, which offers his hapless victim no escape from humiliation. Even in deprecation Berlioz observed the *loi du crescendo*, in a mode of criticism which he recognized as self-destructive but could not quell.[15]

The significance of Berlioz's criticism

It is to Berlioz's awareness of this tension, and to his ultimate inability to resolve it, that we owe much of the poignancy of his concert and opera criticism. We may usefully turn to Berlioz as a chronicler of his times and as an interpreter of the music of his contemporaries, but we must keep in mind that he was chiefly a chronicler of himself. Was he really talking about the arch-classical Henri Reber when he reviewed four of

Reber's symphonies as published by Richault in 1861?[16] Given his Hoffmannesque descriptions of the nocturnal workings of inspiration and the trials of a serious composer trying to convince publishers and orchestras of the quality of his music, I think not. Reber has only a walk-on part in what could be a Berliozian self-portrait dating from the eighteen-thirties. The Beethoven essays of 1837–1838 are similarly auto-biographical in that the details dwelt upon by the critic reveal something of the preoccupations of the composer as he prepared the dramatic symphony *Roméo et Juliette*: the use of thematic fragmentation to conclude a movement (the Funeral March of the *Eroica* Symphony and the Allegretto of the Seventh; Berlioz's opening crowd scene and *Roméo au tombeau des Capulets*); and the problem of finding a "bridge" to link the orchestral and choral portions of a symphonic work (the finale of Beethoven's Ninth; the dramatic symphony's orchestral and choral fugue on "Jetez des fleurs pour la vierge expirée"). Just as he wrote memoirs, confessional stories, and autobiographical compositions, so, too, did Berlioz use criticism to reflect on aspects of his own career.

The interdependence of composition and criticism meant that as soon as he ceased composing – his last significant work, *Béatrice et Bénédict*, was completed in 1862 – Berlioz was free to put down his critic's pen. In October 1863 he reviewed the young Georges Bizet's *Les Pêcheurs des perles*, given at the Théâtre Lyrique, and turned his closing paragraph into one last arrow aimed at the institution that had denied him operatic success in Paris:

> As for the Opéra, from time to time it puts on *La Favorite* and the other masterpieces in its immortal repertory. People are wrong to reproach it for offering nothing new: it has offered its resignation.[17]

But this time the protest was mostly rhetorical. For after forty years of struggle, Berlioz, too, had resigned.

12 The *Grand Traité d'instrumentation*

JOËL-MARIE FAUQUET

When Berlioz's *Grand Traité d'instrumentation et d'orchestration modernes* appeared at the end of 1843, the work was already known to the readers of the *Revue et Gazette musicale de Paris*, for it had been published there as "De l'instrumentation" – sixteen feuilletons that appeared from 21 November 1841 to 17 July 1842. In this series, whose "heroes" are the instruments of the orchestra, Berlioz considers that aspect of musical composition in which he had proven to be particularly inventive. The works that he had already written – three symphonies, the *Requiem*, *Benvenuto Cellini* – demonstrated the essence of what he brought to the art of instrumentation. In fact his interest in the subject seems to have been born with his very first musical impressions, if we are to believe his early letters, his first articles, and especially his *Mémoires*.

Beyond his own taste and intuition, what kind of guidance could be found, in the eighteen-twenties, by a young composer who was fascinated by the alchemy of the orchestra? "My two masters [Lesueur and Reicha] taught me absolutely nothing about instrumentation," writes Berlioz in chapter 13 of the *Mémoires*:

> I regularly attended all the performances at the Opéra. I would take along
> the score of the work to be played and would follow it during the
> performance. In this way I began to see how to write for the orchestra, and
> began to understand something of the timbres and accents as well as of the
> ranges and mechanisms of most of the instruments. By carefully comparing
> the effects produced with the means employed to produce them, I was able
> to see the hidden links between musical expression and the special art of
> instrumentation. But no one told me that this was the way to do it.

In the subject that became so crucial to his later career, it turns out, Berlioz was self-educated.

Such a situation could only reinforce the demands for fresh and sonorous musical invention made by a musician who so disliked everything that was commonplace. Furthermore, everything reveals that Berlioz himself was a most meticulous craftsman of timbres – the care with which he prepared his scores as well as the intransigence he displayed in his role as a critic – because he judged all performers on the basis of one inviolable criterion, namely, absolute respect for what the composer actually wrote.

Thus Berlioz, with his eagle eye, observed utterly everything. As an imaginative symphonist and gifted writer, he personified the "one-man orchestra" to the point of caricature. But of course, like other self-consciously romantic artists, Berlioz knew perfectly well that the very excessive behavior which led to caricature was a highly useful means of drawing attention to himself.

Because of his good relations with those in positions of political authority, Berlioz was solicited by the government to travel to London, in 1851, to judge the musical instruments presented at the first Universal Exposition. The report that he signed in the wake of this visit is somewhat disappointing because it is both general and brief.[1] But behind the conventional style required for this sort of report, one can sense the precision of an ear highly refined by extensive experience as an orchestral conductor. Indeed, it was the fear of having his own musical intentions misunderstood by others that led Berlioz to take up the conductor's baton in the first place. His concert tours abroad, especially his excursions to Germany at a time when wind instruments in particular were undergoing a series of improvements (as they were, also, in France), his associations with orchestra players, and his readings of the *méthodes* that were prepared for use at the Conservatoire – these things completed his education in such a way as fruitfully and intimately to join his identity as a conductor to his identity as a composer. For, unlike the majority of his peers, Berlioz did not compose at the piano; the only instrument he would ever really learn to play was the orchestra.

So it is not at all by chance, as one might imagine, that the high point of his career coincided with a high point in the development of instrumental manufacture, and that a second edition of the *Traité* became necessary only twelve years after publication of the first. This second edition, which appeared in 1855, was augmented by a chapter on new instruments (the saxhorn, the saxophone, Édouard Alexandre's organ-melodium and piano-melodium, the concertina, the octobasse, and others) and by a substantive appendix entitled *The Orchestral Conductor and the Theory of his Art.*

Early on, as we have seen, Berlioz paid close attention to the problems of instrumentation. What were the immediate circumstances that led him to consider them in a special treatise? He gives us a general answer to the question at the beginning of the work: that never before in the history of music had musicians so concerned themselves with this subject. In so saying Berlioz was no doubt thinking of the *Cours d'instrumentation considéré sous les rapports poétiques et philosophiques de l'art à l'usage des jeunes compositeurs*, which Georges Kastner published in 1839 as a complement to his own *Traité général d'instrumentation* of 1837. Kastner was the first to attempt to fill the gap articulated by Joseph Mainzer, in an article entitled "Sur l'instrumentation," in the *Gazette musicale* of 2 March 1834:

> At the present time, even the most polished composers lack a manual that presents the upper and lower limits of each instrument's range, the keys in which each sounds either strong or weak, and the kinds of passage work that are easy, or difficult, depending on the nature of each instrument's mechanism, and not only taken individually, but in combination with others.

In proposing to remedy this situation himself, Berlioz adopted a rather more open approach than did Kastner, inspired as he was (though without ever saying so) by two works of Antonin Reicha: the *Cours de composition musicale ou Traité complet et raisonné d'harmonie pratique* (1816–1818), and the *Traité de haute composition musicale* (1822). Reading these treatises one discovers that, when he was writing his own works, Berlioz not only followed to the letter certain notions articulated by his teacher (Reicha suggests constructing chords from kettle drums tuned to different notes, for example, as Berlioz later did in the *Grande Messe des morts*), but that he also developed his "spatial" notion of timbre, stretched out to the ideal proportions of a perfect orchestra of four hundred and fifty-six players, on the basis of the chapter of Reicha's *Traité* entitled "The Creation and Development of the Musical Idea."

Despite these foreshadowings, Berlioz's conceptions are nonetheless faithful reflections of his own personality. His fundamental principle, in true romantic fashion, is a subjective one, for the characteristic timbre of each instrument is categorized, on an affective scale, with the help of a system of comparisons openly colored by anthropomorphism. However, a second principle reins in the first by exposing it to the rationality of a practice that recalls what the author's imagination owed to the idea of positivism, so dear to the eighteenth century, according to which all forms of productivity depend upon personal experience. One of the reasons that Berlioz's treatise superseded those that had been written earlier – by Vandenbroeck (*c.* 1794), by Francœur as revised by Choron (1827), by Catrufo (1832), to mention but three – is precisely that, for the first time in a consistent manner, the function of each instrument is seen from an "interactive" point of view. That is, the morphological description of the sounding body is seen as inseparable from the particular capacity it possesses to express this or that emotion: the oboe is rustic, tender, timid; the clarinet is the "voice of heroic love"; the horn is noble and melancholy, and so on. The instrument no longer simply colors the musical discourse, it actually engenders it.

Thus, with Berlioz, one passes from instrumentation, which is a science, to orchestration, which is an art. Each instrument takes on its own color in accordance with that multiple entity that constitutes the inner self of the composer. Indeed, in a nineteenth century that charged music with so many purposes, the extent to which Berlioz charged it with *expression* – that key word – is something that hardly needs repeating.

For Berlioz, music first became expressive with Gluck. (Though it did not have to be, expressive music was most commonly associated with text.) Of the sixty-six numbered examples reproduced in the *Traité* and earlier mentioned in "De l'instrumentation," forty-five are taken from operas. In fact the voice itself takes its place in a particularly interesting and extensive chapter of the treatise. This said, however, it is revealing that Berlioz gives no examples from the works of Haydn or from earlier periods. He believes that before Gluck's great tragedies, the orchestra merely muttered a series of literally meaningless formulas. In "De l'instrumentation" there is one allusion to Bach, with reference to the use of the lute, but in the *Traité* the allusion was suppressed. This demonstrates how richly Berlioz's own instrumental style developed and blossomed forth from the emotional relationships the composer maintained with the works of those who first revealed to him the power of music: that "chosen few" of Gluck, Beethoven, Weber, and Spontini.

The larger context of the *Traité* is thus simultaneously rational and subjective. It is, in the true sense of the word, a *poetics*. But if Berlioz breaks new ground, he also breaks with the past rather less than one might be tempted to think. Thus, for example, in the comprehensive chapter devoted to the orchestra as a whole, the mechanistic concept of certain classic music theorists finds new life. In fact, for Berlioz, the orchestra is in itself a "grand instrument" comprised of "machines become intelligent, but subject to the action of an immense keyboard played by the conductor."

One especially provocative phrase in the *Traité* has captured the attention of twentieth-century readers: "Any sounding body employed by the composer is in fact a musical instrument." (This precept was not newly added when the text of the *Traité* was prepared, for readers of the *Revue et Gazette musicale* had already seen it in "De l'instrumentation.") Nonetheless it would be a mistake to insist upon Berlioz's modernity merely on the basis of this cardinal assertion. At most one can conclude from it that the ingenious individual with whom we are dealing was capable of pursuing his reasoning to its logical conclusion without necessarily feeling obligated to put it to a practical test. He would, after all, conclude his career with a mind closed to those whom he had a role in setting on their way, namely Wagner and Liszt – the controversial representatives of what was called at the time the "music of the future." Still, as is well known, the *Traité*, that would-be bible, which was soon translated into Italian, German, and English, and later into Spanish and Russian as well, would exert considerable influence over the years: indeed, a blueprint may be found here for the incomparably rich and abundant sonorities of the orchestras of Mahler and Strauss.

On 10 August 1842 Berlioz wrote to his brother-in-law Marc Suat that he was "putting the finishing touches" on a *Grand Traité d'instrumentation*:

> This is something that has long been lacking in the teaching of music and something that I have often been asked to undertake. My articles on the subject in the *Gazette musicale* only touched the surface, the bloom on the rose, and now I have had to redesign the book from the foundations up, filling in all of the small, technical details.

It should not be concluded from this that the book version of the text in some way invalidates the earlier, periodical version. It is simply that the *Traité* itself is first and foremost addressed to the apprentice composer, while the text of the article, "De l'instrumentation," published without a single note of music, is rather addressed to the cultivated amateur. Even in this form, the enterprise was more than a little daring, because Berlioz feeds the reader a prodigious quantity of technical details by no means easily digested, as the chapters on the flute and the horn demonstrate with particular force. What is more, he relies constantly on the reader's memory whenever he speaks of the instrument in a specific musical context, although here he limits himself to mentioning works most of which come from the grand Germanic tradition.

The inclusion of musical examples in the *Traité*, in full score, was a startling innovation, especially in view of the earlier works on the subject that we have mentioned. Otherwise whole chapters are lifted literally from the series that appeared in the *Revue et Gazette musicale*. At most, in refining his thinking, Berlioz removes certain phrases that were critical of the lacunae in the education offered at the Conservatoire – an understandable bit of repentance, since, if it was to withstand the test of time, a work of such ambition had to be free from the sort of hot-headed irritation produced by exasperation (such as his own) with anything and everything that was routine.

Rather more to be regretted is the omission, in the *Traité*, of certain passages in "De l'instrumentation" where the author speaks of what one might call the "archeology" of timbre, for here he goes so far as to express, at least implicitly, a desire to see the creation of a museum of musical instruments. (As the logic of French officialdom eventually had it, Berlioz did become director of the instrument museum at the Conservatoire, three years before his death, in 1866.) Finally, one may also regret the omission of several instruments considered in "De l'instrumentation": the lute, the baryton, the flageolet, the flute in G, and the dulcimer. Such omissions are compensated in the book publication, however, by the inclusion of articles on the bass tuba, the Russian bassoon, sets of bells, and (apparently a last-minute addition) the saxophone.

It is clear that the *Traité d'instrumentation* bears witness, at a given moment, to an evolution of which Berlioz, more than anyone else, knew how to take advantage – in his correspondence and, especially, in his music criticism. Indeed, the frequent reflections upon instruments and upon the orchestra that one finds in the musician's writings prior to 1840 constitute the ore from which much of the material of the *Traité* was extracted. Early on, and with an original approach, Berlioz begins to reconsider all aspects of the organization, function, and role of the orchestra, beginning with what one might call its disposition "in space." On several occasions he insists upon the fundamental importance of the proper acoustical placement of the orchestra, always in relation to the experience of the listener, something that leads him to deny the very existence of open-air music. For Berlioz it is not that the orchestra fills some preexistent space, it is rather that the orchestra generates its *own* space in accordance with the timbral combinations of the instruments. In this respect it is revealing to see the composer (who attended Alexandre Choron's funeral at the Invalides, on 9 August 1834) actually define in advance what would become the sonic configuration of his *Grande Messe des morts* – by means of the acoustical *dis*equilibrium which on that occasion marred the performance of the Mozart *Requiem*.

Berlioz, it is clear, viewed the orchestra from the vantage point of a sonic architect. His point of view as a critic thus reflected his point of view as a theorist – as may be seen, for example, in his article on the orchestration of Meyerbeer's *Robert le diable*.[2] Furthermore, it is on the basis of the weaknesses he perceived, particularly in theatre orchestras, that Berlioz advances, as from 1834, his own quite precise definition of the *ideal* orchestra. And to designate the person capable of composing for that ideal orchestra, which is at once a unity and a multiplicity, he forges an adroit neologism: the *instrumentaliste*.[3]

In the end we must remember that Berlioz sees the orchestra as sonic structure in and of itself, subject to the physical laws of sounding bodies each one of which, as a member of the larger ensemble, has its own peculiar characteristics. This conception determines the larger organization of the *Traité* into *families* of instruments: strings – plucked, struck, and bowed; winds – with reeds, without reeds, and with keyboard (the organ); brass – with mouthpieces; voices – high and low women's (with children and castrati), high and low men's; and percussion – with instruments both fixed and indeterminate in pitch. Far from resembling a cookbook, the volume embraces the small scale of the instruction manual and the grand scale of the epic. Enriched by numerous musical examples, the *Traité* remains of widespread contemporary interest because it is, above all, a consummate treatise on aesthetics.

Translated by Peter Bloom

PART IV

Execution

13 Performing Berlioz

D. KERN HOLOMAN

Berlioz left posterity an admirable performance legacy. The scores and parts published under his supervision and, for the most part, to his satisfaction, are sources that typically offer unambiguous direction as to his intent. They often reflect years of perfecting the manuscript materials in conjunction with live concerts under his own baton. His personal involvement with multiple performances of the symphonic works, unusual for its time (and far greater, for instance, than Beethoven's), led to meticulous and ongoing recomposition, and with his orchestration and conducting treatises he left useful guides to the performing forces at his disposal and his notions as to their most effective deployment.[1] His sensitivity to the practical issues of live music-making, if not always to the cost of music and musicians, makes his work feel somehow welcoming to those who undertake it. With the exception of perhaps a half-dozen passages of legendary difficulty, the music lies well beneath the fingers and is rewarding to discover and re-create – that is, to perform.

Berlioz the conductor left across Europe a generation of professional musicians schooled in how his music was supposed to go – though too few conductors committed to his cause. By the end of his life, most of the completed works had been well performed. A good proportion of these had been heard often and were familiar to serious listeners both in Paris and elsewhere; a few – the *Fantastique*, the Pilgrims' March from *Harold in Italy*, the *Roman Carnival* Overture, the Hungarian March from *Faust*, and portions of *L'Enfance du Christ* – were even popular: hummed in the streets, known to hundreds. After his death thinking musicians continued to promote the Berlioz legacy, at least so far as they could acquire the performance materials, and those who knew his life's story did it both from enthusiasm for these "lovely pages" and out of a sense of atonement for the difficulties the master had encountered in being understood.

Jules Pasdeloup (1819–1887) began to popularize some of the orchestral excerpts in his mass-market Popular Concerts, from 1861, and can be credited with the universal popularity of the so-called "Three Pieces from *The Damnation of Faust*": the Hungarian March, the *Ballet des sylphes*, and the Minuet of the Will-o'-the-Wisps. Édouard Colonne (1838–1910), whose orchestra concerts began in 1873, premiered a complete, well-rehearsed *Damnation de Faust* in February 1877, repeated it for six consecutive weeks, and eventually conducted more than one hundred and sixty performances of the work. The best orchestra in France was the Société des Concerts du Conservatoire, to which, despite its wary relationship with Berlioz as an active composer and potential conductor, he donated all his performance material in 1863. By 1918 the Société had used his collection to master, in the systematic fashion that was their habit, most of the major works.[2] Their version of *Roméo et Juliette*, undertaken in 1873 with the *Scène d'amour*, was completed in January 1879 under E.-M.-E. Deldevez (1817–1897) and became a staple of their repertory: they were the only orchestra in the world, it was said, capable of playing the Queen Mab Scherzo accurately and at sufficient speed.

The better French conductors (Colonne, Danbé, Taffanel, Gaubert, and, later, Dervaux and Prêtre; the notable exception is Messager) were for the most part familiar with *Les Troyens*, Berlioz's masterpiece, and there were important complete productions in Germany as from 1890.[3] In England, plans for a Covent Garden production were delayed by World War II, but in 1947 Thomas Beecham led a radio broadcast from the Maida Vale studios of the BBC, to which London enthusiasts flocked. In short succession came Sir Jack Westrup's 1950 reading of the work with the Oxford University Opera Club, the Westminster recording of *Les Troyens à Carthage* with the Société des Concerts under Hermann Scherchen (and a post-recording concert performance at the Palais de Chaillot on 10 May 1952), Rafael Kubelik's 1957 Covent Garden production of the complete opera, and a two-year project of the Chelsea Opera Group: concert performances of *La Prise de Troie* in 1963, and *Les Troyens à Carthage* in 1964. These undertakings did much to shape modern enthusiasm for *Les Troyens* in specific and for performing Berlioz in general: among those who participated in the Chelsea Opera Group at the time were David Cairns, Colin Davis, Roger Norrington, and John Eliot Gardiner, all of whom have played critical roles in later stages of the Berlioz "revival." By the time of the Berlioz centennial, in 1969, a coherent and visionary approach to *Les Troyens* was in place, resulting in Hugh Macdonald's publication of the score in the *New Berlioz Edition*, the lavish Covent Garden production of 1969, and the release of the first complete recording as, essentially, the flagship of the Colin Davis Berlioz Cycle for Philips Records. Musicians and music lovers alike thereupon discovered the majesty of *Les Troyens*: as a summary of the composer's art, as the last of the great lyric tragedies, as a worthy companion to *Tristan* and to *Otello*. If live performances remain exceptional, the main reason is the ongoing shortage of tenors trained for and capable of mastering the part of Aeneas – a difficult and taxing role, notably in the fifth act.

Today, as devoted scholars and performers look back on careers of promoting these masterpieces, they have reason to take pride in having established the order and breadth of Berlioz's artistic accomplishment. A vibrant critique of his life and work has replaced the old, unseemly jousting of partisans and detractors. The three operas (*Benvenuto Cellini, Les Troyens*, and *Béatrice et Bénédict*), left in 1869 without anything approaching standard texts, can now be brought to life more or less routinely. Lost works and artifacts of the composer's study, notably the *Messe solennelle* recovered in 1991, have resurfaced and taken their place in the Berlioz lore. Now it seems foolish to argue that Berlioz is any longer "misunderstood and misperformed."

But performing Berlioz still has its particular challenges. For one thing the Berlioz repertory demands rigorous forethought as to venue and personnel – and, as I have written elsewhere, not a little carpentry. The *Te Deum* cannot be done effectively without a pipe organ to the rear, behind the audience, an arrangement common only in French cathedrals and basilicas; *La Damnation de Faust* demands a choral force large enough for the men to be split into two distinct groups for one of its central moments; *Roméo et Juliette* requires its choruses of Capulets and Montagues (and an intermission for them to take their place on stage), a third chorus for the recitatives, and a contralto and tenor soloist who sing briefly at the beginning and then disappear. Berlioz's interest in musical instruments led him to employ novelties of manufacture and curiosities of antiquity that failed to achieve permanence in a typical orchestra's inventory. And still only a half-dozen titles are to be found in its orchestral library: the three pieces from *Faust*, the Royal Hunt and Storm from *Les Troyens*, the *Roman Carnival* and *Corsaire* overtures, the *Fantastique*, and *L'Enfance du Christ*.

So even if performers and listeners can take satisfaction in frequent live performances of the principal compositions and in the wide dissemination of their recordings, it would be wrong to consider the repertory fully discovered or the aesthetic issues of performing Berlioz fully engaged. One would not talk of a rich performance tradition for either the *Te Deum* (requiring its pipe organ and basilica) or *Benvenuto Cellini* (of which there is but a single recording, and for which adequate materials have only recently become available). And there is much fine music to be found among works hardly performed at all, especially in the short vocal works Berlioz developed for his own public concerts. Here, particularly, I think of *Zaïde* and *Sara la baigneuse*, where the only explanation as to why they are so frequently overlooked must be the difficulty of fitting single short works for voice and orchestra onto modern concert programs. Such ceremonial patriotic works as *Le Cinq Mai*, the *Hymne à la France*, *L'Impériale*, and even the *Chant des chemins de fer* are certainly worth an occasional hearing, too.

One might summarize the challenges of performing Berlioz, then, as those of finding the hardware and personnel on the one hand, and the software on the other.

Generally a modern symphony orchestra (ninety-some musicians: a dozen players in each string section, quadrupled winds) with an affiliated large choral society (one hundred and fifty to two hundred singers) is ample for the Berlioz repertory. The Société des Concerts, Berlioz's paradigm, numbered about eighty players and eighty professional singers – including opera virtuosi. Most of the necessary hardware – piccolo, English horn, E-flat and bass clarinet, light percussion – is in keeping with nineteenth-century norms. Among the exceptional requirements are the following:

WOODWINDS. Four bassoons are customary for the French orchestral repertory, owing to the smallish envelope of the instruments of the era; Berlioz occasionally writes four-voice chords for the bassoon section. The contrabassoon part in the *Francs-Juges* Overture may be omitted. There are instances of two and three simultaneous piccolos. While Berlioz arranged the *Chant sacré* (from the *Neuf Mélodies*) for six wind instruments invented or built by Adolphe Sax, including saxophone, the source – from early 1844 – is lost. Saxophones are otherwise nowhere required in Berlioz.

BRASS. Here lie some of the most critical issues of Berlioz performing practice, affecting all the sections. Though the piston- and rotary-valved chromatic horns were claiming a place during the epoch of the *Fantastique*, Berlioz himself preferred to write for natural horns, where the key of the instrument was established once per movement with a crook of appropriate length. (In the *Mémoires*, however, he comes out – not surprisingly – in favor of valved instruments.) Owing to the chromaticism of Berlioz's harmonic rhetoric, he thus often needs horns pitched in multiple keys. In *Roméo et Juliette*, for instance, the Love Scene calls simultaneously for first horn in E, second horn in F, third horn in high A, and fourth horn in D. While such parts are not intrinsically difficult for professional musicians either to read or to play, they do require of the conductor a particular mental gymnastic. Additionally there is a distinct loss of color when out-of-series pitches that would have been achieved by stopping the bell are played in conventional fashion. Be that as it may, it is important to execute the notated *sons bouchés* with the hand and not with a mute.

The Berlioz trumpet section usually consisted of two trumpets and two piston cornets, the latter having a sweeter, somewhat more delicate sound than modern trumpets. It makes sense to try pairs of modern trumpets and cornets in these cases. Additionally there is a lovely solo part for piston cornet in the waltz from the *Fantastique*, a later addition to the score that was probably composed for the great virtuoso Jean-Baptiste Arban (1825–1889).

Many informed listeners think that the greatest loss from the tone-color spectrum of nineteenth-century orchestras is caused by the modern practice of using three large, triggered double trombones in place of the alto–tenor–bass trio favored from Mozart to mid-century; a better compromise is to use two tenor trombones and a bass, or even, as sometimes favored by Berlioz, three tenor trombones. From the *Fantastique* (1830) through *Faust* (1846), Berlioz generally calls for ophicleide (a keyed bugle of airy tone quality and dubious pitch), or ophicleide and the old French revolutionary serpent still in use during that era for ecclesiastical chant. (The *Requiem* calls for *grand ophicléide monstre*, amusing to imagine but impractical to duplicate.) Starting with the *Marche funèbre pour la dernière scène d'Hamlet* (1843) he calls for ophicleide or tuba, or ophicleide and tuba. In the manuscript parts for *L'Impériale*, he replaces *ophicléide* with *saxhorn basse* and *tuba* with *tuba (saxhorn contrebasse)* (see below). Tubas will suffice for all these parts, but the baritone model is sometimes, as in the case of the *Dies irae* in the *Fantastique*, a better solution than the powerful all-purpose double-bass tuba.

Berlioz asks for a double quartet of saxhorns (soprano, contralto, tenor, and contrabass) in the *Marche troyenne* and a quartet of tenor saxhorns in the Royal Hunt and Storm from *Les Troyens*. For visual effect as well as for tone color, the latter – the most frequently performed excerpt from *Les Troyens* – might well be played on baritone horns. One recommended solution for the former is to use the E-flat cornet or trumpet, flugelhorn, French horn, and baritone tuba. The parts for saxhorn *suraigu* in the *Te Deum* and Trojan March are best played on a piccolo trumpet. A number of period-instrument brass bands in the United States own sets of saxhorns (and a matched set is pictured on the 7.7¢ stamp released by the United States Postal Service on 20 November 1976).

PERCUSSION. Each timpanist – Berlioz often calls for multiple players – requires a minimum of three pairs of mallets: hard, medium, and soft, to answer the composer's call for *baguettes de bois, de bois recouvertes en peau,* and *d'éponge*. The implication of Berlioz's sometimes puzzling use of these terms is that the leather-covered medium stick is the norm.[4] Recent developments in coating plastic drumheads duplicate the sound of nineteenth-century skin heads quite satisfactorily.[5] The ordinary orchestral snare drum has little use in Berlioz: for the fourth movement of the *Fantastique*, the *Symphonie funèbre*, the *Marche funèbre pour la dernière scène d'Hamlet*, and the *Marche pour la présentation des drapeaux* of the *Te Deum*, players should use snareless field or tenor drums.

The bells in the last movement of the *Fantastique* present the most celebrated of all the challenges in performing Berlioz, since the symphony is the second most frequently performed of all his works. (The *Roman Carnival* Overture is the first.) The customary acceptable solution is to use large suspended metal plates, available from percussion suppliers by rent; the customary unacceptable solution is to use standard tubular orchestral chimes. A still better course of action is to borrow the largest moveable G and C from a local carillon. (A half-dozen major orchestras in the United States have had their own bronze bells cast for the *Fantastique*, but those of the San Francisco Symphony, for example, sound an octave higher than Berlioz probably intended.)

The tuned antique cymbals in *Roméo et Juliette* and *Les Troyens*, which Berlioz first saw when he visited the museum in Pompeii, are generally replaced by crotales struck with a plastic mallet. (The other "antique" instruments in *Les Troyens* – double flute, sistrum, and tarbuka – are on-stage visual props, matched respectively by oboes, triangles, and the one-headed Provençal *tambourin*.[6]) An anvil (*petite enclume*), struck with "a small sculptor's hammer," is required for one of the smiths' choruses ("Bienheureux les matelots") in *Benvenuto Cellini*. The Hamlet March reaches climax with the arrival of a *peloton* – a firing squad; theatre companies are usually equipped to provide some sort of appropriate effect.[7] The jingling johnny, or *pavillon chinois*, needed for the *Symphonie funèbre et triomphale*, is usually to be found at a local Shriners' band – in France, at the band of the *Légion étrangère*.

HARPS, KEYBOARDS. The nineteenth-century Érard pedal harp was considerably smaller and quieter than the standard modern Lyon & Healey, but the overall effect is roughly the same. Berlioz calls for pairs of harps from the second movement of the *Fantastique* forward; both the solo exposition of *Harold en Italie* and the mezzo-soprano strophes in *Roméo et Juliette* feature important solo harp work, as does Berlioz's orchestration of *L'Invitation à la valse*. In the *Fête chez Capulet* from *Roméo et Juliette* and the scene of the Trojan women in *Les Troyens* ("Complices de sa gloire," in the finale of Act II), some three to six pairs of harps are envisaged. (Wagner probably got the idea for the similar effect at the close of *Das Rheingold* from having heard and seen *Roméo et Juliette* at the Paris première in 1839.)

In *L'Enfance du Christ* Berlioz asks for the harmonium organ he knew as the *orgue mélodium d'Alexandre*, the inventor, Édouard Alexandre (1824–1888), having become a close friend. Purists will need to look around for a foot-pumped model; a more practical solution is the electronic synthesizer or baroque positive.

The guitar is needed for Méphistophélès's scene in *Huit Scènes de Faust* and Somarone's scene at the opening of Act II of *Béatrice et Bénédict*. It was first envisaged for the strophes in *Roméo et Juliette*; two are needed for *Benvenuto Cellini*.

STRINGS. The period from the *Fantastique* to *Les Troyens* saw the complete redesign of the violin family for increased power, a development in which the Parisian violin maker J.-B. Vuillaume (1798–1875) and the bow-maker F.-X. Tourte (1747–1835) took the lead. New instruments were built to bolder specifications and older instruments refitted. Amount and frequency of vibrato certainly increased as the decades elapsed. Berlioz would have been happy enough with this apparent progress, and it makes little sense to ask players to adopt a substantially different approach to bowing, articulation, and vibrato from the one they use for the Beethoven-to-Mahler repertory.

SINGERS. As indicated above, a large chorus of some one hundred and fifty to two hundred – that is, twice the size of the standing chorus of the Société des Concerts – will usually suffice. The problem is the balance of voice parts, since Berlioz typically envisages a little over one-third women, with equal numbers of tenors and basses. For the choruses in *Roméo et Juliette* he suggests seventy Capulets and seventy Montagues (thirty sopranos, twenty tenors, twenty basses); the same sort of force would work for *Sara la baigneuse,* with half of all men and women assigned to chorus I, the remaining women to chorus II, and the remaining men to chorus III. *Faust* calls for similar or larger numbers, but with two significant movements for men alone and added children's chorus for the final *Apothéose*; the *Te Deum* specifies a double chorus (each with forty sopranos, thirty tenors, thirty basses) and a massed children's chorus of six hundred. Works thereafter are for SATB; the cast list for *Les Troyens* calls for "une centaine de choristes surnuméraires" – a hundred choral singers more than the approximately eighty who normally sang at the Opéra (for which theatre Berlioz's opera was conceived).

*

The published Berlioz performance material follows three avenues: (1) scores and parts descended from the original publications contracted with and overseen by the composer; (2) scores and parts descended from the Berlioz *Werke* edited by Charles Malherbe and Felix Weingartner and published in Leipzig by Breitkopf & Härtel (1900–1907), now generally called the *Old Berlioz Edition* (*OBE*); and (3) scores and parts based on the *New Berlioz Edition* (*NBE*), edited by Hugh Macdonald and a team of specialists and published in Kassel by Bärenreiter (see Appendix).

While at least a few copies of the first publications are preserved in research libraries, very little of the performance material available today for hire or purchase descends photographically from the Berlioz originals. (Exceptions are some of the vocal scores and a few sets offered for sale by Kalmus, including those for *La Marseillaise*. But the vocal scores tend toward disorder and aberrant readings, and the parts, lacking rehearsal letters and bar numbers, are viable only for the shortest works.) By contrast, descendants of the Breitkopf & Härtel edition are widely available at attractive prices: parts from Kalmus and Luck's Library, scores from Dover, Kalmus, and Broude. These have become essentially the standard texts, and with a little work by conductor and librarian – addition of rehearsal indications and the blotting out of extraneous text – they remain highly serviceable.

Scholarly considerations aside, the practical triumph of the *New Berlioz Edition* is in how it provides musicians with scores and parts for works that have heretofore been simply unavailable. The project began with two such works, the *Symphonie funèbre et triomphale* (1967) and *Les Troyens* (1969–1970), and has recently unveiled two others: the newly discovered *Messe solennelle* (1994) and, more than one hundred and fifty years after the first performances, *Benvenuto Cellini* in a workable edition of score and parts (1994–1996). (All four are the work of the general editor, Hugh Macdonald.) Bärenreiter's preferred business practice is to rent the performance materials, withholding them from direct sale. End-users dislike this form of capitalism, since it makes it impossible for orchestras or conductors to own sets with their own markings; the corollary – the attempt to control performance rights, practiced aggressively for the first performances of the *Messe solennelle* – seems particularly objectionable. One obvious result is to occasion fewer rather than more performances using these important new materials; another is to favor entertainment cartels and the major opera houses and orchestras over regional, local, and educational institutions. Nevertheless we must be patient as private enterprise recuperates its investment: the cost of preparing these materials is something on the order of $100 per page, and it is said that the parts for *Cellini* alone cost in excess of $50,000. As of this writing, about half the published volumes of the *NBE* have accompanying parts (see Appendix).

Given that on the whole there is comparatively little in the *New Berlioz Edition* that changes the overall sound of the familiar works, it is important to emphasize that the *NBE* achieves a considerably more accurate representation of the composer's notions than did the Malherbe and Weingartner edition, and represents a significant corrective to the misleading characteristics of the materials in common use. For one thing, the old edition attempts, unsuccessfully, to present trilingual readings of titles and lyrics: German at the head, then French and English. In score and parts for the *Fantastique*, for instance, we find at the start of the first movement:

Träumeraien, Leidenschaften
Rêveries – Passions   Visions and Passions

– not all that egregious an English translation, to be sure, but misleading as to the *rêveries* and missing the pointed suggestion that the reveries and the passions are two different parts of the movement (the slow introduction and the Allegro, respectively). The English rhymed texts are barely viable for singing and useless as translations. In the case of *Zaïde*, for example, we have the following:

«Ma ville, ma belle ville,	Granada my native city
C'est Grenade au frais jardin,	'Tis the home of all that's fair
C'est le palais d'Alladin,	Bright as a gem past compare.
Qui vaut Courdoue et Séville.»	Though some may other towns more splendid
[Qui vaut Courdoue,	Perchance prefer,
Qui vaut Courdoue et Séville.]	There's naught fairer than Granada!
Roger de Beauvoir	transl. Percy Pinkerton

["My town, my lovely town, / Is Granada of the cool garden, / Is Aladdin's palace, / Worth as much as Cordoba and Seville [put together]!"]

Including lyrics in three languages not only clutters the voice lines with alternative recompositions to fit the foreign languages, and the vertical layout with the non-Berlioz texts, but in turn forces re-engraving the other stanzas of these simple strophic *mélodies*. Berlioz would merely give the texts of subsequent *couplets* on the last page, sometimes with the adapted melody, sometimes with the lyric text alone.

Then, too, Malherbe and Weingartner adopted principles of layout that actually run counter to Berlioz's musical thought. The chief of these was to place the horn staves above the bassoon, woodwind-quintet fashion, suggesting a philosophy of orchestral choirs that has more to do with Wagnerian ideals than anything Berlioz ever thought or espoused. Further, in my view, Berlioz's manner of notating the trombone parts (often with the bass trombone on one line and the tenor and alto on a second line above) suggests his understanding of voice- and chord-function, such that the Breitkopf re-notating of the two lower parts in the bass clef and the upper part in a C clef can confound the reader as to what is really meant to happen. Jacques Barzun, at the close of his two-volume biography of Berlioz, presents a useful list of dozens of "Errors in the 'Complete' Edition of the Scores"; quite a number of these imply an audible difference between Berlioz's conception and that of Malherbe and Weingartner.[8]

The *New Berlioz Edition* presents no-nonsense, French-only scores, with each staff identified on every page, bar numbers in the upper-left corner of each system, and on the average at least one rehearsal letter for every two-page opening. The guiding principles of editorial policy were formulated with performers in mind: notes and critical apparatus are short, important, and of practical use. (It thus makes sense for conductors to use the full, clothbound *NBE* volumes as opposed to the paperback "Urtext" scores furnished with the rentals but lacking the critical matter.) The overall look of the *NBE* has mutated according to rapid changes in the technology of music typesetting and in the global labor force. The crisp, clean character of the early volumes, prepared in-house in Kassel with presstype (rub-off transfers), was replaced by a bolder and less attractive typeface with scores produced in Asia. Bigger, blacker notes led to wider layout and more frequent page-turns; more pages led to longer volumes and higher prices. (Compare, for instance, pp. 162–163 of the *Fantastique* – *NBE* 16, 1972: seventeen bars – with pp. 266–267 of *Roméo et Juliette* – *NBE* 18, 1990: eleven bars). With *Benvenuto Cellini* (*NBE* 1, 1994) the *NBE* returned to a somewhat tidier look, thanks in large measure to the use of computerized typesetting and page design.

Otherwise there is little to quibble over in the accuracy and usefulness of the *New Berlioz Edition* scores (but for the fact that the silver ink on the spines wears quickly away). One grows accustomed to the minor idiosyncrasies – beams, not flags, for the vocal syllables; slurs, not beams-and-slurs, for melismas; dots dropped for dotted-quarter flagged triplets and dotted-half flagged sextuplets (see the illustrations below) – and one accepts the inevitable discrepancies in widths of wedge accents and crescendo/decrescendos. The clarity of the *NBE* often surpasses that of the precedent publications, and the extra space can be seen to have advantages that perhaps outweigh the frenetic page-turns demanded, for example, by its Queen Mab Scherzo.

Let us compare the first page of the published viola part for *Roméo et Juliette* in the editions of Brandus et Cie (1847), Breitkopf & Härtel

(1901), and Bärenreiter (1990).[9] The musical text is substantially the same in all three, the chief difference being the *divisi* called for in bar 41 of the Brandus part, reflected in neither subsequent edition. (The bar in question is no different, technically, from what precedes and follows. Whether to divide for these effects is best left to the players; professional musicians will generally choose the double stops.) The Brandus part is from a first drawing of the set used by Berlioz for performances in 1846 and corrected in his hand and that of his copyist. (The penciled indication "N° 2" in the upper-right corner is autograph, as are the rubrics on the tissue wrapper, not pictured.) At the top, the part carries the rubber stamp of the Société des Concerts, where it arrived in 1863 and probably served for the performances of 1877 and thereafter; at the bottom it carries the stamp of the Bibliothèque Nationale (where the archives of the Société des Concerts began to arrive in 1974) and, at the lower left, the library shelfmark, Rés. Vma 215, in the hand of the librarian, Jean-Michel Nectoux. One hundred and two bars are given on eleven staves of the first page, compared with sixty-eight bars for the *OBE* and sixty-one bars for the *NBE* parts with ten staves each.

The *NBE* part gives a more accurate representation of Berlioz's intent for the wedge decrescendo as carrying through the sixteenth-note of the main figure in the fugue subject, while the reading in the *OBE* looks more like an accent; by contrast bars 38 and 39 are more successfully represented by the *OBE*. Note, too, the dot-saving scheme the *NBE* uses for the sextuplet figures beginning in bar 24. Both the *OBE* and the *NBE* give a "courtesy" A-natural in bar 44 lacking in the Brandus part. Brandus has no rehearsal or bar numbers; the *OBE* gives rehearsal numbers 1 to 3; the *NBE* gives both bar numbers at the start of each line and rehearsal letters A to F. The cued snippet of the trombone recitative (the "intervention du Prince"; bars 87–91), as given by Brandus at the foot of the page, also appears on p. 2 of the *OBE* part (not pictured); but Brandus lacks the new tempo-character indication, and the *OBE* gives it in Italian: "Fieramente, un poco ritenuto, col carattere di Recitativo misurato." The *NBE* (p. 2, not pictured) gives the correct French original, "Fièrement, un peu retenu et avec le caractère du récitatif," but, curiously, only bars 90–91 of the trombone cue.

Whether these kinds of differences matter to the everyday performing viola player is open to speculation. Though musicians always seem reassured by the traditional Breitkopf & Härtel look, the more spacious layout of the *NBE* does offer a psychological advantage (but yields thirty page-turns as opposed to twenty-eight in the *OBE*). In this particular case the primary advantage of the *NBE* parts would appear to be the line-by-line bar numbers and frequent rehearsal letters. In fact what might make the

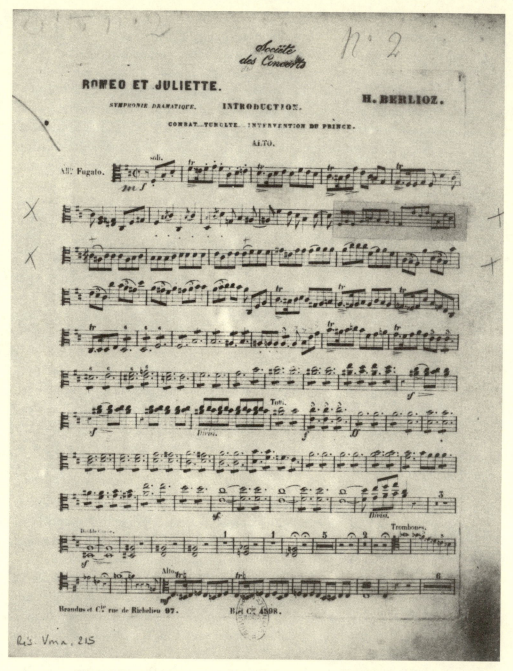

Fig. 13.1 *Roméo et Juliette*, first page of the viola part as printed by Brandus et Cie in 1847.

Fig. 13.2 *Roméo et Juliette*, first page of the viola part as printed by Breitkopf & Härtel (*OBE*) in 1901.

Fig. 13.3 *Roméo et Juliette*, first page of the viola part as printed by Bärenreiter (*NBE*) in 1990.

most positive difference to the overall shape and concept of *Roméo et Juliette* from using the *NBE* parts is simpler still: the proper numbering of the seven movements, as opposed to the *OBE's* contorted and thoroughly wrongheaded attempt to force the structure into four Roman-numeralled symphonic movements.

In sum, one must hire the *NBE* materials for the operas and such less-familiar and available works as the *Messe solennelle*: there is no other viable choice, and the enterprise deserves support. For the symphonic canon it makes good sense to rent the *NBE* materials for works not already in the library, and to base other decisions on considerations of budget and rehearsal strategy. Note that the only parts presently for direct sale by Bärenreiter are those for the *Fantastique*, co-published with Breitkopf & Härtel of Wiesbaden. Since these amount to the old Breitkopf parts with bar numbers added (but no rehearsal numbers or letters), one would make the decision based on the cost of the materials and labor to prepare them for rehearsal.[10]

In the case of the *Requiem* I strongly recommend the full *NBE* materials, with vocal scores purchased by the chorus. All too commonly, modern productions of this work bring together mismatched parts owned by the many groups who need assembling for the final rehearsals and performance: the orchestra plays from descendants of the Breitkopf & Härtel parts, the chorus sings from inexpensive vocal scores from Schirmer and Kalmus, and the conductor reads the *NBE* score, presumably setting afoot three different rehearsal-letter schemes. The vocal scores, descended from a Brandus publication of 1882 based on the 1838 original, embrace a passage in the *a cappella Quaerens me* that was deleted from the 1853 second edition published by Ricordi, as well as dozens of details of voice-part disposition and declamation subsequently improved by Berlioz himself. Further, the timpani parts, as published by Breitkopf & Härtel, have been redistributed and bear little resemblance to Berlioz's own scheme: using them embraces unnecessary compromises to both the visual and (to my ear) audible impact of the timpani choir, particularly if drums are re-tuned, as it were, *en route*. The timpani parts *can* be arranged for four players each controlling four instruments, but who, having assembled the rest of the performing force, would want to bypass this central effect? (Additionally, there is the problem of the disposition of the cornets in the *Sanctus* and the trombone players after the *Lacrymosa* for the final movements – points on which Berlioz is somewhat ambiguous and the parts more ambiguous still.)

Enhanced accessibility to Berlioz materials is not uniquely the work of the *NBE*. In the recent past, for instance, facsimiles of two piano-vocal *mélodies* (the *Élégie en prose* and *La Captive*) were included in Garland's series of *Romantic French Song, 1830–1870*, and Peter Bloom published an edition of the piano-vocal *Nuits d'été* based in part on newly recovered manuscript material. For the French bicentennial ceremonies in 1989, a team of graduate students at the University of California at Davis and I published the newly discovered *Chant du 9 Thermidor* in score and parts, along with editions of the *Marche pour la présentation des drapeaux* and of Berlioz's arrangement of the *Marseillaise*.[11] A facsimile reprinting of the 1863 *Collection de 32 Mélodies* in conjunction with the Berlioz bicentenary in 2003 would go a long way toward making these songs available to singers far and wide.

The performance practice movement reached Berlioz with Roger Norrington's performances and recording of the *Symphonie fantastique* in 1988–1989, a natural outgrowth of his immediately preceding, now famous Beethoven recordings. Norrington's London "Berlioz Experience" of 4 = 6 March 1988 featured, in addition to the *Fantastique* (and lectures, roundtables, and recitals), a vibrant *Roméo et Juliette* – broadcast but not released on disc – and a *Francs-Juges* Overture later released in a collection of *Early Romantic Overtures*. In 1991 John Eliot Gardiner's Orchestre Révolutionnaire et Romantique audio- and video-recorded a *Fantastique* in the Salle des Concerts du Conservatoire, the old hall in which it was first performed in December 1830. Gardiner's period orchestra and Monteverdi Choir released the first-ever *Messe solennelle* in 1993, likewise including a laser-disc; 1998 saw publication of a remarkable pick-and-choose recording of the various versions of *Roméo et Juliette*. Both Norrington and Gardiner were already admired for Berlioz recordings with conventional forces.[12]

Efforts to approximate the conditions of a live performance during the composer's lifetime – the use of period instruments or replicas thereof, corresponding phrase and bowing strategies, and the composer's preferred layout of performing forces and specified tempos – were in the late nineteen-eighties and remain now very much in vogue. The European Community could boast a cohort of properly equipped young professional musicians available to travel the relatively short distances involved to constitute more-or-less authentic performances in the era's main venues. The big recording companies, anxious to acquire novel audio and video "content," arranged for the mixed-media packaging.

All five "performance practice" recordings are worthy additions to the Berlioz discography, the Gardiner *Fantastique* perhaps especially so by

Table 13.1 Performance practice recordings

Symphonie fantastique (Norrington, 1989). London Classical Players, Roger Norrington, conductor. EMI CD CDC 7 49541 2. 1989.

Les Francs-Juges Overture (Norrington, 1990), London Classical Players, Roger Norrington, conductor. *Early Romantic Overtures,* with works of Weber, Mendelssohn, Schubert, and Wagner. Recorded 1988. EMI CD CDC 7 49889 2. 1990.

Symphonie fantastique (Gardiner, 1991). Orchestre Révolutionnaire et Romantique, John Eliot Gardiner, conductor. Recorded and filmed at the Salle des Concerts of the old Conservatoire (now the Conservatoire National Supérieur d'Art Dramatique), September 1991. Philips video 440 070 254–1 (laser disc), . . . 254–3 (VHS cassette). 1991. Philips CD 434 402–2. 1993.

Messe solennelle (Gardiner, 1993). Donna Brown, soprano; Jean-Luc Viala, tenor; Gilles Cachemaille, bass-baritone; Monteverdi Choir, Orchestre Révolutionnaire et Romantique, John Eliot Gardiner, conductor. Recorded live at Westminster Cathedral, London, October 1993. Philips video 440 070 272–1. Philips CD 442 137–2. 1993.

Roméo et Juliette (Gardiner, 1998). Catherine Robbin, contralto; Jean-Paul Fouchecourt, tenor; Gilles Cachemaille, bass-baritone; Monteverdi Choir, Orchestre Révolutionnaire et Romantique, John Eliot Gardiner, conductor. Philips 454 454–2 (2 discs). With alternative and variant readings. 1998.

virtue of a video component that preserves something of the look and feel, if not in fact the acoustic, of a beloved hall now consigned to other uses. Even though the sounds of Beethoven-era strings and old-fashioned woodwind and brass have by now become familiar, one cannot help being intrigued by the woodiness of the woodwind, the stern brass voices of the Berlioz era, the short bow strokes and limited vibrato of the strings. These serve to remind us of a certain loss of personality that resulted from the late nineteenth- and twentieth-century quest for a united, rich-and-round sonic ideal – the near equivalence in tone quality, for instance, of the tenor register in horn, bassoon, saxophone, and even cello – and for the "long line." If the net result seems "stringy" or "harsh" by comparison with traditional recordings, that is in many respects the point.

Norrington's particular focus has been on scrupulous attention to a composer's metronome markings. It does not take much to see the limitations of manuscript metronome marks: composers are notorious for attaching them without actually consulting a metronome; the old-fashioned clockwork mechanism can be unpredictable outside mid-range; and speed as imagined by a composer in his workshop is often markedly different from speed as sensed by working musicians in live concert venues. Berlioz himself favored cautious use of the metronome: music played by imitating the "mathematical regularity of the metronome," he wrote, "would be of glacial rigidity." But in his precedent-setting cycle of the Beethoven symphonies, Norrington demonstrated incontestably (except, perhaps, in the case of the famously slow scherzo of the Ninth) that a fundamentally musical use of the metronome markings, combined with other levels of musical rethinking, could afford intellectually provocative readings of old, familiar works. His readings are surprisingly novel, challenging to the intellect, and – often as not – obviously "right." Norrington's "nice and slow" March to the Scaffold from the *Fantastique* – "because that's the right speed" – has fostered a vogue for such accounts and perhaps a certain rivalry among conductors to see who can go slowest.

But is slow "right," and is Norrington's account of the last movement, at ten-and-a-half minutes, "nice and slow," or simply ponderous? For that matter, do the "performance practice" recordings really follow the composer's scheme? Berlioz's indications are as follows:

Movement IV *Marche au supplice*
   Allegretto non troppo   ♩=72
Movement V: *Songe d'une nuit du sabbat*
   Larghetto   ♩=63
   Allegro   ♩.=112
     ("mockery of the beloved" I, bar 21)
   Allegro assai   o=76
     ("roar of approval," bar 29)
   Allegro   ♩.=104
   ("mockery" II, bar 40; presumably slower owing to technical difficulty)
   sans presser   –
     (*Dies irae*, bar 127)
   animez un peu (from bar 223)   –
   Un peu retenu   ♩.=104
     (*Ronde du sabbat*, bar 241)
   (HB: "The tempo, which should have picked up a little, returns here to that of bar 40:   ♩.=104.)[13]
   animez (bar 492)   –

Both movements consistently struggle to break free of the composer's metronome indication owing, in the March, to the change of character between the lugubrious, sinister first theme and the swashbuckling second, as well as to the mounting frenzy toward the end; and, in the *Ronde du sabbat*, to the general sense that witches must dance faster than ♩.= 104. (A Sousa march in $\frac{6}{8}$ – Marines, not witches – travels at ♩.= 120.)

The received French performance tradition takes both movements considerably faster than Berlioz's metronome marks. Charles Munch, who left the most persuasive Berlioz recordings of the first half of the century (his cycle with the Boston Symphony and the Harvard/Radcliffe/ New England Conservatory choruses has recently appeared as an eight-CD set),[14] begins the March at ♩= 76 and gathers consistently in speed to reach 94 at the end, having skipped the repeat. He takes the "mockery of the beloved" at a relatively strict ♩.= 104 and the Round Dance just short of ♩.= 132 – i.e., a great deal faster than Berlioz says. The young Spanish

Table 13.2 *Symphonie fantastique*

Performance times

	Movement IV	Movement V	All
Munch / BSO RCA 1954; rpt. CD 1996	04:27*	08:42	46:38
Argenta / Société des Concerts London 1955; rpt. CD 1998	06:25	09:39	50:38
Davis / Concertgebouw Philips 1974	06:48	09:57	55:31
Norrington / London Classical Players EMI 1989	07:25	10:37	52:48
Gardiner / Orchestre Révolutionnaire Philips 1991	06:41	11:08	54:45

* Munch does not take the repeat.

conductor Ataulfo Argenta, who left the later of two recordings by the Société des Concerts,[15] follows much the same tempos as Munch. Colin Davis and the Concertgebouw take the March at ♩ = 80, the Round Dance at ♩. = 130.

Norrington, by contrast, begins the March well under ♩ = 72, reaching only 74 by the end; the Round Dance goes at between ♩. = 116 and 120 throughout. Gardiner's March to the Scaffold begins at ♩ = 80 and settles at 84, with a strict ♩. = 104 for the "mockery of the beloved," and a Round Dance at "traditional" speeds, i.e., starting at about ♩. = 120 and reaching 132 toward the end.

During a London roundtable discussion of conducting Berlioz held in October 1995, Norrington, Macdonald, David Cairns, and I discussed the matter of finding workable tempos for these two movements.[16] David Cairns found Norrington's reading of the March to the Scaffold powerful, because it was "more brutal and obscene." (Norrington himself remarked that "I haven't changed since I discovered this lovely metronome marking – how it kind of ponderously goes on.") But Cairns thought even the ♩. = 120 of the last movement, as recorded by Norrington, "too held back."

The conversation turned naturally to other unaccountably slow markings in Berlioz: the ♩. = 76 at the start of *Harold en Italie*, which, according to Macdonald, "has to speed up" at the entry of the viola or else is, according to Norrington, "distressingly slow"; the ♩. = 63 for *La Mort d'Ophélie*, which instead might well go "swingingly along" (Norrington: "She was floating down the river. Very nice; and then she sank."); and the ♩ = 50 for the *Te ergo quaesumus* in the *Te Deum*, a thoroughly impractical speed for the tenor soloist. Both the Love Scene from *Roméo et Juliette* and the Shepherds' Farewell from *L'Enfance du Christ* often seem lethargic in otherwise well-conceived performances, but this is more commonly the result of slipping into a ponderous eighth-note pulse than a function of the calibrations themselves ($\downarrow = 88$; $\downarrow = 50$). The only reasonable explanation of a performance time left in Berlioz's hand for the Queen Mab Scherzo, ten minutes for a movement usually played in seven, is that it reflects an earlier, longer musical text.[17]

Norrington summarized an approach to these questions that amounts to giving first priority to Berlioz's metronome marks, but only so long as they can be made to work:

> People get the impression that one sees a metronome mark or hears of a timing and then uses it for some religious reason. I only do it when they appeal. And sometimes I just don't do it. *Harold* is one of those cases: I don't see how I can do the metronome marking. You have to really be convinced. What's nice is that one so often is. The Beethoven symphonies are a case in point. Except for the Ninth, every single marking in the first eight symphonies is a revelation. It suddenly sounds right.[18]

"It's a revelation," I remarked, "if you're Roger Norrington and if you make such beautiful music from the revelation."

The participants in the London roundtable discussed matters concerning the layout of the Berlioz orchestra, all favoring the composer's preferred antiphonal placement of the two violin sections. Berlioz's attitudes were largely conditioned by the cramped quarters of the Salle des Concerts at the old Conservatoire, where the violins filled the forestage and the chorus continued outward over the covered pit; a desk or two of bass strings was wedged between the violin sections, and the remainder of the orchestra was consigned to steeply rising platforms reaching back to the walls of a removable shell.[19] (The one legible illustration of the nineteenth-century Société des Concerts at work clearly shows the double basses on the top platform, far removed from the violins.[20]) Few of these accommodations to an unusual room seem to merit duplicating for modern performance in more spacious quarters. Even the chorus-in-front strategy for *Roméo et Juliette* (and by extension for the other choral works up to *Faust*), though extraordinary in both visual and acoustic effect, is probably too costly in terms of inherent dangers for conventional modern performance. A large, wrap-around chorus accomplishes the same effect and can be controlled by the chief conductor.

The discussants – all of them conductors – closed by advocating a return to another lost tradition of nineteenth-century performance: applause between the movements. Norrington attributed the demise of applauding between movements, and of on-the-spot encores, to Sir Henry

Wood's discouragement of it beginning in the nineteen-thirties. But "it's wonderful," said Cairns, "when people applaud when they shouldn't."

"It seems to me," said Norrington, "that a concert should be a good deal more fun." Later than evening, in the Royal Festival Hall, I led a salvo of applause after the Pilgrims' March from *Harold en Italie* – over a chorus of shushing from the London regulars. Norrington turned and acknowledged our corner of the *parterre* with a satisfied nod. But he did not grant an encore.

Appendix

Hector Berlioz: New Edition of the Complete Works
General Editor: Hugh Macdonald
Bärenreiter (Kassel, Basel, London, New York, 1967–)

Issued by the Berlioz Centenary Committee London in association with the
Calouste Gulbenkian Foundation, Lisbon. Except for the *Symphonie fantastique* and
the *Te Deum* (which are copublished with Breitkopf & Härtel of Wiesbaden), parts
are identified here with the Bärenreiter edition number (BA 5441*ff.*) plus 72; vocal
scores with edition number plus 90. Scores with rental sets come with paper
bindings and without commentary and notes. An "Index to the New Berlioz
Edition" appears on pp. viii–ix of *NBE* 1a (*Benvenuto Cellini*). For the latest
information, one may search the on-line catalogue at www.barenreiter.com.

1 *Benvenuto Cellini*, ed. Hugh Macdonald (4 vols.: 1a–d). 1994–1996 [vol. 1d
   forthcoming].
   BA 5441. Parts (with the versions Paris 1 and Paris 2/Weimar). Overture
   separately available. Vocal score ed. E. Wernhard and M. Schelhaas (BA 5441a;
   1999).
2 *Les Troyens*, ed. Hugh Macdonald (3 vols.: 2a–c). 1969–1970.
   BA 5442. Parts. Vocal score ed E. Wernhard forthcoming. "Chasse royale et
   orage" ("Royal Hunt and Storm") separately available. Eulenberg pocket score
   EE 6639 (1973); "Chasse royale," EE 1371 (1978).
3 *Béatrice et Bénédict*, ed. Hugh Macdonald. 1980.
   BA 5443. Parts. Vocal score ed. D. Müller, W. Konold, J. E. Durek (BA 5443a,
   1985). Overture separately available.
4 Incomplete Operas. Forthcoming.
   [BA 5444.] *Les Francs-Juges*; *La Nonne sanglante*.
5 *Huit Scènes de Faust*, ed. Julian Rushton. 1970.
   BA 5445. Parts forthcoming.
6 Prix de Rome works, ed. David Gilbert. 1998.
   BA 5446. Parts (by cantata title). Fugue (1826); *La Mort d'Orphée*; *Herminie*;
   Fugue à trois sujets (1829); *Cléopâtre*; *Sardanapale*.
7 *Lélio ou Le Retour à la vie*, ed. Peter Bloom. 1992.
   BA 5447. Parts. Vocal score ed. E. Wernhard (BA 5447a; 2000).
8 *La Damnation de Faust*, ed. Julian Rushton (2 vols.: 8a–b). 1979, 1986.
   BA 5448. Parts. Vocal score ed. E. Wernhard (BA 5448a, 1993).
9 *Grande Messe des morts* (*Requiem*), ed. Jürgen Kindermann. 1978.
   BA 5449. Parts. Vocal score ed. M. Töpul, D. Woodfull-Harris (BA 5449a,
   1992). Study Score TP 332 (1992).
10 *Te Deum*, ed. Denis McCaldin. 1973.
    BA 5450 and 5782 (Parts). Vocal score ed. Otto Taubmann (BA 5782a);
    copublished as Breitkopf & Härtel 8061 (1978).
11 *L'Enfance du Christ*, ed. David Lloyd Jones. 1998.
    BA 5451. Parts. Vocal score ed. E. Wernhard (BA 5451a; 1999).

12   Choral Works with Orchestra. 2 vols.: 12a, ed. Julian Rushton, 1991; 12b, ed.
      David Charlton. 1993. Parts.

   BA 5452/I, vol. 12a: *Resurrexit*; *Scène héroïque*; *Chant sacré*; *Hélène*; *Quartetto
   et coro dei maggi*; *Sara la baigneuse*; *Le Cinq Mai*.

   BA 5452/II, vol. 12b: *Tristia (Méditation religieuse, La Mort d'Ophélie, Marche
   funèbre pour la dernière scène d'Hamlet)*; *Vox populi (La Menace des Francs,
   Hymne à la France)*; *Chant des Chemins de fer*; *L'Impériale*. Parts: *Chant des
   Chemins de fer, Tristia*. Others forthcoming.

13   Songs for Solo Voice and Orchestra, ed. Ian Kemp. 1975.

   BA 5453. Parts. *La Belle Voyageuse*; *La Captive*; *Le Jeune Pâtre breton*; *Les Nuits
   d'été*; *Le Chasseur danois*; *Zaïde*; *Aubade*. Parts for *Les Nuits d'été*. *Les Nuits
   d'été* vocal score with transpositions for mezzo-soprano, ed. D. Woodfull-
   Harris (BA 5784; 1995).

14   Choral Works with Keyboard, ed. Ian Rumbold. 1996.

   BA 5454. *Le Ballet des ombres*; *Chant guerrier*; *Chanson à boire*; *Chant sacré*;
   Le Chant des Bretons; *L'Apothéose*; *Prière du matin*; *Hymne pour la
   consécration du nouveau tabernacle*; *Le Temple universel*; *Veni creator*; *Tantum
   ergo*.

15   Songs for One, Two, or Three Voices with Keyboard. Forthcoming.

   BA 5455. *Le Dépit de la bergère*; *Le Maure jaloux*; *Amitié, reprends ton empire*;
   Pleure, pauvre Colette; *Canon libre à la quinte*; *Le Montagnard exilé*; *Toi qui
   l'aimas, verse des pleurs*; *Nocturne à deux voix*; *Le Roi de Thulé*; *Le Coucher du
   soleil*; *Hélène*; *La Belle Voyageuse*; *L'Origine de la harpe*; *Adieu Bessy*; *Élégie en
   prose*; *La Captive*; *Le Jeune Pâtre breton*; *Les Champs*; *Je crois en vous*;
   Chansonnette; *Aubade*; *Les Nuits d'été*; *La Mort d'Ophélie*; *La Belle Isabeau*; *Le
   Chasseur danois*; *Zaïde*; *Le Trébuchet*; *Nessun maggior piacere*; *Le Matin*; *Petit
   oiseau*.

16   *Symphonie fantastique*, ed. Nicholas Temperley. 1972.

   BA [5456] and 5781. Parts (BA 5781 [65 winds; 74,75,79, 82, 85 individual
   strings], copublished as Breitkopf & Härtel 4929). Study score TP 331
   (1972).

17   *Harold en Italie*, ed. Paul Banks, forthcoming (2001).

   BA 5457.

18   *Roméo et Juliette*, ed. D. Kern Holoman. 1990.

   BA 5458. Parts. Vocal score ed. E. Wernhard (BA 5458a, 1995). Study Score TP
   334 (1996).

19   *Grande Symphonie funèbre et triomphale*, ed. Hugh Macdonald. 1967.

   BA 5459. Parts. Eulenberg pocket score EE 6642 (no. 599) (1975).

20   Overtures, ed. Diana Bickley. 2000.

   BA 5460. *Waverley*; *Le Roi Lear*; *Rob-Roy*; *Le Carnaval romain*; *Le Corsaire*.
   (See *NBE* 1 and 3 for the overtures to *Benvenuto Cellini* and *Béatrice et
   Bénédict*.) Parts forthcoming.

21   Other Orchestral and Instrumental Works, ed. Hugh Macdonald. Forthcoming.

   BA 5461. *Rêverie et caprice*; *Sérénade agreste à la madone*; *Toccata*; *Hymne
   pour l'élévation*; *Marche troyenne*.

22   Arrangements. 2 vols.: 22a: Arrangements of Works by Gluck, ed. Joël-Marie

Fauquet; 22b: Arrangements of Works by Other Composers, ed. Ian Rumbold. Forthcoming.

BA 5462/I. *Orphée*; *Alceste*.

BA 5462/II. *Fleuve du Tage* (Pollet); *Recueil de romances avec accompagnement de guitare*; *Hymne des Marseillais* (Rouget de Lisle); *Chant du neuf Thermidor* (Rouget de Lisle); *Sur les Alpes, quel délice!* (Huber); Recitatives for *Le Freyschütz* (Weber); *L'Invitation à la valse* (Weber); *Marche marocaine* (Meyer); *Plaisir d'amour* (Martini); *Le Roi des aulnes* (Schubert); *Invitation à louer dieu* (Couperin).

23 *Messe solennelle*, ed. Hugh Macdonald. 1994.

BA 5463. Parts. Vocal score ed. E. Wernard (BA 5463a, 1994). Study score TP 333 (1993). "O Salutaris" for chorus, organ, BA 6394.

24 *Grand Traité d'instrumentation et d'orchestration modernes*, ed. Peter Bloom and Hugh Macdonald. Forthcoming.

25 *Catalogue of the Works of Hector Berlioz*, by D. Kern Holoman. 1987.

26 Portraits, ed. Gunther Braam. Forthcoming.

PART V

Critical encounters

14 Berlioz and Gluck

JOËL-MARIE FAUQUET

"The Jupiter of our Olympus was Gluck," Berlioz recalled, when speaking of the feelings he had had as an aspiring twenty-year-old composer. To this youthful metaphor of sincere admiration it is instructive to compare the expression of disillusionment set down in the Postface of the *Mémoires* by the now veteran artist approaching the end of his career:

> There is much that I could say about the two Gluck operas, *Orphée* and *Alceste*, which I was invited to direct, one at the Théâtre Lyrique, the other at the Opéra, but I have discussed them at some length in my book *À travers chants*, and although there are things that I could certainly add to that account ... I prefer not to do so.

This unspoken confession, with its telling ellipsis, leaves us with the impression that there was still unresolved dissonance at the end of Berlioz's long engagement with Gluck. That engagement, always marked by Berlioz's recollections of famous voices such as that of the great dramatic soprano Caroline Branchu, extended from an early, defensive phase – saving the composer from oblivion, on the one hand, and from impertinent arrangers, on the other – to a later, illustrative phase – "reproducing" his works (the word is Berlioz's) and transmitting them to posterity as models of excellence. Berlioz's participation in the revivals of *Orphée* in 1859 and of *Alceste* in 1861 and 1866 marks the culmination of a militant campaign waged by the French composer on behalf of the man whom he recognized, very early on, as both his master and his model.

In order to understand the unique character of the close relationship between Gluck and Berlioz, we must first remember that Berlioz's own creativity was conditioned by certain "poetic shocks," as he called them, which he first experienced as a youth. The works of Gluck and Virgil together were their primary causes, and both had a fundamental impact on the development of the young musician's imagination. Berlioz was not a man of the past, but he was indeed a man of *his own* past, and for him the history of music was above all the history of *his* music: "antiquity" was thus for Berlioz the period in which he discovered its existence – and that was the period of his own adolescence. The music that seems to draw upon the emotional energy of his initial enthusiasms does indeed integrate certain archaic elements into its fabric, for the purpose of characterization, but it never does so in order explicitly to recapture some distant musical era. For Berlioz, therefore, Gluck was not a composer of the past, he was not the last of those of some bygone era; he was rather, as Berlioz put it in 1859, the first of the romantics.

Gluck became such an absolute point of reference because he was the first, as Berlioz saw it, to have used the orchestra in an expressive manner that was entirely in accord with a particular dramatic subject. In addition, Gluck provided Berlioz with the example of a composer who made fundamental revisions of his own works: it is well known, for example, that *Orfeo* (Vienna, 1762) and *Alceste* (Vienna, 1767) were written first in Italian, and then transformed for the French stage by Gluck himself in, respectively, 1774 and 1776. Given such transformations, we may well wonder what it means to speak of the "unique" or "original" work of art – a question of basic importance to the understanding of the attitude later adopted by Berlioz toward these and other works of Gluck.

Finally, the fact that Berlioz never became a teacher of composition must be taken into consideration, for his actions on behalf of Gluck have a decidedly didactic character. One of the few musicians lastingly to benefit from his guidance was the pianist Théodore Ritter, who transcribed, among other works, the version of *Orphée* that Berlioz prepared for the Théâtre Lyrique in 1859.

As early as 1825, and regularly thereafter, Berlioz's music criticism focused upon the name and the works of Gluck in such a way as protectively to surround them with a kind of palace guard: fearing the possible disappearance of what had so inspired him, and what he wished in his own way to transmit, Berlioz denounced the abandon into which the works of Gluck had fallen, urged that the integrity of his idol's musical texts be respected, and thus invoked a tradition of which he considered himself the primary keeper. With the exception of *Telemaco*, to which he devoted an article in the *Gazette musicale de Paris* of 11 January 1835, Berlioz occupied himself exclusively with the so-called "reform" operas of Gluck, including *Armide*, the rehearsals of which he directed, in 1866, with a view towards a revival that in fact never took place. Indeed, *Armide* is the subject of the very first feuilleton – in *Le Corsaire* of 19 December 1825 – that Berlioz devoted to Gluck. So from the very beginning, Gluck became the focal point of Berlioz's musical polemics.

In Berlioz's lifelong struggle on behalf of the earlier composer, the year 1834, when he conceived what became *Benvenuto Cellini*, was especially fruitful. On 1 and 8 June, he offered readers of the *Gazette musicale* a biography of Gluck that situates the composer in his own time. These two articles are highly indicative, for they analyze aspects of the operas that would henceforth serve as the bases of some of Berlioz's "restorative" work on behalf of the composer, including Asteria's monologue from *Telemaco*; the preface to *Alceste* and the modifications of the text and score of the French version of that work (in particular Gluck's own suppression of Alceste's aria "Chi mi parla"); the librettos of *Iphigénie en Tauride* and *Iphigénie en Aulide*; Gluck's self-borrowings, and more. Later that year, Berlioz contributed four further articles to the same journal,[1] which did not seem to him to be too many for an analysis of *Iphigénie en Tauride*. In fact the analysis forms a small and quite remarkable treatise on dramatic composition.

But he directed his primary critical attention to *Alceste*. Berlioz's writings on this work, last performed at the Opéra in 1826, stretch over nearly thirty years, from one article published in 1834 in the *Gazette musicale*[2] to a series of seven published in 1861 in the *Journal des débats*[3] and later reprinted (with some alterations) in *À travers chants*. The latter, to this day one of the most important treatments of *Alceste* and its musical and literary sources, also includes a comparative study of "Gluck's Two *Alcestes*," which Berlioz originally published in 1835 in the *Journal des débats*.[4]

In that same year, the idea of producing *Orphée* (which was almost never seen on stage after the early eighteen-thirties) began to germinate in Berlioz's mind. In an article entitled "On the Gluck Repertory at the Académie royale de Musique,"[5] he considered the varied abilities of the singers engaged by the Opéra to interpret the works of Gluck. He returned to *Orphée* in the *Journal des débats* of 17 March 1839. But it was particularly the revival of 1859 that would lead Berlioz to delve more deeply into this "original" work, which so decisively affected his own musical sensibilities.

As a writer, then, Berlioz never ceased to defend Gluck – and he would do likewise as a conductor. Once again it was primarily *Alceste* that would benefit from his attentions. On 25 November 1838, to the program of the concert he was to give at the Conservatoire, Berlioz added a fragment from the Italian version of *Alceste* that he had reworked in accordance with the wish he had already expressed in his article (mentioned above) of 8 June 1834. In question was the most important alteration that Berlioz hoped to effect in the French version of the work, the reinsertion of the aria "Chi mi parla" (from the second scene of Act II of the Italian score), whose removal he had long deplored. Not only does Berlioz praise the musical qualities of this number, but he also cites its opening words – "Qui mi parla che rispondo! ah che veggo! ah che spavento! ove fuggo! ove m'ascondo! aro . . . gelo . . . manco . . . moro!" – and offers a translation of its most dramatic exclamations: "Qui me parle! [. . .] que vois-je! . . . . où fuir! . . . je brûle . . . je gèle . . . je meurs . . ." The insertion of this number into the third act of the French version, in 1861, would reinforce that act's dramatic character, which Gluck's own contemporaries, starting with Jean-Jacques Rousseau (as Berlioz knew perfectly well), took to be the least persuasive of the three.

Berlioz turned again to the "sublime monologue" from the Italian version of *Alceste*, "Chi mi parla," in one of the series of articles entitled "De l'instrumentation" that formed the basis of his celebrated *Traité d'instrumentation*, using it as a demonstration of the ideal use of muted violins to execute a passage with lightness and rapidity, or to accompany an especially precipitous rhythm.[6]

And on 25 November 1838 Berlioz organized and conducted a concert in which he gave several excerpts from *Alceste* in versions later found in his own rescoring of the work, which was intended for use by Pauline Viardot. The little-known manuscript of this rescoring, clearly prepared before the concert of 10 March 1861 (when Viardot, along with the bass Félix Cazaux, performed at the Conservatoire), gives evidence of the "corrections" Berlioz tended to make as one who claimed properly to understand the tradition in which the score was conceived.[7] Some of these corrections would find their way into the version that Pauline Viardot sang when the work was revived at the Opéra in 1861 – a version that was published by the chef de chant at the Opéra, Vauthrot, in both piano-vocal and piano-solo scores.

The order of the Moldenhauer manuscript is as follows:

No. 1 (Récitatif d'Alceste) "Grands dieux soutenez mon courage"; No. 2 (Aria d'Alceste) "Qui me parle?"; No. 3 Chœur de dieux infernaux invisibles (a copy that corrects the trombone parts of the printed score – something that would become, in 1857, the subject of a heated dispute between Berlioz and the voice teacher François Delsarte); No. 4 Air (Alceste) "Ah! Divinités implacables"; No. 5 Air (Un dieu infernal) "Caron t'appelle" (which reproduces the effect of the two horns facing one-another, bell-to-bell, that had so struck the fourteen-year-old Berlioz when he read Delaulnaye's article on Gluck in Michaud's *Biographie universelle*); No. 6 Air (Alceste) "Divinités du Styx" / "Ombres, larves" (with the French version superimposed upon the translation of the Italian version).

This alternative sequence was reproduced in the piano-vocal score of *Alceste* that conformed to the revival of 1861. As early as 1834 (in the *Gazette musicale* of 8 June), Berlioz had made a comparison of the aria "Ombre, larve," of the Italian version, with "Divinités du Styx," the adaptation in French, finding the former considerably more effective than the latter. It was on this occasion that he made extended reference to the performance of Caroline Branchu:

Who cannot remember the remarkable interpretation of Mme Branchu, when, as the trombones cried out in response to the phrase "Divinités du Styx," she whirled round towards the side of the orchestra whence came those formidable voices and, with energy renewed and eyes wild with might and horror, she proudly roared the final verse: "Je n'invoquerai point votre pitié cruelle"? Her voice was so scathing and forceful, her expression so magisterial, that the mighty orchestra of the Opéra simply disappeared as though vanquished in wondrous battle. Oh, how grand she was at that time! – as grand as Gluck himself, of whom she was *the* sublime interpreter.

Even more than Beethoven, then, Gluck is the musician who seems most frequently to have occupied Berlioz's attention in his various capacities as a composer, conductor, director, and writer. Not only his criticism, but his private correspondence, too, testifies to his overwhelming admiration for Gluck. As early as 1824, he wrote to his friend Édouard Rocher (on 22 June):

> *Alceste*, *Armide*, now *those* are real operas! And they have an advantage over *Orphée* in the sense that those dogs, the *dilettanti*, don't like them, while *Orphée* has the defect of being approved of by that lot.

From comments such as this we can observe with some precision the development of Berlioz's campaign on behalf of the rehabilitation of Gluck. The campaign was essentially three-pronged, with advances in the areas of the aesthetic, the technical, and the fictional.

First, the aesthetic. It is clear that the "Gluck question" posed itself to Berlioz every time that he, himself, was confronted as a composer with the problem of the creation of dramatic music. For example, it was while the Opéra was considering the acceptance or rejection of the libretto of *Benvenuto Cellini*, in mid-October 1835, that he suggested a revival of *Alceste* to the then director, Edmond Duponchel. And it was while the fate of *Les Troyens* was in the balance, in the fall of 1859, that Berlioz agreed to "restore" *Orphée* for performance at the Théâtre Lyrique. Furthermore, it was surely in order to "save" *Les Troyens* from abandonment that, after noisily refusing to intervene in the Opéra's production of *Alceste*, he finally agreed to supervise the "revision" of that work in June 1861.

In the eyes of his contemporaries, Berlioz was viewed early on as a composer who was attempting to prolong the Gluckian tradition, so much so that when *Benvenuto Cellini* failed at the Opéra in 1838, Joseph d'Ortigue rallied to the cause of his friend by writing a polemical volume entitled *De l'école musicale italienne et de l'administration de l'Académie royale de Musique, à l'occasion de l'opéra de M. Berlioz.*[8] Here, d'Ortigue likens Berlioz's efforts at operatic reform to Gluck's, notes how both composers struggled against the invasion of the Italian style, and demonstrates that the "method" which *Benvenuto Cellini* employs is no more or less than the continuation and natural consequence of that of the earlier master. He concludes: "Today, again, we observe a bold composer who is not in the least bit afraid to protest against the very system that Gluck himself attacked head-on."

Second, the technical. Of the musical examples in the *Traité d'instrumentation et d'orchestration modernes* (1843), which comprise one of the most important aspects of the book, the number selected from the works of Gluck is precisely equal to the number selected from the works of Beethoven! Two come from *Orphée*, four from *Alceste*, one from *Iphigénie en Aulide*, eight from *Iphigénie en Tauride*, and two from *Armide*. Additional references to Gluck, without specific musical citations, are furthermore made in the body of the text of the treatise.

Finally, the fictional. In the musical city of Euphonia (in Berlioz's short story of that name),[9] the great musical celebration given in honor of Gluck (whose statue is to be inaugurated) is a performance of *Alceste*, at the end of which the singer Nadira, excluded from singing because of her habit of ornamenting in the Italian manner, finds that the work has revealed to her the true nature of art. She now sees in Gluck a veritable "god of expression." In this discussion of aesthetics, Berlioz imagines the scene as follows:

> Tearing the pearls and gems from her hair, [Nadira] throws them to the ground, tramples them underfoot (as a symbol of recantation), places her hand over her heart, bows her head to Gluck, and in a voice sublime in its accent and quality, begins Alceste's great aria, "Ah! Divinités implacables!"[10]

It is important to note that this scene, in which Nadira is converted to the ideal of Gluckian singing, seems to be based upon an actual incident – namely the concert of 3 February 1839, during the course of which Berlioz first heard the young Pauline Garcia (the future Pauline Viardot) as Euridice, with Gilbert Duprez as Orphée. Indeed, had it not been for the influence of Viardot, Berlioz's desire to hear Gluck in some sort of perfectly ideal form would probably never have come to fruition. For the same reason that prompted Shetland (in *Euphonia*) to refuse to allow Nadira to take the role of Alceste, however, Berlioz qualified Pauline Garcia as a "diva manquée," remarking that at the end of her recitative she made a brief excursion into the lower register of her voice, "whose deeper sonorities she had already allowed us to discover, but at the expense of remaining faithful to the musical text and at the expense of remaining true to the character she had taken upon herself to portray." As for

Duprez: "he would have been perfect had his voice not been extremely fatigued."[11]

Here we find Berlioz confronting the question of performing Gluck in three categories: vocal quality; fidelity to the musical text; truthfulness of dramatic expression.

If we consider the voice as a cultural artifact, we note that the emergence of Pauline Garcia's contralto register, appreciated by Berlioz as early as 1839 (as we see here), and the interest in the repertory of earlier vocal music, particularly Gluck's, that the singer displayed as from that period, would lead Berlioz to come to terms with original Italian version of *Orphée*. Indeed, such an interest in Orpheus' low voice is typical of the romantic era's inclination to favor the contralto register, which, in many nineteenth-century operas, is allotted to evil characters who stand at the dividing-line between the real and the supernatural. (The scenes in the underworld, in both *Orphée* and *Alceste*, are those which, at the time, most attracted both the designers and the critics.) Gilbert Duprez's tenor thus came to be heard as inappropriate to the French version of the opera, which Gluck had specifically prepared for the high tenor voice (*haute-contre*) of Joseph Legros.

Here we see the terms of the problem that Berlioz would solve twenty years later by adapting the role of Orphée to the contralto voice of a woman who would become for him something of a romantic entanglement as well as a close friend, Pauline Viardot. But it should be noted that even earlier, in 1855, Berlioz agreed to indicate to Rosine Stoltz (no romantic entanglement there) the transpositions that she would have to make in order to assume the title role in *Orphée* at the Opéra.

While in his public criticism Berlioz's opinions on the performance of Gluck are firm and clear, they appear to become rather more ambiguous as from 1859. Indeed, his letters to Pauline Viardot at the time reveal a contradictory attitude: reluctant to intervene, for *Orphée*, and refusing (at first) to intervene, for *Alceste*, Berlioz eventually recognized the necessity of doing so. It was then that he opted for the subtle solution of "reproducing" *Orphée*, first, by melding together the Italian version, originally written for the castrato Gaetano Guadagni, and the French version, originally written for the *haute-contre* Legros, and then by smoothing out the synthesis. "That of a maker of mosaics" is the way Berlioz qualified his task here, after having given up on the project he had first envisioned of entirely revising the order of the numbers of the original *Orphée*.[12] The only element that remained of that project, apart from the reordering of a few numbers, was the division of the work into four acts rather than three. It is moreover significant that Berlioz's "purism" further gave way to the cadenza that Pauline Viardot, Camille Saint-Saëns, and Berlioz himself wrote for the concluding aria of Act I, "Amour, viens rendre à mon âme."[13] Like others at the time, Berlioz erroneously attributed this aria to Ferdinando Giuseppe Bertoni – an error that gave him a perfect alibi, as it were, for music written by someone other than Gluck could obviously be modified without reservation!

Still, the desire to return *Orphée* to its original purity led Berlioz piously and attentively to make a number of small adjustments in the vocal part of the title role. Cuts, by shortening the work, strengthened the synthesis of the two versions. To fit the tonalities of the Italian version, Berlioz had to transpose (usually down by fourth or fifth) the numbers from the French version that he had decided to retain. He further modified some of the recitatives and made a number of changes in the text. For the original final chorus, "L'amour triomphe," he substituted a chorus from *Echo et Narcisse*, "Le dieu de Paphos et de Gnide," which had been popular during the First Empire. Finally, he removed from the score several sections that seemed particularly dated, such as the *airs de ballet* and the *chaconne* – for Gluck, to Berlioz's way of thinking, was a musician of the present who deserved to be liberated from the bonds of a now superseded past. The scores and parts used for the 1859 revival further-more reveal that, contrary to what he proclaimed, Berlioz made several changes to the orchestration, most notably in No. 3, Orphée's *romance* and recitative "Objet de mon amour": here, besides adding two clarinets to the ensemble, he placed a violin, oboe, and cello on the stage in order to effect a dialogue with the orchestra and thus reinforce the echo effect upon which the structure of the piece is based.

The reappearance at the Théâtre Lyrique of *Orphée*, literally *re*-pro-duced by Berlioz, on 18 November 1859, was a cultural event of consider-able consequence. Its success was largely due to the extraordinary dramatic authority of Pauline Viardot, who fascinated painters and sculptors as much if not more than she did musicians. Eugène Delacroix, for example, himself little attracted to Gluck, designed the costume for Viardot's Orpheus.

Berlioz's version of Gluck's *Orphée* was long and continues to be sung as the "original" version of the opera. But even Berlioz's version has undergone several transformations. In 1859, Léon Escudier published what he called the "only version entirely in conformity with the per-formance." This was a reduction for voice and piano made by Théodore Ritter, with a preface by Berlioz – now quite rare – that appeared only with the first printing of that score.[14] Here the composer offers a justification for his fusion of the French and Italian versions of the opera while other-wise wholly minimizing his contributions in comparison to those of the director of the Théâtre Lyrique, Léon Carvalho, and of the leading lady, Pauline Viardot. Apart from the replacement of the work's finale, he indicates as his principal modification the restitution to Act I of a recitative from the Italian version that Gluck removed from the French: Orfeo's "Che disse?" For reasons unknown, this preface disappeared from the second printing of the score, which was made shortly after the first few performances. The "version Berlioz" thus became "unrecognized" or "unacknowledged" by its author. Nevertheless, building upon the success of the Paris performances, Viardot went on to sing *Orphée* in England and in Germany, and no one was unaware of the fact that Berlioz was the mastermind of this absolutely stunning revival.

In 1866 Berlioz was asked by the German publisher Gustav Heinze to revise the work that he had done for the Théâtre Lyrique by reinstating those numbers which had been suppressed. When Berlioz refused, Heinze gave the task to Alfred Dörffel, who did indeed take up Berlioz's revision and add the bits set aside in 1859. It is *this* version, published by Peters and still in wide circulation, that passes for the authentic source of the original French version. However, the rehabilitation in recent times of the original Italian version of 1762, along with performers' and conductors' total abandonment of the original French version of 1774, has had the salutary effect of once again drawing attention to the "true" Berlioz version of 1859, which in its own turn may be seen to have the status of an "original."[15]

The tremendous success of *Orphée* in 1859 led the directors of the Opéra to undertake *Alceste*, with Pauline Viardot in the title role. Even more than with *Orphée*, Berlioz was preoccupied with *Alceste* from the moment of that "poetic shock" he felt on first encountering the work through some twenty-five years of writings, which illustrate for us the various factors that led him to bring the opera to life. In this case, however, the transposition of the title role is not justified in the way that it is in *Orphée* because the tessituras of the Italian and French versions of *Alceste* are the same. Despite his public refusal to modify the work, Berlioz agreed privately, if reluctantly, to make a few changes, among them the insertion of the aria "Chi mi parla."

Perhaps one can best explain Berlioz's apparently ambiguous attitude as follows: although he disapproved, as a purist, of making transpositions that altered the tonal plan of the score, he nonetheless allowed himself to make small modifications, additions, and corrections (of the sort he had been calling for since 1834) in the effort to perfect a work that he already considered exemplary.

In addition to motivations of an "exterior" sort, as we might wish to call them, Berlioz was also impelled to act for reasons of a private and even sentimental sort. In the case of *Orphée*, he no doubt wished to atone for the "sin" committed by Offenbach with his *Orphée aux enfers* of 1858. And in the case of *Alceste*, by altering the vocal text (most frequently by transposing it down a minor third), he may well have wished to rediscover, in Pauline Viardot's rendition, the force of one of those "original" voices he so much prized, in this instance, that of Caroline Branchu. It is also possible that, with *Alceste*, he wished to retaliate, on behalf of the Opéra, after the recent, scandalous failure there of *Tannhäuser* – some of whose set designs were reused for the underworld scene of *Alceste* – by setting Gluck in opposition to Wagner! Be this as it may, the success of the revival of *Alceste* at the Opéra, though considerable, was not as great as that occasioned by the revival of *Orphée* at the Théâtre Lyrique.

Five years later, in 1866, Berlioz was invited by Émile Perrin (director of the Opéra since 1862) to supervise another revival of *Alceste*, which opened on 12 October, with Marie Battu in the title role. This provided the composer with an opportunity to reestablish the original tessitura of the role and to restore the many cuts that had been made in the score in 1861. But contrary to what one might think, apart from a few of the 1861 transpositions, Berlioz continued to believe wholeheartedly in some of the earlier changes, including the arrangement of the aria "Divinités du Styx" in Act I and the arrangement of the aria "Qui me parla" in Act III. In addition, he suppressed Hercules' aria "C'est en vain que l'enfer" (from Act III), which he and others wrongly attributed to Gossec. Still, on completing his restoration, Berlioz had the satisfaction of feeling that his task had been well done. Even his old enemy François-Joseph Fétis sent his compliments, writing that Berlioz had "profoundly understood the thinking of *Alceste*'s great composer," to which Berlioz courteously replied that he was pleased to be able to defend their mutual gods.[16] Berlioz had manifested a similar zeal in this regard, two years earlier, when, in 1864, by fitting new words to the vocal line, he assisted his friend Humbert Ferrand to transform the *Marche religieuse* from *Alceste* into a strictly Catholic *Chant pour la communion*, which was published by Brandus in 1865.

Berlioz's work on behalf of Gluck is obviously not the first example, nor is it the last, of one composer "reinventing" another. Ought we in this case, however, take such reinvention as evidence that Berlioz, the quintessential romantic, wished now to adopt a more classical artistic posture? In his efforts to produce the works of Gluck in an ideal fashion, Berlioz was actually under the influence of the grand idea that was in fact the credo of Second Empire society – that *progress* was possible in the arts as it was in all human endeavor. Such an idea resulted from two convictions: first, that modern copies, given their technical excellence, were superior to their ancient models; and second, that *all forms of expression* tended constantly to evolve towards perfection. So it is erroneous to think that Berlioz's attention to the past is an unmistakable signal of a retreat into conservatism. On the contrary, to his contemporaries, Berlioz's concern with "antiquity" was an aspect of a mentality in which the use of the past was but one element of a modern vocabulary designed to engender expression of a kind that was advanced and up to date.

From this point of view, Berlioz's innovative personality is no less present in *Les Troyens* than it is in the *Symphonie fantastique* and *Roméo et Juliette.* And the emotions painted by Gluck are no less contemporary than those painted by Virgil. Even if one sees in *Les Troyens* the apotheosis of Gluckian tragedy, then, one must not take that work as some kind of retraction of an earlier, more obviously romantic aesthetic. As early as 1839, comparing Gluck to Virgil, Berlioz wrote that "if it were not anachronistic to say so, one might suggest that Gluck attempted to depict the ever-suffering ghost of the Queen of Carthage, of that Dido whom Virgil has us discover *indignata sub umbras* and who, in the face of the Trojan warrior who was the cause of all her anguish, fled to the edges of the dark fields in order to hide her wound and her grief."[17] In this way Berlioz demonstrated his conviction that perceiving a work in purely aesthetic terms could give access to what time had rent obscure, and could place that work in a kind of eternal present. It remains to be seen whether, in his capacity as an "arranger" of Gluck, Berlioz believed he had attained the same perfection that he strived for in his own compositions, or whether, on the contrary, he was doubtful of having done so, and thus preferred, on closing his *Mémoires*, to say nothing more.

Berlioz's editorial efforts on behalf of Gluck would in any event ensure that modern musicologists would engage with the work of the earlier master. "In Europe," Berlioz wrote in *Les Grotesques de la musique* (1859),

> no one has dared to undertake a new, carefully prepared, annotated edition,
> properly translated into German and Italian, of Gluck's six grand operas.
> And no one has made a serious attempt to find subscribers for such an
> edition. No one has even contemplated risking twenty thousand francs [...]
> to fight against the ever more numerous tendencies that threaten to destroy
> such chefs-d'œuvre. Thus, despite the great resources that are available to art
> and to industry, these masterpieces, thanks to everyone's monstrous
> indifference to the well-being of the art of music, will perish.

These touching lines had the salutary effect of inspiring Fanny Pelletan, a wealthy and well-trained musician, to undertake a first complete edition of Gluck's operas. Pelletan, aided by her teacher, Berlioz's friend Berthold Damcke, brought out the two *Iphigénies*, *Alceste*, and *Armide* between 1873 and 1876 (the year of her death). What was Gluck's salvation was Berlioz's salvation as well.

Translated by Peter Bloom

15 Berlioz and Mozart

HUGH MACDONALD

"J'adore Mozart" wrote Berlioz in 1856.[1] Ten years later, at a time when he took pleasure in *not* going to operas any more, he attended eight performances of *Don Giovanni* at the Théâtre Lyrique, where he was seen to "cover his face and cry like a child."[2] Yet neither Berlioz himself nor his biographers are ever inclined to include Mozart among the select pantheon of historical figures who inspired him most deeply, the names being more usually Shakespeare, Goethe, Virgil, and among musicians Gluck, Beethoven, sometimes Weber, sometimes Spontini. Mozart never displaced Gluck in Berlioz's mind as the greatest of eighteenth-century composers, a preference which very few would admit to in the present century when an admiration for Mozart has been a solid *donné* among professionals and amateurs alike. Where did Mozart stand in his critical perspectives, and what part did Mozart play in his work as conductor and composer?

The matter was admirably summed up by Berlioz himself in chapter 17 of the *Mémoires*, which is devoted entirely to his regard for Mozart. Written probably in 1848, or soon after, it describes the fiery passions of his student years: "I have said that [...] I was taken up exclusively with the study of great dramatic music. I should rather have said, of lyric tragedy; and it was for this reason that I regarded Mozart with a certain coolness." Gluck was performed in French at the Opéra while Mozart was sung in Italian at the Théâtre Italien, and that was sufficient to assign him to the enemy camp. The only Mozart opera to be heard in French at the Opéra was *Les Mystères d'Isis*, a garbled version of *Die Zauberflöte* which Berlioz always held up as an example of a work of art travestied by a meddling posterity. Berlioz's most regular attitude to Mozart in his early years was not as a master whose works inspired his own creative flame but as a figure whose heroic integrity had to be defended against the impostures of interfering editors. And although the *Mémoires* indicate that "the marvelous beauty of his quartets and quintets and one or two of the sonatas" later converted him to the earlier master's celestial genius, his experience of Mozart was, like that of many of his contemporaries, distinctly incomplete.

The two works that he most consistently admired were *Don Giovanni* and *Die Zauberflöte*; he also valued *Le Nozze di Figaro*, one of the few operas he ever conducted, and he included his rather lukewarm notice of *Die Entführung* in the collection *À travers chants* in 1862. It is uncertain whether he ever heard a performance of *Così fan tutte* or more than a few extracts from *Idomeneo* and *La Clemenza di Tito*. Of the choral works both the *Requiem* and *Ave verum corpus* were frequently performed in his time, and the last four symphonies featured regularly in the more classically oriented concert series such as that of the Société des Concerts. He had very little to say about the instrumental music – nothing about the piano concertos, for example – and regarded Mozart as primarily a composer for the stage. He often repeated the anecdote that Mozart failed to win a commission from the Paris Opéra, partly as an illustration of the crassness of administrators in the face of genius, partly, one suspects, in disappointment that Mozart did not leave posterity a French opera, like those of Gluck, where his expressive style might have been allied to classical French drama.

Knowledge of Mozart's life and character remained largely anecdotal in Berlioz's time. The volume of Michaud's serial *Biographie universelle* which contained the entry on Mozart came out after Berlioz left La Côte-Saint-André, so that Gluck had the alphabetical advantage of inflaming the boy's imagination in his father's library. The sole works in French available to Berlioz were Winckler's *Notice biographique sur Jean-Chrysostyme-Wolfgang-Théophile Mozart* (1801, based on Schlichtegroll's *Nekrolog* of 1793) and C. F. Cramer's *Trente-deux anecdotes sur Mozart* (1800, translated from Rochlitz's articles about Mozart in the *Allgemeine musikalische Zeitung* of 1798). The Mozart section of Stendhal's *Vies de Haydn, de Mozart et de Metastase*, published in 1814, was a shameless theft of Cramer's book. Nonetheless Mozart occupied a remarkably honored place in critical opinion under the Empire and was already perceived to have a certain canonic quality.[3] Nearer 1830, Fétis's adulation of Mozart in the *Revue Musicale* raised public consciousness of the instrumental music, and the craze for Hoffmann's stories chimed with the success of *Don Giovanni* on the French stage.[4]

When Oulibicheff's *Nouvelle Biographie de Mozart* appeared in 1843, Berlioz reviewed it generously,[5] complaining only that Oulibicheff's enthusiasm for Mozart compelled him to denigrate Beethoven. Another biographer, Edward Holmes, whose *Life of Mozart* came out in 1845, became one of Berlioz's most eloquent admirers and a staunch friend at a time when his view of Mozart seems to have broadened. But few – and Berlioz was no exception – were ready to bestow upon Mozart the halo of universal genius that has adorned him since the beginning of the twentieth century, for few were willing to look beyond the romantic, and especially demonic, qualities of *Don Giovanni*, which meshed so well with the image of the misunderstood prodigy cut down in his prime and pitched into an unmarked grave.

Don Giovanni shared a distinction Berlioz accorded to *Der Freischütz*, *La Vestale*, *Fidelio*, *Il Barbiere di Seviglia*, *Iphigénie en Tauride*, and *Les Huguenots*; when those works are being played, the imaginary orchestral players in his *Les Soirées de l'orchestre* concentrate on their duties and do not swap stories and idle chatter. But his profound admiration for *Don Giovanni* was by no means uncritical; he could never accept Donna Anna's second act aria "Non mi dir" and devoted much of the Mozart chapter of the *Mémoires* to explaining why:

> It is an aria of intense sadness, full of a heartbreaking sense of loss and sorrowing love, but towards the end degenerating without warning into music of such appalling inanity and vulgarity that one can hardly believe it to be the work of the same man. [...] I could not readily forgive Mozart for such a blunder. Today I feel that I would give some of my own blood to erase that shameful page and a few more of the same kind which one is forced to recognize among his works.

Far from softening the fury of his attack, he later felt it should to be intensified, adding as a footnote: "Even shameful seems to me too light a word. Mozart in this passage has committed one of the most odious and idiotic crimes against passion, taste, and common sense of which the history of art provides an example." In 1857 Delacroix noted sourly in his journal how Berlioz had quite spoiled a dinner party at Pauline Viardot's by going on at great length against *fioriture* in opera, picking on "Non mi dir" as a prime culprit.[6]

He was never in any doubt, however, that the opera was a great masterpiece. He may well have consulted the full score of the opera published in Paris by Frey in about 1820 and thus been familiar with the work before he heard it performed in French at the Odéon in December 1827 (soon after the English Shakespeare season) as an adaptation of Molière's *Le Festin de pierre*.[7] The crucial revelation for Parisians was the Opéra production of 1834, less thoroughly mangled than its 1805 production, but nonetheless considerably reshaped to suit the tastes and exigencies of the time and a marked success in the repertory.[8] It was preceded by a performance in Italian at the Théâtre Italien only a few weeks before, with Tamburini as the Don, Rubini as Ottavio, and Grisi as Donna Anna. This was attended by Berlioz in his capacity as critic for *Le Rénovateur*, and here he laid out his admiration in the plainest terms:

> Everything is so wonderfully beautiful in this score! The forms are so pure, the contours so rounded and so graceful, and the style so Raphaelesque! [...] The partisan of the old Italian school will show you how Mozart's melodies

are very close to the style of that glorious era. The Gluckist will quote you twenty passages where declamation outweighs melodic feeling, and will even prove that in the first bars that the Commendatore's statue sings from his plinth Mozart reveals a distinct reminiscence of *Alceste*. The classicist will claim Mozart as his own by focusing on the purity of the harmony and the restraint with which the composer handles the orchestra, while the romantic, enchanted by the fantastical nature of the subject, the boldness of the drama, and the *truth* with which the composer has expressed them, will find in it further proof in support of his artistic religion. But everyone will agree in proclaiming the German composer's work to be sublime.[9]

The review Berlioz wrote of *Don Juan* in March 1834 was the first full-scale review he ever wrote of a major Opéra production.[10] He offered no scene-by-scene analysis but launched into panegyric:

The success of *Don Juan* at the Opéra is an event of the highest artistic interest. It proves beyond a doubt that the public can now absorb deeply thought-out music which is conscientiously written, tastefully orchestrated, and always expressive, dramatic and true, without getting bored. This music is free of catchy tunes, it bears the stamp of the most exalted poetic ideas, it is free and proud, never servilely bowing to the gallery, and it seeks only enlightened approbation, scorning the applause of ignorant crowds.

With Dérivis as the Commendatore, Levasseur as Leporello, Falcon as Anna, Gras-Dorus as Elvira, and Cinti-Damoreau as Zerlina, it had a fine cast. The fact that the tenor Nourrit sang the baritone title role elicited little comment from Berlioz. He was more preoccupied by interpolations in the score, the most offensive of which was the ballet sequence introduced before the supper scene, using various instrumental works by Mozart grossly reorchestrated with bass drum and ophicleide. The *Dies irae* from the *Requiem* was sung just before the final scene to accompany an extraordinary tableau in which a procession of young girls dressed in white bring forward Donna Anna's bier. The black-veiled corpse of Donna Anna half rises from the bier, while Don Juan goes insane. The final scene in Mozart's score was not sung at all. In his second notice of the production, in November 1835, Berlioz was deeply impressed by the impact of the chorus as Don Juan is driven to destruction. By 1839, with the same production still on show, Berlioz was convinced that if he were alive Mozart would rather it were not played at all.[11]

Rage at what Mozart's score suffered at the hands of meddling interference springs from the pages of Berlioz's letters and feuilletons in the following years. The *Don Juan Quadrille* concocted by the showman-conductor Musard drew some bitter jibes, exacerbated by the similarity of their names when pronounced in French and by the fact that Musard was making a fortune while Mozart died a pauper. Berlioz repeatedly complained that the Serenade should be accompanied by a mandolin, and not by two guitars, or pizzicato violins, or any other substitute. In London in 1848 (and again in 1851) he was horrified by Costa's reorchestrations of *Don Giovanni* and *Figaro* with extra trombone parts, plenty of bass drum, and even an ophicleide in the supper scene. But he found Henriette Sontag an enchanting Zerlina: "It is impossible, I think, for the liveliest imagination to conceive a more complete realization of Mozart's ideal."[12] A revival of *Don Giovanni* at the Théâtre Italien in 1863, with Adelina Patti as Zerlina, was apparently "shameful,"[13] but when the Théâtre Lyrique mounted it in 1866 (almost simultaneously with less successful revivals at the Opéra and the Théâtre Italien), Berlioz finally found a production that gave him infinite pleasure, with its superb array of female singers: Charton-Demeur as Donna Anna, Nilsson as Donna Elvira, and Miolan-Carvalho as Zerlina.

The Mozart opera that pleased him second only to *Don Giovanni* was *Die Zauberflöte*.[14] Once again he found fault with certain sections of the work and again felt the need to defend its integrity against the invasion of arrangers. As *Les Mystères d'Isis* it enjoyed enormous success at the Opéra almost continuously from 1801 to 1827. This was a pastiche arranged by the Bohemian composer Lachnith, using extracts from *Don Giovanni*, *Figaro*, and *La Clemenza di Tito*, even a tune from a Haydn symphony, along with selected sections of *Die Zauberflöte* itself.[15] Berlioz was first able to see it in the summer of 1823, with Mme Branchu in the cast. He was impressed by its "religious splendors"[16] and always tended to think of it as a quasi-spiritual work. But studying the score in the Conservatoire library he discovered how profoundly garbled the current version was and thereafter always denounced Lachnith as an assassin.[17] He was delighted when a company visiting from Aachen played the opera in German in its original form at the Théâtre Italien in May 1829 – original, that is, allowing for the insertion of "O wie ängstlich" from *Die Entführung* by the tenor, Haitzinger. Being then firmly entrenched against the vocal excesses of Italian opera, Berlioz found the Queen of the Night's music unacceptable and always coupled it with "Non mi dir" as an example of Mozart's occasional but fatal lack of judgment. One discovery that surprised him was the overture's brilliant demonstration of the effectiveness, even expressiveness, of fugues, the procedure he consistently decried in its stricter forms.[18]

He heard the opera in Hamburg in 1843, with the great bass Reichel singing Sarastro, and again at Covent Garden in 1851, with Mario as Tamino, Grisi as Pamina, Viardot as Papagena, and Formes as Sarastro. His review of that performance contains the most eloquent Mozart criticism he ever wrote. Not even in his writings on Gluck does admiration find so poetic expression as this. He differentiated three styles in the opera: the passionate, the comic, and the antique-religious, and of these it is the antique-religious that moved him most:

> This style is all found in the second act, with five numbers – five miracles – for which any admiration is merely pale and inadequate. These are the instrumental March, Sarastro's air with chorus "O Isis und Osiris," his second air with two verses "In diesen heil'gen Hallen," the moralities sung by the two men in armor to a chorale accompanied by the orchestra in fugal style, and lastly two choruses of priests. This, as I say, is of incomparable beauty and immensely elevated in style and thought. Everything about it is superb: expression, melody, harmony, rhythm, orchestration, and modulation. No one before Mozart came even close to such perfection in this manner, and I fear that no one has done so since. It would be folly to attempt it. These are the Egyptian pyramids of music; they exist, they defy time and feeble imitations. Most to be admired is the sovereign majesty, the lordly calm of Sarastro, whom everyone in the temple of Isis must obey. No high priest of any ancient religion ever equaled this in grandeur, serenity, force, and tenderness all at once. He sings of the goodness of the gods and the charm of virtue, and everything responds sympathetically to his voice; even the monument he inhabits seems to respond with mysterious echoes. One can imagine walking with him in the holy courts of heaven, breathing unknown scents in an atmosphere flooded with new and sweeter light; the earth and its sorrowful passions are forgotten. Sarastro himself falls into a state of sublime ecstasy as he sings. The grandeur of his voice gets more and more monumental in its calm gravity; the sound dims and dies; a profound silence falls, full of mystery all around; everything is wrapped in contemplative silence. We are at the doorway to the Infinite.[19]

Other aspects of the opera pleased him less. He regarded Schikaneder's libretto as stupid and absurd (like many before and since); he objected not only to the Queen of the Night's roulades but also to two bars of elaboration in Pamina's "Ach ich fühl's"; he found the music for the Three Ladies and the Three Boys too ordinary, and somewhat surprisingly felt that the orchestra intrudes too much on the vocal line. But he was delighted by Papageno's music and by much in Tamino and Pamina's roles.

As part of its wide-ranging Mozart series in the eighteen-sixties, the Théâtre Lyrique gave one hundred and seventy-two performances of *La Flûte enchantée* between 1865 and 1868. Berlioz certainly went to see it, although he had given up writing reviews and made no mention of it in his correspondence. Not as crudely manhandled as *Les Mystères d'Isis*, this version nevertheless strayed freely from the original text, which would have distressed him. Equally saddening for Berlioz was to see some discarded sets from *Les Troyens à Carthage* recycled to represent the Egyptian temple. Berlioz observed sourly to his neighbor in the theatre that the public applauded these sets in *La Flûte enchantée*, though they had not applauded them in *Les Troyens*. "They are a remarkable people, the Parisians," he was overheard to say.[20]

Since it lacks the dramatic force of *Don Giovanni* and the solemnity of *Die Zauberflöte*, *Le Nozze di Figaro* never made quite the same impression on Berlioz. He heard it at the Théâtre Italien in 1823 and assigned it, perhaps unthinkingly, to the Italian school. He heard it again in 1826, this time in French at the Odéon. In 1839, when it was revived at the Théâtre Italien, he wrote a notice which included some fine sentiments:

> It is a long time since we have heard music at the Théâtre Italien as pure, expressive, witty, clever, and natural as this. Never have I felt such admiration for the creative power of Mozart's genius nor for the constant lucidity of his mind. There is something despairing, I was almost going to say vexing, about this unfailing beauty, always calm and sure of itself and forcing us to acknowledge our obeisance from beginning to end of a very long work.[21]

He saw *Figaro* again in Berlin, in 1843, but he was suffering at the time from the "black philosophy" which caused him (as he was well aware) to adopt some perverse opinions: "I might [...] announce that it was time to have done with this adulation of Mozart, with his operas that are all alike and his maddening imperturbability, and that Cimarosa's *Il Matrimonio segreto* [...] is nearly as boring as *Le Nozze di Figaro*." This passage in the *Mémoires*, from the Seventh Letter describing his travels in Germany, is alarmingly open to misinterpretation, though we should recognize a pre-echo of the same "maddening imperturbability" in his 1839 review of the opera. In 1867 he remarked to Cui that Mozart's operas "are all alike. His imperturbable composure (*beau sang-froid*) irritates and exasperates."[22]

In 1848 he conducted two performances of *Figaro* at Drury Lane Theatre, London, though without any special excitement to be doing so. He was proud not to permit the kind of "trombonization" that Costa inflicted on Mozart's operas a few yards away at Covent Garden. A performance at the rival house, Her Majesty's Theatre, in 1851, was again "trombonized and ophicleided," but at least it had two performers who enchanted Berlioz: Cruvelli as Cherubino, and Sontag as Susanna. The latter drew some evocative writing from Berlioz:

> When in the garden scene at night Mme Sontag sang that divine monologue for a woman in love, which I had only ever heard crudely done ["Deh vieni"], in her *mezza voce*, so tender, soft, and mysterious all at once, this secret music (which I nonetheless understood) seemed to me a thousand times more bewitching. "That's it!" I thought to myself, being careful not to exclaim aloud, "that's the perfect faithful rendering of Mozart's admirable

piece! That's the true song of solitude, of ecstatic reverie, of the night's mysteries; that's how a woman's voice should murmur in such a scene; that's true subtlety in singing, the half-shade, the true *piano* and *pianissimo* that composers can get from an orchestra of a hundred players or from choruses of two hundred voices, but which they cannot get from most singers, whether competent or incompetent, Italian or French, intelligent or stupid, human or divine, either for gold or jewelry, or by flattery or threat, or with kisses or blows."[23]

He included this aria in a concert he gave in Baden in August 1858, sung by Anne Charton-Demeur, and again in one of his last concerts, in St. Petersburg on 28 November 1867, sung by Anna Regan. The last staging of the opera he saw was a very successful version given at the Théâtre Lyrique in May 1858, with Beaumarchais's text versified by Barbier and Carré and the music more or less intact. Berlioz devoted very little space to it in his review.

To the remaining Mozart operas he paid little attention. He seems not to have attended either of the two productions of *Così fan tutte* given in Paris in his time, the first at the Théâtre Italien in November 1862, the second four months later at the Théâtre Lyrique in an unsuccessful rehash fitted approximately to Shakespeare's *Love's Labour's Lost* by the indefatigable Barbier and Carré. Berlioz was in Germany when it opened and may not have troubled to see it on his return. But he at least knew the magnificent quintet from Act I since he conducted it in a concert in London on 6 July 1855 with the stellar line-up of Grisi, Bosio, Mario, Tamburini, and Lablache.

His notice of *Die Entführung aus dem Serail*, when it was staged at the Théâtre Lyrique as *L'Enlèvement au sérail* in 1859 on a double bill with Weber's *Abu Hassan*, was contemptuous of its feeble libretto and juvenile music, making exception only for the Constanze–Belmonte duet near the end ("Meinetwegen sollst du sterben").[24] He was nonetheless angry at the reorganization and adaptation the opera had undergone and stood up for the composer's integrity once again.

Parts of *Idomeneo* were used in a pastiche entitled *Louis XII ou la Route de Reims*, staged at the Odéon in 1825, but that Berlioz heard it or knew what it was is unlikely. Fragments from the opera were quite frequently performed by the Société des Concerts in the years 1836–1849 without provoking much response from Berlioz's pen; he seems not to have grasped the opera's manifest debt to Gluck, or at least not to have commented on it in print. He heard the overture and the opening aria in a concert in January 1863.

La Clemenza di Tito provided substantial sections of *Les Mystères d'Isis*, so Berlioz was probably as well acquainted with it as with *Idomeneo*.

He included an aria (which?) in a concert he conducted in Paris on 24 April 1842, and in his lengthy essay on *Fidelio* written in 1860 he stepped aside briefly to rebuke Mozart for allowing the basset horn to indulge in over-elaborate concertante figures in Vitellia's aria "Non più di fiori" at a moment when the singer is contemplating her own death.[25]

Berlioz had the opportunity to see *Der Schauspieldirektor* in Paris in 1856, but since it was rewritten by a couple of boulevardier wordsmiths and mounted by Offenbach, he stayed away.[26]

Of the two choral works in general circulation Berlioz deeply admired the motet *Ave verum corpus* but had reservations about the *Requiem*, although he recognized it to be a masterpiece. The fugal *Kyrie* was naturally not to his taste, and the *Tuba mirum*, with its single trombone where only a thousand could convey a sufficiently overwhelming vision of the Last Judgment, struck him as puny and inadequate.[27] The *Requiem* was often heard at funerals, at Choron's and Chopin's for example, and for the return of Napoléon's ashes to Paris in December 1840. The *Ave verum* he cited complete in the *Grand Traité d'instrumentation* as a fine example of writing for voices in the middle register, and he included it in his concerts at least five times, including his monster concerts for the 1855 Exposition Universelle and in two of his final concerts in Russia in 1867–1868. In taking issue with his friend Joseph d'Ortigue's view that religious music should aspire to the nature of plainchant and not be infected by expressiveness, he used the *Ave verum*, "that sublime expression of ecstatic adoration," as evidence that the composition of true sacred music did not have to confine itself to the old church modes.[28] "God dictated it, an angel wrote it down," he wrote.[29]

It is in the area of instrumental music that Berlioz's regard for Mozart is most ambiguous. Despite his admission in the *Mémoires* that his eyes were eventually opened to the "marvelous beauty of the quartets and quintets," he had nothing to say about those works, nothing to say about the concertos, and little comment on the symphonies. He conducted the *Jupiter* Symphony just once, in London, on 24 March 1852. Ganz, citing unnamed sources, reports that in the "swift movement of the fugal finale the players reached the 'acme of execution'. Berlioz's interpretation was faultless in clarity, balance of phrase and rare nobility of style."[30] Since he was insistent on clarity and precision as essentials of the art of conducting – in contrast to the more impulsive style advocated by Liszt and Wagner – it is surprising that he did not conduct more Mozart, where these qualities must have been most helpful and effective. He proposed to include the C-Minor Piano Concerto, K. 491, in his first St. Petersburg concert in 1867, but in fact did not do so.[31] The last four symphonies appeared regularly in the programs of the Société des Concerts in the years when Berlioz reviewed them, so he was familiar with them, even though he had little critical insight to offer. In 1839, after a performance of the *Prague* Symphony, he could only feel the immense distance which separated this work from the "sublimities" of Beethoven.[32] The G-Minor Symphony was "an admirable masterpiece," although the minuet he took to be some kind of crude joke, and the finale of the E-flat Symphony he regarded as definitely inferior to the rest.[33]

He was aware of seventeen symphonies, but only considered the last three to be worth playing.[34] In 1844 he wrote dismissively that in his symphonies Mozart, like Haydn, made no attempt to break out of old formulae, with the "more or less clever succession of pretty phrases, little melodic fancies and some witty and piquant orchestral touches. These works are simply there to divert the ear. There is never the least tendency towards what we call poetic ideas. [. . .] Their sense of expression was unawakened and seems to have come alive only when they were setting words to music." Their orchestration too, he noted, was unadventurous.[35] Gluck, who never wrote symphonies and sonatas, was innocent of this fatal weakness.

As for Mozart's juvenile works, he felt Leopold made a great mistake in preserving them.[36] On seeing the overture to *Die Entführung* (which Berlioz believed to have been composed at the age of fifteen) he should have said: "My son, you have just written a truly awful overture. You said the rosary before beginning, I'm sure, but you will now go and write another, and this time you will tell your rosary to get the saints to inspire you a bit better."[37] When Joachim said he had deliberately sought to sustain a lengthy dissonance in one of his overtures, Berlioz remarked to the Princess Wittgenstein that he would prefer Mozart's early piano sonatas, which was *not* intended as a compliment.[38]

Mozart's chamber music certainly stood below Beethoven's in Berlioz's estimation, and although he had many opportunities to hear it he felt no special resonances with it, at least none that he ever wrote about in his feuilletons or correspondence. Baillot's series of chamber concerts in the eighteen-twenties and thirties included many performances of Mozart quartets and quintets, and later ensembles continued to do so.[39] Berlioz's strictures against Fétis in the monologues of *Lélio* must certainly refer to Fétis's "corrections" of Beethoven's Fifth Symphony, but he surely also knew that Fétis had rewritten Mozart's C-Major Quartet (K. 465, the "Dissonance") in order to remove the dissonances, a matter which was widely discussed at the Conservatoire in 1830.[40]

It remains to consider whether Mozart's music had any direct or indirect impact on Berlioz's own. Berlioz himself denied it, in all essentials, but it is tempting nonetheless to see Mozartian influences at work here and there. One piece by Mozart, the duet "Là ci darem la mano" from *Don Giovanni*, inspired him to compose a set of variations for guitar, published in 1828 but now lost;[41] "inspired" is perhaps misleading, since he was simply using a melody borrowed by every other composer of the day for variations with no affinity implied. In at least two elements of the *Sérénade* in *Harold en Italie*, we may begin to trace a line to Mozart. The gurgling low sixteenth-notes in the second clarinet that starts at bar 48 of the *Sérénade* may come from a similar passage in the Maskers' Trio in the first act finale of *Don Giovanni*, especially since Berlioz drew attention to this effect in the *Traité d'instrumentation*, commending that particular use of the low clarinet; something similar had already appeared at bar 61 of the *Quartetto e coro dei maggi* of 1831, coupled with a bassoon. It seems also to be no coincidence that Berlioz should attempt a complex combination of three different meters in the *Sérénade* in the very year, 1834, that he was thinking deeply about the Opéra's production of *Don Juan*. He drew his readers' attention, after all, to the sophistication of the first act finale with its three off-stage bands in different meters, a passage which he also gives advice about in his brochure on conducting, *Le Chef d'orchestre*. When he came to review the third act of *Les Huguenots* in 1836 he lauded Meyerbeer's clever combination of three different choruses – a chorus of soldiers, a chorus of women at prayer, and a chorus of Catholics exclaiming in alarm – and acknowledged that it far surpassed Mozart's three off-stage orchestras in complexity. Whether indebted to Mozart or Rossini (*Guillaume Tell*) or Meyerbeer, Berlioz remained fond of combining two or more different strata of music that have been heard individually in advance. The three off-stage orchestras in the first act finale of *Les Troyens* should perhaps be seen as legitimate descendants of *Don Giovanni*.

Some observers perceive a Mozartian grace in Berlioz's last works, especially *Béatrice et Bénédict*. Andrew Porter has compared the duet "Nuit paisible et sereine" with "Deh vieni" (in *Figaro*) and the trio "Soave sia il vento" (in *Così*),[42] while David Cairns identifies as Mozartian a "general ideal of lucidity, lyrical grace, and wit combined with dramatic expressiveness" rather than in characteristics of style or form.[43] The difficulty is that Berlioz was apparently untouched by that side of Mozart's genius, and I would myself be more inclined to perceive Mozartian characteristics when Berlioz aims at the Gluckian solemnity and religiosity which he so admired in *Die Zauberflöte*. Many pages in the last act of *Idomeneo* anticipate Berlioz's world, and I believe that in the last part of *L'Enfance du Christ* he modeled the Ishmaelite father's high moral tone on Sarastro, especially after St.Joseph, like Tamino, has had to knock on three doors before gaining admittance to the Ishmaelite's house. The closing chorus of *L'Enfance du Christ* might be considered in the spirit of the *Ave verum*. Sarastro is certainly present in the figure of Priam in *Les Troyens*, and the solemnity of the last pages of the opera owes as much to Mozart as to Gluck.

Berlioz's fuller knowledge of Mozart came late in life. In 1862 he told Cornelius "We are beginning to understand Mozart,"[44] reflecting the fact that throughout his working life Berlioz never had the opportunity to see beyond the adaptations that shielded the true Mozart from public view. Thus although Berlioz persistently championed the integrity of Mozart's work, it was as if the composer's integrity meant more to him than the music itself. It was almost worse that Mozart should be played everywhere but played wrong while Gluck, whose works had never been disfigured to the same degree, was not being played at all. "Mozart," he wrote in 1839, "is far from Gluck in dramatic music, whatever anyone may say, enormously far." "I admire Mozart profoundly, but he *moves* me less than those three composers [Gluck, Beethoven, and Weber]."[45] Whereas in his earlier years Berlioz did not hesitate to rank Gluck above his younger contemporary, by the end of his life he was no longer quite so sure.

16   Berlioz and Beethoven

DAVID CAIRNS

In the reminiscences of Berlioz which he addressed to Eduard Hanslick in the *Revue et Gazette musicale* ten years after the composer's death, Stephen Heller recalled his friend's response to a performance of Beethoven's E-Minor Quartet (the second "Rasumovsky"), which they attended together in the eighteen-sixties:

> During the adagio there was a look of rapture, of ecstasy on his face; it was as if he had experienced a "transubstantiation." One or two other fine works still remained to be played at the concert, but we didn't wait for them. I accompanied Berlioz to his door. On the way no word was exchanged between us: we were still hearing the Adagio and its sublime prayer. As I said good-bye he took my hand and said: "That man had everything . . . and we have nothing!"[1]

To that anecdote we may add Berlioz's account of a rehearsal of a late Beethoven quartet, perhaps Op. 127, which was in the repertory of the Bohrer Quartet when they played in Paris in February and March 1830:[2]

> To my mind Anton Bohrer feels and understands the popularly supposed eccentric and unintelligible works among Beethoven's output as few men do. I can see him now, at quartet rehearsals, with his brother Max (the well-known cellist, now in America), Claudel, second violin, and Urhan, viola, in ardent support. Max, at the strains of this transcendental music, would smile with the sheer pride and delight of playing it; he had the relaxed, contented air that comes from breathing one's native element. Urhan worshipped in silence, eyes averted as though from the radiance of the sun; he seemed to be saying, "God willed that there should be a man as great as Beethoven, and that we should be allowed to contemplate him. God willed it." Claudel admired the others for the depth of their admiration. But with Anton Bohrer, the first violin, it was a sublime passion, an ecstasy of love.
>
> One evening, in one of those unearthly Adagios where Beethoven's spirit soars vast and solitary like the huge bird above the snows of Chimborazo, Bohrer's violin, as it sang the heavenly melody, seemed to become possessed with the divine fire and, suddenly taking on a new force and eloquence of expression, broke into accents unknown even to it, while his face lit up with the light of pure inspiration. We held our breaths, our hearts swelled – when, abruptly, he stopped, put down his bow and ran from the room. Mme Bohrer, worried, went after him; but Max, still smiling, said, "It's nothing – he couldn't contain his feelings. Leave him to calm down a little, then we'll start again. You must forgive him." We forgive you – dear great artist.[3]

The image of the bird soaring to unknown heights (taken from the passage on the condor in Alexander von Humboldt's *Tableaux de la nature*, a copy of which was in Berlioz's father's library) recurs more than once in his writings on Beethoven. For Berlioz, Beethoven's spirit and sovereign art inhabit regions beyond the reach of other composers, even of his beloved Gluck. At times he will seem to place the two on an equal footing.[4] But Beethoven is the greatest. It was the discovery of his music, in the winter and spring of 1828, that set Berlioz consciously on a new compositional path, and that would soon inspire him to become one of Beethoven's most dedicated and articulate champions.

The shock of that discovery can be compared only to the experience of hearing the full orchestra and chorus of the Paris Opéra six years earlier, after a boyhood in which the summit of musical life was the band of the local Garde Nationale. But the impact must have been in some ways even more powerful and profound on a sensibility as acute as Berlioz's and on a musician whose musical experiences had been quite circumscribed. There had been a vigorous French tradition of symphonic writing at the turn of the century, but it had petered out by the time Berlioz came to Paris in 1821. The French tradition he acquired, in the opera house and the library, was that of Gluck and his lesser followers, and Cherubini and Spontini. (Weber's *Der Freischütz*, at the Odéon throughout 1825, alone suggested perspectives beyond the confines of classicism.) The occasional Haydn or Mozart symphony, performed without conviction on the bare stage of the Opéra at the Lenten *concerts spirituels*, left little impression. The story of Berlioz exclaiming, after the first night of the English company's *Romeo and Juliet* in September 1827, that he would "write his greatest symphony on the play" (reported in chapter 18 of the *Mémoires*) – a story he himself denied – cannot possibly be true. At that stage, six months before the first Conservatoire concert, he would not have thought in those terms. An operatic *Romeo* could have been in his mind: a symphonic *Romeo* would not have occurred to him.

Exactly when Berlioz first became aware of Beethoven is uncertain. In his *Mémoires* (in chapter 14) he speaks of having seen two of the symphonies in score, and of "sensing" that Beethoven was a "sun," though "a sun obscured by heavy clouds." It is very likely that he knew of the Beethoven symphony rehearsals going on in the months preceding the inaugural season of the Société des Concerts du Conservatoire – many of the players were friends of his – and that it excited his curiosity. But nothing can have prepared him for the reality, encountered in the flesh in the resonant acoustics and intimate ambiance of the Conservatoire Hall – the *Eroica* and the Fifth played by the orchestral élite of Paris, diligently prepared under the violinist-conductor François-Antoine Habeneck and animated by a passionate belief in the holiness of their cause.

By the time Berlioz left for Italy three years later he had heard the first eight symphonies, some of them several times, as well as various other works including the *Coriolan* Overture (and the C-sharp-Minor Quartet), had studied the Ninth in the Conservatoire library, and had taken Beethoven to his heart and soul and mind. In Beethoven's music, in the rages and lightning emotions of the Fifth, the pantheistic joys of the *Pastoral*, the slow movement of the Seventh, "that inconceivable achievement of the great master of somber and profound meditation,"[5] he found the mirror of his own innermost self and the catalyst his creative being had been waiting for.

The revelation was both formal and expressive, or rather an interfusing of the two. It did not make him forswear Gluck or abandon the artistic beliefs by which he had lived. That would have been out of character in someone of such tenacious loyalties, and in any case not necessary. He remained a dramatist. But his whole conception of the dramatic was enlarged to include the symphonic, which, he saw at once, had become in Beethoven's hands a medium for dramatic music of a scope and on a scale not encountered before. Berlioz (like Liszt) was wrong when he accused Haydn of slavishly adhering to formal stereotypes in his symphonies; but he was right to see that the Beethovenian revolution was for him a crucial liberation. Beethoven's symphonic dramas were living organisms. Their endless variety of compositional procedures was the musical equivalent of what Shakespeare's plays taught – the formal freedom, after years of French classical drama turned out according to set rules. Form was each individual work's unique response to the poetic idea and material it embodied. Each work – the *Eroica*, the Fifth, the *Pastoral*, and the others – was a fresh dramatic utterance, with its own character and color, its own laws and structure.

This "pensée poétique" governing a whole symphony yet subordinate to purely musical logic was for Berlioz one of the revelations of Beethoven. Complementary to it was the revelation of the limitless expressive possibilities of the symphony orchestra. The language of instruments spoke. It was as eloquent as human speech – more so, in fact: when Berlioz wrote his love scene for Romeo and Juliet he entrusted it to the orchestra alone.

The consequence of 1828 was an upheaval in Berlioz's artistic being. Beethoven widened not only Berlioz's idea of what was possible in music but of what he himself could achieve. Like Columbus, Beethoven had discovered a new world. Why should he not be its Cortez or Pizarro? From now on, the Beethovenian symphony – what Berlioz calls the *genre instrumental expressif* – is at the forefront of his thoughts and ambitions. Already by the end of 1828 the symphony that will become the *Fantastique* is active within him.

The resulting work, and its successors, show us that Beethoven's influence on Berlioz was general rather than specific. Certainly the many detailed innovations – the harmonic freedom, the emancipation of the timpani, the combination of different rhythms and meters, and such things as the melodic disintegration at the end of *Coriolan* and the *Eroica*'s Funeral March, used as an image of death – were not lost on him. Particular echoes of Beethoven may strike us in the *Fantastique*, notably in the slow movement, the *Scène aux champs* – the *Pastoral*'s quail-call on the oboe, the successive *fortissimo* diminished sevenths of the opening movement of the Fifth, Florestan's ebbing paroxysm in *Fidelio*; and Berlioz has, clearly, learned from what Wilfrid Mellers calls "Beethoven's technique of thematic generation and transformation."[6] But the formal processes are quite different. Berlioz does not follow the Viennese classical tradition exemplified, however radically, by Beethoven's symphonies. The reprise of the *idée fixe* two-thirds of the way through the first movement is in the dominant; it represents not a sonata-form recapitulation but a stage in the evolution of the theme from monody to its integration with the orchestral tutti beginning at bar 410. The structure of the finale is like nothing in Beethoven – nor anyone else: the Witches' Sabbath not having been used as the subject of a symphonic movement before, Berlioz had to invent a form for it.

In short, though Beethoven's influence is paramount, it is a matter of inspiration more than imitation. Beethoven himself may sometimes dispense with orthodox recapitulation (for example, in *Coriolan* and in *Leonore* No. 2, which, as it happens, were Berlioz's favorite Beethoven overtures); but Berlioz goes much further. In the opening Allegro of his second symphony, *Harold en Italie*, the second theme only hints at the dominant; the movement is soon merging exposition, development, and recapitulation in a free-flowing continuum. Even the echo of the finale of the Ninth Symphony – the recall of earlier themes – which begins the finale of *Harold* is adapted to ends opposite to those of Beethoven, as a means not of justifying the introducing of new elements – voices and text – into an instrumental work, but of sanctioning the excluding of elements previously integral to the score, the solo viola and its motto theme.[7]

Similarly, the Dramatic Symphony *Roméo et Juliette* takes Beethoven's Ninth only as its stimulus and starting point. The concept of a symphony with a big choral finale, introduced by instrumental recitative, is extended, if not altered, to one in which the vocal element and the overtly dramatic content are present from the beginning: graphic orchestral depiction of the street battles in Verona, brass recitative leading to choral prologue which sets out the action, and voices not entirely forgotten even in the central orchestral movements, so that the full-scale choral dénouement will be heard as the natural culmination of the work.

Berlioz summed up what was to be his relationship to Beethoven, and the decisive effect of the discovery of his music, in a letter written to his friend Édouard Rocher on 11 January 1829, during that first momentous initiation:

> Now that I have broken the chains of routine, I see an immense territory stretching before me, which academic rules forbade me to enter. Now that I have heard that awe-inspiring giant Beethoven I realize what point the art of music has reached; it's a question of taking it up at that point and carrying it further – no, not further, that's impossible, he attained the limits of art, but as far in another direction.

Beethoven, for Berlioz, is a "benefactor," a tutelary spirit, both household god and "friend."[8] The decision, in 1845, to write a major work, after six years in which he has produced only small-scale compositions, is taken immediately after the Bonn Beethoven festival, in the solitude of Königswinter, the village where Beethoven used to go as a young man. And the shape of the opening phrase of *La Damnation de Faust* will reflect, consciously or not, in the calm stepwise ascent to the keynote followed by a falling sixth, its Beethovenian inheritance.[9]

By that time Berlioz was a devoted apostle of Beethoven; he had been expounding him in print for the past sixteen years.[10] That was not necessarily regarded in France as a respectable thing to do, especially where the works of Beethoven's final period were concerned. Fétis, in the *Revue Musicale*, made much of the many false harmonic progressions – some of them no better than schoolboy howlers – in the late quartets (Berlioz's soaring bird, he might have said, had crash-landed); even the Seventh Symphony, in its first and last movements, was "the improvisation of a gifted composer on an off day." Adolphe Adam considered Beethoven too flawed to be – as some misguidedly claimed – the leading composer of the century (that honor belonged to Auber). Rellstab, in the *Revue et Gazette musicale*, deplored the ruin of Beethoven's once noble genius, as exemplified by the follies of the Ninth Symphony.

Dismissive criticism of the sort, however, was quite untypical of the *Gazette* under Maurice Schlesinger's editorship. The journal's regular writers worked on the assumption that music of the highest quality by definition challenged the listener and might well not reveal itself immediately. Foremost among composers of such music was Beethoven; and foremost among his advocates Berlioz. For him, the symphonies – the Ninth above all – were the beginning of modern music. In the eighteen-thirties Berlioz published "critiques admiratives" of all nine. He had first enunciated the idea in December 1825 when in a letter to *Le Corsaire* he took issue with Castil-Blaze's strictures on Gluck's *Armide*. The critic's duty was to write a reasoned appreciation of the music he admired, to "reveal the strokes of genius in a work," many of which may have "escaped the notice of a public blinded by the prejudices of the moment."[11]

This principle, essentially, informs all Berlioz's writings on Beethoven. From time to time his admiration is qualified by a touch of Conservatoire pedantry (such as, ironically, will characterize subsequent French criticism of Berlioz's music). He is not immune to prejudices himself. He fails to respond to the humor of the sudden, brusque conclusion of the Eighth Symphony's Allegretto scherzando ("How can this ravishing idyll finish with the commonplace for which Beethoven had the greatest aversion, the Italian cadence? [. . .] I have never been able to explain this vagary").[12] Equally mystifying to him, and even more disagreeable, is the dissonance which opens the finale of the Ninth, and which is repeated, still more discordantly, just before the entry of the voice. The bee in his bonnet about "obligatory" fugues in religious works buzzes so loudly that it deafens him to the glories of "In gloria Dei Patris, Amen," and "Et vitam venturi saeculi, Amen," in the *Missa Solemnis*; the fugal treatment of "Amen" is like a red rag to a bull.

Such failures, however, are exceptional. In general he respects what Beethoven does, even when he can't see the reason for it. As he says in the Postscript of the *Mémoires*, "[I am] a freethinker in music, or rather I am of the faith of Beethoven, Weber, Gluck, and Spontini, who believe and preach, and prove by their works, that everything is 'right' or 'wrong' according to the effect produced." At the end of his long and detailed *critique admirative* of the *Pastoral* Symphony, he concludes:

> After that, can one speak of oddities of style in such a work – of groups of five notes in the cellos opposed to four-note phrases in the double basses without combining into a genuine unison? Does one have to point out the horn-call on an arpeggio of the chord of C while the strings sustain the chord of F? Must one search for the reason for such harmonic anomalies? I confess I am incapable of it. For that, one must be cool and rational – and how can one keep ecstasy at bay when the mind is engaged with such a subject![13]

Berlioz's method aims to lead the reader/listener into the music by a mixture of the two modes of criticism first defined by E. T. A. Hoffmann, the poetic and the pedagogic. He uses literary analogy and evocative imagery seasoned with technical description. A representative example, combining both modes, is this account of the second movement of the Seventh Symphony. Here he takes in his stride the unresolved chord which begins and ends the movement. Elsewhere he defends the chord against critics who, failing to see the reason for it, "point out as a fault one of Beethoven's finest inspirations."

Rhythm – a rhythm as simple as that of the first movement – is again the chief element in the incredible effect produced by the Andante [*recte* Allegretto]. It consists entirely of a dactyl followed by a spondee, repeated uninterruptedly, now in three parts, now in one, now all together, sometimes as accompaniment, often focusing attention solely on itself, or providing the main subject of a brief double fugue in the stringed instruments. It is heard first on the lower strings of the violas, cellos, and double basses, played *piano*, then repeated shortly afterwards in a mysterious and melancholy *pianissimo*. From there it passes to the second violins, while the cellos utter a sort of sublime lament, in the minor mode. The rhythmic figure, rising from octave to octave, reaches the first violins which, while making a crescendo, hand it to the wind instruments at the top of the orchestra, where it bursts out with full force. The plaintive melody, now more energetic, becomes a convulsive wailing. Conflicting rhythms clash painfully against each other. We hear tears, sobs, suffering. But a ray of hope shines. The heartrending strains give way to a vaporous melody, gentle, pure, sad yet resigned, "like patience smiling at grief." Only the cellos and basses persist with their inexorable rhythm beneath this rainbow-like melodic arc: to borrow once again from English poetry, "One fatal remembrance, one sorrow that throws / Its bleak shade alike o'er our joys and our woes."

After further alternations of anguish and resignation the orchestra, as though exhausted by its struggle, can manage only fragments of the main phrase, before giving up the ghost. The flutes and oboes take up the theme with dying voice but lack the strength to go on; the violins complete it with a few barely audible pizzicato notes – after which, flaring up like the flame of a lamp about to go out, the wind instruments give a deep sigh on an incomplete harmony and ... "the rest is silence." This plaintive exclamation, with which the Andante opens and closes, is produced by a chord, that of the six-four, which normally resolves. In this case the placing of the tonic note in the middle of the chord, while the dominant is above and below it, is the only possible ending, leaving the listener with a sense of incompleteness, and intensifying the dreamlike sadness of the rest of the movement.[14]

Berlioz's Beethoven symphony analyses, as we have seen, appeared in the *Revue et Gazette musicale* (and subsequently in the *Voyage musicale* and *À travers chants*). The *Gazette* had a specialist readership. But he could also treat the subscribers to the *Journal des débats* to just as demanding a course of instruction. The long crescendo in the opening movement of the Fourth Symphony prompted one of his most detailed technical pages, which originally appeared in a feuilleton in the *Débats*:

The second part of this same Allegro contains a totally new idea whose first bars seize the attention and which, after carrying one away by its mysterious development, astonishes one by the unexpectedness of its conclusion. This is what happens. After a vigorous tutti the first violins break up the main theme and make a game out of it with the second violins. Their *pianissimo* dialogue leads to two sustained dominant-seventh chords in the key of

B-natural, each interrupted by two silent bars during which all that is heard is a quiet roll of the drums on B-flat, the enharmonic major third of the bass note F-sharp. The drums then stop, leaving the strings to murmur other fragments of the theme and then, by a new enharmonic modulation, to arrive on a six-four chord of B-flat. The drums, reentering on the same note, which instead of being a leading-tone as it was the first time is now a genuine tonic, go on with their roll for a further twenty bars. The force of the key of B-flat, barely perceptible to begin with, becomes stronger and stronger the more the roll continues; and while the drums rumble on, the momentum of the other instruments, scattering fragments of phrase as they go, culminates in a great *forte* which finally establishes B-flat in all its majestic energy.

This prodigious crescendo is one of the most extraordinary inventions in music. To find another like it you have to go to the one that concludes the famous scherzo of the C-Minor Symphony; and even then, despite its immense effect, the latter is conceived on a less spacious scale. It starts *piano* and proceeds straight to its climax, never leaving the main key – whereas the one we have just described starts *mezzo forte*, sinks down for an instant to a *pianissimo* colored by harmonies that remain deliberately imprecise, then reappears with more clearly defined chords, and bursts forth only at the moment when the cloud which veiled the modulation is completely dispersed. It is like a river whose calmly flowing stream suddenly goes underground, from where it reemerges with a roar, as a foaming cascade.[15]

Berlioz's account of the crescendo in the scherzo of the Fifth is perhaps too well known to be quoted here, though it provides a further example of his method and must have delighted the Beethoven-lovers among his readers and astonished those who were yet to be converted: the trio's theme, "played by cellos and basses with the full force of the bow, whose ponderous gait makes the desks of the whole orchestra shake, and suggests the gamboling of a herd of high-spirited elephants" – as "the sound of this mad stampeding gradually fades, the motif of the scherzo reappears, pizzicato, the silence deepens and all that is left are a few notes plucked by the violins and the strange gobble of the bassoons, playing high A-flat against the jarring juxtaposition of the octave G, the bass note of the dominant minor ninth" – "the ear hesitates, unsure where this enigmatic harmony will end" – "the dull pulsation of the drums gradually growing in intensity" – and so on.[16]

Almost his last Beethoven article, the *critique admirative* of *Fidelio*, in the *Débats* of May 1860, contains some of his most arresting images and at the same time a final declaration of faith:

[*Fidelio*] belongs to that powerful race of maligned works which have the most inconceivable prejudices and the most blatant lies heaped on them, but whose vitality is so intense that nothing can prevail against them – like those sturdy beeches born among rocks and ruins, which end by splitting the stone and breaking through the walls, and rise up proud and verdant, the more solidly rooted for the obstacles they have had to overcome in order to force their way out; whereas the willows that grow without effort on the banks of a river fall into the mud and rot, forgotten.

Its time will come:

> Who knows that light may not dawn sooner than one thinks, even for those whose spirits are closed at the moment to this beautiful work of Beethoven's, as they are to the marvels of the Ninth Symphony and the last quartets and the great piano sonatas of that same inspired, incomparable being? Sometimes, when one looks at a particular part of the heaven of art, a veil seems to cover "the mind's eye" and prevent it from seeing the stars that shine there. Then, all of a sudden, for no apparent reason, the veil is rent, and one sees, and blushes to have been blind so long.[17]

The need to expound Beethoven was for Berlioz the most important *raison d'être* of his work as a critic, and a compensation for the mental and psychological burden that criticism and his financial dependence on it increasingly became. He surely hoped, too, that initiating readers into the mysteries and splendors of Beethoven's music would help to make his own works more intelligible – works which Paganini was not alone among musicians in regarding as inheriting the mantle of Beethoven. But above all he celebrated Beethoven because he had to: he must share his enthusiasm, communicate to others the wonder of the discovery. He could not do otherwise. And it is clear that he often did, verbally and in private. Ernest Legouvé never forgot hearing Berlioz explain to him the Ninth Symphony:

> His articles, admirable as they are, give an imperfect idea of it, for they contain only his opinions. When he spoke, the whole of him was in it. The eloquence of his words was enhanced by his expression, his gestures, tone of voice, tears, exclamations of enthusiasm, and those sudden flashes of inspired imagery which are sparked by the stimulus of a listener hanging on every word. An hour spent in this way taught me more about instrumental music than a whole concert at the Conservatoire – or rather, when I went to the Conservatoire the following Sunday, my mind full of Berlioz's commentaries, Beethoven's work suddenly opened before me like a great cathedral flooded with light, the whole design of which I took in at a glance and in which I walked about as though on familiar ground, confidently exploring every recess and corner. Berlioz had given me the key to the sanctuary.[18]

There was, of course, another way of expressing his feelings about Beethoven and of communicating his understanding of the Ninth and the other symphonies to a wider audience: conducting. Berlioz's emergence, in the eighteen-thirties, as a conductor of a new school, who beat time with a baton, not with a violin bow, and who rehearsed the orchestra sectionally and with numbered parts, was significant first of all for his own music, which till then he had generally had to hear performed "approximately" under the bow of Habeneck or Narcisse Girard. But as his renown spread he came to be in demand as a conductor of music other than his own, which to him meant, above all, Beethoven.

Opportunities, by modern standards, were admittedly infrequent for someone who, though regarded by many musicians as the finest conductor of the day, was never attached to a regular concert-promoting body. The first Beethoven symphony he is known to have conducted – the *Pastoral* – was part of a one-off Beethoven program put on by Liszt at the Paris Conservatoire on 25 April 1841, to raise money for the fund which Liszt had set up to pay for a statue of the composer in his native town, Bonn. (The *Emperor* Concerto, played by Liszt, the *Kreutzer* Sonata, with Liszt and Lambert Massart, and the overture *The Consecration of the House*, were the other works.) In January 1845, at the Cirque Olympique, Berlioz accompanied Charles Hallé in a Beethoven concerto (No. 4 or the *Emperor*, the evidence is conflicting).[19] And in London in November 1847 he opened the inaugural season of Jullien's Grand English Opera, of which he was music director, with *Leonore* No. 2, his excuse being that *Lucia di Lammermoor*, the main item of the evening, did not have a proper overture of its own.

He had more scope in the eighteen-fifties, with the founding of the Société Philharmonique, under his leadership, and then of the New Philharmonic Society, created for him by his London admirers. In 1850, in Paris, he gave the Fifth Symphony, and in 1852, with the New Philharmonic, the Fifth, the Triple Concerto, *Leonore* No. 2 again, and two performances of the Ninth which were reckoned incomparably the best ever given in London, with a first-rate orchestra and a choir far superior to its Parisian counterpart. Of those performances *The Morning Post* wrote:

> The most worthy execution of Beethoven's magnificent symphony, and at the same time the best orchestral performance, ever heard in this country. [...] We never before heard so much accent and true expression from an English orchestra.[20]

And the *Illustrated London News* wrote:

> [T]he greatest victory ever yet attained in the development of Beethoven's intentions. [...] We heard on Wednesday night professors of no little note, whose sneers and scoffs at the Ninth Symphony years back we had not forgotten, make avowal that it was incomparably the grandest emanation of Beethoven's genius. [...] [H]onor and glory to the gifted conductor, who wielded Prospero's wand and subdued all the combined elements to one

harmonious whole. Well did Berlioz earn the ovation bestowed by the moved thousands who filled the hall on this memorable occasion, one to be for ever treasured in our musical annals.[21]

Such revelations were not achieved without much more thorough rehearsal than was customary in London then or for long afterwards. Berlioz had six for the Ninth, and it was partly because the cost was higher than the New Philharmonic's sponsors expected, and also because of the machinations of one of the sponsors, the aspiring but mediocre conductor Dr. Henry Wylde, that Berlioz was not invited back to the orchestra except briefly in 1855. In the late eighteen-fifties, owing to ill health and preoccupation with composing and then promoting *Les Troyens*, he virtually gave up conducting, except for an annual gala concert at Baden-Baden (where excerpts from Beethoven figured on some of the programs). But not long before he died, his career as a conductor enjoyed a belated flowering, thanks to an invitation to Russia in the winter of 1867–1868. Though chronically sick and in pain, he directed six concerts in St. Petersburg and two in Moscow. The main content of the programs was divided among Beethoven, Gluck, and his own music. He conducted the *Eroica*, the Fourth, the Fifth, the *Pastoral*, the *Emperor*, and the Violin Concerto. Ill as he was, the experience rejuvenated him. After the series opened he wrote to his uncle Félix Marmion (on 8 December 1867):

> At the first concert I directed Beethoven's *Pastoral* Symphony, with profound adoration for the poor great man who had the power to create so amazing a poem in music. And how we sang that poetry! What a splendid orchestra! They do what I want, these fine artists.[22]

What were Berlioz's Beethoven performances like? We have no way of knowing. All we have are fleeting indications. The composer and critic César Cui wrote in the St. Petersburg *Gazette*:

> What a grasp he has of Beethoven, how exact, how thoughtful his performances are, how effective yet without the slightest concession to the false and the tawdry. I prefer Berlioz as an interpreter of Beethoven to Wagner (who, with all his excellent qualities, is at times affected, introducing sentimental rallentandos). [...] Of all the conductors we have heard in Petersburg, Berlioz is unquestionably the greatest.[23]

From Berlioz's and Wagner's comments on each other's conducting, their interpretations and style of music-making seem to have been as different as Toscanini's and Furtwängler's (Berlioz being more like the Italian maestro and Wagner like the German). Where his music was concerned, Berlioz set great store by the metronome, but there is no evidence of how much importance he attached to Beethoven's metronome marks. His calling the second movement of the Seventh Symphony (a work he never conducted) Andante instead of Allegretto may indicate that Habeneck took it more slowly than the score's ♩= 76, and that he too thought of it like that. On the other hand the press reports of the New Philharmonic's Ninth mention the very rapid tempo of the trio and of the finale's concluding variations – a startling difference from the Old Philharmonic's plodding performances, thrown on with one rehearsal, which London audiences had had to make do with till then.

All we can say for certain is that Berlioz found great joy in repaying something of what he owed to the mighty mentor who, together with Gluck and Shakespeare, had pointed the way for his own music.

17 Berlioz and Wagner: Épisodes de la vie des artistes

PETER BLOOM

> Glaub' mir – ich *liebe* Berlioz [...]: er *kennt* mich nicht, – aber *ich* kenne *ihn*.
> (WAGNER TO LISZT, 8 SEPTEMBER 1852)
>
> Wagner est évidemment fou.
> (BERLIOZ TO HIS SON LOUIS, 5 MARCH 1861)

"Au Grand et cher auteur de *Roméo et Juliette*, l'auteur reconnaissant de *Tristan et Isolde*" – so reads the dedication on the copy of the full score of *Tristan* that Wagner sent to Berlioz, on 21 January 1860, accompanied by a brief and touching letter:

> Cher Berlioz,
>   Je suis ravi de vous pouvoir offrir le premier exemplaire de mon *Tristan*.
>   Acceptez-le et gardez-le d'amitié pour moi.
>   A vous.
> Richard Wagner.

"I am delighted to be able to offer you the first copy of my *Tristan*," writes Wagner, who urges Berlioz to accept the score "as a token of friendship." Such attentiveness is a small indication, I think, that even as a mature composer nearing his forty-seventh birthday, Wagner continued to regard Berlioz, then fifty-six, as his senior and by no means conventionally benevolent colleague.[1] In fact the gift was one of extraordinary generosity, both because this was indeed a first, and rare, pre-publication copy, sent by the publishers to Wagner only one week earlier, and because it was a costly item, whose list price of thirty-five thalers, or one hundred and forty-four francs, was equivalent at the time to the monthly income of many a professor, government functionary, or itinerant musician. What led Wagner to bestow such bounty upon Berlioz? And why, for Wagner, was the Frenchman still the "grand and dear author of *Roméo et Juliette*" – the now more than twenty-year-old dramatic symphony of 1839?

It may be because French Wagnerianism flourished in the period immediately following Berlioz's death – in remarkable counterpoint with French Germanophobia – that subsequent generations have tended to pair Berlioz and Wagner as they have Bach and Handel (who were born in the same year) and Haydn and Mozart (who reached compositional maturity in the same decade). But apart from their differing views of the world (broached in Jacques Barzun's contribution to this volume), the nature of the relations between the composer of *Roméo et Juliette* and the composer of *Tristan und Isolde* are best understood in light of the differences between their ages and between the trajectories of their careers.

Early impressions

It is logical to assume that Wagner knew the name Berlioz well before arriving in Paris in 1839. If the winner of the Academy's Prix de Rome in 1830 was not mentioned in the vivid accounts of the July Revolution that made history "come alive" for the seventeen-year-old German reading the *Leipziger Zeitung*, he *was* mentioned in reports from Paris carried by such music journals as Leipzig's celebrated *Allgemeine musikalische Zeitung*, where Berlioz's name occurs as early as December 1829, and later, in the *Neue Zeitschrift für Musik*, where, in July and August of 1835, Robert Schumann published his astonishing review of the *Symphonie fantastique*. Berlioz's overture to *Les Francs-Juges* was played in Leipzig in November 1836, but by then Wagner had left his native city for Königsberg, there to make preparations for his marriage to Minna Planner.

Three years later Wagner arrived in Paris, in the autumn of 1839, with letters of introduction provided by Meyerbeer to some of the city's musical luminaries. He first encountered Berlioz at Maurice Schlesinger's shop, in the rue de Richelieu, a meeting place and gossip-mill for musicians foreign and domestic,[2] and he soon attended one of the three successive performances, probably the first, of Berlioz's new dramatic symphony.[3] On p. 64 of the autograph of *Roméo et Juliette*, there is a note in Berlioz's hand that reads: "Mr Wagner / rue Monmartre." The suggestion – even though Richard Wagner's official address at the time was 3, rue de la Tonnellerie (in the same neighborhood) – is that Wagner made himself known to Berlioz at a time when the composer, who conducted from the manuscript, had the score in hand.

Roméo et Juliette, the greatest success of Berlioz's career to date, was thus the first work of his that Wagner heard. Now, Wagner tells us that he experienced an epiphany on hearing the first three movements of Beethoven's Ninth Symphony rehearsed by the Société des Concerts in the first two weeks of December 1839 – perhaps on 7 December 1839, when Habeneck rehearsed something of Wagner's as well – but obviously the revelation was enhanced by hearing, at almost precisely the same time, Berlioz's *Roméo et Juliette*.[4]

Further works by Berlioz that were performed during Wagner's stay in Paris include the *Symphonie fantastique*, *Harold en Italie*, the overture and

Teresa's cavatina from *Benvenuto Cellini*, excerpts from the *Requiem*, the *Symphonie funèbre et triomphale*, *Sara la baigneuse*, *Le Cinq Mai*, the recitatives for *Der Freischütz* along with the orchestration (for the ballet) of Weber's *L'Invitation à la valse*, and the *Rêverie et Caprice*. In his three years in the French capital Wagner thus came into possession of almost the entirety of the repertory of Berlioz's most fertile decade. When he departed, on 7 April 1842, it was to prepare performances of the two operas he had miraculously managed to complete during what had been a period of such urgent financial need that he had even had to seek meager employment as a chorister in a popular theatre on the boulevard: "I came off worse than Berlioz when he was in a similar predicament," he later told Edward Dannreuther. "The conductor who tested my abilities discovered that I could not sing at all, and pronounced me a hopeless case all around."[5] *Rienzi* and *Der fliegende Holländer* soon secured for their composer a brilliant reputation of his own, however, and a secure position as Kapellmeister at the court of the King of Saxony.

By curious coincidence, Berlioz, too, departed from Paris in 1842, in an official capacity, to investigate and report upon musical conditions in Germany, with assistance from the Ministry of the Interior, and in an unofficial capacity, to seek acceptance for his own brand of dramatically expressive instrumental music, to establish his reputation abroad, and thereby to improve his standing at home. Between December 1842 and May 1843 Berlioz visited the cities, some more than once, of Frankfurt, Stuttgart, Hechingen, Karlsruhe, Mannheim, Weimar, Leipzig, Dresden, Brunswick, Hamburg, Berlin, Magdeburg, and Hanover. "Here I am, home from my long travels throughout Germany," he subsequently reported to his father, on 5 June 1843:

> I am still extremely tired (which I would have been even had my efforts been
> less demanding) because in five months I directed fourteen concerts and
> forty-three rehearsals. Fortunately, the results of my labors were highly
> beneficial in terms of my musical reputation, and perfectly satisfactory in
> terms of my financial gain, which could not under the best of circumstances
> have been very great in view of the enormous expenses entailed by such a
> venture – one without precedent in the history of art. This musical journey
> created a tremendous stir in the German press and, as a result, in the French,
> English, and Italian presses as well. A composer traveling across Germany to
> mount and to direct by himself a series of concerts devoted exclusively to the
> performance of his own works is something that has simply never before
> been seen.

Berlioz then adds a note characteristic of such communications to his family, suggesting epigrammatically an artistic, financial, and political creed:

> If I had been born in Germany, if I were Saxon, or Prussian, I would by now
> have a post guaranteed for life with a salary of ten or twelve thousand francs
> and a pension that would, after my demise, satisfy the needs of my family . . .
> In France I have . . . a liberal constitution.[6]

– a constitution, Berlioz goes on to say, whose "liberality" would allow to starve not only those who might shower honor upon their country (among them himself), but even those who might more coldly be seen as *materially* useful to it. In June 1843 it seems fair to conclude that he was still feeling the loss of his protector, the duc d'Orléans, Louis-Philippe's eldest son and the heir to the throne, who had been killed the year before in an accident that deprived the country of a widely admired successor.

When he later made a formal report on his German trip to the Minister of the Interior, comte Duchatel, on 23 December 1843, Berlioz again voiced a concern for the welfare of the artist, this time less cynically, by accentuating the positive aspects of what he had just observed:

> A pension plan for artists has been established at all of the German courts,
> and is responsible for the zeal and assiduousness with which their chapel
> services are conducted. Instrumentalists and chorus members there are paid
> livable wages and can count on a kind of future security that is simply
> unavailable to artists in France. The composer-chapelmaster is able to create
> and to reflect upon his creations without undue distraction. He does not
> have to compose in order to live: the sovereign upon whom he depends has
> rather made it possible for him to live in order to compose.[7]

With Berlioz's favorable view of the princely support of the arts in mind, we may better read the specific account of his visit to Dresden, where he spent twelve days, from 7 to 19 February 1843, where he found resources richer than those available in many of the other German towns, where he conducted eight rehearsals and two concerts and, finally, where he encountered Richard Wagner – now on far more familiar turf and stable ground than during his years in Paris. On the 7th Berlioz heard the fourth Dresden performance of *Der fliegende Holländer*, under Wagner's direction, and on the 19th he heard *Rienzi*, under the baton of the senior Dresden Kapellmeister, Carl Gottlieb Reissiger. In fact what he heard was *Rienzi's Fall* – the last three acts of the original opera – which, like *Les Troyens* at a later date, was considered too long for one evening's entertainment and was thus hewn in half.

Berlioz's report from Dresden first appeared as an open letter in the *Journal des débats* of 12 September 1843: the "recipient" was Heinrich Wilhelm Ernst, the German violinist whom Berlioz had known in Paris for some ten years. This letter was soon incorporated into his *Voyage musical en Allemagne et en Italie* (1844), with some small changes, and was later entered into the *Mémoires*. In it Berlioz speaks of Wagner in some detail, for the latter's first official duties had been to assist the visiting Frenchman with his rehearsals – something Wagner did, Berlioz tells us, "with zeal and excellent good will." Berlioz describes Wagner's pleasure and "glowing satisfaction" when he was formally installed as associate master of the chapel, and goes on to speak of his work:

> Having endured in France the untold hardships and all the mortifications that come when one is a little known artist, Richard Wagner, now back in his native Saxony, had the audacity to embark upon and the good fortune to complete the composition of both the words and music of a five-act opera, *Rienzi.* This work had a brilliant success in Dresden. It was soon followed by *Le Vaisseau hollandais*, a two-act opera whose theme is the same as that of *Le Vaisseau fantôme* (given two years ago at the Opéra de Paris), and for which he again wrote both words and music.[8] Whatever one's opinion of these works may be, it must be conceded that there are not many men capable of successfully accomplishing a double feat of this kind, and thus that M. Wagner has a remarkable capacity to focus interest and attention upon himself. This is precisely what the King of Saxony understood. And on the day that he gave to his senior Kapellmeister a colleague in the person of Richard Wagner, thereby guaranteeing the latter an honorable livelihood, lovers of art must have spoken to His Majesty the very words that Jean Bart replied to Louis XIV when the king informed the intrepid old sea-dog that he had appointed him commodore: "Sire, you have done well."[9]

Here Berlioz underlines the still remarkable fact that the librettos of *Rienzi*, premiered in Dresden on 20 October 1842, and *Der fliegende Holländer*, premiered there on 2 January 1843, one month before Berlioz's arrival, are among the first written by *any* composer of the music. (Wagner was already, of course, the "double" author of *Die Feen* and *Das Liebesverbot*.) But he more prominently underlines the action of Friedrich August II, King of Saxony from 1836 to 1854, to whom he returns in the following paragraph: "we must honor the enlightened king who, by according [Wagner] his active and total protection, has in effect saved a young artist of rare talents."

Wagner himself, aware of the possible servitude to which such a position might condemn him, and awake to the psychological distance between campestral Dresden and cosmopolitan Paris, had at first been fearful of accepting it. But three months after doing so he would write proudly to his friend Samuel Lehrs, in Paris, that "I now have tenure for life with a handsome salary [of 1,500 thalers, or 5,550 francs per annum] and the prospect that it will continue to increase, and I control a sphere of influence such as has been granted to few men."[10] In the same letter (of 7 April 1843) Wagner speaks of King Friedrich August as "an honest man with none of the usual airs and graces, but totally sincere in his approach to everything," and as taking in his new Kapellmeister "a genuine and good-natured delight."

Thus, when he likened Friedrich August's promotion of Wagner to Louis XIV's promotion of the celebrated seaman Jean Bart (1650–1702) – whose disarmingly simple manners had so charmed the King and his court at Versailles that he was able to use without offense the now celebrated phrase, "Sire, vous avez bien fait" – Berlioz's judgment was sound. In fact Berlioz enjoyed likening *himself* to Jean Bart: he did so, for example, when he invited the duc d'Orléans to his concert of 25 November 1838,[11] and he did so again, in 1853, when he imagined what he would have said to Napoléon had the Emperor required a command performance of the *Requiem* – which is, he told Franz Liszt on 23 February, what "Jean Bart replied to Louis XIV: 'Sire, vous avez raison.'" Berlioz's leitmotivic use of the saying is a sign of his awareness, I think, that a cantata in honor of Jean Bart was commissioned in 1845, for the inauguration of the statue in the Atlantic city of Dunkerque that to this day speaks of Jean Bart as its "glorious son." More broadly, it is a sign of his sincere respect for enlightened aristocratic patronage.

It may seem odd that Berlioz's writerly account of his encounter with Wagner is nowhere prefigured in his private correspondence immediately contemporary with the visit to Dresden. But he was busy with rehearsals in Leipzig and even found it necessary to take the morning train to Dresden (on 2 February 1843), to make concert arrangements there, and to return to Leipzig on the same afternoon – "Puissance des chemins de fer!" he exclaimed to his father on 14 March, impressed as he was by the rail line that, since only 1839, spanned those now diminished seventy miles. He was also under surveillance by his traveling companion, Marie Récio, with whom relations were mercurial and public appearances awkward. Correspondence of the period is in any event somewhat cautious and restrained.

Eleven years later Berlioz flirted seriously with an invitation to become Kapellmeister in "Wagner's" Dresden, in the spring of 1854, when he gave four concerts there and planned a revival of *Benvenuto Cellini*. The opera was not performed, however, and Berlioz did not became master of the chapel. The senior Kapellmeister was still in office, and Berlioz – whose high regard for Reissiger stands in stark contrast to Wagner's carping estimation of the talent of his superior officer – presumably wished neither to encroach upon Reissiger's position nor to accept one of subordinate status. Furthermore, Dresden was still a relatively undeveloped backwater, despite Berlioz's assertions of the excellence of its musical establishment. Did a sufficiently generous offer not materialize due to the accidental death of the king? Like Berlioz's earlier patron, the duc d'Orléans, Friedrich August II, too, was killed in a fall from a carriage, on 9 August 1854. For Berlioz, this was "a fatality worthy of the ancients."[12]

There is no indication that the composer pursued the matter with Johann, Friedrich August's brother, who now became King of Saxony. Marie, Berlioz's wife since 19 October 1854, and her mother, the Frenchified Spaniard whose company Berlioz would later come to appreciate, were probably little inclined to expatriate. And Berlioz's election to the Académie des Beaux-Arts two years later made the question of any such emigration academic, for members of the Institute had to reside in France. It seems nonetheless clear that Berlioz, in the eighteen-fifties, was temperamentally more suited to become a Saxon court musician than had been Wagner, in the eighteen-forties. How odd that Wagner, in the eighteen-sixties, should become the God-sent "child of Heaven" to the twenty-year-old King of Bavaria.[13]

Artistic rapports

To trace the impact of Berlioz on Wagner (aware that there are no certainties in matters of "influence") it would seem appropriate to start with the scores the German composer was drafting when he first encountered the Frenchman's music in Paris in the winter of 1839 – the overture on Goethe's *Faust* (completed on 12 January 1840) and the operas *Rienzi* and *Der fliegende Holländer*. Of these much-written-about works let me set down here only some suggestions I have not seen elsewhere. The overture to *Rienzi* begins quite remarkably with a single note from the trumpet, the fifth of the triad on D that is the tonic of the work as a whole. The only prior instances of this procedure that I am aware of occur in Weber's *Oberon* Overture (1826), and in Berlioz's own *Waverley* Overture (1828), the latter having been published in Paris in the autumn of 1839, and probably come to Wagner's notice when he was working on *Rienzi*. The decorative turns with which the strings punctuate the presentation by wind and brass of the *Rienzi* Overture's principal D-Major theme (bars 50–65) might furthermore have been lifted from the passage in the first movement of *Harold en Italie* (given contemporaneously in Paris, on 6 February 1840) in which Berlioz's orchestra for the first time takes up the soloist's *idée fixe* (from bars 73 to 84).

It is for employing such *idées fixes* (tranquilly in *Harold*, obsessively in the *Fantastique*) that Berlioz was already celebrated in 1839, and many have proposed that herein lie the origins of the emblem of Wagner's larger aesthetic experiment, the leitmotif. But the French composer was even more satisfied, I think, by the deployment, at moments of dramatic intensity, of a combination of two earlier, vital tunes, which he troubled to label as a *réunion*. In the finale of the *Fantastique*, for example, we see the explicit notation "Dies Irae et Ronde du Sabbat *ensemble*"; in the finale of the second tableau of *Benvenuto Cellini*, we hear three separately announced ideas openly and artfully combined in the following delightful episode;[14] and in the second movement of *Roméo et Juliette* (at bar 226), we see the principal melody of the *Fête chez Capulet* combined with an earlier conspicuous melody of leisurely pace into an unabashed "réunion des deux thèmes, du Larghetto et de l'Allegro."

For Act V of *Rienzi*, Wagner sketched a similar *réunion des thèmes* that consisted of the melody of Rienzi's Prayer, at the opening of the first scene (used in the overture), and a version of the opening melody of the subsequent duet between the title character and his sister, Irene. Wagner abandoned the sketch, as John Deathridge has shown, because he could not bring these tunes into harmonious unity.[15] He did manage an effective superimposition in Act III of *Der fliegende Holländer*, when the Norwegian sailors attempt to drown in sound the Dutchman's motley crew. By transforming an exercise in academic counterpoint into a moment of dramatic expression, was Wagner paying homage to Berlioz? The Frenchman was famously antipathetic to schoolmasterish rules yet filled his scores with fugue and fugato. Wagner, too, later wrestled overtly with the question of musical law and liberty in what became *Die Meistersinger von Nürnberg*.

For many observers, Berlioz's most obvious role as a model for Wagner was as a student of novel and expressive instrumental sonorities and (in Berlioz's words) as a "player of the orchestra." The one hundred musicians of Berlioz's *Roméo et Juliette* orchestra of 1839, with its eight harps, offstage choirs, and other spatial effects, could not have failed to impress Wagner, whose previous experience was with orchestral ensembles of classical proportion. The expansion of the orchestra that we witness in *Der fliegende Holländer* was, for Eduard Hanslick, an imitation of "the gaudiest achievements of Meyerbeer and Berlioz."[16] But for Richard Strauss, revising the *Traité d'instrumentation et d'orchestration modernes*, Berlioz's orchestration was "full of ingenious visions [...] whose realization by Richard Wagner is obvious to every connoisseur."

Interrogating Berlioz's later musical influence upon Wagner is to be recommended as edifying and non-addictive. Seeking Berlioz's literary influence upon Wagner should be equally productive. The latter we may sense in as early a piece as Wagner's first fictional essay, *Eine Pilgerfahrt zu Beethoven*, which initially appeared in French as *Une Visite à Beethoven*. In November and December of 1840, readers of Maurice Schlesinger's *Revue et Gazette musicale* would have immediately recognized the explicitly Berliozian resonance of Wagner's subtitle – *Épisode de la vie d'un musicien allemand* – echoing that of Berlioz's first symphony, *Épisode de la vie d'un artiste*.

Social calls

Wagner later saw Berlioz on visits to Paris in 1849, 1850, and 1853, and Berlioz, after Dresden, heard much about Wagner during his visits to Weimar in 1852 and 1854. They exchanged few letters, but their communications with Franz Liszt made it inevitable that the one always knew what the other was up to. Wagner and Liszt spoke of Berlioz on more than two dozen occasions in the decade after 1851, and Liszt did not hesitate to quote from Berlioz's letters in his correspondence with his German colleague.[17]

It was in London, in the spring of 1855, when Berlioz was engaged as conductor to the New Philharmonic Society, and Wagner to the Old, that they had their closest meeting of minds. After Wagner's last concert, on 25 June 1855, Berlioz and Marie went to see him with five other friends. All returned to Wagner's rooms, conversed, drank champagne punch, and departed, after effusive embraces all around, at three o'clock in the morning. How did the *maestri* converse? One witness, whose observations ring true, tells us that "Berlioz was reserved, self-possessed, and dignified," and that his "clear, transparent delivery was as the rhythmic cadence of a fountain," while "Wagner was boisterous, effusive, and his words leaped forth as the rushing of a mountain torrent."[18] Wagner's gift for self-dramatization was clearly manifest in person, and Berlioz found him full of enthusiasm, warmth, and heartfelt emotion. Indeed, the Frenchman was deeply moved even by Wagner's passionate outbursts (*ses violences*),[19] while his own gift for self-dramatization was usually more apparent in writing. Wagner tended to take his vantage point at the top of the mountain; Berlioz, at the edge of the grave.

What did they talk about on that Monday evening in London? Women? In the presence of Marie and Mme Praeger, this is unlikely. Birds? Like Flaubert and Courbet, Berlioz had a pet parrot at one time or another, and so, too, did Wagner. (Later, in 1878, Wagner chose "Berlioz" as the name of a pet rooster.[20]) Critics? Berlioz pilloried the leading Parisian critic of the eighteen-twenties and thirties, F.-J. Fétis, in his mélologue, *Le Retour à la vie*; Wagner lampooned the leading Viennese critic of the eighteen-sixties, Eduard Hanslick, in a (not-final) version of the libretto of *Die Meistersinger*. Both composers did so under the rubric of comic relief, but both critics reacted with whatever is the opposite of good humor.

Did they talk about Jews? Among others, Dieter Borchmeyer has argued that Wagner's anti-Jewish sentiments were more French than German in origin, having been stirred up during his first, celebratedly miserable sojourn in Paris, and by the sometimes open hostility expressed by such friends of Berlioz as Vigny and Balzac.[21] But Berlioz would presumably hear nothing of Wagner's animadversions *contra* Meyerbeer, with whom the French composer long remained on perfectly cordial terms.

Conducting? This is a point of critical importance, for the two men's approaches set the stage for much future interpretive debate (Berlioz conducted from score, Wagner from memory). The young pianist-conductor Karl Klindworth, among the guests, would have lent an ear to such a discussion, but in the competitive circumstances that prevailed in London in 1855, the subject was probably too hot to handle. Violinists? Wagner's host and concertmaster, Prosper Sainton, was among the company; perhaps they talked of *tremolo*. Oboe players? This is not as silly as it sounds, for Wagner's former oboist in Dresden, Rudolf Hiebendahl, was at precisely that moment applying legal pressure to obtain repayment of a loan he had made to the composer some ten years earlier.[22] Berlioz could not have forgotten this fellow, for it was he who had spoiled the *Scène aux champs* by adding trills and grace-notes to the off-stage solo that opens the third movement of the *Fantastique* when Berlioz gave the work in Dresden in 1843. (Warned against executing such melodic niceties, Hiebendahl refrained from doing so at the rehearsals, but let loose again at the concert, knowing that in the presence of the king, Berlioz would not punish such perfidy in public.[23])

Did they talk about the piano? Berlioz seems always to have had one – he had purchased a spinet in his student days in the eighteen-twenties, and in 1851 took possession of a rosewood grand that was a gift from Pierre Érard. Mme Érard bestowed a similar gift upon Wagner, in 1858. In fact neither man composed at the instrument: Berlioz, who did not play fluently, sometimes plunked out a few notes; Wagner, who did, used the piano primarily to test what he had composed at his desk.[24]

Did they talk about books? Berlioz was an avid reader of *literature*, while Wagner preferred history and philosophy. To understand the sources of Wagner's inspiration we must read Feuerbach and Schopenhauer; to plumb the wellsprings of Berlioz's imagination, we must plunge into Chateaubriand, Hugo, and Vigny, to say nothing of Virgil and Molière, which he knew by heart.

We can be fairly sure that they talked about Beethoven – hoping individually to gain by the comparison – and we can be sure that they talked about Liszt, that great mid-century friend and advocate of both. A reading of Berlioz's letter to Liszt of 25 June, and of Wagner's letter to Liszt of 5 July, suggests that the two had finally come to understand one another. Berlioz says that "on his word of honor" (as though in some way hoping to reassure Liszt), "I believe that [Wagner] loves you every bit as much as I do, myself." Wagner, reporting ten days later, admits that he had discovered a Berlioz quite different from the one he had earlier imagined – a veritable *Leidensgefährte*, a companion in misfortune.

Late reflections

In the ensuing years, as Wagner developed from an extraordinary composer of romantic opera into the unparalleled creator of music drama, and from a wandering fugitive into the eventual "savior" of the Bavarian monarch, relations with Berlioz inevitably cooled. The Frenchman's later years were clouded by ill health and by the ill fortunes of *Les Troyens*, which ought to have crowned his success. And yet when Berlioz died, on 8 March 1869, Wagner (who appears to have received the news on the 11th) felt compelled to memorialize the occasion. On 14 March Cosima noted in her diary that the obituaries they had read were embarrassed, or confused (*verlegen*). On 7 April (by which time she may have been reading the *Mémoires* – an advance copy seems to have been given to the couple by their French friend, the writer Édouard Schuré), she wrote that Wagner "is quite unable *now* to write about Berlioz. He would have liked to do it, and the impact of such an essay would perhaps have been good, but nobody should expect it of him."[25]

Cosima's emphasis on the word *jetzt* suggests that Wagner had recently begun but failed to realize a substantial necrology. Of this we have only what appears to be the prologue – undated, but presumably written in early April 1869. It is a tortured piece of writing in the original German, and it is equally convoluted in William Ashton Ellis's translation. I offer a paraphrase of the first, full-to-bursting sentence:

> Even if, during his lifetime, a person has been discussed in generally negative terms, it is still our sacred duty, after his death, to speak about him in a positive manner. And yet, to ensure that posterity not be misled, we must also assume the distressing obligation of exposing as false some of the flattering images of the man, which he, himself, had done much to encourage. [26]

This is followed by a straightforward thought: were the true worth of an artist easy to assess, the making of a proper judgment would be unproblematical. But the making of a proper judgment is especially difficult when the *impact* of an artist is dubious, or suspicious (*zweifelhaft*) – even when certain qualities of his work are beyond question (*unzweifelhaft*).

Wagner underlines the tendency of posterity to inflate previous appraisals, and urges those who wish to behold what is beautiful and significant in purely human terms to make judgments without the constraints of *any* particular historical period. "We choose Hector Berlioz," he writes, "to try to gain from his example the kind of disinterested judgment that transcends time and circumstance."

Here ends the fragment. Was this in fact to be an obituary? Or, as one might gather from the "we choose" phraseology, was it to be a treatise on the philosophy of criticism? In either case, it is a prolegomenon to something obviously conflicted and bittersweet. Wagner had always found "uneasiness," "chaos," "confusion," and "mistakes" in the work of Berlioz, and yet now – as in 1852, when he told Liszt, "Believe me, I *love* Berlioz, even though he distrustfully and obstinately refuses to come near me: he does not *know* me, but *I* know *him*" (I give the original in the epigraph of this chapter) [27] – even now, in 1869, he was clearly drawn to the French composer. In May of that year he read Berlioz's *Mémoires* with considerable sympathy, and told his companion that the book had "strengthened his resolve never again to have anything to do with Paris."[28] Six months later Wagner was writing his treatise on conducting – the first of any importance since Berlioz's *L'Art du chef d'orchestre* of 1855. Is the French musician's conspicuous absence from *Über das Dirigieren* (1869) a paradoxical sign of his presence in Wagner's imagination? Be this as it may, for years thereafter, Berlioz was a topic of conversation between Richard and Cosima, whose diaries are filled with fascinating *aperçus* – complimentary, critical, contradictory – regarding both the man and his music.

That music, Wagner knew well. It was presumably during his years in Dresden, when he amassed a considerable library, that Wagner began purchasing Berlioz's published scores. By the end of his life, he possessed an impressive collection of first editions, as we know from the current Berlioz holdings in the Wagner museum at Wahnfried, which include the *Symphonie fantastique*, *Harold en Italie*, the *Requiem*, *Roméo et Juliette* (in both full score and in Theodor Ritter's piano reduction), the *Symphonie funèbre et triomphale*, *La Damnation de Faust*, the *Te Deum*, and the overtures *Le Roi Lear*, *Benvenuto Cellini* (in both full score and in Fumagalli's piano arrangement), and *Le Carnaval romain*. Wagner also possessed the Witzendorf edition of Liszt's arrangement of the *Symphonie fantastique*, the first edition of the *Mémoires* (as we have seen), and the *Instrumentationslehre* as translated by Alfred Dörffel.

The precise contents of Berlioz's library have never come to light. The only works by Wagner that we may be certain were in his possession are *Lohengrin* (which I mention in the introduction to this volume, and which Berlioz mentions in his letter to Wagner of 10 September 1855) and *Tristan* (with which we began this inquiry). In Paris in 1860 Wagner offered the latter score to Berlioz as a tribute to his colleague and rival whose work he had attempted to transcend –

Does the "confession of love" motif at the beginning *Tristan* (A²) evolve from what Berlioz called *Roméo seul* (A¹) at the opening of the second movement of the dramatic symphony? Does the "magic casket" motif of Wagner's opera (B²) derive from the second half (B¹) of the love theme from Berlioz's *Scène d'amour*? Does Isolde's "Mild und leise" (C²) arise from the extended melody (C¹) between Berlioz's *Roméo seul* and *Grande Fête chez Capulet*?

– and in the hope of winning both the French composer's private affection and public approval of a radically new musical style. But Berlioz's approval (his influential column, that is, in the influential *Journal des débats*) could never be purchased, not even by the elegant gift of the handsome new score of *Tristan*. While he reacted in many favorable ways to parts of *Rienzi, Der fliegende Holländer, Tannhäuser,* and *Lohengrin* (whose overture he considered a *chef-d'œuvre*), Berlioz could not find it in his heart – because he could not find it in his *ear* – to lavish praise upon *Tristan*, whose prelude, soon to become the most intensely scrutinized hundred bars in the entire musical canon, he failed to grasp.

What Berlioz wrote in reaction to the prelude – "I have read and reread this curious page; I have listened to it with scrupulous attention and with a sincere desire to discover its meaning; but alas, I must admit that I do not yet have the slightest idea of what the author was attempting to do" – has caused him to become known as one of Wagner's detractors. But if we read and reread this sentence, we see that it is not mere disparagement, for the crucial words *pas encore* ("not yet") suggest that Berlioz understood the possibility that the deficiency was not Wagner's, but *his*. It is well to remember that the dissonances at the opening of the finale of the Ninth Symphony – hardly a work that the French composer abhorred – caused Berlioz to use a quite similar formula: "I have long sought the reason for this idea, but I am compelled to admit that it remains to me inexplicable."[29]

The remainder of the article on Wagner deals with the so-called "music of the future"; here, too, Berlioz's objections, read coolly, are directed not so much at Wagner as at the "religion" of *la musique de l'avenir*, to whose prophets he would say *non credo*. Like Rossini, whose music Berlioz respected but whose proselytes he disdained, Wagner was for Berlioz a man to be reckoned with, the Wagnerians, men to be spurned.

Of the many aspects of this multi-dimensional relationship – almost all of the stories you might wish to tell can be told along with the story of Berlioz and Wagner – let me reiterate one that brings both men together. This concerns the phenomenon that so impressed Berlioz on his initial encounter with *Rienzi* and *Der fliegende Holländer* – Wagner's two-fold authorship of the text and the music. The encounter surely added fuel to the fire that eventually led Berlioz, too, to compose his own librettos. In this way Berlioz was able to give his music "the first and final say," as Katherine Kolb has persuasively written, "while simultaneously declaring the text so crucial that the composer alone could be relied on to do it justice."[30]

Would Richard Wagner have put it this way? In the eternal debate over the primacy of the one or the other, he tended, at least in theory, to exclaim *prima le parole, dopo la musica*. He diagnosed Berlioz's problem as advocating the opposite, as we see in his letter to Liszt of 8 September 1852, with its analysis of the weakness of Berlioz's *Benvenuto Cellini* couched in explicit sexual imagery that a "new" musicologist might wish to pursue:

> If ever a *musician* needed *a poet*, it is Berlioz, and it is his misfortune that he always adapts his poet according to his own musical whim, arranging now Shakespeare, now Goethe, to suit his own purpose. He needs a poet to fill him through and through, a poet who is driven by ecstasy to violate him, and who is to him what man is to woman.[31]

It is true that the libretto of *Benvenuto Cellini*, like those of the dramatic symphony *Roméo et Juliette* and the dramatic legend *La Damnation de Faust*, fails to rise to Goethean or Shakespearean heights. (*Les Troyens* and *Béatrice et Bénédict* were not yet written.) What is striking is Wagner's "solution" to Berlioz's "difficulty": that he take over Wagner's *own* prose outline of the story of *Wieland der Schmied*, the three-act mythical-legendary-Germanic-heroic opera sketched in the winter of 1849–1850 and abandoned in favor of the Nibelungs. We may find this ludicrously self-centered, for Berlioz, who contemplated setting many tales, was unlikely to warm to such a subject.[32]

But Wagner was perfectly serious. More droll, Wagner suggests that the French libretto of *Wieland* be prepared by, of all persons, Henri Blaze. Now, it is not clear whether Wagner refers to Berlioz's predecessor at the *Journal des débats*, the critic known as Castil-Blaze, or to his son, Henri Blaze de Bury. For Berlioz, both were incarnations of all that was wrong with French musical life – the former because of his arrangements of Mozart and Weber, which Berlioz called *dérangements* and *castilblazades*; the latter because of his "De l'école fantastique de M. Berlioz," a misguided essay that itemized Berlioz's "faults" in an insidious way that misinformed an entire generation.[33] Wagner may have liked Berlioz, he may have admired and felt sympathy for him, but he did not *know* him, contrary to what he explicitly claimed to Liszt, for no one who knew him could possibly have suggested that he traffic with a Blaze.

Wagner's diagnosis of the converse, however, was wise: "How unfortunate for me that you do not understand German," he wrote to Berlioz on 6 September 1855, recognizing that on that account he would always remain a stranger to the French composer. Throughout his lifetime Wagner was consumed with the question of "Was ist deutsch." And because he saw his own music as "merely an illustration" of the poem and the underlying poetic concept – the *poetische Entwürfe* – he assumed that

Berlioz would always be estranged from his music as well. Berlioz replied sympathetically – with humor, without linguistic chauvinism, without philosophical baggage:

> In *true* music, there are accents that require their particular words, and there are words that require their particular accents. To separate the one from the other, to give equivalents that are merely approximate, is to have a puppy suckled by a goat and vice-versa.[34]

Afterword

Near the end of the love scene in Act II, Tristan and Isolde entreat the love-night (*Liebesnacht*) to bring about their love-death (*Liebestod*) – the desired fruit of their love-passion (*Liebeslust* – the last word of the scene). Because German loves *Liebes*-compounds, let us choose *Liebesangst* to represent Wagner's feelings about Berlioz. The gift of *Tristan* was no doubt a display of affection. But it is also possible to see it as a demonstration of anxiety, which he expressed candidly to Liszt, and which resulted in part from what he called "his horrible French."[35] The psychological state in which Wagner encountered Berlioz was manifest in his larger encounter with the French nation, which now he would now adopt, now he would defeat. How curious that, unlike Berlioz's later reception (warm abroad, mixed in France, everywhere free from ideological excess), Wagner's afterlife – from the time of Nietzsche to the time of the Holocaust and beyond – should become an incarnation of *Liebesangst* itself.

PART VI

Renown

18 Berlioz's impact in France

LESLEY WRIGHT

"Impact" – the forceful contact or collision of one body against another – is a particularly appropriate word to describe Hector Berlioz's effect upon his contemporaries, whether the composers of his own or of the next generation, the public, or colleagues in the press. Many in France acknowledged the genius of Berlioz the musician, but in his own time true appreciation of his achievement tended to reside mainly with a few ardent admirers, for Berlioz cultivated a style that was so distinctive, subjective, and exploratory that general audiences did not embrace the bulk of his works.

In 1870, only a year after his death, a youthful Adolphe Jullien stressed the personal character of Berlioz's music by characterizing the man and his art as one and the same: "he acts, he thinks, he lives in his works. Each page of his music is made in his own image."[1] Younger composers, intent on building their careers, tended to avoid the risky course of adopting wholesale his innovations and individual style. In 1871 Georges Bizet expressed both the deep admiration and the wariness symptomatic of his generation's attitude toward Berlioz as a model:

> [W]hat makes for success is the talent and not the idea. The public [. . .] only understands the idea later on, but to make it to this "later on" the artist's talent has to make the road accessible to the public, by means of appealing forms, and not to put people off from the start. In such a way Auber, who had so much talent and so few ideas, was almost always understood, while Berlioz, who had genius but no talent, almost never was.[2]

Berlioz foresaw the battles he would face and, early in his career, armed himself with a powerful weapon to advance his reforms – the prose of a well-placed music commentator and critic. Although he made enemies as he carried on a columnist's campaign for serious music, including his own, he was also protected by the powerful owners – the Bertin family – of the respected newspaper that employed him from 1835 to 1863, the *Journal des débats*. Still, even in 1886, when bitterness over the trenchant power of his pen must have begun to recede, the subjectivity and originality of his music limited his place in the repertory of French performing institutions to only a handful of favored works. Oscar Comettant, himself a sometimes dogmatic composer-critic whose taste ran rather to Halévy, Meyerbeer, and Rossini, articulated the conservative point of view:

No, my dear Berlioz, my dear master, I do not think that your music will ever be played, with the exception of two or three scores whose subjects are marvelously suited to the strengths of your musical and extra-musical imagination, but your genius was great and your discoveries have entered into the public domain of art, which you have thereby enriched; your name will never die and your glory is eternal.[3]

As Comettant predicted, Berlioz's name has never died, but his import in his own country has long been and is still debated. This study examines Berlioz's impact in France by focusing, first, on the assessments made at the time of his death. It then considers the renaissance of the eighteen-seventies (spearheaded by such figures as the composer-critic Ernest Reyer and the conductors Édouard Colonne and Jules Pasdeloup), the semi-canonization by supporters in 1886 (who characterized him as a French ancestor and as a bulwark against the Wagnerian invasion), and the appraisals made on the centenary of his birth in 1903. Composers' reactions in France and elsewhere give us further insight into the nature of Berlioz's standing during these three decades, as do certain works of those composers, touched by Berlioz's conception of the work of art, by his unique style, or by the musical gestures and sonorities of his individual movements.

In the twentieth century scholarly texts and reference books have widely recognized that composers in the Western tradition, French and not French, adopted certain general aspects of Berlioz's style.[4] His orchestration treatise as well as his revelation of the "boundless expressive potential of the orchestra" were seminal.[5] Carl Dahlhaus credits him with the "emancipation of timbre," one of the decisive evolutionary features of the nineteenth century.[6] Berlioz's striking use of thematic transformation and program provided models for later programmatic symphonies, symphonic poems, and cyclic works: a standard textbook would have us believe that "All subsequent composers of program music, including Strauss and Debussy, would be indebted to him."[7] But Jacques Barzun underlines a paradox: Berlioz did indeed influence "all those who came after," but he did so "without being imitated by any."[8]

In an opera-loving culture, Berlioz moved toward a new symphonic concept by synthesizing the arts in symphonies and mixed-genre pieces, despite a muse "strongly rooted in the Gallic vocal tradition."[9] Initially inspired by Beethoven, he stood apart from the German-dominated mainstream and marked the end of a tradition stemming from Gluck and Lesueur. Hugh Macdonald stresses this isolation in noting that Berlioz should be seen "for what he was and what he did rather than for where he stood in relation to others. [. . .] In France Berlioz's style effectively had no influence on the succeeding generations."[10] Julian Rushton's study of Berlioz's musical language, on the other hand, finds a way to reconcile Barzun's and Macdonald's statements: because Berlioz never repeated his own inventions, "he produced no *class* of works capable of serving as a general model for others," even if *one work* could have a "specific influence" upon another (my emphasis). At the same time, like Barzun, Rushton points to "a certain general influence" that he limits to the French school of the generation that followed Berlioz, which included Gounod, Saint-Saëns, Bizet, and Chabrier. And finally, like Macdonald, he acknowledges Berlioz's isolation and concludes that we cannot neatly relate him to the trends of the nineteenth century, since he "stands perpendicular to the line of their development and is not part of them."[11]

In the wake of Berlioz's death

The first large body of articles to assess Berlioz's career cluster in the weeks and months immediately after his death on 8 March 1869. With emphases and perspectives quite different from those of modern critics, their authors, too, speak to Berlioz's originality and his place in history, though their views are clearly influenced by the near immediacy of his publications and personality. Writers in these newspapers and periodicals, for example, all refer to his importance as a critic, although Berlioz had resigned from this position at the *Débats* some six years before his death. Though *Les Troyens* was finally staged in a mutilated version at the same time, in 1863, his earlier program symphonies and mixed-genre works – which, except via excerpts, had receded from the concert stage in Paris – formed the basis of most generalizations about his music. Berlioz as innovator in orchestration and in "descriptive" music, Berlioz as an erudite and indefatigable reformer armed for battle, Berlioz as a "Germanic" figure, unappreciated at home but beloved abroad – these are the principal themes that were enumerated in 1869.[12] Partisans complained that Berlioz had never been adequately recognized in France, but some, like Gustave Chadeuil, pointedly referred to the numerous official honors that should have tempered Berlioz's bitterness: "Despite all the injustices he suffered, he died as librarian of the Conservatoire, member of the Institute, officer of the Legion of Honor, and knight of innumerable orders."[13] Still, on virtually every issue, this one included, the attitudes of the writers ranged from fervent support to open hostility.

Berlioz's own prose occasionally served as the basis for appraisals of his achievement. Mathieu de Monter, for example, based his description of Berlioz's style on precisely what the composer had written in the Postscript of the *Mémoires*:

> In Berlioz the composer, men of the next generation have before them a bold style that enlarges the number of constituent elements in art: a veritable luxuriance of melodies, [...] inward intensity, rhythmic impetus, unexpectedness, sincerity, and passionate expression bent on reproducing the inner meaning of its subject, even when that subject is the opposite of passion.[14]

Many expressed admiration for Berlioz's lifelong battle on behalf of his beliefs, and yet, in a substantial portion of the 1869 notices, it is easy to sense an uncomfortable ambivalence. In his extended essay, published on the anniversary of Berlioz's death, even Adolphe Jullien expressed admiration with reserve:

> Berlioz yielded too often to the desire to write descriptive and imitative music; too often he wanted to use sounds to express inexpressible feelings. Enamored of originality, always on the lookout for new combinations, Berlioz, next to many inspired pages, left others on which one is too conscious of the researcher.[15]

Oscar Comettant, while conceding originality, also maintained a certain distance from Berlioz's aesthetic:

> Whatever may be posterity's judgment of Berlioz's work, he will remain one of the boldest personalities of the romantic school of music, one of the most poetic and original minds of our century. His whole life was a fight for the triumph of a musical poetics that can be disapproved of, but that he nonetheless invented and that has had no lack of imitators, beginning with Richard Wagner.[16]

In 1869, attempts to situate Berlioz in the history of music often depended on a list of German composers – perhaps an acknowledgment that his principal achievements lay outside the realm of opera as well as a tacit admission that he had brought to French music both the seriousness of German orchestral music and the enriched orchestral palette of Weber. As Daniel Bernard remarked, "Berlioz will have his appointed place, well above Cherubini, and immediately behind Weber and Beethoven."[17] On the other hand, Armand de Pontmartin, writer for the royalist *Gazette de France* and no friend to Berlioz, located him entirely outside the pale, as have some modern writers, finding it impossible "to assign him a clearly defined place between Beethoven and Mendelssohn [or] between Rossini and Meyerbeer," and yet finding it "completely unjust to call him a musical 'outcast.'"[18] Despite evident respect for his intellect, some blamed his lack of success in France on what was perceived as the essentially non-French character of his music: "Berlioz the musician too often spoke a foreign language, and I think that the striking pages spread among his works can be likened to those unusual and powerful turns of phrase that foreigners sometimes transmit from their idiom to ours."[19]

Berlioz's great success in Germany, in contrast to his lonely prestige in France, was commonly mentioned at the time of his death. David de Closel deftly sketched Berlioz's isolation with metaphors: "In Paris he manifested the sadness of a missionary among the savages; he was Jesus among the Jews. A stranger among us, he appeared truly at ease only in Germany."[20] A more thoughtful and knowledgeable critic, Arthur Pougin, attributed this situation to national taste and training: "The Germans, whose temperament and musical abilities have developed differently from ours, truly knew how to appreciate the worth of this eminent man, and Berlioz was always welcomed by them as one of the most original, most personal, and most valiant artists that this century has produced."[21]

Wagner was the only living German composer regularly compared to Berlioz in 1869, and Berlioz's enemies made a point of stressing this controversial tie. Closel felt Berlioz had abandoned melody in favor of harmony (like Wagner) and had thus betrayed his audience: "Berlioz was our French Wagner. Those waves of erudite, complex harmonies upon which there is not even one knot of melody per hour – they caused displeasure and led one to exclaim (creating a wall between the composer and the listener): 'I don't understand!' "[22] Even Berlioz's adversaries could not have foreseen the extent to which his voice would soon be combined with, subsumed under, or muted by the widespread adoption of Wagnerian rhetoric and syntax. Pontmartin made the prophetic observation that "for the last eight or ten years in Europe Wagner has usurped or conquered that importance, that breadth, that burning zeal of the musical revolutionary, of the musician of the future, which Berlioz ardently dreamed of but pursued in vain." He felt that Beethoven's shadow had stood in the way of Berlioz's career at the beginning, and that Wagner's had done the same at the end.[23]

Since the authors of the obituaries in the newspapers and music periodicals were virtually all music and/or drama critics, it is not surprising that they made reference to Berlioz's journalism. Berlioz himself called his journalistic duties his "ball and chain"; he told his sister on 11 May 1856 (when making the rounds to members of the Académie des Beaux-Arts), "My articles have done me more harm than good; someone was saying to me again yesterday that without them I should have been elected to the Institute eight or ten years ago."[24] Philarète Chasles, among others, agreed that this was indeed the principal reason for Berlioz's difficulty:

It is specifically his ardent, violent, acid-tipped, vengeful, and militant polemics, attacked and attacking in turn; it is his prejudice, his use of the newspaper as a weapon of attack and defense; his epigrams, satire, and irony – which diminished and weakened Berlioz. If his talent, or rather his genius, resisted this, it is because he had a great deal of it.[25]

Closel remarked that while Berlioz's music was not always understood, his criticism was, because with his pen Berlioz could wash and dissect a work like a body on a marble table.[26] In the low-budget, small-format *Petit Journal*, Timothée Trimm made it clear that he liked the artist more than the man; characterizing Berlioz as a soaring eagle who, as a bird of prey, could also make use of his beak and claws.[27] The Marquis de Thémines, himself a librettist and translator, admired the talent of the critic but sniped that his "impartiality was not always up to the level of his competence."[28] Others pointed out that his position at the respected *Journal des débats* (widely read by members of the élite and haute bourgeoisie) gave Berlioz considerable power that he used to great advantage: Berlioz had

> remarkable talent as a writer, which he did not hesitate to press into service to second his ambitions as a composer and which, when settled into the fortress of his feature article in the *Journal des débats*, he could use each morning to rally the troops, defeat his enemies, glorify his doctrines [...], recruit the artists whom he needed, or take revenge upon those whom he resented.[29]

Evaluations of Berlioz's accomplishments as a musician and of his impact on other composers were relatively sparse in 1869, when, as we have seen, writers focused more on the man and the critic. Still, the more thoughtful ones, like Pougin, discussed Berlioz's particular interest in program music: "[Berlioz] persuaded himself that music must have a subject, a program, and that the triumph of art was to express this program by means of colorful effects, be it with the help of voices and words or with instruments alone."[30] Compliments to Berlioz's musical achievement tended to refer either to individual works or to orchestration in general, where he was characterized as having "a genius for *sonority*, just as certain painters have a natural genius for chiaroscuro."[31] When Félicien David, successor to Berlioz at the Académie des Beaux-Arts, read the obligatory tribute to his predecessor, he, too, took up this line of praise:

> While in the search for melody he manifested an indomitable repugnance for banal ideas and conventional forms, in his orchestration he showed himself to be a bold and powerful innovator, and achieved the rank of a true master. It is by this that he gained the right to be admired; it is by this that he lives and will live for a long time.[32]

Berlioz's staunchest supporters in the press – Ernest Reyer of the *Journal des débats* and Johannès Weber of *Le Temps* – foresaw a resurgence of interest in Berlioz's music. Reyer, a close friend to Berlioz and himself a respected composer, summarized the views of the opposing camp and predicted their eventual enlightenment:

> If those who deny the progress made by Hector Berlioz in orchestration and in the variety of new elements that he introduced into symphonic music; if those who reproach him for the oddity of his rhythmic combinations and rebuke him for the childishness of the imitative effects that are found in some of his compositions; if those who accuse him of lacking melody and wanting all sense of the dramatic; if those people live a few years longer, as I sincerely hope they do, then they will witness a reaction that will enlighten them on the true worth of their judgments.

Reyer's goal in the eighteen-seventies was to return Berlioz's work to the repertory full and uncut: the public "must get to know it not in fragmentary or mutilated form, but complete and in all its perfection."[33]

Johannès Weber, another composer-critic who supported a Berlioz revival, also predicted a turnaround:

> I've always been convinced that there will eventually be a reaction in Berlioz's favor. [...] This reaction will result from two things: the composer's own merit, and French chauvinism. [...] The time will come when everyone will call Berlioz, and with reason, the French Beethoven.[34]

"The French Beethoven," whatever its literal significance, is a fine compliment. Is it not difficult to imagine a candidate for that title other than Berlioz?

The Berlioz revival

Johannès Weber claimed that the rehabilitation of Berlioz began as soon as he was placed in the grave: the "defiance" and "turbulence" of his reception, at the Pasdeloup concerts, had now turned to "reserve" and "respect."[35] Near the beginning of the revival, Ernest Reyer wondered whether the effects of the Franco-Prussian War were helping to resuscitate Berlioz for a populace stung by military defeat: "Would the war that banned Richard Wagner have led us directly to Berlioz?"[36] And in the following decade Adolphe Jullien speculated that "without the War of 1870 and the sudden awakening of national spirit," the public "would have gone straight over to Richard Wagner, after tossing a few bravos of condolence to the author of *Roméo*."[37]

The Berlioz revival, though tirelessly encouraged by Reyer, did not begin with the memorial concert that he and Henry Litolff organized at the Opéra on 22 March 1870: the audience there was reserved and respectful to the point that, as one reviewer remarked, Berlioz would have "preferred to be less venerated and more *disrespectfully* applauded."[38] The movement ought rather to be dated from the time at which Pasdeloup began frequently to program Berlioz's works. Colonne joined suit, and so, too, did Lamoureux and the Concerts du Conservatoire. Brief selections gave way to longer sections and, by the mid-eighteen-seventies, to complete works, including the first three symphonies and, most successful of all, *La Damnation de Faust.*[39] In fact the winter of 1877 featured rival performances of the *Damnation* by both Pasdeloup and Colonne. A failure in earlier decades, it suddenly became a favorite – perhaps rendered more palatable by the public's familiarity with Gounod's now celebrated opera, perhaps by the demise of critics' personal grudges.[40]

Frequent performances of some of Berlioz's works did continue into the next decade, but of the larger works only *La Damnation de Faust* and the *Symphonie fantastique* were securely in the repertory by the eighteen-eighties. Still, prior to 1878 the Berlioz revival was so remarkable that Arthur Pougin noted "a considerable reversal of opinion" when he updated Fétis's *Biographie universelle des musiciens*: "[T]oday the crowd rushes to hear Berlioz's works whether they are presented at the Concerts populaires, the Châtelet concerts, or even those at the Conservatoire."[41]

Comparisons with Wagner become gradually more frequent in the Berlioz literature in the eighteen-eighties and nineties and largely displace references to all other composers. In 1883, for example, Georges Noufflard classified Berlioz as the precursor to *all* modern music and asserted that his work contained all the elements that would be assembled and systematically coordinated in Wagner's music dramas.[42] Reviewing the book, Johannès Weber vehemently disagreed, finding that the two composers were similar in only certain general and personal characteristics.[43]

The statue of Berlioz

Wagner's shadow was present, though not welcomed, at the inauguration of Alfred Lenoir's statue of Berlioz in the Square Vintimille, on 17 October 1886. In the seventeen years since his death, the press had gradually shifted away from focusing on personal qualities to concentrating on artistic characteristics, from emphasizing German qualities to concentrating on French ones, and from speaking in a reserved manner to articulating views with more enthusiasm.[44] Two parts of the ceremony excited particular comment in the press. One was Reyer's moving tribute to his friend, whom he acknowledged as a man of both principle and genius:

> Berlioz did not produce students, but he did produce disciples – and we are among them. If we took no lessons with him, if he did not teach us directly, he did offer us a great deal of instruction – by demonstrating himself that an artist's primary duty is to maintain his dignity, particularly in his relations with others as imposed upon him by the necessities of his career. He told us that to genuflect before those brought to power merely by chance was to demonstrate a shameful weakness, and that to make concessions to popular taste was to manifest nothing but cowardice.

Though Reyer referred to the asperity of Berlioz's pen, he credited Berlioz with a "great and legitimate influence on the musicians" of the generation following his death:

> Who among us [. . .] has not profited from the precious innovations that came from his instrumental palette! Who among us has not felt himself irresistibly drawn to the cult of ideal beauty by the eulogistic praises he sang in honor of some of the most glorious and noble representatives of our art – of Gluck and Beethoven, of Spontini and Weber?[45]

While Reyer's speech was widely praised for its sincerity and power, Charles Grandmougin's poem, "À Berlioz," recited by an actor from the Comédie française, was found inappropriate for its mention of Richard Wagner. (In his eleventh stanza, Grandmougin refers to Wagner's triumph and urges that France defend her native son from this imminent invasion.[46]) Albert Wolff snarled that Berlioz was "great enough through his own genius to stand on his own without a dig at Wagner by a meek poet who has probably never heard *Lohengrin*."[47] Fourcaud, elevating Berlioz to the status of "veritable restorer and founder of our school of music," replaced the comparison to Wagner with a new one – to two literary giants – of his own:

> [W]e are overwhelmed by the power of [Berlioz's] poetry [. . .] What he felt, we feel. [. . .] From this moment onward we must say of him what we say of Balzac and Victor Hugo in literature: all composers owe him something. He is no longer a solitary figure; he is an ancestor.[48]

Saint-Saëns, too, suggested that promoting Berlioz was a patriotic gesture: "true patriotism consists of bringing our own richness to light."[49]

But not everyone who attended the inauguration was willing to hail Berlioz as the father and exemplar of modern French music. The anonymous writer for *Le Petit Journal* pointed out that the majority of the public still did not understand his music, and, reflecting the view of his humble readership, asserted that in fact Berlioz was no martyr: he had had success, his music had been heard, he had had a regular newspaper column, and he had had access to the major institutions.[50] Taking a different tack, the conservative critic Simon Boubée conceded that Berlioz's works had brought colorful elements to the French tradition, but blamed him for inducing young composers erroneously to view the art of music as nothing more than the art of "description."[51]

To the centenary

Assessments over the next seventeen years, to the centenary of 1903, include Adolphe Jullien's monumental and richly illustrated study, the first based on extensive use of primary sources. Jullien concentrated more on determining what Berlioz himself had accomplished than on what he had inspired others to do.[52] In 1890 Hippeau called Berlioz the "leader" of French music, but admitted that French composers were little willing to acknowledge his stature because of Wagner's growing artistic presence.[53] Lavoix's history of music in France (1891) also designates Berlioz the head of the French Romantic school.[54] But reviewing this book and elsewhere, Johannès Weber continued his refusal to see Berlioz as the progenitor of modern French music, saying that he was rather merely the creator of the (possibly "spurious") genre of the "dramatic symphony":

> Berlioz was Berlioz. That is his glory, but let us surely not crown him head of a school, for if we do, then woe to art! There are men who, despite their genius or their talent, should never be accorded this title. Meyerbeer and Berlioz are among them.[55]

At the time of the centenary celebrations in 1903, a few scholars examined Berlioz's achievement from the point of view of its impact upon other musicians. In the grand *Livre d'or du centenaire*, Eugène de Solenière noted that Berlioz's ideas, writings, and actions had at least as much influence as had his music, and rehearsed in new words the old idea that his presence in the work of younger composers was muted because of the simultaneous presence of Wagner:

> Berlioz was a revolutionary whose cries were covered by those of another revolutionary whose voice was stronger than his. In fact they did not say the same things, but they had the same hatreds, the same aversions, the same animosities, and while using different means for different purposes, they essentially fought for the same ideals. Thus was Berlioz Wagner's precursor.[56]

Julien Tiersot, one of the early fine Berlioz specialists, also admitted that the brilliance of Wagner's star dimmed Berlioz's radiance soon after the posthumous revival of the eighteen-seventies and eighties had brought him to glory. But for Tiersot, "the eclipse he suffered by the approach of the brighter star that was Wagner was far from total, and was only temporary."[57] To underline Berlioz's importance as an artist, Tiersot made sport of Wagner while evoking the figure of one of Berlioz's earliest musical gods:

> Berlioz was no *Uebermensch*. He always remained on earth [...] Leaving Wagner alone in outer space, Berlioz remained among us, holding out his hand to the greatest of all, to the hero of genius and suffering, to his first and true forebear, Beethoven.
>
> In their everlasting song, united as son to father, Berlioz and he have expressed the purest, most sincere and most profound essence of humanity.[58]

Camille Saint-Saëns used equally exalted terms to glorify Berlioz in the temple of high art. In a speech prepared to be read in Berlioz's home town of La Côte-Saint-André at the time of the hundredth anniversary of his birth, he wrote that "il est Lui," the capital L suggesting god-like stature, and went on:

> [H]e was the incomparable initiator of the entire generation to which I belong. He opened the golden door through which soared into and invaded the world that host of dazzling and enchanting fairies that is modern orchestration; he offered the admirable example of a life entirely devoted to pure art. Glory to him, glory forever.[59]

Composers on Berlioz

As we have seen, few critics considered Berlioz's music to have served as a model for the works of other composers. Today, it would be difficult to write a book on *After Berlioz* that would deal with later composers' readings and misreadings of Berlioz's principal compositions – as Mark Evan Bonds has done, for the composer of the Ninth Symphony, in *After Beethoven*.[60] Where might we find the "anxiety" of Berlioz's influence? At the peak of his career, Charles Gounod chose candidly to take on a subject strongly associated with Berlioz, *Roméo et Juliette* – and Berlioz's reaction confirms that he felt a challenge: "Have you not read the numerous newspapers which spoke of my score of *Roméo et Juliette* in comparison with Gounod's opera," he wrote to his friend Ferrand on 11 June 1867, "and in a way that could hardly be flattering to him?" The press referred to the challenge as well, though Gustave Bertrand, for one, felt that Gounod had deliberately avoided a head-on confrontation.[61]

Some in the press found memories of Berlioz's setting to be distracting, especially in the introduction and in the Queen Mab aria, where Gounod seems in fact to have concentrated obeisance to his predecessor. For Reyer, the unaccompanied chorus of the introduction was analogous to Berlioz's in the general sense of the form.[62] But fugal exposition, choral recitation, and instrumentation suggest that Gounod's reading of Berlioz was rather more explicit. This is not the place to consider Gounod's larger debt to Berlioz – there is Eugène Scribe's libretto, *La Nonne sanglante*, which Berlioz worked on in the early eighteen-forties, and which Gounod set in 1853; and there is *Faust* – but debt, as we learn from Gounod's generous preface to the *Lettres intimes*, there clearly was.[63]

Nor is it the place to consider others whom one might wish to speak of under Harold Bloom's famous title. Georges Bizet owned the full score of *L'Enfance du Christ*, so one might logically wish to relate the flute and harp sonority, the tessitura of the opening melody, the quiet dynamics, the slow tempo and, especially, the mood of utter peace of the prelude to Act III of *Carmen* to the trio for two flutes and harp performed by the young Ishmaelites in Part III of *L'Enfance du Christ* – even if some similarities evaporate upon closer analysis. It is easier to link a piece such as Franck's March of the Moabites in his oratorio *Ruth* (revised in 1871) to the Pilgrims' March of *Harold en Italie*, since not just the atmosphere but the form and pedal points all indicate that model.[64] Are these "anxious" incidents of influence?

Over the years many French composers expressed opinions of Berlioz, though not always in the public arena. Near the beginning of the Berlioz revival, a teenaged Ernest Chausson confided an emotional bond to his diary:

> I feel that even if the whole world were against me my admiration would always remain the same. How could I not love the man who has caused me to shed tears, who has surely procured for me the sweetest pleasures that life has to offer?[65]

Repeating what then became the standard assessment, Alfred Bruneau judged Berlioz to be the intellectual father of the symphony in France and the initiator of diverse and colorful forms of program music; but he reserved his highest tribute for Berlioz's character:

> For today's composers, for his sons, he is a marvelous and incomparable professor of energy and courage. It is in this way, I believe, that Berlioz will most lastingly exert his estimable influence on our art.[66]

In the later eighteen-eighties, Wagner's presence obviously loomed large in French musical circles. But the mature Emmanuel Chabrier found no difficulty in expressing admiration for Berlioz:

> Berlioz, a Frenchman above all else (he was not old hat in his era!), put variety, color, and rhythm into the *Damnation, Roméo* and *L'Enfance du Christ*. They lack unity, you say? I say *merde!* If to be number one you absolutely have to be boring, then I prefer to be number two, three, four, ten, or twenty; indeed, I prefer to have ten colors on my palette and to grind up all the different keys... I want beauty everywhere and beauty takes a thousand different forms.[67]

The leading composers of the following generation, sometimes willing to acknowledge aspects of Berlioz's mastery, tended to recoil from his harmony, forms, and romantic excesses. In the anniversary year of 1903 Claude Debussy claimed that Berlioz had always found his greatest admirers among non-musicians and denied that he had had any influence at all on modern musicians, with only a single exception:

> Because of his concern with color and curiosities, Berlioz was immediately adopted by the painters; indeed one can say without irony that Berlioz was always the musician preferred by those who did not know music very well.
> [...] Professional musicians are still horrified by his harmonic "liberties" (which they call "awkwardnesses"), and by his "go-to-hell" forms. Is this the reason that his influence on modern music is practically nil? and that he will remain essentially unique? In France, only in Gustave Charpentier do I see the possibility that one might find a little of this influence.[68]

Elsewhere Debussy claimed that he did not find much that was particularly "French" in Berlioz.[69]

Maurice Ravel also disparaged Berlioz's methodology:

> My contention is that Berlioz was the only composer of genius who conceived his melodies without hearing their harmonization, and proceeded to discover this harmonization afterwards.[70]

Like Debussy, he claimed that Berlioz's influence was practically non-existent. And yet some of his contemporaries saw Ravel's own technique as stemming in part from Berlioz. Writing in 1913, Gaston Carraud suggested that

> the influence of Berlioz – even given the differences between their temperaments and their works – appears in the limitless virtuosity of [Ravel's] orchestral writing, in the pursuit and accumulation of surprising effects, and in the frequent use of extra-musical means.[71]

Another contemporary, Charles Koechlin, who admired Berlioz and used his *Traité d'instrumentation* as a model for his own, took issue with the specific point that Ravel had raised:

> I am convinced that if composers . . . made more use of *writing a melody first* (without worrying about its harmonization), they would write more alive and significant music. Berlioz worked thus: people may joke about this, but I have never found it at all ridiculous, and I have often followed his example without having had any cause to regret it.[72]

Berlioz's enormous impact on the history of orchestration has never been contested. Composers of France, Germany, Russia, and elsewhere found inspiration for instrumental sonorities both in his works and in his celebrated *Traité d'instrumentation*. Virtually all the biographies of later nineteenth-century musicians – among them Mahler, Elgar, Delius, Busoni, d'Indy, Debussy, and Puccini – mention that their subjects read and profited from the treatise. Musorgsky, for example, kept the treatise with him until his death.[73] Richard Strauss made his own version of the book, in 1904, updating Alfred Dörffel's translation (of 1864) by adding to Berlioz's original sixty-six examples eighty-four of his own, selected from his own works along with some by Liszt, Marschner, Verdi, Debussy, and, overwhelmingly, Wagner.

In a period when most critics heard nothing but echoes of Wagner in modern scores, Ernest Reyer heard Berlioz. In the rich polyphony and large orchestra of Chabrier's *Gwendolyne* (1886), for example, many heard *Die Meistersinger*. But because, in the brilliant overture, Chabrier had placed the love theme (from Gwendoline's aria) above a rapid and persistent rhythm in order to insert light into an otherwise dark picture, Reyer rather found a sonic response to Berlioz's overture to *Les Francs-Juges*.[74]

In the year of Strauss's version of the *Traité d'instrumentation*, Berlioz's one-time disciple Saint-Saëns felt he had to defend his *maître* from the pen of Gabriel Fauré, who in a review of a performance of the overture to *Benvenuto Cellini* had attacked the work's supposedly uninspired themes, contorted form, and vulgar sonority. He asked Fauré whether people ever spoke of the vulgarities and platitudes in *Tannhäuser* and *Lohengrin* and suggested to him that the procedure at the climactic section of the Berlioz – where the trombones in unison play the grand theme from the Adagio while the violins play the lively second theme from the Allegro – was appropriated by Wagner and on this account alone merited "a certain deference."[75]

From Berlioz's death to the hundredth anniversary of his birth and beyond, composers and critics most regularly associated with Berlioz the broad notion of "descriptive orchestral music" – music characterized by the presence of an autobiographical subject, by the use of a recurring theme representative of a person or idea, and by the impression of narrative or theatrical or visual intent. Urged on by Balakirev, Tchaikovsky provided one of the most successful tributes to Berlioz in his *Manfred Symphony* (1885): here, as in *Harold en Italie*, a recurring theme represents the wandering of the Byronic hero; and here, as in *Harold*, an opening melancholy is supplanted by a closing bacchanal.[76]

Harold was also the model (Debussy would have agreed) for Gustave Charpentier's *Impressions d'Italie* (1887–1889). With its detailed program, homage to Berlioz seems clearly intended, as the youthful composer allied himself with the "French school" just as Berlioz was first being dubbed the leader and the ancestor of all French musicians. The reviewer for *Le Ménestrel* makes the comparison explicit:

> In these two compositions the viola plays a role of primary importance and is used to translate similar emotions; in both works there is a serenade and a march across the mountains; there is also a musical description of the feelings one has at the summit. [. . .] As in Berlioz's composition, we find in the finale reminiscences of the previous movements.[77]

Liszt's symphonic poems derive from Berlioz, it is often said, and Strauss's *Ein Heldenleben* (1899) is as much a descendant of Berlioz's symphonies as of any of Liszt's descriptive compositions. Mahler, too, was a champion of Berlioz, and some suggest that his own programmatic symphonies hearken back to the composer of the *Symphonie fantastique* (with which Mahler made a splash as conductor in Vienna and New York). And the list goes on. For in all biographies, including the modern ones by Barzun, Bloom, Cairns, Macdonald, and others, and in the more narrowly focused studies of the music by Primmer and Rushton, among others, Berlioz's "impact" is treated in various ways that cannot help but reflect how these authors simply happen to hear music "after" Berlioz.

In his authoritative life-and-works, Holoman makes a point that would suggest a separate study – and that is that "by 1870 royalty and empire were all but things of the past, as was their ceremonial music."[78] The advent of the Third Republic did indeed mark a decrescendo of formal, stately occasions of the sort for which Berlioz had provided appropriate musical monuments with such works as the *Requiem* and the *Te Deum*. Napoléon III never did a great deal on behalf of our composer, but had he remained in power, others might well have looked to Berlioz for precedents to whatever sorts of grand ceremonial music the aging emperor might have required.

Scholars, musicians, and commentators have never wholly agreed on the extent of Berlioz's impact in France. At first, the residue of his acerbic pen colored the assessment of his achievement and encouraged the portrayal (as he did himself) of an artist isolated from the mass. As memories faded, bitterness was replaced by respect for his integrity as an artist. But in the matter of musical style, Berlioz's habits were so personal and so controversial that composers of younger generations largely avoided or shied away from open emulation. When Berlioz's imagination touched other musicians, it was in the realm of sonority, color, and idea. Of course a concern with sonority does not obscure an individual style. Thus works so typically German as Strauss's, so Russian as Tchaikovsky's, or even so Wagnerian as Franck's, can be seen to acknowledge Berlioz, as it were, without obscuring national or personal character.

Berlioz achieved a broadened concept of genre, a new legitimacy in France for orchestral music as a vehicle for serious expression, and a widespread acceptance of an infinitely enriched palette of instrumental color. If he did not preside over a school of composition, he nonetheless opened minds to many possibilities little explored.

Notes

Introduction: Berlioz on the eve of the bicentenary

1 The album-leaf, formerly in the collection of Edward H. Wannemacher, is reproduced in Barzun, *Nouvelles Lettres de Berlioz* (Westport, Conn., 1974), after p. 41. Barzun dates the item as *c.* 1865, on the assumption that this is when Berlioz might have been in contact with the album's owner, "M. Mendès" – presumably Catule Mendès (1841–1909), who arrived in Paris in 1859, became a libertine and a fervent Wagnerian (Wagner contributed to his *Revue fantaisiste*), and married Judith Gautier, daughter of Berlioz's friend Théophile Gautier, in 1866. The musical manuscript suggests an earlier date, however (and thus a different Mendès), possibly 1844, when Vincendon-Dumoulin's study of Tahiti appeared in Paris (as did Gustave Bourdin's collection of satirical articles entitled *Voyage autour de Pomaré, Reine de Mabille*); possibly 1847, when Élise Sergent died suddenly of tuberculosis; possibly 1849, when Berlioz joked with Théodor von Döhler about *his* being named pianist and composer to the Queen (in a letter of 14 July of that year); possibly 1855, when Berlioz addressed a hilarious review of the Exposition Universelle, in broken French "as it is spoken at the Tahitian court" (a now politically incorrect technique), to "sa Majesté Aïmata Pomaré, reine de Tahïti" (*Journal des débats*; 19 October 1855; reprinted in *Les Grotesques de la musique*, pp. 83–86); possibly 1857, when, in a letter of 21 December, Berlioz again joked about the court of Queen Pomaré as a fine place to seek musical employment. See Adrien Bertrand, *Catulle Mendès* (Paris, 1908); Jean Ziegler, *Gautier Baudelaire Un Carré de dames* (Paris, 1977); and Pierre Enckell, "Petite chronique des dames galantes," *L'Avant Scène Opéra*, 51 (*La Traviata*), pp. 4–9.

2 See Gautier, *Correspondance générale*, III, ed. Claudine Lacoste-Veysseyre (Geneva, 1988), pp. 118–119.

3 See Claude Pichois and Jean Ziegler, *Baudelaire* (Paris, 1987), pp. 212–214.

4 *Romanzero* (1850–1851). For another amusingly detailed portrait of La Pomaré, see Léon Séché, *La Jeunesse dorée sous Louis-Philippe* (Paris, 1910), pp. 254–268.

5 See *Selected Letters of Berlioz*, ed. Hugh Macdonald (New York, 1997), p. x.

6 Tysczkiewicz published his complaints in *Le Constitutionnel* on 19 October 1853 and in *L'Indépendance belge* on 2 November 1853. Accounts appeared subsequently in the *Berlin Musik-Zeitung* (6 November), *La France musicale* (27 November), the *Journal des débats* (9 December), and the *Süddeutsche Musik Zeitung* (19 December). The court proceedings were reported in *La France musicale* and the *Revue et Gazette musicale* of 11 December 1853. The editors of the latter journal, to which Tysczkiewicz had first appealed, had already suggested (in the issue of 16 October 1853) that he take the matter to the courts. For Berlioz's letters of protest, see *CG* IV, pp. 431–436, 446–447.

7 This score is found in the Bibliothèque Nationale de France (hereinafter BNF), Musique, FS 21. I am grateful to Jean-Michel Nectoux for drawing it to my attention.

8 See Mark Evan Bonds, *After Beethoven* (Cambridge, Mass., 1996), chapter 1 (here, p. 13).

9 In my translation I have adjusted the text, with the author's permission, to fit the current context.

10 His remark on reviewing a text submitted to the Académie des Sciences in 1865, quoted in my "Berlioz à L'Institut Revisited," *Acta Musicologica*, 53 (1981), p. 197. Particularly in the *Traité*'s chapter on the concertina, which includes a discussion of enharmony, does Berlioz ridicule certain theoretical concepts.

11 David Brown, *Tchaikovsky*, vol. 1 (New York, 1978), p. 125.

12 The Dumas story explains why, in Berlioz's otherwise inexplicable account, the municipal officer insisted that the composer, leaning back against a tree (like Armand Duval), approach and inspect the open coffin: in such circumstances, the law required that before any translation could take place, a body had officially to be "recognized."

The musical environment in France

1 Masset and Deschamps, *De M. Paër et de Rossini* (Paris, 1820).

2 [Annibal Bérenger de Labaume], *Observations désintéressées sur l'administration du Théâtre Royal Italien adressées à M. Viotti, Directeur de ce théâtre, par un dilettante* (1821). On Stendhal's role, see François Michel, "Un

mélomane ami de Stendhal: Bérenger de Labaume," *Études Stendhaliennes* (Paris, 1958), pp. 33–43.

3 As explained by Carl Dahlhaus, *Nineteenth-Century Music*, transl. Bradford Robinson (Berkeley, 1989), pp. 8–9, who cites Kiesewetter's use of the expression in 1834. Both were, in practice, ideal types.

4 *Le Correspondant*, 4 and 11 August, 6 October 1829; *CM* I, pp. 47–61.

5 On 2 September 1844, in a version by A. Royer and G. Waëz, and on 9 December 1853, in a version by Castil-Blaze.

6 *Mosè in Egitto* was given at the Opéra on 20 October 1822, *La donna del lago* on 7 September 1824, and *Semiramide* on 15 September 1825. *La gazza ladra* was given there on 18 September 1821, only a short while before Berlioz's arrival in Paris.

7 "[L]e jour précédent j'avais vu s'élever triomphant *Rossini*, encore accompagné des *Pages du duc de Vendôme*" (*CM* I, p. 442). Scholars have assumed, on the basis of a letter to Nanci of 13 December 1821, that Berlioz first saw *Iphigénie* when it was given at the Opéra on 26 November 1821. But this appears to contradict not only the assertion in the *Mémoires* that the *first* two operas Berlioz heard in Paris were *Les Danaïdes* and *Stratonice*, but also the account published on 9 November 1834 in the *Gazette musicale de Paris* (cited here) that before hearing the Gluck Berlioz had already discovered the Conservatoire library – an event Berlioz scholars have set in mid-1822. Could the letter of 13 December 1821, first published by Tiersot, be misdated?

8 In chapter 44 of the *Mémoires*, he tells the story of discovering willful errors in Fétis's edition of the Beethoven symphonies while proofreading the score of *Guillaume Tell*.

9 In articles for *Le Rénovateur* and other journals he spoke of *La gazza ladra*, *Le Comte Ory*, and *Mosè in Egitto*.

10 *CM* I, p. 443.

11 The Théâtre Allemand played in the Salle Favart, which was the home of the Théâtre Italien.

12 Stendhal, *Life of Rossini*, transl. Richard Coe (London, 1985), p. 107. The reviews in question were reprinted in his book from among the several he published anonymously in *Le Miroir des spectacles* (this one on 5 August 1821) beginning immediately upon his arrival in Paris some four or five months before Berlioz. See (in chapter 36 of the *Mémoires*) Berlioz's allusion to the *Vie de Rossini* and to Stendhal as an "homme d'esprit" who wrote "the most irritating stupidities about music, for which he fancied he had a feeling."

13 Gluck, letter to the *Mercure de France* (February 1773), in *Source Readings in Music History, The Classic Era*, ed. Oliver Strunk (New York, 1965), p. 107.

14 *CM* I, pp. 248–249.

15 Berlioz's essay first appeared in the *Revue et Gazette musicale* on 1 and 8 January 1837. I cite Jacques Barzun's translation as reprinted in Berlioz, *Fantastic Symphony* (Norton Critical Score), ed. Edward T. Cone (New York, 1971), p. 43.

16 See Louis Véron, *Mémoires d'un bourgeois de Paris* (Paris, 1856–1857), vol. 3, p. 320.

17 *Pandore* (7 June 1824), pp. 324, 326. In his study of *Iphigénie en Tauride* Berlioz admitted that the dilettanti were "in their way just as fanatical as I could be in mine" (*CM* I, p. 443).

18 See the *Dictionnaire théâtral, ou douze cent trente-trois verités*, 2nd ed. (Paris, 1825), a parody of the Dictionary of the Academy.

19 See *Annales de la littérature et des arts*, V, vol. 18 (Paris, 1825).

20 Cited in Paulo Fabbri, "Rossini the Aesthetician," transl. Tim Carter, *Cambridge Opera Journal*, 6 (1993), pp. 26–27.

21 *Ibid.*, p. 20.

22 "Aperçu sur la musique classique et la musique romantique," *Le Correspondant* (22 October 1830); *CM* I, p. 63.

23 See *CM* I, p. 474; and Berlioz's essay on the current state of the art of singing in *À travers chants*, pp. 113–127.

24 Legouvé, *Soixante ans de souvenirs* (Paris, 1886), vol. 1, pp. 298–299.

25 *Ibid.*, p. 305.

26 *Les Soirées de l'orchestre*, Twenty-fifth Evening.

27 Legouvé, *Soixante ans*, vol. 1, pp. 297–298.

28 See *Le Chef-d'œuvre inconnu, Gambara, Massimilla Doni*, ed. Marc Eigeldinger (Paris, 1981), p. 221.

29 See *CM* I, p. 42.

30 *À travers chants*, p. 94.

31 See his comparison of Gluck's, Spontini's, and Rossini's use of the bass drum in the essay on "The Current State of the Art of Singing" in *À travers chants*; and *CM* I, p. 140.

32 *Journal de Delacroix, 1822–1863*, ed. André Joubin (Geneva, n.d.), entry for 4 March 1824. See also the entry for 26 January 1824: "painting, as well as music, are *beyond* thought – this, their indefiniteness, constituting their advantage over literature."

33 In *Racine et Shakespeare*, I (Paris, 1823), chapter 3. See Alan B. Spitzer, *The French Generation of 1820* (Princeton, 1987); and André Jardin and André-Jean Tudesq, *Restoration and Romanticism, 1815–1848*, transl. Elborg Forster (Cambridge, 1983).

34 See the article of 5 August 1821 reprinted in the *Vie de Rossini*.

35 As Nina Maria Athanassoglou-Kallmyer suggests in her chapter "Rossinisme as Modernism," in *Eugène Delacroix: Prints, Politics and Satire, 1814–1822* (New Haven, 1991), p. 139.

36 See *CM* I, p. 67; *CG* I, p. 244, and the *Mémoires*, chapter 13.

37 Cited in Jean Mongrédien, *La Musique en France des Lumières au Romantisme (1789–1830)* (Paris, 1986), p. 71.

38 See his account in chapter 5 of the *Mémoires*. Later, Berlioz himself would not hesitate to "modernize" the operas of Gluck. (See, for example, the essay in this volume by Joël-Marie Fauquet. – *Ed.*)

39 *CM* I, p. 113.

40 *Mémoires*, chapter 15.

41 Méhul's *Dansomanie* parodied the various styles, which tended toward the acrobatic.

42 Lincoln Kirstein, *Four Centuries of Ballet: Fifty Masterworks* (New York, 1984), p. 131; and Marian Hannah Winter, *The Pre-Romantic Ballet* (London, 1974).

43 *Mémoires*, chapters 1 and 5.

44 *Mémoires*, chapter 15.

45 According to Athanassoglou-Kallmyer, *Eugène Delacroix*, pp. 78–82, to whose readings of Delacroix's lithographs my own are partially indebted.

46 Joël-Marie Fauquet, *Les Sociétés de musique de chambre à Paris de la Restauration à 1870* (Paris, 1986), p. 42.

47 See *À travers chants*, p. 311.

48 Athanassoglou-Kallmyer, *Eugène Delacroix*, p. 85. See also her chapter 3, "*Voltigeurs* and Weathervanes, Crayfish and Candle-extinguishers."

49 *Guerre aux rossinistes par un amateur du Morvan* (Paris, 1821), p. 3.

50 Berton's articles were reprinted as a pamphlet in 1826 along with a verse "Épître à un célèbre compositeur" lauding Boieldieu, whose works had sustained the Opéra Comique during the first quarter of the nineteenth century. *La Dame blanche* was turning out to be one of the most popular French operas ever written.

51 See Anselm Gerhard, *The Urbanization of Opera*, transl. Mary Whittall (Chicago, 1998), p. 58.

52 We see the continued force of these allegorical images in the aftermath of Berlioz's review of *Robert Bruce*, a pastiche of Rossini's music given with his consent on 30 December 1846. This so outraged Rossini's wife, Olympe Pélissier, that she sent Berlioz and his editor, Armand Bertin, a pair of realistic ass's ears packaged in hay.

53 See Athanassoglou-Kallmyer, *Eugène Delacroix*, pp. 89 and 140n. (The author misidentifies Isabella as Rosina.)

54 Berlioz quotes the remark at the end of chapter 14 of the *Mémoires*.

55 See F. W. J. Hemmings, *Culture and Society in France, 1789–1848* (Leicester, 1987), pp. 181, 177. (Baudelaire's comment is from his *Salon de 1846*.)

56 It might nonetheless be noted that proximate models for Juliet's funeral procession and for the *Joie délirante* of the sixth movement may be found in Bellini's operatic version of the story, *I Capuleti et i Montecchi*, which Berlioz saw in Florence and protested too much in his review for the *Revue européenne* of 15 March 1832 (*CM* I, pp. 69–72).

Genre in Berlioz

1 The autograph of *La Damnation de Faust* originally bore the more precise term "opéra de concert." See *NBE* 8b, p. 457.

2 See *ibid.*, p. 458; and Frederic V. Grunfeld, "Berlioz: 'Not two flutes, you scoundrels,'" *Horizon*, 12 (1970), p. 106 – a facsimile of a contemporary biographical dictionary in which Berlioz entered many corrections, among them the crossing out of the second word of the *Damnation*'s designation as a "légende symphonique."

3 In a manuscript of 1845 Berlioz lists "Symphonies: Fantastique / Mélologue / Harold / Funèbre / Roméo et Juliette." See Holoman, *Catalogue*, p. 509. The work was later re-titled *Lélio*, and re-subtitled *monodrame lyrique*.

4 See Julian Rushton, "*Les Nuits d'été*: Cycle or Collection," in *Berlioz Studies*, ed. Peter Bloom (Cambridge, 1992), pp. 112–135; and "Berlioz and Irlande: From Romance to Mélodie," in *Irish Musical Studies*, ed. Patrick Devine and Harry White, vol. 5 (Dublin, 1996), pp. 224–240.

5 The idea reminded Hugh Macdonald of opéra comique. See Macdonald, *Berlioz* (London, 1982), p. 81.

6 Jim Samson, "Genre," *The Revised New Grove Dictionary of Music and Musicians*, ed. Stanley Sadie (forthcoming). I am indebted to the author for an advance view of this valuable text.

7 Self-borrowing may simply have been less well concealed in Berlioz's early career – see Hugh Macdonald, "Berlioz's Self-borrowings," *Proceedings of the Royal Musical Association*, 92 (1965–1966), p. 27 – but the recent discovery of the *Messe solennelle* did not produce any additions to the slight quantity of self-borrowings detectable in music written after 1850: see Macdonald, "Berlioz's *Messe*

solennelle," Nineteenth-Century Music, 16 (1993), p. 267.

8 The music of the love duet in *Benvenuto Cellini*, which found its way into *Le Carnaval romain,* originated in the 1829 cantata *Cléopâtre.*

9 The aria is published for the first time in *NBE* 1a, pp. 168–186.

10 The poem by Florian begins: "Je vais donc quitter pour jamais / Mon doux pays, ma douce amie." For a convincing fitting of these words to the melody, see *NBE* 16, p. 194.

11 In the first version of the symphony, the *Dies irae* was played by the ophicleide and serpent, the latter an instrument much used in church services. It is possible that enough of the sacred association of trombones remained for the first parody (from bar 147) to have been more of a generic shock in Berlioz's time than it is in ours.

12 See Frits Noske, *French Song from Berlioz to Duparc*, transl. Rita Benton (New York, 1970), pp. 92–115.

13 See Wotton, *Berlioz* (London, 1935), pp. 82, 130.

14 See *NBE* 2c, p. 784.

15 In chapter 7 of the *Mémoires* Berlioz describes the *Messe solennelle* as "une imitation maladroite du style de Lesueur"; elsewhere, he calls it "platement imitée des messes de Lesueur" (see Grunfeld, "Berlioz," p. 106).

16 At bar 56 of the *Rex tremendae*, the words "voca me" should be followed by "cum benedictis"; instead, text from the Offertory (grammatically incomplete) occupies bars 57–75. The normal text resumes at bar 76.

17 On the "grand perspective" of the *Requiem*, see Edward T. Cone, "Berlioz's *Divine Comedy*," in *Music: A View from Delft* (Chicago, 1989), pp. 139–157.

18 The music is taken, with little alteration, from *Cléopâtre*, but the score bears a line from Shakespeare's *Romeo and Juliet* – a characteristic intertextual inspiration.

19 See Jeffrey Langford, "The Byronic Berlioz: *Harold en Italie* and Beyond," *Journal of Musicological Research*, 16 (1997), pp. 199–221; and Mark Evan Bonds, "*Sinfonia anti-eroica:* Berlioz's *Harold en Italie* and the Anxiety of Beethoven's Influence," *Journal of Musicology*, 10 (1992), pp. 417–463.

20 On *Roméo et Juliette* as covert opera, see Julian Rushton, *Berlioz: Roméo et Juliette* (Cambridge, 1994), pp. 80–86.

21 For the various versions of the forging scene, see *NBE* 1c; and, for the use of tags for Cellini, Balducci, and Fieramosca, *NBE* 1a, 1b, and 1c.

22 See Richard Pohl, *Hektor Berlioz: Studien und Erinnerungen* (Leipzig, 1884), p. 58.

23 On the relationship of Berlioz's work to "grand opera," see the articles by Ian Kemp and David Charton in *Hector Berlioz: Les Troyens*, ed. Kemp (Cambridge, 1988).

The symphonies

1 This is how Berlioz referred to his third symphony, *Roméo et Juliette*, but the expression is usefully applied to all but the last.

2 Berlioz's "De l'imitation musicale" appeared in the *Revue et Gazette musicale* on 1 and 8 January 1837. Jacques Barzun's translation of the essay is reprinted (with editorial additions) in Berlioz, *Fantastic Symphony*, ed. Edward T. Cone (New York, 1971), pp. 36–46.

3 For comment on *Lélio*, see the chapter here by Julian Rushton. – *Ed.*

4 On the relationship between the symphony and the poem, see Jeffrey Langford, "The Byronic Berlioz: *Harold en Italie* and Beyond," *Journal of Musicological Research*, 16 (1997), pp. 199–221.

5 The review appeared in the *Revue européenne* of 15 March 1832; it is reprinted in *CM* I (see esp. pp. 69–73).

6 For a detailed "programmatic" reading of the symphony, see Ian Kemp, "Romeo and Juliet and *Roméo et Juliette*," in *Berlioz Studies*, ed. Peter Bloom (Cambridge, 1992), pp. 37–79.

7 *Avant-propos de l'auteur, NBE* 18, p. 2 (my translation).

The concert overtures

1 The second part of Beethoven's *Wellington's Victory* also opens with an *Intrada*. Did Berlioz know this oddly popular work?

2 Jacques Barzun, *Berlioz and the Romantic Century* (New York, 1969), vol. 2, pp. 49–50.

3 Berlioz explicitly mentions reading the poem in the article he wrote published in *L'Europe littéraire* on 8 May 1833. See *CM* I, p. 91 and note.

4 *De l'Opéra en France* (Paris, 1920), vol. 2, p. 12.

5 *Revue musicale*, 6 (November 1829), p. 349.

6 See David Levy, " 'Ritter Berlioz' in Germany," in *Berlioz Studies*, ed. Peter Bloom (Cambridge, 1992), pp. 136–147.

7 *CM* I, pp. 66, 250, 271, 367.

8 See Basil Deane, "The French Operatic Overture from Grétry to Berlioz," *Proceedings of the Royal Musical Association*, 99 (1972–1973), pp. 67–80.

9 Macdonald, *Berlioz* (London, 1982), p. 81.

10 See *NBE* 7, p. xi.

11 Cairns, *Berlioz, 1803–1832: The Making of an Artist* (London, 1989), p. 382.

12 *Revue musicale*, 9 (13 November 1830), p. 25.

13 Donald Francis Tovey, *Essays in Musical Analysis*, vol. 4 (London, 1937), p. 83.

14 Cairns, *Berlioz*, p. 425.

15 The English horn playing, by Sidney Green, is particularly admirable on the CD recording by Yoav Talmi and the San Diego Symphony Orchestra (Naxos 8.550999). – *Ed.*

16 *NBE* 1b, pp. 579–580.

17 *NBE* 23, p. 50.

18 *NBE* 1a, pp. 218–220.

19 *The Musical World* (London), 27 June 1848. On this occasion the piece in question was *Le Carnaval romain*.

The operas and the dramatic legend

1 Claude Debussy, *Monsieur Croche et autres écrits*, ed. François Lesure (Paris, 1971), pp. 169–170.

2 Charles Merruau in *Le Temps* (17 September 1838); see *Hector Berlioz, Benvenuto Cellini: Dossier de presse parisienne (1838)*, ed. Peter Bloom (Heilbronn, 1995), p. 148.

3 F. Sauvo in *Le Moniteur universel* (12 September 1838); see *Cellini: Dossier de presse*, p. 107.

4 Nestor Roqueplan in *Le Constitutionnel* (9 November 1863); see *Hector Berlioz, Les Troyens à Carthage: Dossier de presse parisienne (1863)*, ed. Frank Heidlberger (Heilbronn, 1995), p. 14. Roqueplan, for a time one of the directors of the Paris Opéra, was never a friend to Berlioz.

5 J.-G. Chaudes-Aigues in *L'Artiste* (16 September 1838); see *Cellini: Dossier de presse*, p. 10. On Chaudes-Aigues (1814–1847), a writer and critic of talent and a quintessentially *Jeune France* character, see P. Larousse, *Grand Dictionnaire universel du XIXe siècle*, 17 vols. (Paris, 1866–1879; repr. Geneva, 1982), III, 2, p. 1094.

6 See *NBE* 1, 2, 3, and 8. Among recordings, those conducted by Sir Colin Davis, who has undertaken a complete-works series of discs for Berlioz, are outstanding.

7 Although some sources give the date set down here, there is in fact some question as to the date of Berlioz's first encounter with *Iphigénie en Tauride*. This is mentioned in Janet Johnson's contribution to this Companion. – *Ed.*

8 Five movements of the work survive; of these only the overture has had an independent existence in performance. See D. Kern Holoman, "Les Fragments de l'opéra 'perdu' de Berlioz: *Les Francs-Juges*," *Revue de musicologie*, 63 (1977), pp. 77–88; and David Cairns, *Berlioz, 1803–1832: The Making of an Artist* (London, 1989), pp. 214–219.

9 On this subject see Leo Schrade, *Beethoven in France: The Growth of an Idea* (New Haven, 1942), part I.

10 François Piatier, *Hector Berlioz: Benvenuto Cellini ou le mythe de l'artiste* (Paris, 1979), p. 21.

11 Auguste Morel, writing in the *Journal de Paris* (11 September 1838), notes that Cellini is "un des héros de prédilection de Berlioz." See *Cellini: Dossier de presse*, p. 71.

12 As several contemporary reviewers noted, this scene is not taken from Cellini's autobiography but is based (as is the opera's opening scene) on E. T. A. Hoffmann's tale "Signor Formica [Salvator Rosa]," in part four of *Die Serapions-Brüder* (1819–1821). Hoffmann's works appeared in French translation in 1830 (one of the translators was Berlioz's friend P.-A. Richard) and were widely read and imitated in the next few years.

13 The recording is based on the version performed at Covent Garden, London, in 1966.

14 Joseph d'Ortigue, *Journal des débats* (10 December 1863); see *Les Troyens à Carthage: Dossier de presse*, p. 80.

15 This air was newly composed in 1838 and substituted for one written earlier; the change was made at the request of the soprano, Mme Dorus-Gras.

16 See D. Kern Holoman, *Berlioz* (Cambridge, Mass., 1989), p. 160. The song, to appear in *NBE* 15, is printed in the *Old Berlioz Edition*, the *Werke*, ed. Charles Malherbe and Felix Weingartner, 20 vols. (Leipzig: Breitkopf & Härtel, 1900–1907), vol. 17, p. 123.

17 Franz Liszt, "Le Persée de Benvenuto Cellini," *Revue et Gazette musicale de Paris* (13 January 1839); reprinted in Piatier, *Hector Berlioz: Benvenuto Cellini*, pp. 5–11. Berlioz had himself seen the statue when he passed through Florence in 1831.

18 The 1893 staging was done by Raoul Gunsbourg, who adduced a (fictitious) note by Berlioz saying that the work *should* be a staged opera. See Julien Tiersot, *Hector Berlioz. Le Musicien errant, 1842–1853* (Paris, 1927), p. 164. Sir Thomas Beecham's staged performance was given a regretfully negative review by W. McNaught, "*La Damnation de Faust* as an Opera," *The Musical Times*, 74 (1933), pp. 645–646.

19 For Berlioz's letters to Scribe, from August through December 1847, see *CG* III, pp. 445–485. The work was to be called *Méphistophélès*, partly because of the existence of a *Faust* by Spohr but also in recognition, I think, of the real central character of the drama. Gounod was of course to revert to *Faust* as the title in 1859.

20 See *NBE* 8, p. 458. The failure of the 1846 performance was partly redeemed for Berlioz by a highly successful one under his direction in Vienna in 1866.

21 For Berlioz's rueful comment on this, see his "Est-ce une ironie?" in *Les Grotesques de la musique*, pp. 49–50.

22 See Holoman, *Berlioz*, pp. 372–379.

23 Among the most enthusiastic reviews were those of Marie Escudier in *La France musicale* (8 November 1863), who called Berlioz the heir of Gluck and Beethoven, and "equal to the most illustrious composers for the operatic stage"; and Auguste de Gasparini in *Le Ménestrel* (8 and 15 November 1863), who wrote "Whatever may be the fate reserved to it in our own day, *Les Troyens* is an imposing work, one of the glories of our century; it will not perish." See *Les Troyens à Carthage: Dossier de presse*, pp. 53, 59, 98.

24 Ian Kemp, "Antique and Obsolete Instruments," in *Hector Berlioz: Les Troyens*, ed. Kemp (Cambridge, 1988), pp. 204–212.

25 The melody of this dance resembles that of a song Berlioz wrote and published before he reached the age of sixteen, *Le Dépit de la bergère* (to appear in *NBE* 15; published in Berlioz, *Werke*, vol. 18, pp. 2–5). If the reference was deliberate, Berlioz shows us at once the unity of his musical thought and its magnificent development over a period of forty years.

The religious works

1 Descriptions of concerts in France are cited in Ralph P. Locke, "Paris: Centre of Intellectual Ferment," in *Man and Music: The Early Romantic Era*, ed. Alexander Ringer (London, 1990), pp. 60–61. Prostitutes often found clients in theatres and concert halls, as reported by Karen Ahlquist, *Democracy at the Opera: Music, Theater, and Culture in New York City, 1815–60* (Urbana, 1997), pp. 3–11.

2 See Locke, "Paris," pp. 32–40. A *Hymne à l'agriculture* (1796) by Xavier Lefèvre is recorded on a Nimbus CD, NI-5175.

3 The royalist use of the victory *Te Deum* is memorably portrayed in the finale of Act I of Puccini's *Tosca* (1900). The enemy whose downfall is celebrated is, of course, none other than Napoléon.

4 On that sacred repertory, notably at the Tuileries Chapel, see Jean Mongrédien, *French Music from the Enlightenment to Romanticism 1789–1830*, transl. Sylvain Frémaux (Portland, Oreg., 1996), pp. 159–204, esp. p. 168.

5 See Jean Mongrédien, "La Musique du sacre de Napoléon Ier," *Revue de musicologie*, 53 (1967), pp. 137–174. The music that was sung on this occasion is recorded on a Koch CD, 3–1208–2.

6 See Howard Smither, *A History of the Oratorio*, vol. 3 (Chapel Hill, 1987), pp. 577–601.

7 Jean Mongrédien, *Jean-François Le Sueur: Contribution à l'étude d'un demi-siècle de musique française (1780–1830)*, vol. 2 (Bern, 1980), pp. 912–914, 965–966.

8 Hugh Macdonald, "Berlioz's *Messe solennelle*," *Nineteenth-Century Music*, 16 (1993), pp. 267–285, here p. 268. The work is recorded on Philips CD 442–137–2. Julian Rushton nots significant resemblances to Lesueur's *Oratorio de Noël* in "Ecstasy of Emulation: Berlioz's Debt to Lesueur," *Musical Times* (Autumn 1999), pp, 11–18.

9 Cited in Jacques Barzun, *Berlioz and the Romantic Century* (New York, 1969), vol. 1, p. 277.

10 Edward T. Cone, "Berlioz's Divine Comedy," in *Music: A View from Delft*, ed. Robert P. Morgan (Chicago, 1989), p. 144.

11 On Berlioz's use of such "intermittent" elements, see Julian Rushton, *The Musical Language of Berlioz* (Cambridge, 1983), pp. 128, 138; and Charles Rosen, *The Romantic Generation* (Cambridge, Mass., 1996), p. 545.

12 On the work's relationship to French traditions, see Frank Reinisch, *Das französische Oratorium von 1840 bis 1870* (Regensburg, 1982), pp. 275–292.

13 Alec Robertson, *Sacred Music* (London, 1950), p. 68.

14 Cited in *Anton Bruckner: Ein Handbuch*, ed. Uwe Harten (Salzburg, 1996), p. 458. By contrast, he considered Berlioz's *Requiem* one of the highpoints of modern art and particularly admired its instrumentation and counterpoint.

For their helpful comments and advice, I should like to thank Antonius Bittmann, Donna Di Grazia, D. Kern Holoman, Hugh Macdonald, Alfred Mann, James Parakilas, and Jean Pedersen.

The songs

1 Among those who particularly underline Berlioz's importance to the development of French song are Frits Noske, *French Song from Berlioz to Duparc*, transl. Rita Benton (New York, 1970); Laurenz Lütteken, " '. . . erfordert eine ziemlich große Sensibilität bei der Ausführung': Anmerkungen zum Liederzyklus *Les Nuit's d'Eté* von Hector Berlioz," *Musicologica Austriaca*, 8 (1988), pp. 41–64; Peter Bloom, "In the Shadows of *Les Nuits d'été*," in *Berlioz Studies*, ed. Bloom (Cambridge, 1992), pp. 81–111; Julian Rushton, "*Les Nuits d'été*: Cycle or Collection?" in *Berlioz Studies*, pp. 112–135.

2 For a consideration of the *romance* as part of the regular musical diet of the era, see, for example, Austin Caswell, "Loïsa Puget and the French *Romance*," in *Music in Paris in the*

Eighteen-Thirties, ed. Peter Bloom (Stuyvesant, N.Y., 1987), pp. 97–115.

3 See David Charlton, "A Berlioz Footnote," *Music & Letters*, 52 (1971), pp. 157–158. Charles Rosen deconstructs Berlioz's and his idolaters' claims for romantic "immediacy" in *The Romantic Generation* (Cambridge, Mass., 1995), pp. 542–568.

4 See, for example, Rainer Gstrein, *Die vokale Romanze in der Zeit von 1750–1850* (Innsbruck, 1989); Andreas Ballstaedt and Tobias Widmaier, *Salonmusik: Zur Geschichte und Funktion einer bürgerlichen Musikpraxis* (Stuttgart and Wiesbaden, 1989); Annegret Fauser, *Der Orchestergesang in Frankreich zwischen 1870 und 1920* (Laaber, 1994); and David Charlton, "The *Romance* and its Cognates: Narrative, Irony and *Vraisemblance* in Early Opéra Comique," in *Die Opéra Comique und ihr Einfluß auf das europäische Musiktheater im 19. Jahrhundert*, ed. Herbert Schneider and Nicole Wild (Hildesheim, 1997), pp. 43–92.

5 Charlton, "The *Romance* and its Cognates," p. 43.

6 Fauser, *Der Orchestergesang*, pp. 7–20, esp. p. 14.

7 Laura Mason, *Singing in the French Revolution: Popular Culture and Politics, 1787–1799* (Ithaca and London, 1996).

8 Wagner, "Pariser Amüsements," *Europa* (April 1841), cited by Ballstaedt and Widmaier, *Salonmusik*, pp. 33–34.

9 Sophie Gay, *Salons célèbres* (Brussels, 1837), p. 192.

10 See *NBE* 13, p. xiii.

11 Noske, *French Song*, pp. 93–96.

12 Adolphe Boschot, *La Jeunesse d'un romantique* (Paris, 1906), p. 364.

13 *Mémoires*, p. 238 (translation modified by the editor).

14 See Macdonald, *Berlioz* (London, 1982), p. 87; Holoman, *Berlioz* (Cambridge, Mass., 1989), p. 97. Julian Rushton has studied these songs in "Berlioz and Irelande: From Romance to Mélodie," in *Irish Musical Studies*, ed. Patrick Devine and Harry White, vol. 5 (Dublin, 1996), pp. 224–240.

15 The highly problematical groupings in the *Old Berlioz Edition* and the *New Berlioz Edition* are due to the changing forces required for each successive number and to the existence of more than one version of the second, fourth, sixth, and eighth songs. For this paper I have used the copy of the first edition of the score preserved in the British Library (Hirsch IV. 699).

16 The engraver of *Huit Scènes de Faust* is identified as E. Alhoy; the engraver of the *Neuf Mélodies* as E. A. – probably the same person.

17 The seriousness of some salon music, among other things, is evidence that the common image of a bunch of lovesick teenagers sitting around moaning about *baisers*, evoked earlier, is in need of repair, for a good deal of intellectual life took place in the salons. On the concept of "private mythology," see Carl Dahlhaus, *Die Musik des 19. Jahrhunderts* (Laaber, 1980), p. 138.

18 See, for example, David Cairns, *Berlioz, 1803–1832: The Making of an Artist* (London, 1989), pp. 318–320. An affinity to Moore's artistic concepts is suggested in Berlioz's letters of 10 January 1828 and 2 March 1829.

19 See *CG* I, pp. 534–535. On hearing *La Captive*, in Rome, "the ladies," Berlioz reports to his sister, "simply fell all over me to ask for more."

20 Cited by Berthold Hoeckner, "Schumann and Romantic Distance," *Journal of the American Musicological Society*, 50 (1997), p. 55.

21 Translation from Cairns, *Berlioz*, p. 321.

22 See *CG* I, p. 312.

23 *Gazette musicale de Paris*, 1 (1834), pp. 169–171. (David Charlton very kindly provided me with a copy of this review.)

24 On the genesis and structure of *Les Nuits d'été*, see the articles by Peter Bloom and Julian Rushton in *Berlioz Studies* (see note 1).

25 *CM* II, p. 68.

26 See, for example, Lütteken, "Anmerkungen," p. 46.

27 Méry, *Les Nuits de Londres* (Brussels, 1840), vol. 1, p. 1. I am grateful to Joël-Marie Fauquet for bringing this reference to my attention.

28 Rushton, "*Les Nuits d'été*," p. 119. Bars here refer to the orchestral score of 1856 as published in *NBE* 13. A critical edition of the original version, for voice and piano, was published by Les Éditions musicales du Marais (Paris, 1992), ed. Peter Bloom.

29 Cited in *NBE* 13, p. xx.

30 Holoman, *Berlioz*, p. 515.

31 I borrow the term "aesthetic autobiography" from Suzanne Nalbantian, *Aesthetic Autobiography: From Life to Art in Marcel Proust, James Joyce, Virginia Woolf and Anaïs Nin* (London, 1994); see esp. p. ix.

32 Macdonald, *Berlioz*, p. 38. Even Lütteken, who goes further than most writers, remains cautious on this point.

33 Nalbantian, *Aesthetic Autobiography*, p. 39.

For assistance in the preparation of this article I am deeply grateful to Peter Bloom, Tim Carter, David Charlton, and Katharine Ellis.

The short stories

1 Besides the three main stories or *nouvelles* – *Le Premier Opéra*, *Le Suicide par enthousiasme*, and *Euphonia, ou la ville musicale* – the volume contains five others designated as *nouvelles*, two of which I shall also discuss here. The rest are

mere anecdotes, though all eight bear distinctive tags (such as "a grammatical tale," "a necrological tale," "an improbable tale," "a downstage tale," etc.). In this paper I use the translation of *Les Soirées* as *Evenings with the Orchestra* by Jacques Barzun (reissued by the University of Chicago Press in 1999), who adds his own tag, "a fantastic tale," to the Eighteenth Evening's story of *Le Piano enragé*.

The generic term "short story" does not exist in French; usage alternates between *nouvelle* and *conte*, often interchangeable: E. T. A. Hoffmann's *Novellen*, for example, appeared in French as *Contes fantastiques*. "Story" translates as *histoire*. Strictly speaking, *conte* (tale) evokes the older, oral, and – especially in French – fairy-tale tradition of storytelling. Thus the narrator of the Twelfth Evening's *Suicide par enthousiasme* insists that this is not a *conte* (a "tall tale") but *une histoire vraie* (a "true story"). The *nouvelle*, or "novella," is, in contrast, usually written: Berlioz's musicians *read* most of their stories. Barzun designates all as "tales," a choice that matches the idiom of the descriptive tags and suits the storytelling atmosphere.

2 The "necrological tale" of the Fourth Evening, *Un Début dans le Freischütz*, is a revenge story in a humorous vein. In the *Fantastique* it is "betrayal," and not merely unrequited love, that provokes the artist-hero to imagine murdering his beloved. He is betrayed because he has specifically imagined (in the program of the third movement) that she has been unfaithful to him.

3 On the role of fiction in the journal, see Katharine Ellis, *Music Criticism in Nineteenth-Century France: La Revue et Gazette musicale de Paris, 1834–1880* (Cambridge, 1995), pp. 48–52 and, for a listing of the stories published, pp. 262–265.

4 Berlioz used similar language after his fiancée's (and her mother's) breach of promise in 1831. "There is no justice in heaven when such crimes stay unpunished," he wrote (see *CG* I, p. 432; see also pp. 436, 444). The heroines of Berlioz's two other major stories (*Le Suicide* and *Euphonia*) are clearly modeled on this fiancée, Marie Moke (known as Camille), who left Berlioz in 1831 to marry the wealthy piano manufacturer Camille Pleyel, and who, as Mme Pleyel, became a celebrated pianist.

5 Berlioz was personally acquainted with Mme Branchu, whom he heard towards the end of her career, though never in *La Vestale*. (See Joël-Marie Fauquet's essay on "Berlioz and Gluck" elsewhere in this volume. – *Ed.*)

6 Poor and emaciated at the end, Adolphe is related to the starving artists of Vigny's *Chatterton* (1835) and Wagner's "An End in Paris" (1841). In theory, such artist-victims of an uncomprehending society are unrelated to the artists-*manqués* that haunted Balzac (Wenceslas Steinbock in *La Cousine Bette*) or Flaubert (Frédéric Moreau in *L'Éducation sentimentale*). In practice the types are not easily separable.

7 Berlioz scholarship has tended to gloss over the love story. Replacing the utopia within the larger narrative discloses problems of gender and power implicit in the Euphonian model, which (comic exaggeration aside) is entirely in keeping with the values implicit in Western classical music.

8 The freedom from emotion necessary to create emotion is the paradox analyzed by Diderot in *Le Paradoxe sur le comédien*. On the issues involved, see my "Primal Scenes: Smithson, Pleyel, and Liszt in the Eyes of Berlioz," *Nineteenth-Century Music*, 18 (1995), pp. 211–235.

9 Stendhal showed infinitely more sympathy for the Italian performance-based aesthetic than Berlioz, who associated it with castratos and effeminacy as the antithesis of drama. Yet even Stendhal found it difficult to avoid some implicit disparagement of the sensuous Italians – twice conquered by the French since the renaissance – relative to the verbal, rational French. See his *Vie de Rossini*, chapter 2.

10 For Rousseau as for Shakespeare, the entire social fabric, if not the cosmos, hangs on the sexual fidelity of women. The faithless wife, declares Rousseau, "destroys the family and breaks the bonds of nature [. . .] her crime is not infidelity but treason [. . .] it is the source of dissension and crime of every kind." See *Émile*, transl. Barbara Foxley (New York, 1933), p. 372.

11 This Evening also contains a parody of Adolphe's "suicide from enthusiasm." Barnum offers a reward to desperate men willing to commit their intended suicide after a concert by Jenny Lind: they are to declare it impossible to return to ordinary life after such bliss.

12 Margaret Miner deals with such ambiguities in "Phantoms of Genius: Women and the Fantastic in the Opera-House Mystery," *Nineteenth-Century Music*, 18 (1994), pp. 121–135.

13 Another minor story published separately, as such, is *Rubini à Calais*, which appeared first in the *Gazette musicale* (5 October 1834) and then in the *Journal des débats* (10 October 1834). Owing to some of the aforementioned ambiguities, Berlioz was obliged to publish a factual *Historique de la représentation de Rubini à Calais*, in the *Gazette musicale* of 2 November 1834, demonstrating to some who took offense that *Rubini à Calais* was indeed a fiction: "une espèce de conte fantastique."

14 In the first published version of the story (in

L'Europe littéraire, 8 May 1833), Berlioz explicitly says that he "recognized" himself in the character of Vincenza. He speaks movingly of his beloved Dido in chapters 2 and 3 of his *Mémoires.*

15 In the 1844 version of *Euphonia*, Xilef also faints (see *Les Soirées de l'orchestre*, p. 260).

16 On the exclusion of women from creative genius (as opposed to performance), see, for example, *Cecilia Reclaimed: Feminist Perspectives on Gender and Music*, ed. Susan C. Cook and Judy S. Tsou (Urbana and Chicago, 1994), p. 1 and *passim.*

The criticism

1 In Section C of the Catalogue of Prose Works, Holoman, in the *Catalogue*, lists 936 items (counting single installments individually and including articles attributed to Berlioz by Katherine Reeve Kolb and Kerry Murphy). A complete edition of Berlioz's criticism – *CM* I and *CM* II (see the list of abbreviations) – has only recently begun to appear.

2 For further discussion of this point, see my *Music Criticism in Nineteenth-Century France: La Revue et Gazette musicale de Paris, 1834–1880* (Cambridge, 1995), pp. 48–50.

3 For more on this term, see Kerry Murphy, *Hector Berlioz and the Development of French Music Criticism* (Ann Arbor, 1988), pp. 17–18; and Katherine Reeve Kolb, "Hector Berlioz," in *European Writers: the Romantic Century*, ed. W. T. H. Jackson, George Stade, and Jacques Barzun, vol. 6 (New York, 1985), pp. 771–812, esp. p. 786. This extended essay gives the most comprehensive and nuanced account of Berlioz's criticism to date.

4 The expression occurs in Berlioz's review of Beethoven's Ninth Symphony, which first appeared in the *Revue et Gazette musicale* of 4 March 1838 and was later incorporated into *À travers chants.*

5 For further discussion of this technique, see Katherine Reeve Kolb, "Rhetoric and Reason in French Music Criticism of the 1830s," in *Music in Paris in the Eighteen-Thirties*, ed. Peter Bloom (Stuyvesant, N.Y., 1987), pp. 537–551.

6 For sources of this idea, see Edmund Burke, *A Philosophical Inquiry into the Origin of our Ideas of the Sublime and the Beautiful* (London, 1757), which influenced Kant. Relevant extracts from both authors are given in *Music and Aesthetics in the Eighteenth and Early-Nineteenth Centuries*, ed. Peter Le Huray and James Day (Cambridge, 1988), pp. 60–65 (Burke) and 160–167 (Kant). Schlesinger's journal was an important outlet for such ideas, as applied to music, in the Paris of the eighteen-thirties.

7 Berlioz never attempted to hide his elitism, which resulted from a conception of artistic nobility stemming largely from Hoffmann and frequently exploited in Schlesinger's *Revue et Gazette musicale.* See my *Music Criticism*, pp. 50–51.

8 Originally published in the *Revue et Gazette musicale*, and reprinted with slight revisions in *À travers chants.*

9 *À travers chants*, pp. 64–65; translated by Elizabeth Csicsery-Rónay as *The Art of Music* (Bloomington, 1994), pp. 27–28. In letters and articles Berlioz was fond of citing "The rest is silence," Hamlet's last words in Act V scene 2 of the play. The expression "like patience smiling at grief" is surely Berlioz's recollection of Viola's words in Act II scene 4 of *Twelfth Night.*

10 Only in extreme cases, such as those of Bellini's *I Puritani* and Halévy's *La Juive*, did Berlioz ask to be excused from reviewing altogether. On 15 April 1835 Berlioz told his friend Humbert Ferrand that he had not wanted to review those works because he had too much ill to speak of them and feared being accused of expressing only jealousy.

11 This famous passage, from the *Journal des débats* of 10 November 1836, is translated in Murphy, *Hector Berlioz*, p. 127.

12 *Journal des débats*, 8 March 1862.

13 See Murphy, *Hector Berlioz*, pp. 154–155. In fact the term gives little indication of the ferocious ends to which Berlioz was able to use superficially tepid language.

14 Berlioz's important essay on this subject – "De l'Opéra-Comique," *Revue et Gazette musicale*, 18 September 1836 – is discussed in David Charlton, "*Opéra-comique:* Identity and Manipulation," in *Opera and Ballet Criticism from the Revolution to 1848*, ed. Roger Parker and Mary Ann Smart (forthcoming).

15 Such recognition threads its way like a leitmotif through the *Mémoires.* See, in particular, chapters 23, 47, 53, and the *Post-scriptum.*

16 *Journal des débats*, 23 July 1861; reprinted in *À travers chants.*

17 *Journal des débats*, 8 October 1863.

The Grand Traité d'instrumentation

1 See Hector Berlioz, *Rapport sur les instruments de musique, fait à la Commission française du Jury international de l'exposition universelle de Londres* (Paris: Imprimerie Impériale, 1854). This report is reproduced in Frédéric de La Grandville, *Recueil complémentaire des exemples d'orchestration cités dans le texte du Grand Traité d'instrumentation d'Hector Berlioz* (Reims:

Faculté des Lettres et Sciences humaines, 1978), pp. 251–254.

2 In the *Gazette musicale de Paris* of 12 July 1835 (reproduced in *CM* II, pp. 209–216).

3 In English we would have to say not "instrumentalist" – that is the French word *instrumentiste* – but "instrumenter," one who "instruments" (i.e., one who "orchestrates"). So the neologism is best left in French. – *Ed.*

Performing Berlioz

1 See the *Grand Traité d'instrumentation et d'orchestration modernes* (Paris, 1843). A conducting treatise, *Le Chef d'orchestre*, was added for the second edition, 1855. See Holoman, *Catalogue*, pp. 431–432. I have treated some of these same issues in "The Present State of Berlioz Research," *Acta musicologica*, 67 (1975), pp. 31–67; and in *Berlioz* (Cambridge, Mass., 1989), notably pp. 348–361. For clarifying various points in 1999 I am grateful to David Cairns, Hugh Macdonald, Michael Steinberg, and the editorial staff of Bärenreiter Verlag, Kassel.

2 To summarize: the *Ballet des sylphes* from *La Damnation de Faust* (from 1849), the duo-nocturne from *Béatrice et Bénédict* (from 1863), *La Fuite en Égypte* (Part II of *L'Enfance du Christ*, from 1864), *Le Carnaval romain* (from 1873), the *Francs-Juges* Overture (from 1874), *La Mort d'Ophélie* (from 1875), excerpts from *Roméo et Juliette* (from 1877) and the complete work (1879), *Le Corsaire* (from 1880), *Benvenuto Cellini* Overture (from 1895), *Le Roi Lear* (from 1899), the *Marche funèbre pour la dernière scène d'Hamlet* (from 1899), *Sara la baigneuse* (from 1903), the Pilgrims' March from *Harold en Italie* (from 1874) and the complete work – a vehicle for the celebrated violist Maurice Vieux (from 1907), and the *Symphonie fantastique* (from 1917).

3 To summarize: Karslruhe (1890, Mottl), Munich (1895, Levi; 1907, 1908, Mottl), Cologne (1898, Klessel), Leipzig (1900, Gorter). A list of performances of *Les Troyens* through 1987, compiled by Louise Goldberg, appears in the Cambridge Opera Handbook *Hector Berlioz: Les Troyens*, ed. Ian Kemp (Cambridge, 1988), pp. 216–227.

4 Nicholas Temperley treats the matter of timpani sticks, citing relevant passages from the *Traité d'instrumentation*, in Appendix VIII of *NBE* 16, p. 221.

5 For instance, new lines by Remo Percussion.

6 See Ian Kemp, "Antique and Obsolete Instruments," in *Hector Berlioz: Les Troyens* (see note 3), pp. 204–212.

7 In a 1979 performance with the Orchestre de Paris at the Kennedy Center, Washington, D.C.,

Daniel Barenboim pulled a revolver from his belt and fired it. This silliness provoked laughter from the audience at large and particular guffaws from those who made a connection with the conductor Artur Rodzinksi, said to have packed a pistol at orchestra rehearsals.

8 Jacques Barzun, *Berlioz and the Romantic Century* (New York, 1969), vol. 2, pp. 358–381.

9 I am particularly grateful to the *NBE* for the loan of a set of parts for *Roméo et Juliette*, from which Fig.13.3 was photographed.

10 My figures for the *Fantastique*, at 1999 exchange rates, are as follows, for a complete set including six of each string part: *NBE*: $462, Kalmus: $607.50. Details: *NBE*: score, 110 DM; wind parts 230 DM, strings parts (36 x 12 DM = 432) DM; total 772 DM = $412, plus $50 labor (the adding of rehearsal letters); this does not include a copy of the clothbound vol. 13. Kalmus: score, $70; set of parts, $250; extra strings, $187.50, labor, $100 (adding of bar numbers and rehearsal letters); this does not include shipping and handling.

11 *French Romantic Song, 1830–1870*, ed. David Tunley (New York: Garland, 1994), pp. 49–60; *Les Nuits d'été*, ed. Peter Bloom (Paris: Les Éditions Musicales du Marais, 1992); *Chant du neuf Thermidor* and *La Marseillaise*, ed. D. Kern Holoman, *Marche pour la présentation des drapeaux*, ed. Dennis McCauldin (Davis: University of California, 1989).

12 Gardiner has issued two different important recordings of the Berlioz *Mélodies* (Oiseau-Lyre, 1968; Musifrance, 1990), *L'Enfance du Christ* (Erato / RCA, 1988), *La Damnation de Faust* (Philips, 1989), and Gluck's *Orphée et Eurydice* in Berlioz's arrangement (EMI, 1989); Norrington has issued *Songs for Chorus* (Argo, 1969).

13 This footnote appears in only the first edition of the score (1845).

14 Christian Wasselin notes, "I don't think that Charles Munch was a great Berliozian conductor . . . [He] was very different from one evening to another. When you hear the different recordings of the *Symphonie fantastique* by Charles Munch, you have three or four different conceptions with different timings and different tempos." See the question-and-answer sessions following Wasselin's paper on "The Culture of Paris at the Time of Berlioz," *Berlioz Society Bulletin*, 155 (1996), p. 26.

15 The other is a 1939 recording with Bruno Walter, widely available in CD reprint (VAI, Grammofono, Iron Needle, Enterprise).

16 The roundtable is transcribed (with some inaccuracies) in "Performing Berlioz's Music," *Berlioz Society Bulletin*, 155 (1996), pp. 27–50.

17 See *NBE* 18, p. 365 (last paragraph).
18 I have edited these conversational remarks for clarity but not altered their substance.
19 See Berlioz's "Observations" for *Roméo et Juliette*, *NBE* 18, p. 383; a similar layout is described in the final chapter, "L'Orchestre," of the *Traité d'instrumentation*.
20 *L'Illustration*, 15 April 1843; reproduced in *Musée de la Musique: Guide* (Paris, 1997), p. 25.

Berlioz and Gluck

1 In the issues of 9, 16, and 23 November and 7 December 1834. All the articles mentioned here, through 1836, are reproduced in *CM* I and *CM* II.
2 8 June 1834.
3 12, 15, 20, 24 October, 6 and 23 November, and 8 December 1861. The article of 24 October is a review of the première at the Opéra.
4 16 and 23 October 1835.
5 *Le Monde dramatique*, 8 August 1835.
6 *Revue et Gazette musicale*, 28 November 1841. Example 4 in the *Traité d'instrumentation* is an excerpt from "Chi mi parla."
7 The manuscript is in the Moldenhauer Collection of the Library of Congress, in Washington, D.C.
8 Paris, 1839 (in fact the book appeared in December 1838).
9 *Euphonia* was first published in eight installments in the *Revue et Gazette musicale* of 1844; it was later reprinted in *Les Soirées de l'orchestre*.
10 *Les Soirées de l'orchestre*, pp. 358–359. The translation is largely that of Jacques Barzun, *Evenings with the Orchestra* (Chicago, 1999), p. 280. In *Euphonia*, Berlioz appears under the name of Shetland, an exact anagram of the name Stendhal, oddly enough, and chosen, perhaps, in order to take "revenge" against the celebrated author of *Le Rouge et le noir*, who was a passionate *amateur* of Italian singing. (In her contribution to this collection, Katherine Kolb takes the name Shetland to be vaguely suggestive of British reserve and control. – *Ed.*)
11 *Journal des débats*, 17 March 1839, and, again, in the *Revue et Gazette musicale*, 24 March 1839.
12 See Joël-Marie Fauquet, "Berlioz's Version of Gluck's *Orphée*," in *Berlioz Studies*, ed. Peter Bloom (Cambridge, 1992), pp. 189–253.
13 "L'espoir renaît dans mon âme" in the original French version. The aria was reorchestrated by Saint-Saëns.
14 See Fauquet, "Berlioz's Version of Gluck's *Orphée*," pp. 217 et seq.
15 For this reason, Berlioz's version will be included in *NBE* 22a.
16 The letters of Fétis (13 October 1866) and

Berlioz (14 October 1866) are printed in *Le Ménestrel*, 21 October 1866.
17 See note 11.

Berlioz and Mozart

1 *CG* V, pp. 310–311.
2 *The Orchestra* (19 May 1866); cited in T. J. Walsh, *Second Empire Opera* (London, 1981), p. 209.
3 See Katharine Ellis, *Music Criticism in Nineteenth-Century France: La Revue et Gazette musicale de Paris, 1834–1880* (Cambridge, 1995), pp. 19–21.
4 See Herbert Schneider, "Probleme der Mozart-Rezeption im Frankreich der ersten Hälfte des 19. Jahrhunderts," *Mozart-Jahrbuch* (1980–1983), pp. 25–26.
5 *Journal des débats*, 27 March 1849.
6 *CG* V, p. 418n.
7 Berlioz referred to this performance in reviews of *Don Giovanni* at the Opéra in March 1834 and in May 1841.
8 For details of these adaptations, see Rudolph Angermüller, "'Les Mystères d'Isis' (1801) und 'Don Juan' (1805, 1834) auf der Bühne der Pariser Opera," *Mozart-Jahrbuch* (1980–1983), pp. 32–97.
9 *CM* I, p. 129.
10 It appeared in two parts in *Le Rénovateur* on 16 and 23 March 1834 (*CM* I, pp. 191–202). A later notice of *Don Juan*, in the *Journal des débats* of 15 November 1835, is better known, having been reprinted in compilations by André Hallays (*Les Musiciens et la musique* [Paris, 1903]) and Gérard Condé (*Cauchemars et passions* [Paris, 1981]); it borrows many passages from his earlier notices almost verbatim.
11 *CG* II, p. 570.
12 See A. W. Ganz, *Berlioz in London* (London, 1949), pp. 108–109.
13 *CG* VI, p. 403.
14 Although he told Rellstab in 1838 that he thought it was Mozart's masterpiece (*CG* II, p. 433), he is consistent elsewhere in ranking it behind *Don Giovanni*.
15 See Angermüller, "Les Mystères," and *Mémoires*, chapter 16; also Jean Mongrédien, "*Les Mystères d'Isis* (1801) and Reflections on Mozart from the Parisian Press at the Beginning of the Nineteenth Century," in *Music in the Classic Period: Essays in Honor of Barry S. Brook*, ed. Alan Atlas (New York, 1985), pp. 195–211.
16 *Mémoires*, chapter 17.
17 His study of *Les Mystères d'Isis* appeared as an article in the *Journal des débats* on 1 May 1836, some nine years after it had disappeared from the repertory. Some of this article was used in chapter 16 of the *Mémoires*; the full text

was reprinted by Hallays, *Les Musiciens*, pp. 14–21.

18 See *CM* I, p. 190.

19 *Journal des débats*, 12 August 1851. Different extracts were reprinted by Ganz, *Berlioz in London*, pp. 110–112, and Condé, *Cauchemars et passions*, pp. 207–212. In the *Revue et Gazette musicale* of 27 February 1840 Berlioz had earlier stated that the solemn music in *Die Zauberflöte* surpassed anything in *Don Giovanni* or *Figaro*, but that he was not able to regard the opera as superior to those two as a whole.

20 *Le Figaro*, 5 March 1865; cited in Walsh, *Second Empire Opera*, p. 191.

21 *Revue et Gazette musicale*, 10 March 1839.

22 V. V. Stasov, *Selected Essays on Music*, transl. Florence Jonas (London, 1968), p. 163.

23 *Les Soirées de l'orchestre*, p. 447; *Les Grotesques de la musique*, p. 256.

24 The review is in *À travers chants*, pp. 266–269.

25 *À travers chants*, p. 97.

26 *CG* V, p. 310.

27 *Les Soirées*, p. 367; *CM* I, p. 376; and *CG* II, p. 671.

28 *À travers chants*, p. 276.

29 *Revue et Gazette musicale*, 28 March 1841.

30 Ganz, *Berlioz in London*, pp. 126–127.

31 Octave Fouque, *Les Révolutionnaires de la musique* (Paris, 1882), p. 239.

32 *Revue et Gazette musicale*, 28 March 1839.

33 *Revue et Gazette musicale*, 9 April 1840, 28 February 1841, and 13 February 1842.

34 *CG* VI, p. 278.

35 *Journal des débats*, 15 December 1844; cited in Condé, *Cauchemars et passions*, pp. 95–96.

36 *CG* V, p. 570; and *Les Soirées*, p. 401.

37 *À travers chants*, p. 266.

38 *CG* V, p. 448.

39 See Joël-Marie Fauquet, *Les Sociétés de musique de chambre à Paris de la Restauration à 1870* (Paris, 1986).

40 See Julie Anne Vertrees, "Mozart's String Quartet K. 465: The History of a Controversy," *Current Musicology*, 17 (1974), pp. 96–114.

41 See Holoman, *Catalogue*, p. 56.

42 *The New Yorker*, 17 December 1979; see also Wilfrid Mellers, *Man and His Music* (London, 1962), p. 768.

43 Cairns, *Memoirs* (New York, 1975), p. 555.

44 *CG* VI, p. 289.

45 *CG* II, pp. 531, 433.

Berlioz and Beethoven

1 *Revue et Gazette musicale*, 9 March 1879.

2 See Joël-Marie Fauquet, *Les Sociétés de musique de chambre à Paris* (Paris, 1986), p. 117.

3 *Mémoires,* Premier Voyage en Allemagne, 10e lettre.

4 See, for example, *CG* V, pp. 244–245.

5 *CG* I, p. 238.

6 *Man and his Music* (London, 1962), p. 762.

7 Paul Banks makes this point in "Byron, Berlioz and *Harold*," an unpublished paper delivered at a conference of the Royal Musical Association in Birmingham in 1982.

8 "Benefactor" and "friend" are words Berlioz uses in his evocation of Beethoven when reporting the Bonn celebrations. See *Les Soirées de l'orchestre*, p. 425.

9 Cf. the opening bars of Beethoven's *An die ferne Geliebte*.

10 His first feuilleton for the *Journal des débats*, of 25 January 1835, included a long analysis of the *Eroica* (*CM* II, pp. 35–38), and his articles in *Le Rénovateur*, the previous year, frequently discussed and extolled Beethoven. In 1829 Berlioz published a three-part biography of Beethoven in *Le Correspondant* (*CM* I, pp. 47–62).

11 *CM* I, p. 9.

12 *Revue et Gazette musicale*, 18 February 1838.

13 *Revue et Gazette musicale*, 4 February 1838.

14 *Revue et Gazette musicale*, 11 February 1838. The English quotations derive, respectively, from Shakespeare's *Twelfth Night* and from the poetry of Thomas Moore.

15 *Journal des débats*, 12 April 1835 (*CM* II, pp. 113–118).

16 See *À travers chants*, pp. 52–54.

17 *Journal des débats*, 19 and 22 May 1860 (*À travers chants*, pp. 87–103).

18 Ernest Legouvé, *Soixante ans de souvenirs* (Paris, 1883), vol. 1, pp. 306–307.

19 According to the *Life and Letters of Sir Charles Hallé* (London, 1896), p. 68, he played the Fourth Concerto; Holoman, in *Berlioz* (Cambridge, Mass., 1989), p. 618, lists the *Emperor*.

20 13 May 1852.

21 15 May 1852. Berlioz's earlier doubts about the vocal writing in the finale of the Ninth (see Katharine Ellis, *Music Criticism in Nineteenth-Century France* [Cambridge, 1995], p. 111) may have been partly allayed by the excellent singing of the New Philharmonic Chorus in these performances.

22 This letter, unpublished, will appear in *CG* VII.

23 Quoted in Vladimir Vasilevich Stasov, *Selected Essays on Music*, transl. Florence Jonas (London, 1968), p. 166.

Berlioz and Wagner

1 Wagner's letter is included in *CG* VI, p. 111.

2 See Wagner, *My Life*, transl. Andrew Gray, ed. Mary Whittall (Cambridge, 1988), p. 191. Schlesinger's business (at 97) was just up the road from the Brockhaus shop, at 60, rue de Richelieu, where the proprietor was Eduard

Avenarius, Cäcilie Wagner's fiancé in 1839 (and husband in 1840).

3 Wagner, whose name figures on the list of guests invited to the opening (Julien Tiersot, *La Musique aux temps romantiques* [Paris, 1930], p. 174), may have accompanied Meyerbeer to the concert. The two were together on frequent occasion in November, as Meyerbeer's diary reveals. See Giacomo Meyerbeer, *Briefwechsel und Tagebücher*, vol. 3, ed. Hans and Gudrun Becker (Berlin, 1975), p. 209.

4 Wagner's Parisian experience of Beethoven and the controversy surrounding it are rehearsed by Klaus Kropfinger, *Wagner and Beethoven*, transl. Peter Palmer (Cambridge, 1991), pp. 33–35. See also John Deathridge, *Wagner's Rienzi* (Oxford, 1977), pp. 40, 130.

5 Dannreuther, "Wagner," in George Grove, *A Dictionary of Music and Musicians*, 1st ed., vol. 4 (London, 1895), p. 351. The comment shows that Wagner was familiar with the anecdote Berlioz recounts in chapter 12 of the *Mémoires*.

6 *CG* III, p. 98. The ellipses here are original.

7 See Peter Bloom, "La Mission de Berlioz en Allemagne: Un Document inédit," *Revue de musicologie*, 66 (1980), p. 83.

8 Although Wagner himself employed the literal translation, *Le Hollandais volant*, the expression, which sounds silly in French, fell out of use. *Le Vaisseau fantôme* is the work by Pierre-Louis Dietsch, on a libretto by Paul Foucher and Henri Révoil, premiered at the Opéra on 28 October 1842.

9 *Journal des débats*, 12 September 1843 (a copy of this article was kindly provided to me by Joël-Marie Fauquet). My translation borrows much from that of David Cairns.

10 *Selected Letters of Richard Wagner*, transl. and ed. Stewart Spencer and Barry Millington (New York, 1988), p. 107. Spencer mentions the actual salary in "Wagner behind bars?" *Wagner*, 19 (1998), p. 95.

11 The draft of this invitation is on the verso of a draft of the program of the concert of 25 November 1838 (Bibliothèque Nationale de France, Musique, Berlioz, Lettres autographes).

12 Letter to Hans von Bülow, 1 September 1854: "and one might say of the king what Virgil said of Dido: 'Thrice did she rise, supporting herself on her elbows; and thrice did she fall back upon her bed'" (*CG* IV, p. 574).

13 See Manfred Eger, in *The Wagner Handbook*, ed. Ulrich Müller and Peter Wapnewski, transl. John Deathridge (Cambridge, Mass., 1992), p. 318.

14 *NBE* 1b, p. 557.

15 Deathridge, *Rienzi*, pp. 134–135.

16 Quoted in Richard Wagner, *Der fliegende Holländer*, ed. Isolde Vetter; *Sämtliche Werke*, Band 4/I (Mainz, 1983), p. vii.

17 See *Franz Liszt–Richard Wagner Briefwechsel*, ed. Hanjo Kesting (Frankfurt, 1988).

18 Ferdinand Praeger, *Wagner as I Knew Him* (London, 1892), p. 94. Praeger and his wife (who was French) were in the group on that occasion, as we know from Wagner's letter to Minna of 26 June, in Richard Wagner, *Sämtliche Briefe*, vol. 7, ed. Hans-Joachim Bauer and Johannes Forner (Leipzig, 1988), p. 233.

19 Letter to Liszt of 25 June 1855; *CG* V, p. 116.

20 See *Cosima Wagner's Diaries*, ed. Martin Gregor-Dellin and Dietrich Mack, transl. Geoffrey Skelton, vol. 2 (New York, 1977), entries for 1 June, 8 and 12 September 1878. I should like to thank Gunther Braam for bringing these references to my attention.

21 Borchmeyer, in *The Wagner Handbook*, p. 178.

22 See, for example, Wagner's letter to Wilhelm Fischer of 4 June 1855; *Sämtliche Briefe*, vol. 7, pp. 196–197.

23 *Journal des débats*, 12 September 1843; taken over in the *Mémoires*, Premier Voyage en Allemagne, 5e lettre.

24 Robert Bailey, "The Method of Composition," in *The Wagner Companion*, ed. Peter Burbidge and Richard Sutton (New York, 1979), p. 273.

25 See *Cosima Wagner's Diaries*, vol. 1 (New York, 1978), pp. 73, 83; or Cosima Wagner, *Die Tagebücher*, vol. 1, ed. Martin Gregor-Dellin and Dietrich Mack (Munich, 1976), pp. 69, 81.

26 See Richard Wagner, *Entwürfe, Gedanken, Fragmente. Aus nachgelassenen Papieren zusammengestellt* [by Hans von Wolzogen] (Leipzig, 1885), pp. 77–78. The autograph of Wagner's fragment on Berlioz is found in the Nationalarchiv der Richard-Wagner-Stiftung Bayreuth (B ll e V). William Ashton Ellis's translation is found in *Richard Wagner's Prose Works*, vol. 8 (London, 1899), p. 376. Neither Wolzogen nor Ellis could date this fragment because Cosima's diaries were not available at the time. My rendering is much indebted to those of my distinguished colleagues Hans Rudolf Vaget and Philipp Otto Naegele.

27 *Selected Letters*, p. 268; letter of 8 September 1852, with "ich *liebe* Berlioz" translated, I think wrongly, as "I *like* Berlioz."

28 *Cosima Wagner's Diaries*, vol. 1, p. 217.

29 Berlioz, *À travers chants*, p. 76. This article originally appeared in the *Revue et Gazette musicale* on 4 March 1838.

30 Katherine Reeve Kolb, "*The Damnation of Faust*, or the Perils of Heroism in Music," in *Berlioz Studies*, ed. Peter Bloom (Cambridge, 1992), p. 151.

31 The original is in *Sämtliche Briefe*, vol. 4, ed. Gertrud Strobel and Werner Wolf (Leipzig,

1979), p. 459; translation, *Selected Letters*, p. 268.

32 Of all persons, none other than Adolf Hitler once planned to make a setting of *Wieland der Schmied*. See Ulrich Müller, "Wagner in Literature and Film," in *The Wagner Handbook*, p. 385. In *Wagner Androgyne* (Paris, 1990), Jean-Jacques Nattiez argues that *Wieland* is an illustration of Wagner's views, set down in *The Artwork of the Future*, regarding the relative importance of music and poetry in opera (p. 76). Such a philosophical question, even if the French composer interpreted the tale in this way, was not what Berlioz prized in a libretto.

33 Henri Blaze's essay appeared in the *Revue des deux mondes* on 1 October 1838.

34 *CG* V, p. 151. The autograph of Berlioz's letter (which was unavailable to the editors of *CG*), is preserved in the Archiv Richard Wagner, Gedänkstätte Bayreuth.

35 *Sämtliche Briefe*, vol. 5, ed. Gertrud Strobel and Werner Wolf (Leipzig, 1993), p. 425 (7 October 1853): "ich fürchte mich vor Berlioz, mit meinem schlechten Französisch bin ich verloren."

Berlioz's impact in France

1 Adolphe Jullien, "Hector Berlioz," in *Airs Variés* (Paris, 1877), pp. 39–40. This piece was first published in the *Revue contemporaine* on 15 March 1870 to coincide with Reyer's festival of works by Berlioz at the Opéra.

2 Georges Bizet, *Lettres de Georges Bizet: Impressions de Rome (1857–1860): La Commune (1871)*, ed. L. Ganderax (Paris, 1907), pp. 322–323.

3 Oscar Comettant, "Hector Berlioz," *Le Ménestrel*, 17 October 1886, p. 370.

4 See, for example, *The New Grove Dictionary of Music and Musicians*, s.v. "Symphony," pp. 459–460.

5 David Cairns, *Berlioz 1803–1830: The Making of an Artist* (London, 1989), p. 390.

6 Carl Dahlhaus, *Nineteenth-Century Music*, transl. J. Bradford Robinson (Berkeley, 1989), p. 243.

7 Donald J. Grout and Claude V. Palisca, *A History of Western Music*, 5th ed. (New York, 1996), p. 575.

8 Jacques Barzun, "Hector Berlioz," in *Atlantic Brief Lives*, ed. L. Kronenberger (Boston, 1965), p. 57.

9 Alan Houtchens, "Romantic Composers Respond to Challenge and Demand," in *The Orchestra: Origins and Transformations*, ed. Joan Peyser (New York, 1986), p. 188.

10 *The New Grove*, s.v. "Berlioz," and similar statements in *Berlioz* (London, 1982), pp. 204–205.

11 Julian Rushton, *The Musical Language of Berlioz* (Cambridge, 1983), p. 258.

12 Comments are based on obituaries and other articles of 1869–1870 from *L'Art musical*, *Le Constitutionnel*, *Le Figaro*, *Figaro-Programme*, *La France*, *La France musicale*, *Le Gaulois*, *La Gazette de France*, *Le Journal des débats*, *Le Ménestrel*, *Le Moniteur universel*, *La Patrie*, *Le Pays*, *Le Petit Journal*, *La Presse*, *Revue contemporaine*, the *Revue des deux mondes*, the *Revue et Gazette musicale*, *Le Temps*, and *L'Union*.

13 Gustave Chadeuil, "Revue musicale," *Le Siècle*, 16 March 1869, p. 1.

14 Ém. Mathieu de Monter, "Hector Berlioz," *Revue et Gazette musicale*, 3 July 1870, p. 210 (the final article of a series of thirty-two).

15 Jullien, "Hector Berlioz," *Airs variés* [March 1870], p. 57.

16 Oscar Comettant, "Échos," *Le Siècle*, 11 March 1869, p. 3. See also Comettant's "Hector Berlioz," *Le Ménestrel*, 14 March 1869, p. 113.

17 Daniel Bernard, "Hector Berlioz," *L'Union*, 29 April 1869, p. 1. Near the end of his short life Bernard edited the first collection of Berlioz's correspondence, the *Correspondance inédite* (Paris, 1879). Calmann-Lévy, the publisher, had earlier brought out Berlioz's *Les Soirées de l'orchestre*, *À travers chants*, and *Mémoires*.

18 Armand de Pontmartin, "Semaines littéraires, CCXVIII: Hector Berlioz, Homme de lettres," *Gazette de France*, 21 March 1869, p. 1.

19 P. Lacôme, "Berlioz et le Romantisme," *L'Art musical*, 20 May 1869, p. 197.

20 David de Closel, "Revue de Quinzaine," *Le Consitutionnel*, 21 March 1869, p. 1.

21 Arthur Pougin, "Hector Berlioz," *Figaro-Programme*, 9 March 1869, p. 1.

22 Closel, *Le Constitutionnel* (see note 20).

23 Pontmartin, "Semaines littéraires," pp. 1–2.

24 Quoted from *Selected Letters of Berlioz*, ed. Hugh Macdonald, transl. Roger Nichols (New York, 1997), p. 343. Berlioz was elected to the Institute on 21 June 1856.

25 Philarète Chasles, "Berlioz," *L'Art musical*, 31 March 1870, p. 137.

26 Closel, *Le Constitutionnel*, p. 1.

27 Timothée Trimm, "Hector Berlioz," *Le Petit Journal*, 10 March 1869, p. 1.

28 M. de Thémines (Achille de Lauzières), "Revue musicale," *Le Siècle*, 16 March 1869, p. 2.

29 Pontmartin, "Semaines littéraires," p. 1.

30 Pougin, "Hector Berlioz," p. 1.

31 Chasles, "Berlioz," p. 137.

32 Félicien David, *Notice sur Hector Berlioz* (Paris, 1870), p. 11. The text was read at the meeting of the Académie des Beaux-Arts on 30 July 1870.

33 Ernest Reyer, "Hector Berlioz," *Journal des débats*, 31 March 1869, p. 3.

34 Johannès Weber, "Critique musicale," *Le Temps*, 1 April 1869, p. 2.

35 Johannès Weber, "Critique musicale," *Le Temps*, 26 June 1877, p. 1.

36 Ernest Reyer, "Revue musicale," *Journal des débats*, 13 December 1872, p. 2. For a description of Reyer's efforts on behalf of his friend, see Elizabeth Lamberton, "The Critical Writings of Ernest Reyer" (Ph.D. diss., University of British Columbia, 1988), pp. 266–313.

37 Adolphe Jullien, *Hector Berlioz: Sa Vie et ses œuvres* (Paris, 1888), p. 356.

38 "Festival dédié à la mémoire d'Hector Berlioz," *Revue et Gazette musicale*, 27 March 1870, p. 98.

39 See the list in Adolphe Jullien, *Berlioz*, Appendice 1, pp. 367–371.

40 See Adolphe Boschot, *Le Faust de Berlioz: Étude sur la Damnation de Faust et sur l'âme romantique* (Paris, 1945), esp. "La Résurrection d'un chef-d'œuvre," pp. 120–159; Jullien, *Berlioz*, p. 353; and Weber, "Critique musicale," *Le Temps*, 17 January 1872, p. 1.

41 Arthur Pougin, *Supplément* to Fétis, *Biographie universelle des musiciens* (Paris, 1878), s.v. "Berlioz."

42 Georges Noufflard, *Berlioz et le mouvement de l'art contemporain* (Florence, 1883), pp. 87ff.

43 J. Weber, "Critique musicale," *Le Temps*, 27 February 1883, p. 2.

44 Comments are based on articles found in *Le Constitutionnel, L'Écho de Paris, Le Figaro, La France, Le Gaulois, La Gazette de France, Le Journal des débats, Le Matin, Le Ménestrel, Le Moniteur, La Patrie, Le Pays, Le Petit Journal, Le Petit Parisien, Le Siècle, Le Soleil*, and *Le Temps*.

45 Ernest Reyer, "La Statue de Berlioz," *Journal des débats*, 17 October 1886, p. 1 (also quoted in *Le Temps*, 18 October 1886, and elsewhere).

46 Stanza XI: "A cette heure où Wagner triomphe jusqu'en France, / Où son art, caressé d'une chaude espérance, / Sur notre sol aimé veut germer et fleurir, / Il faut, ô Berlioz, Français à la grande âme, / Que ton pays entier te défende et t'acclame, / Toi qui sus, avant lui, réformer et souffrir!" (At this hour, when Wagner is triumphant even in France, when his art, imbued with high hopes on our beloved soil, would take root and flourish, it is essential, O Berlioz, French to the depths of your soul, that your entire country defend and exalt you – you who knew so much, before him, of reform and of suffering!)

47 Albert Wolff, "Courrier de Paris," *Le Figaro*, 18 October 1886, p. 1.

48 Fourcaud, "Le Roman d'un musicien," *Le Gaulois*, 17 October 1886; "Inauguration de la Statue Hector Berlioz," *Le Gaulois*, 18 October 1886.

49 Saint-Saëns, "La Statue de Berlioz," *La France*, 24 October 1886, p. 1.

50 "La Statue de Berlioz," *Le Petit Journal*, 19 October 1886, p. 2.

51 Simon Boubée, "Musique," *La Gazette de France*, 18 October 1886, p. 2.

52 See Jullien, *Berlioz*, pp. 317ff.

53 Edmond Hippeau, *Berlioz et son temps* (Paris, 1890), p. 400.

54 Henri Lavoix, fils, *La Musique française* (Paris, 1891).

55 J. Weber, "Critique musicale," *Le Temps*, 7 October 1890, p. 1.

56 Eugène de Solenière, "L'Influence de Berlioz," in *Le Livre d'or du centenaire d'Hector Berlioz* (Paris, 1907), pp. 180–181.

57 Julien Tiersot, *Hector Berlioz et La Société de son temps* (Paris, 1904), p. 320.

58 *Ibid.*, p. 321.

59 Camille Saint-Saëns, "Discours de M. Saint-Saëns," *Le Guide musical*, 6 and 13 September 1903, p. 627. Saint-Saëns's better-known portraits of Berlioz are included in Saint-Saëns, *Regards sur mes contemporains*, ed. Yves Gérard (Paris, 1990).

60 Cambridge, Mass., 1996.

61 Gustave Bertrand, "Semaine théâtrale," *Le Ménestrel* (12 May 1867), p. 187.

62 Ernest Reyer, "Revue musicale," *Journal des débats*, 5 May 1867, p. 1.

63 Berlioz, *Lettres intimes* avec une préface par Charles Gounod (Paris, 1882).

64 See Léon Vallas, *César Franck*, transl. Hubert Foss (London, 1951), p. 73.

65 Ernest Chausson, *Journal*, 3 November 1871; this unpublished diary is cited by Jean Gallois, *Chausson* (Paris, 1994), p. 64, n. 42.

66 Alfred Bruneau, "L'Influence de Berlioz sur la musique contemporaine," *Musica*, 7/66 (1908), p. 36.

67 Emmanuel Chabrier, *Correspondance*, ed. Roger Delage and Frans Durif (Paris, 1994), p. 412; letter of 17 July 1887.

68 Claude Debussy, in *Gil Blas*, 8 May 1903. See Debussy, *Monsieur Croche et autres écrits*, ed. François Lesure (Paris, 1971), p. 165.

69 Debussy, *Monsieur Croche*, p. 273.

70 Arbie Orenstein, "Maurice Ravel on Berlioz: An Interview by M. D. Calvocoressi," in *A Ravel Reader* (New York, 1990), p. 461. Virtually the same criticism appears in one of Robert Craft's interviews with Stravinsky. See *Conversations with Igor Stravinsky* (New York, 1959), p. 27.

71 Gaston Carraud "La musique

symphonique," in *Rapport sur la musique française contemporaine*, ed. Paul-Marie Masson (Rome, 1913), p. 99.

72 See Robert Orledge, *Charles Koechlin* ([Newark, N.J.], 1989), p. 234.

73 Mikhail Ivanov, "From Musorgsky's Obituary," in *Musorgsky Remembered*, ed. Alexandra Orlova, transl. V. Saytzeff and F. Morrison (Bloomington, 1991), p. 138.

74 See Ernest Reyer, "Revue musicale," *Journal des débats*, 18 April 1886, p. 2.

75 See Saint-Saëns' letter to Fauré of 24 November 1904, in Gabriel Fauré, *Correspondance*, ed. Jean-Michel Nectoux (Paris, 1980), p. 251. The moment – a

characteristically Berliozian *réunion de deux thèmes* – occurs at bar 401 (see *NBE* 1a, p. 55).

76 See John Warrack, *Tchaikovsky* (New York, 1973), pp. 191–192.

77 Amédée Boutarel, "Revue des grands concerts", *Le Ménestrel*, 27 March 1892, p. 100–101.

78 Holoman, *Berlioz* (Cambridge, Mass., 1989), p. 510.

For their enthusiastic assistance in the preparation of this article, I should like to thank my students Andra Hawks, Lynne Johnson, Leilynne Lau, Rosa Lewis, Xiaole Li, Mae Masuda, Mitchell Moriwaki, Leslie Tagorda, Scott Takata, and Robert Wehrman.

Bibliography

JEFFREY LANGFORD

This bibliography is arranged by broad topics and is intended to introduce the reader to some of the most important research and writing on Berlioz in English. Its emphasis is on scholarship of the last ten years, although some older works are included to fill out topics less well represented by recent research. Annotations are brief and selective. Those interested in earlier writings on Berlioz, and writings in other languages, should consult Jeffrey Langford and Jane Graves, *Hector Berlioz: A Guide to Research* (New York: Garland, 1989), which gathers many different primary and secondary research sources into particular categories for ease of access. It includes a simplified list of works by Berlioz as well as annotated citations of books and articles in several languages on different aspects of his life and work.

Nine articles listed below appear in *Berlioz Studies*, ed. Peter Bloom (Cambridge: Cambridge University Press, 1992). Only the title of that volume, *Berlioz Studies*, is given in the references here.

Works by Berlioz
Music
The works of Berlioz are most readily (and inexpensively) available in a series of miniature scores published by Kalmus. This set is a reduction and reprinting (in paperback) of the first critical edition of Berlioz's works edited by Charles Malherbe and Felix Weingartner and published between 1900 and 1907 by Breitkopf & Härtel. Its original title was *Hector Berlioz Werke* but is now generally referred to as the *Old Berlioz Edition* (*OBE*). The edition is full of inaccuracies and editorial emendations that detract from its value as a tool for the close study of Berlioz's music.

The need for a revised critical edition soon became apparent, and the centenary of Berlioz's death (1969) marked the appearance of *Hector Berlioz: New Edition of the Complete Works* under the general editorship of Hugh Macdonald and published by Bärenreiter. This edition, known as the *New Berlioz Edition* (*NBE*), presents Berlioz's musical œuvre in carefully edited, extensively annotated, and beautifully printed hard-bound volumes. These are itemized in the List of Abbreviations in this Companion.

Essays and treatises
Apthorp, William, transl. *Hector Berlioz: Selections from his Letters, and Aesthetic, Humorous, and Satirical Writings.* New York: Holt, 1879. Reprint, Portland: Longwood, 1976.
   –Includes the most complete translation of a collection of Berlioz's satirical anecdotes titled *Les Grotesques de la musique.*

Berlioz, Hector. *The Art of Music and Other Essays.* Ed. and transl. Elizabeth
Csicsery-Rónay from *À travers chants.* Indianapolis: Indiana University Press,
1994.
– The newest translation of Berlioz's final collection of essays and journal articles
on subjects including Beethoven, Mozart, Gluck, Weber, Wagner in Paris, and
miscellaneous others, with a thoughtful Foreword by Jacques Barzun.
The Conductor: The Theory of his Art. Transl. John Broadhouse from *Le Chef
d'orchestre, théorie de son art.* London: William Reeves, n.d. Reprint, St. Clair
Shores, Mich.: Scholarly Press, 1976.
– Also printed as part of *Treatise on Instrumentation* (see below).
Evenings With the Orchestra. Transl. and ed. Jacques Barzun from *Les Soirées de
l'orchestre.* New York: Knopf, 1956. Reprint, Chicago: University of Chicago
Press, 1973. Reprint, with a new Foreword by Peter Bloom, Chicago: University
of Chicago Press, 1999.
– Fictional, satirical stories, biographies, and anecdotes; Berlioz the critic at his
best.
"Fêtes musicales de Bonn: Report on the Unveiling of the Beethoven Monument in
1845." Transl. and ed. Kevin Bazzana. *Beethoven Newsletter,* 6/1 (1991), 1–11,
29–36.
– Includes an introduction to the translation on pp. 1, 12–14.
"On Imitation in Music." Transl. Jacques Barzun from "De l'imitation musicale," in
Berlioz: Fantastic Symphony. New York: Norton [Norton Critical Scores], 1971.
– One of Berlioz's most significant essays on the question of program music.
Berlioz, Hector, and Richard Strauss. *Treatise on Instrumentation.* Transl. Theodore
Front from *Grand Traité d'instrumentation et d'orchestration modernes.* New
York: Kalmus, 1948. Reprint, New York: Dover, 1991.
– Strauss did not alter Berlioz's treatise but expanded it by adding a number of
examples, primarily from the works of Richard Wagner.

Memoirs

Newman, Ernest, annot. and rev. *Memoirs of Hector Berlioz.* Transl. Rachel and
Eleanor Holmes. New York: Knopf, 1932. Reprint, New York: Dover, 1966.
– The Newman edition remains in wide circulation, but the Cairns translation,
below, is preferable.
Cairns, David, ed. and transl. *The Memoirs of Hector Berlioz.* London: Gollancz,
1969; New York: Norton, 1975; various other editions including London:
Cardinal, 1990.
– David Cairns's knowledgeable translation and commentary are exemplary and
invaluable.

Letters

Berlioz's collected correspondence is published in French by Flammarion, in Paris,
as enumerated in the List of Abbreviations. In English the general collections of
letters are as follows:
Barzun, Jacques, ed. and transl. *New Letters of Hector Berlioz, 1830–68.* New York:
Columbia University Press, 1954. Reprint, Westport: Greenwood, 1974.

   –A bilingual edition, with exemplary translations.

Macdonald, Hugh, ed. *Selected Letters of Berlioz*. Transl. Roger Nichols. London: Faber and Faber, 1995; New York: Norton, 1997.

   –A generous selection, with commentary by one of today's most knowledgeable specialists.

Searle, Humphrey, ed. and transl. *Hector Berlioz: A Selection from his Letters*. New York: Vienna House, 1973.

   –A useful selection, but superseded by the Macdonald edition (above).

Works About Berlioz

Bibliographies and research tools

Cairns, David. "The Reboul–Berlioz Collection." In *Berlioz Studies*: 1–16.

   –An overview of letters and diaries, in the important collection of the Berlioz family, which have affected recent biographical scholarship.

Holoman, D. Kern. *Catalogue of the Works of Hector Berlioz. New Edition of the Complete Works*, vol. 25. Kassel: Bärenreiter, 1987.

   –The definitive catalogue of all Berlioz's works, musical and literary.

Wright, Michael. *A Berlioz Bibliography: Critical Writing on Hector Berlioz from 1825 to 1986*. Farnborough: Saint Michael's Abbey, 1988.

   –A thorough bibliography that is arranged chronologically and is therefore somewhat difficult to access by topics.

Biographies

Barzun, Jacques. *Berlioz and the Romantic Century*, 2 vols. Boston: Little, Brown and Co., 1950. Revised in one volume as *Berlioz and his Century: An Introduction to the Age of Romanticism*. Cleveland: World, 1956. Reprint, Chicago: University of Chicago Press, 1982. Reissued as a third edition (revised from the first), with a new preface by the author, New York: Columbia University Press, 1969.

   –The first serious English biography of Berlioz, written by one of America's greatest cultural historians. Particularly useful for its attention to the sociological environment in which Berlioz lived and worked, its extensive bibliography, and its wisdom.

Bloom, Peter. *The Life of Berlioz*. Cambridge: Cambridge University Press, 1998.

   –A concise overview of Berlioz's life intended for the general reader and especially rich in its depiction of the composer as a product of the political and cultural milieu in which he lived. Discussion of major works is presented in non-technical language.

Cairns, David. *Berlioz 1803–1832: The Making of an Artist*. London: Deutsch, 1989. Revised ed., London: Penguin, 1999. *Berlioz 1832–1869: Servitude and Greatness*. London: Penguin, 1999.

   –The most carefully researched and detailed English biography to date. Elegantly written and insightful throughout; general discussion rather than analytical treatment of the music.

Holoman, D. Kern. *Berlioz*. Cambridge, Mass.: Harvard University Press, 1989.

   –A thorough but less leisurely biography than that of Cairns. Especially useful for

its detailed musical analysis, treatment of a Berlioz's compositional process, and
annotated bibliography.

Macdonald, Hugh. *Berlioz.* 2nd ed. London: Dent, 1991.

–A comprehensive life and works in Dent's "Master Musicians" series by one of
the world's leading Berlioz scholars.

"Hector Berlioz." In *The New Grove Early Romantic Masters* 2. New York: Norton,
1985.

–An accessible and perceptive short survey, revised from the article in the *New
Grove Dictionary.*

Biographical studies on specialized topics

Bloom, Peter. "Berlioz in the Year of the *Symphonie fantastique." Journal of
Musicological Research,* 9 (1989), 67–88.

–Surveys Berlioz and "politics" in the period before and during the composition
of his most celebrated symphony.

"Episodes in the Livelihood of an Artist: Berlioz's Contacts and Contracts with
Publishers." *Journal of Musicological Research,* 15/4 (1995), 219–273.

–Includes an attempt to clarify the picture of Berlioz's financial resources.

"Berlioz's Directorship of the Théâtre Italien." *Échos de France & d'Italie. Liber
amicorum Yves Gérard.* Ed. Marie-Claire Mussat, Jean Mongrédien, and Jean-
Michel Nectoux. Paris: Buchet/Chastel, 1997: 137–152.

–Closely examines the events that led to Berlioz's nomination (not confirmed) as
director of one of the leading theatres of the French capital.

Boursy, Richard. "The Mystique of the Sistine Chapel Choir in the Romantic Era."
Journal of Musicology, 11/3 (1993), 277–329.

–Contrasts Berlioz's dislike of Palestrina and ancient music in general with the
more common nineteenth-century reverence for this music.

Cockrell, William D. "A Study in French Romanticism: Berlioz and Shakespeare."
Journal of Musicological Research, 4/1–2 (1982), 85–113.

–Traces the French understanding of Shakespearean form in the early nineteenth
century and Berlioz's adoption of it in *Les Troyens.*

Currie, Norman. "Hector Berlioz, Robert Schumann, Felix Mendelssohn: Three
Early Romantic Composers and Their Publishers." Ph.D. diss., City University of
New York, in progress.

–Examines Berlioz's business and personal relations with two French publishers,
Maurice Schlesinger and Simon Richault, and their effect upon his career.

Grattan-Guinness, I. "A Note on Hector Berlioz and the Université Royale de
France." *Music Review,* 50/3–4 (1989), 181–184.

–Supplies the most accurate and detailed information about Berlioz's enrollment
in medical school and his earning of a bachelor's degree in 1824.

Williams-Gartrell, Judith. "Hector Berlioz as Conductor." D.M.A. diss., University of
Washington, 1987.

–A study of Berlioz's role, technical and more broadly musical, in the
development of the modern conductor, with an evaluation of his contribution
based in particular upon the pamphlet appended to the *Traité d'instrumentation*
entitled *Le Chef d'orchestre* and upon contemporary reviews of Berlioz's
conducting in performance.

Biographical studies of Berlioz in relation to other composers

Covell, Roger. "Berlioz, Russia and the Twentieth Century." *Studies in Music,* 4
(1970), 40–51.
  –Considers Berlioz's influence on nineteenth-century Russian composers.

Fauquet, Joël-Marie. "Berlioz's Version of Gluck's *Orphée.*" In *Berlioz Studies*:
189–253.
  –A close examination of Berlioz's amalgamation of the French and Italian
  versions of Gluck's score.

Geiringer, Karl. "Hector Berlioz and Gluck's Viennese Operas." In *Essays in
Musicology: A Tribute to Alvin Johnson.* Ed. Lewis Lockwood and Edward
Roesner. Philadelphia: American Musicological Society, 1990: 258–265.
  –A short summary of Berlioz's critical evaluation of Gluck.

Gross, Ernest. "The Influence of Berlioz on Contemporary Nineteenth-Century Use
of Brass Instruments." *Brass Bulletin,* 67 (1989), 20–31; 68 (1989), 34–44; 69
(1989), 88–92; 70 (1989), 62–67.
  –Surveys Berlioz's attitude toward and use of all brass instruments and claims an
  influence on Wagner and Strauss.

Ramalingan, Vivian S. "Berlioz, Beethoven, and 'One Fatal Remembrance.' " In
Beyond the Moon: Festschrift Luther Dittmer. Ottawa: Institute of Mediaeval
Music, 1990: 394–409.
  –Investigates the emotional connotations of Berlioz's quotation in the Lacrymosa
  of his *Requiem* of a few bars from the second movement of Beethoven's Seventh
  Symphony and of the phrase "One fatal remembrance" from Thomas Moore's
  Irish Melodies.

Reeve [now Kolb], Katherine. "Primal Scenes: Smithson, Pleyel, and Liszt in the Eyes
of Berlioz." *Nineteenth-Century Music,* 18/3 (1995), 211–235.
  –Analyzes the role of three performers in creating the kind of violent visceral
  reaction to masterpieces of music that Berlioz describes in the opening chapter
  of *À travers chants.*

Watson, Derek. "Liszt, Berlioz, and Wagner: Critical Reappraisals of the New
German School." *Wagner,* 10/2 (1989), 39–48.
  –Discusses Franz Brendel's role in coining the term "New German School" and
  lists eight points of common interest among its three major composers.

Criticism

Barzun, Jacques. "Overheard at Glimmerglass ('Famous Last Words')." In *Berlioz
Studies*: 254–271.
  –A fictional conversation among three erudite friends who debate matters of
  style, meaning, and musical aesthetics in Berlioz.

Bloom, Peter. "Berlioz and the Critic: 'La damnation de Fétis.' " In *Studies in
Musicology in Honor of Otto E. Albrecht.* Ed. John W. Hill. Kassel: Bärenreiter,
1980: 240–265.
  –Summarizes the complex relationship between Berlioz and the influential
  French critic François-Joseph Fétis.

Ellis, Katharine. *Music Criticism in Nineteenth-Century France: La Revue et Gazette
musicale de Paris, 1834–1880.* Cambridge: Cambridge University Press, 1995.
  –The first extended treatment of the leading musical periodical of Berlioz's day,

including an attempt to unravel the system of belief that grounded its critical practice.

Levy, David. "'Ritter Berlioz' in Germany." In *Berlioz Studies*: 136–147.

–Discusses the critic Wolfgang R. Griepenkerl's enthusiastic support of what he saw as the Germanic elements in Berlioz's music, especially his adoption of Beethoven's technique of creating humor.

Murphy, Kerry. *Hector Berlioz and the Development of Music Criticism*. Ann Arbor: UMI Research, 1988.

–Presents Berlioz's criticism in the context of musical journalism in nineteenth-century Paris, concentrating on his views of contemporary operas and of concerts at the Conservatoire.

"Joseph Mainzer's 'Sacred and Beautiful Mission': An Aspect of Parisian Musical Life of the 1830s." *Music & Letters*, 75/1 (1994), 33–46.

–Discusses Berlioz's reviews of the amateur choral singing classes established by Mainzer in Paris *c.* 1837–1838.

Payzant, Geoffrey. *Edward Hanslick and Ritter Berlioz in Prague: A Documentary Narrative*. Calgary: University of Calgary Press, 1991.

–Explains why the young Hanslick, under the influence of the critic Bernhard Gutt, changed his opinion of Berlioz's music from supportive to hostile within only one year.

Reeve [Kolb], Katherine. "Hector Berlioz." In *European Writers: The Romantic Century*. Ed. Jacques Barzun. Vol. 6 (*Victor Hugo to Theodor Fontane*). New York: Charles Scribner's Sons, 1985: 771–812.

–Justifies Berlioz's rightful place in the pantheon of the century's major French writers.

Dramatic works

Albright, Daniel. "Berlioz's Faust: The Funeral March of a Marionette." *Journal of Musicological Research*, 13/1–2 (1993), 79–97.

–Suggests that Berlioz created his Faust after the model of the Byronic hero destined for self-destruction.

Goldberg, Louise. "Aspects of Dramatic and Music Unity in Berlioz's *Les Troyens*." *Journal of Musicological Research*, 13/1–2 (1993), 99–112.

–Demonstrates how this episodic opera is unified by parallel dramatic structures in each act and by recurring musical ideas.

Kemp, Ian. "*Romeo and Juliet* and *Roméo et Juliette*." See "Symphonies."

Reeve [Kolb], Katherine. "*The Damnation of Faust*: The Perils of Heroism in Music." In *Berlioz Studies*: 148–188.

–Explores aspects of masculinity and femininity in Berlioz's musical depiction of Faust.

Robinson, Paul. "The Idea of History: Hector Berlioz's *The Trojans*." In Robinson, *Opera and Ideas: From Mozart to Strauss*. Ithaca: Cornell University Press, 1985: 103–151.

–Hypothesizes that *Les Troyens* reflects a Hegelian concept of history.

Rushton, Julian. "Berlioz's Swan-Song: Towards a Criticism of *Béatrice et Bénédict*." *Proceedings of the Royal Musical Association*, 109 (1982–1983), 105–118.

–Analyzes Berlioz's drastic but nonetheless musically coherent adaptation of Shakespeare's *Much Ado About Nothing*.

"The Overture to *Les Troyens*." *Music Analysis*, 4:1/2 (1985), 119–144.

–Suggests that the opera's first number acts as an overture by introducing four significant musical images from the larger drama.

"Misreading Shakespeare: Two Operatic Scenes of Berlioz's." In *The Opera and Shakespeare*. Ed. Holger Klein and Christopher Smith. Lewiston: Edwin Mellen, 1994: 213–227.

–Considers the love scenes from *Les Troyens* and *Roméo et Juliette*.

Schmidgall, Gary. "Some Ado about Berlioz." In *Shakespeare and Opera*. New York: Oxford University Press, 1990: 272–279.

–Analyzes Berlioz's relationship to Shakespeare and his adaptation of *Much Ado About Nothing* for *Béatrice et Bénédict*.

Werth, Kent. "'Nature Immense,' A Sketch from Berlioz's *La Damnation de Faust*: A New View of the Composer at Work." *Musical Quarterly*, 74/1 (1990), 74–82.

–A study of the sketch for the *Invocation à la nature* showing how attention to the text determined the working out of Berlioz's musical ideas.

Performance practice

Appert, Donald. "Berlioz, the Conductor." D.M.A. diss., University of Kansas, 1985.

–Includes a history of baton conducting in the early nineteenth century and contemporary critiques of Berlioz's conducting.

Bayard, Michael. "Finally a Solution to Berlioz." *Percussive Notes*, 28/4 (1990), 44–48.

–Suggests the use of large tubular carillon bells for the fifth movement of the *Symphonie fantastique*.

Bowen, José. "The Conductor and the Score: The Relationship Between Interpreter and Text in the Generation of Mendelssohn, Berlioz, and Wagner." Ph.D. diss., Stanford University, 1993.

–Compares Berlioz's theoretical account of the technique of conducting with his actual practice as recounted in the London newspapers.

"Mendelssohn, Berlioz, and Wagner as Conductors: The Origin of the Ideal of 'Fidelity to the Composer.'" *Performance Practice Review*, 6/1 (1993), 77–88.

–Contrasts Berlioz's view of conducting as a "recreative" art with Wagner's view of it as a "creative" art.

Davies, Joyce. "The *Cornet à Pistons* in French and French-Influenced Orchestration From 1830–1936." D.M.A. diss., Ohio State University, 1990.

–Suggests that Berlioz's adoption of the valved cornet as the standard chromatic high-brass instrument of the orchestra, in and around 1830, established a tradition important in France and Russia for the remainder of the century and until the valved trumpet became widely accepted.

Del Mar, Norman. *Conducting Berlioz*. New York: Oxford University Press, 1997.

–A practical guide to conducting Berlioz's orchestra music, with bar-by-bar suggestions for each work covered.

Macdonald, Hugh. "Berlioz and the Metronome." In *Berlioz Studies*: 17–36.

—The first comprehensive look at Berlioz's metronome markings and their relation to the character of his music.

O'Neal, Melinda. "Berlioz's *L'Enfance du Christ: trilogie sacrée,* Op. 25: A Conductor's Analysis for Performance." D. Mus. diss., Indiana University, 1987.
—Historical background and structural analysis.

Schroeter, Sheridan Jean. "Singing Berlioz: A Study in 19th-century Performance Practice." D.M.A. diss., Stanford University, 1991.
—Explores issues of musical expressiveness and the role of an empathic relationship between singer and composer in achieving a "vital performance."

Style analysis

Barzun, Jacques. "The Meaning of Meaning in Music: Berlioz Once More." *Musical Quarterly,* 66/1 (1980), 1–20.
—Maintains that all Berlioz's music is in a sense programmatic.

Collins, William. "Berlioz and the Trombone." D.M.A. diss., University of Texas at Austin, 1985.
—Compares Berlioz's writing for trombone with that of his predecessors and successors.

Macdonald, Hugh. "Berlioz's Orchestration: Human or Divine?" *Musical Times,* 110 (1969), 255–258.
—Explores some "weaknesses" in Berlioz's orchestration.

Primmer, Brian. *The Berlioz Style.* London: Oxford University Press, 1973.
—An articulate attempt to capture the essence of Berlioz's style by focusing on the nature of the composer's melody and his deployment of tonality and harmony.

Rushton, Julian. *The Musical Language of Berlioz.* Cambridge: Cambridge University Press, 1983.
—A comprehensive and complex examination of such matters as instrumentation, counterpoint, rhythm, melody, and formal schemes in Berlioz's œuvre.

Zonis, Ella. "Berlioz as Melodist: A Study of Thematic Treatment and Form in his Symphonic Works." M.M. thesis, New England Conservatory, 1961.
—Suggests that Berlioz's forms result from the song-like nature of his melodic invention.

Symphonies

Austenfield, Thomas. "'But Come, I'll Set Your Story to a Tune': Berlioz's Interpretation of Byron's *Childe Harold.*" *Keats-Shelly Journal,* 39 (1990), 83–94.
—Claims that the Berlioz is not a "translation," but a "reaction" to Byron's poem that uses Byronic techniques in treating a dramatic persona.

Banks, Paul. "Berlioz's 'Marche au supplice' and *Les Francs juges* – a Re-examination." *Musical Times,* 130 (1989), 16–19.
—Supports the theory that the *Marche au supplice* was not a part of the original *Les Francs-Juges* but a later addition to the score.

Bonds, Mark Evan. "Sinfonia Anti-*Eroica:* Berlioz's *Harold en Italie* and the Anxiety of Beethoven's Influence." *Journal of Musicology,* 10/4 (1992), 417–463.
—Suggests that Berlioz viewed Beethoven both as a "model to be emulated and a

precursor to be overcome"; that *Harold en Italie* is a "contradiction" of
Beethoven's Ninth Symphony.

Holoman, D. Kern. "Berlioz." In *The Nineteenth-Century Symphony*. Ed. Holoman.
New York: Schirmer, 1997.
  –A fine general survey of the symphonies.

Kemp, Ian. "*Romeo and Juliet* and *Roméo et Juliette*." In *Berlioz Studies*: 37–79.
  –Analyzes the relationship of the musical structure of the symphony to the play in
the various versions of it that Berlioz actually knew.

Langford, Jeffrey. "The Byronic Berlioz: *Harold en Italie* and Beyond." *Journal of
Musicological Research*, 16 (1997), 199–221.
  –Suggests that both Berlioz's life and his music were permeated with the influence
of Byron.

Olson, Karen. "The Solo Viola's Role in Berlioz's *Harold en Italie*." Ph.D. diss., New
York University, 1999.
  –Examines Berlioz's depiction of characteristics of the romantic hero as
represented by *Childe Harold's Pilgrimage* and shows how Berlioz's solo viola
mirrors Harold's attainment of self-realization.

Richardson, Brian. *Berlioz: Symphonie Fantastique*. Leeds: Mayflower, 1990.
  –Contains biographical background, general style analysis, and a detailed analysis
of the symphony.

Rushton, Julian. *Berlioz: Roméo et Juliette*. Cambridge: Cambridge University Press,
1994.
  –A Cambridge Music Handbook giving historical background with detailed
musical analysis.

Vocal music (see also dramatic works)

Bloom, Peter. "In the Shadows of *Les Nuits d'été*." In *Berlioz Studies*: 81–111.
  –Explores the date of composition, aspects of the autograph manuscripts, and
Berlioz's relationship to the poet Théophile Gautier.

Johnson, April. "An Exploration of Unity in Hector Berlioz's *Les Nuits d'été*
Through Analysis of Structural and Stylistic Elements." D.M.A. diss., University
of Texas at Austin, 1991.
  –Examines musical and extra-musical factors that bear upon the conception of
the work as a unified cycle.

Lee, Namjai. "Orchestral Accompaniment in the Vocal Works of Hector Berlioz."
Ph.D. diss., University of North Texas, 1994.
  –Searches for the orchestrational patterns and rationales of Berlioz's music in
relation to the mostly vocal tradition of French music.

Macdonald, Hugh. "Berlioz's *Messe solennelle*." *Nineteenth-Century Music*, 16/3
(1993), 267–285.
  –An account of the rediscovery of the work, in 1991, and a detailed description of
its various movements and of their use in later compositions.

Rushton, Julian. "*Les Nuits d'été*: Cycle or Collection?" In *Berlioz Studies*: 112–135.
  –Explores the notion of the song cycle and the properties of Berlioz's songs that
suggest they belong to this category.

Index